ESSAYING THE ESSAY

Essaying
the Essay

······························

EDITED BY DAVID LAZAR

WELCOME TABLE PRESS

Welcome Table Press is an all-volunteer, nonprofit independent press dedicated
to the publication and celebration of the essay, in all its forms. The essay is a
chameleon, at once formal and scholarly, lyrical and narrative, personal and
political, educational and secretive, humorous and curmudgeonly, loud and quiet.
It is endangered and dangerous, adaptable and perishable.

This anthology is in your hands because of the words, efforts, and contributions
representing a confluence of people whose generosity is unparalleled. To them, we
offer our deepest gratitude.

Welcome Table Press
Gettysburg PA 17325
Copyright 2014 Welcome Table Press
www.welcometablepress.org
Printed in the United States of America

Printed on acid-free paper.

Library of Congress Control Number: 2013950520

Includes bibliographical references.
isbn-13: 978-0-9885926-1-2

Design by Richard Hendel
Set in Scala and Scala Sans
Production by Bare Hands Design
Proofreading by Kate Gorton, Elizabeth Fallon
Printed and bound by BookMobile.

CONTENTS

· · · · · · · · · · · · · · · · ·

DAVID LAZAR
....

Somewhat Smithian

dialectical nature of a story

A reader must synthesize assumpt. between authors intent/ perception of author's and his/her own framework

ontological nature → truth in fiction ↳ complications in the power of narrative, real or unreal

AN ESSAY UPON ESSAYS
UPON ESSAYS UPON ESSAYS

APOLOGIES TO HILLAIRE BELLOC

> *The world is everywhere whispering essays.*
> — *Alexander Smith "On the Writing of Essays"*

Writing the introductory essay to a collection of essays about the essays, I feel, inevitably, as though I were embarking on an infinite regression. Hillaire Belloc's amusing essay title, "An Essay Upon Essays Upon Essays," sums up the scene, and also speaks to the essentially self-referential nature of essay writing, generally. In a sense, almost all essays are about the essay, because essays are so hopelessly, or better yet, hopefully, self-reflexive. If essays are considerations, thought processes, meditations, whether critical, lyrical, dialectical, philosophical, personal, fragmented, epistolary, or manifested, they tend to betray self-consciousness of form. It is a genre, if it is a genre—some of our essayists express doubts—whose slip is always showing, or shall I say, being shown.

"likinds" of essays

Reading essays that speak more or less explicitly to the form over a four hundred year period, it's a bit eerie to see how certain themes have recurred with consistency. Among these are the generic and ontological status of the essay as work of art; the epistemologies of truth-telling and seeking in the essay; the essay's relationship to the persona and selfhood of the writer; the resistance to systematic thought, closed systems, and accepted belief on mere convention; the necessity of establishing a mood or atmosphere, using heightened or poetic language, pursuing a complicated and rich, textured wordscape; the essay as a readerly form, but also a form with deep engagement with the world, the moment, circling back around: the self. Chance, or accident also shows up crucially—we might consider these today as motions of the subconscious, but accidents seem to intrigue essayists consistently whether or not they're stirred tectonically. Hélène Cixous brings together many of the historical strands in the history of essays on the essay, how the form ventures inside and outside,

what isn't the essay?

what can/'t it do?

straying far from the self while staying close. Her reading of Thomas Bernhard reading Montaigne highlights the essay as ~~hermeneutical~~ in its relationship to other texts; it reforms and recreates objects, others, worlds inside itself; essays are themselves little worlds that have been nudged, prodded, questioned into being . . . they are reactions and refuges, completely incomplete.

This anthology begins with Montaigne, since even though precursors of the form are clearly available, the self-consciousness of form begins with Montaigne essaying, and begins with him nominally: *essais,* essayer. To paraphrase Rachel Blau DuPlessis, when one is overcome with abundant American essays, one only has to scratch the surface of the history of the essay to reveal the Shakespearean necessity of Montaigne to the form: "one begins muttering Montaigne, Oscar Wilde, Montaigne, Christa Wolf, Montaigne, Walter Benjamin, Montaigne, Primo Levi, Montaigne." Shakespeare read Montaigne, as did every essayist who has written the form, and he shows up everywhere in these essays as the form's first and greatest theorist.

Our job isn't to claim truth but illuminate reality

Montaigne writes passages that have been essential to many essayists' manifestoes: "Others shape the man; I narrate him, and offer to view a special one, very ill-made, whome, could I fashion him over, I should certainly make very different from what he is . . . ("Of Repenting").

That note of severe self-reflection and correction is a necessity to the way most essayists think on the page. If you can't be your own most severe critic, who can? If it's left to the reader, the essay marches down the road of dramatic irony, which is the province of the short story. Behind all self-questioning, of course, is the Montaignian motto *"Que sais-je,"* which he imprinted on his coin, an emblem of free judgment and his adapted skepticism. (It's also, startlingly, a perfume, first made by Georges Patou, in 1925.) Montaigne says in "Of the Education of Children":

Essay list realizes his fallibility

> For likewise there are the humours and opinions personal to me; I give them out as what I believe, not as what is to be believed; I aim here only at revealing myself, who may perchance be different tomorrow, if fresh experience changes me. I have no authority to be believed, nor do I desire to be so, feeling myself too poorly instructed to instruct another.

Montaigne introduces a subject that doesn't seem to want to go away:

truth, and its cousin, honesty. Contemporary writers may tire of this subject, tied as it is to the nonfiction-fiction binary (and the continuum of relative of "nonfictiveness" or "fictiveness" in the essay that others slide along). But many of the essayists who write about the essay, beginning with Montaigne, assert the value of finding truth or truths in their work, writing truthfully, assuming a truthful persona (or not!), as part of the essence of essay writing. Montaigne writes, for example, in "Of Repenting," "I do indeed contradict myself, but the truth, as Demades said, I in no wise contradict." Famously, in his opening, "To The Reader," Montaigne tells us, "This is an honest book." Hazlitt says of Montaigne that he wrote "to satisfy his own mind of the truth of things" ("On the Periodical Essayists"). Cornwallis writes of his attempt in the essay, "to clothe her [the essay] in truth, and plainness." Johnson, in the *Rambler*, addressing the question to the use of persona (as Montaigne does by implication in "To the Reader") writes, "'A mask,' says Castiglione, confers a right of acting and speaking with less restraint, even when the wearer happens to be known. He that is discovered . . . cannot be rigorously called to justify those sallies or frolics . . . . But I have been cautious lest this offence should be frequently or grossly committed." Virginia Woolf reminds us, understatedly, that "To tell the truth about oneself, to discover oneself near at hand, is not easy." And Lukács, whose dense vision of the essay as critical art form is ripe, difficult, essential, says that, "were one to compare the forms of literature with sunlight refracted in a prism, the writings of the essayists would be the ultra-violet rays." I want to simply quote this line by Lukács any time a hint of defensiveness for the essay's virtues as art creeps in, as it does, in fact, in some essays. (Sometimes the essay's status as genre is denied as a kind of backhanded grab for higher ontological power: the essay is an "anti-genre"—I'll return to this). Lukács speaks, as well, of the essay as, "a struggle for truth, for the incarnation of a life in which someone has seen in a man, an epoch or a form." Adorno speaks to the essay's engagement with truth by telling us that, "In the emphatic essay thought divests itself of the traditional idea of truth." I assume he means the dialectical essay (aren't most essays?), the philosophical essay which finds truths transient, ephemeral, thinking against itself. But this truth is also a process, a way of essay-thinking: "the essay's innermost formal law is heresy," Adorno writes, in one of the notable lines about the form.

Graham Good, a fine, lesser-known theorist of the essay, notes that, "The essay makes a claim to truth, but not permanent truth. Its truths are particular, of the here and now." Good says, implicitly linking truth and knowledge, "In so far as its utterances are not presented as fictional, the essay does imply a claim to count as knowledge." The epistemology of knowledge, and its relationship to fiction, becomes rather thorny here. From David Shields' "Reality/Persona": [What is true for you in private is true for all men."] Even our last essayist, Brian Lennon, writing on the lyric essay, comments that, "To negate fiction is, in a sense, to create truth." He also argues that the lyric essay "positizes the negative," which sounds delightfully like Cole Porter.

Montaigne writes, in "On Giving the Lie, "Painting myself for others, I have painted myself in colours more distinct than were mine originally. I have no more created my book, than my book has created me—a book of the same substance as its author." He goes on to write that, "Every motion reveals us." He desires to be seen, he tells us in "To the Reader," and this, despite subterfuge, playful or distorted personae, may hold much of the essay's drive. How not to be thrilled, still, reading these lines again, also in "Of Repenting":

> I am the first to do this with my general being, as Michel de Montaigne, not as grammarian or poet or jurisconsult.

[Cornwallis refers to his work as, ["The inward discourse of an honest mind."] Such plain English prose. By Johnson's time, the movements of self-consciousness had already acquired their clichéd gestures; he parodies the the essayist's cheeky formulae in the *Rambler*'s "First Address." Hazlitt, though, speaks with a fresh metaphor in "On the Periodical Essayists," referring to, "This kind of personal authorship among the moderns, in which the reader is admitted behind the curtain . . . ." Thrown forward two hundred years, we see the projection of the essay persona thrown up on Oz's screen.

According to Alexander Smith, "It is this egotism, this perpetual reference to self, in which the charm of the essayist resides." Virginia Woolf, writing her encomium to Beerbohm's essays, says that, "What Mr. Beerbohm gave, was, of course, himself." She goes on to lament the absence of the hauntingly memorable self in the English essay between Lamb and Beerbohm. And in "The Decay of Essay-writing" she avows that, "Almost all essays begin with a capital 'I.'" Interesting since many (though certainly not all) of Woolf's essays shy away from the first person. She did give us one of the greatest extended personal essays of the twentieth century. I am speaking, of course, of *A Room of One's Own*. Cynthia Ozick

[margin notes: "or essence to larger humanity"; "Remembering now Reader To the reader on a header"; "An essay should show itself as well intentioned"; "Egotism vs. charm vs. modesty? Balance?"; "Role of 'I'"]

* side note about linguistic cap. of I
→ interesting dialectical essay somewhere
in this

→ Body as an Archive

in "Self-Portrait of the Essay as a Warm Body," "speaks of how essays,
"unlike novels, emerge from the sensations of the self." She says that,

Pursuing the work of Art

tagonist, the secret self's

"I never enjoyed crime shows, hadn't the stomach for gore or vio

psychoscos

part of the discourse by
lf confronting Value, the *philosoph.*
n of Stupidity . . . ." Cer- *capital objects*
ristopher Morley, whose *signify*
essays is utterly charm- *high— order*
scious revelation of self *concept*

Now that I'm older, I've become ever more sensitive to violence. I see it the museum galleries and the caryatids which look down

supply variations on the
self. It is built into the
r, beaming the self onto
assuming a divorce be-
r time, have clearly be-
ssays in some essential

★

epistemology
→ Truth
of the
self
↓ could
closest we
exist self
perc.

form, despite personae
that may be largely or lightly fictionalized (Addison's De Coverly, Lamb's
Elia, Your version of you), the question of who is speaking, and how truly
that persona represents the writer, doesn't seem to ever go away. It is the
quality of "the essay voice": intimate, digressive, discursive, intellectual,
which confounds genre, and can make fiction, especially novels, read like
extended essays, especially in the work of twentieth century writers like
Sebald, Sarraute, Kundera. David Shields addresses this head on, poly-
phonically, in the "Persona" section of "Reality/Persona": "Most of all, we
expect personal essayists to speak to us from behind a stylized version of
themselves." And: "I'm not interested in myself, per se. I'm interested in
myself as theme carrier, as host."

And here we come to what the essay is in itself: if writers have inscribed *what is the Essay*
themselves, one way or another, what in? Certainly, the essay takes many
forms. Whether it *is* a form, a genre (a species?), a series of subgenres
spoking out from Montaigne's first essais: the critical essay, the personal
essay, the philosophical essay, the familiar essay, the informal and formal
essays . . . the more familiar essay, which inscribes the personal voice and
creates a identifiable persona, dominates the musing on the essay over
time. Phillip Lopate, in "What Happened to the Personal Essay," says, *→ prioriti2. or import. for versatilit*
"The personal or familiar essay is a wonderfully tolerant form, able to ac-
commodate rumination, memoir, anecdote, diatribe, scholarship, fantasy, →

and moral philosophy."

Montaigne suggests his essay is, "a record of varying and mutable incidents and uncertain thoughts, and it may happen, contradictory ones" ("Of Repenting"). The roots of diary, of commonplace book show through, as does the Heraclitian temperament that essays frequently move by (and movement, motion is central: Jean Starobinski's elegant *Montaigne in Motion* is the best exploration of this.) It's easy to see Virginia Woolf's attraction to the form, to its wavering moments. Stephen Toulmins, in *Cosmopolis*, rightly stresses how embodied Montaigne is, how distinct his essays are from much of the Western philosophy that followed, and the body tends to never let the mind, well . . . disembody in the essay. Cornwallis speaks of his "undigested motions" and notes, "How feeble the succors of the body are . . . . for words but clothes, matters substance. . . Rhetoric cookery, is the vomit of the pedant, which to make saleable, he imitated the dyer."

Culpepper strikes the note of the essay's unboundedness: "Though they gather some honey from the best flowers of wit and learning, they have a limitation from none . . ." And it is the essay's tensions between "wit" and "learning," "the material world of the body and the ideation of the mind and the imagination, critical endeavors and flights of fancy, that many essayists speak to when trying to say what they think the essay is, or what balance of these qualities the form should ideally have." Hume, in his essay "Of Essay Writing," complains that, "The Separation of the Learned from the conversible World seems to have been the great Defect of the last Age, and must have had a very bad Influence both on Books and Company . . ." He also, striking a note that will be picked up by DuPlessis, Mairs, Cixous and others, suggests that at least the critical essay might be better taken up by women than men: "Women of Sense and Education . . . are much better Judges of all polite Writing than Men of the same degree of Understanding . . . ."

Hazlitt thinks that the essay, "makes up its general accounts from details, its few theories from many facts." For him, ideas are what make essays reverberate. In pallid essays, "objects are not linked to feelings, words to things, but images revolve in splendid mockery, words represent themselves in their strange rhapsodies" ("Familiar Style"). Emerson, too, who considers how the essay is, "The superior mind," of which Montaigne is the exemplar, is skeptical, but looks for "the permanent in the mutable."

In contrast to Emerson, Alexander Smith's "On the Writing of Essays" is much about the essay's mood, its feeling and images, and is prescient,

6 DAVID LAZAR

Handwritten margin notes:
Interesting. motion. truth. peripetics. Importance in staying anchored. corporeal

materiality ↑↓ abstraction

role of metaphor

Hume / pure logic resulted in poor scholarship

Gender & critical essay

Essay as mind

rational ↕ sensual

perhaps the first essay to specifically call the form lyrical. It pulls away from the stress on ideas, on rhetoric. This tension may be the central one in the essay, at least for the last hundred and fifty years, between ideas, argument, critical judgment, and mood, poetic language, atmosphere. Of course many essays incorporate both. Why shouldn't they? But there is a bit of uneasiness in the descriptions of what the form is, might be, should be, at times. "The essayist is a kind of poet in prose . . . he will hang the mantle of his thought, heavily brocaded with with the gold of rhetoric," Smith writes. Doesn't quite sound the Hazlittian note. Though he continues to speak of the common subjects, "the reference to thought," which most essayists agree upon. He also writes, "The essayist is a chartered libertine, and a law unto himself." This lawlessness, Culpepper's "unboundedness," is also there in Lukács's claim that "each [essay] creates a different world," and Adorno's that "The essay . . . does not let its domain be prescribed for it." This emergent sense builds in the twentieth century that the essay form is somehow centrally ungraspable, self-renewing, ever expanding, formally anti-formal, yet retaining some essential quality (movement, thought, persona linked to writer) that can allow one to identify work as marked broadly by its qualities. At times, the arguments are dizzyingly contradictory (should we be surprised in a form marked by contradiction?).

freedom in the essay

Repulse? is and isn't contrad.?

In the twentieth century, the essay is also theorized formally in two essays that become a kind of locus classicus for the theoretical essay on the essay: Lukács's "On the Nature and Form of the Essay" and Adorno's "The Essay as Form." These two essays engage the question of the essay as art form, but also the relationship of the essay to theory. Lukács argues for the essay, "as work of art, a genre?" derived from Plato and engaged in an attempt to articulate a critique, penetrate ideological and aesthetic conventions through irony and the process of judging. Adorno agrees that the essay is an instrument for the critique of ideology, that it is, "A form whose suspiciousness of false profundity does not protect it from turning into slick superficiality" (This fear of the essay's superficial whimsy, its bourgeois complacency, shows up as early as Johnson). Adorno thinks the essay is almost art, thinks the essay most successful, and practices it, dialectically. But both Adorno and Lukács agree that the essay is an open, anti-systematic, albeit, rigororously thought form. They are not precisely referring to the familiar essay, nor are they excluding it from their considerations. The essayist on the essay who seems to respond to and extend them most directly is Rachel Blau DuPlessis, who in her remarkable es-

Form meets Theory

importance of some seriousness (critical)

say, "*f*-words: An Essay on the Essay," incorporates legions of essayists who are conventionally omitted from the canon, and discusses the symbolic and ethical ways of being that the essay has traditionally represented and might emerge to represent. Adding to this dialogue, consider the title of Robert Atwan's essay, "The Essay: Is it Literature?" Atwan's plastic sense of the form not only notes the generic complications of pinning down the essay itself ("A fly itself will serve my purpose—perhaps the essay is, at times, that fly") but also notes how the essay insinuates itself into other forms. He writes, "In this alternate history of the essay, a novelist like Henry Fielding, who was proud of the way he had interlaced the periodical essay into his fiction, has as much to contribute to the genre as does Addison. There is no term that I know of that conveniently describes the pervasive presence of the essay within other genres, its intrageneric character."

Carl Klaus, in "Essayists on the Essay," feels that the essay is a "profoundly fictive kind of writing." Christopher Morley finds a kind of manifest destiny in the essay, writing: "the essay is a mood rather than a form; the frontier between the essay and the short story is as imperceptible as is at present the once famous Mason and Dixon line." Deborah Tall and John D'Agata had said in their 1997 Seneca Review introduction to the Lyric Essay, that it didn't "expound," that it was "coy." Cynthia Ozick finds the essay "closer in kind to poetry than to any other form." Language is crucial to her, and distinguishes the essay. Even if "An essay is reflection and insight," "the secret self's personification" the essay's depth charge, "sublime language" is the tuning fork, without which the essay falls from the shelf of literary art. Phillip Lopate agrees: "it in fact seeks to persuade more by the delights of literary style than anything else."

No wonder that Lydia Fakundiny, in the introduction to her wonderful anthology of essays, says, charmingly: "Tell me what it is, or failing that, show me how to make one." After all: "Every essay is the only one of its kind." Speaking to the point of our work here, she points out: "Essays, it seems, insist on being thought about only in essays."

Taking a breath with Réda Bensmaïa (I'd love to title an essay that!), we might ask whether it is indeed true that ". . . Essay constantly refers to a wide variety of works that have nothing in common but the absence of system and relative 'brevity.'" According to Bensmaïa, "A unique case in the annals of literature, the Essay is the only literary genre to have resisted integration, until quite recently, in the taxonomy of genres. No other genre ever raised so many theoretical problems concerning the origin and the definition of its Form . . . ." But as many suggest, the essay's transgressiveness *is* its nature: "The nature of the essay asks one to resist categories, starting with itself" (DuPlessis, "*f*-words: An Essay on the Essay"). DuPlessis and Mairs mostly agree, finding qualities in the form they would call feminine. Roland Barthes, near the end of his life, admitted ambiguously that he had written "only essays, an ambiguous genre." To Brian Lennon, at the end of this anthology—end of the line—essays are "the negation of genre."

With so much uncertainty, it is no wonder that Montaigne should see his compositions "guided . . . by chance." That, according to Adorno, "Luck and play are essential to it." That Bensmaïa notes the role of "chance," and Lia Purpura says, "The luck, the stories, the courting of unknowns— mean 'essay' to me."

Luck
chance
play

But, really, then, what are essays? Here are some aphoristic possibilities:

✷ rather an answer, in part, to Fakundiny (on ps. 8)

"I am, myself, the subject of my book . . . ."
    (Montaigne, "To the Reader")
"The inward discourse of an honest mind . . . . "
    (Culpeper, "Of Essayes")
"The essay can be short or long, serious or trifling,
    about God and Spinoza, or about turtles and Cheapside."
    (Woolf, "The Modern Essay")
"The essay is a mood rather than a form . . . ."
    (Morley, "Preface")
"The essay is a judgment, but the essential, the value-determining
    thing about it is not the verdict . . . but the process of judging."
    (Lukács, "On the Nature and Form of the Essay")

etymologic reality

"The bad essay tells stories about people instead of elucidating
    the matter at hand."
    (Adorno, "The Essay As Form")
"The essay is a remembering form, whether in the narratives
    of personal reminiscence we call autobiographical or in the
    affectionate awareness essayists have always shown of their
    predecessors."
    (Fakundiny, "Introduction")
"It is the movement of the free mind at play."

Not only tell but arise a story is the form to bring about some complic.

Spaziersans

(Ozick, "Self-Portrait of the Essay as a Warm Body")
"Essays are acts of writing-as-reading."
(DuPlessis, "*f*-words: An Essay on the Essay")

If one wanted an all-inclusive definition, I think one could say something like: the essay is a prose form in which we move, intimately, across a landscape of thoughts, ideas, and images, with a persona that is usually closely identified with the writer. We might add something like: it is frequently digressive, resists closure, and many of its practitioners pay attention to common subjects, and have a tendency to be ironists. But the second sentence, and all subsequent ones, would begin narrowing the pool of essays one might want to consider, historically. *One* might want to do that elsewhere, but *I* don't want to do it here.

[margin, handwritten: should complicate (not be complicated) and unsettle]

[margin, handwritten: How do you diachronically define something?]

A few words on my selections: on some levels all essays are about essays, so I faced a plenitude. I chose as many essays as possible that spoke to the essay directly, and very few essays that one might be considered "scholarly," though that distinction is . . . shall we say, academic. Several of the essays speak to the form through the work of essayists on their companions in the field, Hazlitt on Montaigne, Lamb on Hazlitt, Woolf on Montaigne, and so on. I found this useful, and revealing. We create and recreate our forms through literary genealogy. I'm sure I have left out work that is wonderful, lively, fascinating and useful. One always does. I make no attempt to be thorough, comprehensive, universal in ways other than those that seem to speak to certain urgent and interesting questions of the form which has intrigued me for so long. Anthologies are always cognates of the essay, or they are if they're interesting. Occasionally, they're like borrowed poems.

[margin, handwritten: critique and illumination through essayist review and reflection on their own task via the work of others.]

A couple of essays I invoke in the introduction—Graham Good's, Lydia Fakundiny's—were omitted due to the intransigence of their publishers in requiring permissions payments beyond our scope. Please seek them out. I hope that what is here makes you want to read more essays. I'm wanting to, always.

[margin, handwritten: Role of economics in essay's develop]

Finally, a few choice favorites from among the many lines in this volume that I haven't already squeezed in—the aphoristic soul may be sharp or lyrical, but it is wide and deep:

[margin, handwritten: Serialization to full publish of novel changed concept.]

Beuesuns → german preserves "the way" in the action of moving

"Every motion reveals us,"
 (Montaigne, "On Giving the Lie")
"Why exaggerate the power of virtue,"
 (Emerson, "Montaigne, or the Skeptic")
"A world in the hand is worth two in the bush,"
 (Emerson, "Montaigne, or the Skeptic")
"Let us say what comes into our heads, repeat ourselves,
 contradict ourselves, fling out the wildest nonsense,
 and follow the most fantastic fancies without caring
 what the world does or thinks or says."
 (Woolf, "Montaigne") *we are mad. This is the truth of thinking wildly, always*
"The essay is like the Serpent, smooth and graceful and
 easy of movement, also wavering or wandering."
 (Chesterton, "On Essays")

And fittingly, for the last words:

"If a subject is unfamiliar to me, for that very reason I essay it."
 (Montaigne, "Of Giving the Lie")

NOTES
Fakundiny, Lydia. *The Art of the Essay*. New York: Houghton Mifflin College
 Division, 1990.
Good, Graham. *The Observing Self*. London: Routledge Kegan & Paul, 1988.

MICHEL DE MONTAIGNE
·······(··································

TO THE READER   [1580]

[handwritten margin: Ray's writing is not described as an adornment but a peeling back, a mode of access (unrestricted) to some mortal and true self]

[handwritten margin: Addresses the reader as well as says that the book has been written for him]

This is an honest book, <u>reader</u>. It gives you to know, at the outset, that I have proposed to myself only an intimate and private end; I have <u>not</u> considered <u>what would be serviceable for you</u> or for my renown; my powers are not equal to such a design. I have devoted these pages to the particular pleasures of my kinsman and friends; to the end that, when they have lost me (which they must do ere long), they may find herein some touches of my qualities and moods, and that, by this means, they may cherish more completely and more vividly the knowledge they have had of me. Had I purposed to seek public favour, I should have better adorned myself, and presented myself in a studied attitude. I desire to be seen in my simple, natural, everyday guise, <u>without effort and artifice</u>; for it is my own self that I portray. <u>My imperfections</u> will be seen herein to the life, and my personal nature, so far as respect for the public has permitted this. I assure you that, had I been living among those nations which are said still to dwell under the benign license of the primal laws of nature, I should very readily have <u>painted</u> myself quite completely, and quite naked. Since, reader, I am thus, myself, the subject of my book, it is not reasonable that you should employ your leisure on so trivial and empty a matter.

So, farewell. From Montaigne, this first March, 1580.

[handwritten margin: Can one name intention while recognising alterior?]

[handwritten margin: persona was mentioned primarily essay]

Judgement is human,
we should not avoid
but refine our
related faculties

OF DEMOCRITUS AND

HERACLITUS [1580]

essayer

The judgement is a tool for all subjects, and enters into every thing. For this reason, in the essays I here make of it, I employ it on every sort of occasion. If a subject is unfamiliar to me, for that very reason I essay it, measuring the depth of the ford from afar; and when I find it too deep for my stature, I remain on the shore; and in this recognition of my inability to cross over is a form of its action, aye, one of those of which it is most proud. Sometimes, with a hollow and empty subject, I essay to see if it can find any thing to give it substance and with which to support it and prop it up. Sometimes I direct it to a famous and much-travelled subject about which it can find nothing original, there being such a beaten way that it must needs travel in the track of others. There it plays its game in selecting the road which seems to it the best, and of a thousand paths it says that this one or that one has been the better choice.

critique
substance
givings

I take by chance the opening theme, since one is as good as another in my eyes, and I never plan to produce them completely. For I do not see the whole of any thing; nor do those who promise to make us see it. Of a hundred members and aspects that every thing has, I take one, sometimes to taste it, sometimes to skim it, and sometimes to squeeze it even to the bone. I stab into them, not as widely, but as deeply, as I know how. And I like in most cases to seize them by some unfamiliar side, I might venture to go to the bottom of some subject, if I knew myself less well. Scattering a word here, another there, bits taken from the whole, set by themselves, without plan and without pledge, I am not responsible for them, nor bound to hold to them without changing if I so please, nor to refrain from giving myself up to hesitation and uncertainty, and to my dominant characteristic, which is ignorance.

essay as object

death r knowledge

montaigne effect

Every motion reveals us. That same mind of Caesar's which manifests itself in organising and arranging the battle of Pharsalia, manifests itself also in arranging idle and amorous matters. We judge a horse, not merely by seeing him when racing, but also by seeing him walk, aye, and by see-

motion as reality

Truth arises in transient moments between states

ing him at rest in the stable.

Among the offices of the soul there are some that are inferior. He who does not see her in that wise does not know her wholly; and perchance we observe her best when she is jogging quietly along. The gusts of passion affect her more on her higher planes; moreover, she gives herself wholly to every matter, and wholly busies herself in it; and she never treats more than one subject at a time, and treats it, not in accordance with its qualities, but in accordance with her own. Things by themselves have, it may be, their weights and measures and conditions; but within us, she fashions them as she thinks best. Death is terrifying to Cicero, desirable to Cato, indifferent to Socrates. Health, conscience, authority, learning, wealth, beauty, and their opposites, are stripped on entering, and receive from the soul new apparel and such colouring as pleases her—dark, light, dim, glaring, soft, deep, superficial—and as pleases each of our souls; for they have not agreed in common upon the titles, laws, and nature of their qualities; each soul is queen in her own domain.

Wherefore let us no more find excuse in the external qualities of things; it is for us to estimate their value to ourselves. What is well and bad for us depends wholly on ourselves. Let us offer our gifts and our prayers to ourselves, not to Fortune: she can not affect our moral nature; on the contrary, that draws her in its train and moulds her to its likeness. Why shall I not judge of Alexander at the table, talking and drinking heavily? or, when he played chess, what chord of the mind does not that foolish and puerile game touch and employ? I dislike it and shun it, because it is not play enough, and it is too serious a pastime; I feel ashamed to give it the attention which would suffice for some worthy thing. He was no more completely engrossed in preparing for his glorious expedition to the Indies; nor is another man in solving the difficulties of a passage on which the salvation of the human race depends. See how heavy and compressed that absurd amusement makes our mind, if all her sinews do not stiffen themselves; how amply it permits every one to know himself and judge himself rightly. I do not behold myself and feel myself more completely in any other situation. What passion does not therein play upon us? anger, vexation, hatred, impatience, and a vehement ambition to conquer in a matter in which it would be more excusable to be ambitious of being conquered; for rare excellence, above the common, in frivolous things is unbecoming for a man of high standing. What I say regarding this example may be said of all others. Every particle, every occupation of a man betrays and displays him equally with every other.

14 MICHEL DE MONTAIGNE

Democritus and Heraclitus were two philosophers, the former of whom, deeming the human state vain and ridiculous, never appeared in public but with a mocking and laughing countenance; Heraclitus, having pity and sympathy for that same state of ours, wore an unchangeably sad visage, and his eyes were full of tears.

The one laughed every time he stepped over the threshold; the other, on the contrary, wept.

I like best the first humour, not because it is more agreeable to laugh than to weep, but because it is more contemptuous and condemns us more than the other; and it seems to me that we can never be despised as much as we deserve. Lamentation and commiseration are commingled with some estimation of that which we lament; the things we laugh at we esteem valueless. I do not think that we have so much ill fortune as inconstancy, or so much bad purpose as folly; we are not so full of evil as we are of insanity; we are not so wretched as we are base. This Diogenes, who in idle solitude passed his time rolling himself about in his tub, and flouting the great Alexander, esteeming us as but flies or bladders full of wind, was a judge much more bitter and sharp-tongued, and consequently, to my feeling, more just, than Timon—he who was called the hater of men; for what we hate we take seriously. This man wished us ill, was passionately desirous of our destruction, shunned intercourse with us as dangerous, we being wicked and depraved; the other thought so little of us that we could neither disturb him nor by our contagion harm him; he forsook our company, not from fear, but from contempt for our society; he thought us capable of doing neither well nor ill.

Of the same stamp was the reply of Statilius, when Brutus spoke to him to secure his aid in the conspiracy against Caesar; he thought the enterprise as a just one, but did not think that men deserved that any trouble should be taken for them. This conforms to the rule of Hegesias, who said: "The wise man should do nothing except for himself, inasmuch as he alone deserve to have things done for him"; and that of Theodorus: "It is unreasonable that the wise man should risk his life for the good of his country, and that he should imperil wisdom for fools." Our peculiar condition is as ridiculous as risible.

[handwritten marginalia: to see and understand laws and the absurdity in disapproval · *laughter > sad not b/c better but b/c more critical* · *positive spin on human intent + suffering* · *virulent* · *impotent* · *smithian? Not for the bener. of the sake*]*

[handwritten note at bottom: I'm very fascinated by this print of never relieving of contempt as we deserve. So often, I realize that I'm the one imagining all the reasons while someone would spite me — when in honestly they are likely too busy to even think twice about me.]

OF GIVING THE LIE [1580]

Yes, but I shall be told that this plan of making use of oneself as a subject to write about would be excusable in exceptional and famous men, who, by their reputation, had caused some desire for their acquaintance. It is beyond question; I admit it; and I know well that, to look at a man of the common sort, an artisan will hardly lift his eyes from his task; whereas, to see a great and renowned personage enter a city, the workrooms and shops are deserted. It is unfitting for any other to make himself known save him who has something to invite imitation, and whose life and opinions may serve as a pattern. Caesar and Xenophon had the wherewithal to base and strengthen their narratives on the magnitude of their deeds, as on a reasonable and enduring foundation. And it is to be wished that we had the daily records of Alexander the Great, and the notes that Augustus, Cato, Sylla, Brutus, and others may have left of their actions. Of such personages the figures are admired and studied even in copper and in stone.

This remonstrance is very just, but it concerns me very little:

> I do not recite my verses except to friends, and that only when invited; not everywhere, or to every one. But there are many who, in the middle of the forum, or when bathing, recite their writings.

I am not erecting here a statue to be set in a city street, or in a church, or in a public square.

> Truly, I do not study to swell my page with pretentious trifles. . . . We talk together privately.

It is for the corner of a library, and for the entertainment of a neighbour, a kinsman, or a friend, who may have pleasure in renewing acquaintance and familiarity with me through this picture. Others have taken courage to speak of themselves from having found the subject worthy and fruitful; I, on the contrary, from having found it so sterile and meagre that no suspicion of ostentation can attach to it.

I freely pass judgement on the acts of others; of my own I give little ground for judgement because of their nullity. I do not find so much good in myself that I can not tell it without blushing. What pleasure it would give me to hear some one thus describe to me the manners, the appearance, the demeanour, the most ordinary speech, and the fortunes of my ancestors! How attentively I should listen! Truly, it would give evidence to a bad nature, to hold in contempt even the portraits of our friends and predecessors. A dagger, a harness, a sword, which they have used, I preserve so far as I can from the inroads of time, for love of them; and I have not banished from my own room some long staves which my father usually carried in his hand. *The garment and the ring of a father are dear to his children in proportion to their love for him.* If, however, my posterity be of another mind, I shall have wherewith to be revenged; for they can not make less account of me than I shall of them in those days. All the dealing that I have with the public in this matter is that I borrow the tools of their writing as being quicker and more agreeable. As compensation, I shall perhaps prevent a pound of butter in the market-place from spoiling.

That the tunny may not lack a coat, nor the olives hoods.
And I shall often furnish a cloak for the mackerel.

And, if no one shall read me, have I wasted my time in being occupied so many idle hours in such useful and agreeable thoughts? Modelling this figure after myself, I have been obliged so often to trim myself up and arrange myself, in order to give my outline, that the model has consequently strengthened and, in some degree, shaped itself. Painting myself for others, I have painted myself in colours more distinct than were mine originally. I have no more created my book, than my book has created me—a book of the same substance as its author, with an occupation of its own, with its own business, a member of my life; not with an external and alien business, like all other books. Have I wasted my time in taking account of myself so constantly, so minutely? For those who consider themselves in thought only, and in words now and then, do not examine themselves so exactly, or enter into themselves, as he who makes this his study, his business, and his occupation; who binds himself to a lasting record, with all the faithfulness and strength that he has.

The most delightful pleasures, being inwardly recognised, avoid giving any sign of themselves and avoid the observation, not only of the multitude, but of any one. How many times has this occupation diverted me from troublesome thoughts! and all trifling thoughts should be reckoned as troublesome. Nature has endowed us with a great faculty of conversing with ourselves apart; and often invites us to do so, to teach us that we owe ourselves in part to society, but for the most part to ourselves. To the end that I may school my imagination even to muse according to some order and plan, and to keep it from going astray and wandering at random, it is needful only to give shape to all the petty thoughts that offer themselves to it, and place themselves on record. I listen to my musings because I have to register them. How many times, being vexed by some act which civility and good sense forbade me to reprehend openly, have I unburdened myself, not without a purpose of public instruction! And indeed these poetic scourges—

> One in the eye, one on the snout,
> One on the back of the pig!

make an even greater impression when on paper than when given on the living flesh. What if I lend my ear a little more attentively to books, since I have been on the watch to see if I can filch from them something wherewith to adorn or prop up my own? I have not at all studies to make a book; but I have studies somewhat because I had made it, if it be in any wise studying to select the best, or to catch hold by the head or by the teeth, now of one author, now of another; not at all to form my opinions, but to aid those long ago formed, to second and support them.

But whom shall we believe when speaking of himself in such debased times, seeing that there are few, or none, whom we can believe when speaking of others, where there is less to gain by lying? The first feature of corruption of morals is the banishment of truth; for, as Pindar said, being truthful is the beginning of great virtue; and it is the first qualification that Plato requires in the governor of his republic. Our truth nowadays is not what is, but what others may be persuaded of; as we call coin, not only that which is of good alloy, but also the counterfeit which passes current. Our nation has long been reproached with this vice; for Salvianus Massiliensis, who was of the time of the Emperor Valentinian, said that to the French lying and perjury were not vices, but mere forms of speech. He who would enhance his testimony might say that it is now a virtue in their eyes. Men form and fashion themselves to it as being an honourable practice; for dissimulation is among the most renowned qualities of this age. Consequently, I have often considered whence could arise this habit, which we retained so religiously, of feeling ourselves more bitterly injured by being charged with this vice, which is so common with us than any other; and that it is the greatest insult that can be offered us in words, to charge us with falsehood. Whence I conclude that it is natural to defend ourselves most earnestly for the faults to which we are most addicted. It seems that in resenting the accusation and in being moved by it, we in some measure rid ourselves of the trespass; if we have it in fact, we condemn it to save appearances.

May it not be, also, that this reproach seems to involve cowardice and faint-heartedness? Is there any more manifest expression of this than to belie one's word—nay, to belie one's knowledge? Lying is a villainous vice, and an ancient writer depicts it as most shameful when he says that to lie is to manifest contempt of God together with fear of man. It is not possible to represent more fully the horror, the vileness, the outrageousness of it. For what can be conceived more villainous than to be cowardly with respect to men and audacious with respect to God?

Certain nations of the new Indies (there is no need to note their names; they no longer exist; for the desolation of that conquest has extended even to the entire abolition of names and of the former knowledge of places; a wonderful and unheard-of instance) offer to their gods human blood, but no other than that taken from the tongue and ears, by way of expiation of the sin of falsehood, as well listened to as spoken. That Greek worthy said that children play with huckle-bones, men with words.

As for our different methods of giving the lie, and our laws of honour in that matter, and the changes they have undergone, I will postpone to another time saying what I know of them; and I will meanwhile learn, if I can, when this habit began of weighing our words so carefully, and of making our honour dependent upon them. For it is easy to judge that it did not exist of old among the Romans and the Greeks. And it has often seemed to me novel and strange, to see how they gave the lie and insulted one another, without consequently entering into a quarrel. The laws of what was due took some other course than ours. They called Caesar, to his face, sometimes a thief, sometimes a drunkard. We see the freedom of the invectives they used against one another,—I mean the greatest warchiefs of both nations,—when words were avenged solely by words, and involved no other consequence.

MICHEL DE MONTAIGNE

······································

OF REPENTANCE [1585–88]

normative *descriptive*

Others shape the man; I narrate him, and offer to view a special one, very ill-made, and whom, could I fashion him over, I should certainly make very different from what he is; but there is no doing that. Now the lines of my portrait do not err, although they change and are now this, now that. That world is but personal motion; all things in it move incessantly,—the earth, the rocks of Caucasus, the pyramids of Egypt,—both with the universal motion and with their own; fixedness itself is only a more lingering motion. I can not anchor my subject: he is always restless, and staggering with an unsteadiness natural to him. I catch him in the state that he is in at the moment when I turn my attention to him. I do not paint his being; I paint his passing—not the passing from one age to another, or, as the common people say, from seven years to seven years, but from day to day, from moment to moment; my narrative must be in accordance with the hour; I may change immediately, not merely by chance, but also by intention. My narrative is a record of varying and mutable incidents and of uncertain thoughts, and, it may happen, contradictory ones, whether because I am different myself, or because I apprehend the subjects by other circumstances and considerations. So it is that, peradventure, I do indeed contradict myself, but the truth, as Demades said, I in no wise contradict. If my soul could find a foothold, I should not exert myself in attempts, I should free myself from perplexity; it is still in pupillage and on trial.

I set forth a life humble and without glory—it comes to the same thing; all moral philosophy may be connected with a common and private life as fitly as with a life of richer substance; every man has in himself the whole form of human nature. Writers of books commune with the world with some special and peculiar badge; I am the first to do this with my general being, as Michel de Montaigne, not as grammarian or poet or jurisconsult. If the world finds the fault that I speak too much of myself, I find the fault that it does not even think of itself.

But is it reasonable that, being so private in my way of life, I undertake to make myself publicly known? Is it reasonable also that I produce to the world, where manner and art have so much influence and authority,

very Krausian

results of nature both imperfect and simple, and of nature, besides, of very little force? Is it not like building a wall without stone, or something of that sort, to build books without learning? The compositions of good music are guided by art, mine by chance. I have this at least in accord with doctrine, that never did a man treat a subject which he understood or knew better than I do this that I have undertaken, and that therein I am the most learned man alive; secondly, that no one ever went deeper into his subject, or by full examination of it more distinctly pointed out its different parts and its issues, and arrived more exactly and more completely at the end which he had proposed to himself of his work. To perfect it, I have need to bring to it only fidelity; that I give to it, the most sincere and purest that can be found. I tell the truth, not to my full satisfaction, but as much as I venture to utter; and I venture a little more as I grow old; for it would seem that custom concedes to age more liberty of garrulity and indiscretion in speaking of oneself. It can not here happen as I often see it happen, that there is contrariety between the artisan and his work; a man of such an excellent course of life, can he have written such a foolish book? or such learned writings, have they proceeded from a man of such weak conduct? If a man be commonplace in intercourse, and his writings remarkable, it means that his ability is somewhere whence he borrows it, and not in himself. A learned person is not learned throughout; but the able man is able throughout, and even in not knowing.

My book and I, we here proceed in conformity with one another and in one course. In other cases, the work may be praised or blamed apart from the workman; in this case, not: who touches the one touches the other. He who shall pass judgement on it without becoming acquainted with the workman will wrong himself more than me; he who comes to know him will wholly satisfy me. Fortune beyond my deserts if I have only this much public approbation, that I make people of intelligence feel that I could have profited by learning had I had it, and that i deserve more aid from memory.

Let me be excused for saying here what I often say, that I rarely repent, and that my conscience is content with itself, not as the conscience of an angel or a horse, but as the conscience of a man; adding this unfailing qualification,—not a qualification on convention but of true and essential submission,—that I speak as one who is ignorant and seeking, referring myself for decision purely and simply to common and legitimate opinion. I do not teach, I narrate.

There is no sin that is unquestionably sin which does not do harm, and which a sound judgement does not reprove; for it has such manifest vileness and unseemliness that, per adventure, they are right who say that it is chiefly begotten by stupidity and ignorance, so difficult it is to conceive that it can be recognised without being hated. Wickedness swallows the greater part of its own venom, and poisons itself therewith. Vice, like an ulcer in the flesh, leaves repentance in the soul, which is forever scratching and lacerating itself. For reason does away with other sadnesses and pain, but it engenders that or repentance, which is the more grievous inasmuch as it is born within; as the chills and heat of fevers are more severe than those which come from outside. I regard as vices (but each in its degree) not only those which reason and nature condemn, but those also which the opinion of mankind, false and erroneous indeed, has created, if the laws and custom give authority to that opinion. Even so, there is no goodness which does not rejoice a well-dowered nature. There is surely I know not what self-gratification in doing well, which rejoices us ourselves, and a noble pride which attends a good conscience. A boldly vicious character may perhaps obtain for itself security, but it can not supply itself with this complacency and contentment. It is no slight pleasure to feel oneself preserved from the contagion of so rotten an age, and to say within oneself: "Whoever could see me to my very soul would not find me guilty, either of causing the affliction or the ruin of any one, or of revenge or envy, or of public violation of the laws, or of innovation and disturbance, or of being false to my word; and whatever the license of the age may permit and teach to every one, yet have I not laid hands on either the property or the purse of any Frenchman, and have lived solely upon what is mine, not less in time of war than in peace, and have made use of no man's labour without payment." These testimonies of the conscience are gratifying; and this natural enjoyment is very beneficial for us, and the only recompense that never fails us.

To the base the reward of virtuous actions on the approbation of others is to choose a too uncertain and obscure foundation. Especially in a corrupt and ignorant age like this, the good opinion of the vulgar is offensive; to whom do you trust to perceive what is praiseworthy? God preserve me from being a man worth according to the description which I see given every day by each one doing honour to himself! *What were formerly vices have become habits.* Some of my friends have sometimes undertaken to school me frankly and spiritedly, either of their own motion or at my invitation, as a service which, to a well-informed mind, surpasses, not in utility only, but in kindness as well, all the other services of friendship. I have always welcomed it with the most open arms of courtesy and gratitude. But, to speak of it now in all honesty, I have found in their reproofs and their praise so much false measure, that I should hardly have done wrong to do wrong, rather than do rightly after their fashion. We, especially, who live a private life that is in view only to ourselves, ought to have a model established within us, by which to test our actions and, according to it, sometimes make much of ourselves, sometimes correct ourselves.

I have my laws and my court to judge me, and I resort to them more than elsewhere. I restrain my actions, indeed, according to others, but I enlarge them only according to myself. It is only you who know whether you are cowardly and cruel or loyal and pious; others do not at all see you, they guess about you by uncertain conjectures; they see not your natural disposition so much as your artificial one. Therefore, rely not on their judgement; rely on your own. You must make use of your judgement about yourself. *Great is the importance of one's own consciousness of virtues and vices; that discarded, all is laid low.* But this that is said, that repentance follows close on the heels of sin, seems not to regard sin when, armed from head to foot, it dwells within us as in its own abode. When we can disown and forbid the vices which surprise us, and to which passions impel us; but those which by long habit are rooted and anchored in a strong and sturdy will are not submissive to being thwarted. Repentance is no other than a forbidding of our will and opposition to our inclinations, which stirs us up on all sides. It makes this man repudiate his past virtue and continence:

> Why was not my mind the same when I was a boy that it is to-day? Or why, with my thoughts of to-day, do not my cheeks become as they were?

That is a life of consummate excellence which preserves an orderly bearing even in private. Every one may take part in play-acting, and represent the honourable personage on the stage; but the point is, inwardly and in one's own breast, where all things are permissible, where all things are hidden, there to be subject to rule. The next step is to be so in one's own house, in one's every-day actions, of which we have not to render account to any one; where there is nothing studied, nothing artificial. And therefore Bias, describing a surpassingly worthy family condition, says: "The master is the same, when in his house alone, as when out of it, from fear of the law and of men's speech." And that was a fit saying of Julius Drusus to the workmen who offered for three thousand crowns so to arrange his house that his neighbors could no longer look into it as they had done: "I will give you six thousand," he said, "and do you manage so that every one can look into every part of it." We note as honourable the custom of Agesilaus, of taking up his quarters in temples, when he was travelling, so that the people and the gods themselves could witness his private actions. A man may appear wonderful to the world, in whom his wife and his servant see nothing even remarkable; few men have been admired by their household.

No man was ever a prophet, not merely in his own house, but in his native place, declares the teaching of history. Even so with things of naught; and in the following humble instance may be seen the image of greater ones. In my region of Gascony, it seems droll to people to see me in print. In proportion as knowledge of me extends farther from my abode, I am rated the higher: in Guienne I pay the printers, elsewhere they pay me. Those who hide themselves when alive and here, rely on this fortune to bring themselves into repute when dead and gone. I would rather have less of it; and fling myself into the world only for what I wrest from it. When I leave it, I quit it all.

The crowd escorts him from public state, with admiration, to his door; he puts off, with his gown, the part he plays, and falls as much the lower as he had been uplifted; within, in himself, all is commotion and of no account. Even if discipline existed there, it would need a keen and special judgement to perceive it in these mean and secret acts. Moreover, regularity is a dull and dismal virtue. To enter a breach, to conduct an embassy, to govern a people—these are brilliant actions. To chide, to laugh, to sell, to pay, to love, to hate, and to hold intercourse with one's family and with oneself, gently and justly, not to give way, never to derogate from oneself—that is something more rare, more difficult, and less observable. Retired lives, whatever may be said, maintain in these ways duties as severe and exacting as do other lives, or more so. And private persons, says Aristotle, observe a more difficult and higher virtue than they who are in authority. We prepare ourselves for great occasions more for the sake of glory than for the sake of conscience. The shortest way to attain glory would be to do for conscience what we do for glory. And the virtue of Alexander seems to me to exhibit somewhat less strength in its scene of action than does that of Socrates in its humble and obscure exercise. I can easily imagine Socrates in Alexander's place, but Alexander in that of Socrates, I can not. To him who shall ask Alexander what he knows how to do, he will reply: "Subjugate the world"; he who shall ask this of the other will be answered that he knows how "to lead human life in conformity with its natural condition"—a knowledge much more general in its scope, more important, and more legitimate.

The worth of the soul does not consist in moving at a height. but fittingly. Its grandeur is not brought into play in grandeur. but in mediocrity. Thus those who judge and examine us within make no great account of the lustre of our public acts, and see that they are but threads and drops of clear water springing from a source otherwise slimy and thick; even so, those who judge us by this brave outward show equally come to conclusions about our internal character, and can not yoke together faculties that are common and like their own and those other faculties, so far from their scope, which astound them. Thus we ascribe to demons monstrous shapes; and who does not endow Tamburlane with lifted eyebrows, open nostrils, a grim visage, and a stature as huge as the stature of the idea conceived of him from the report of his fame? Had I been taken in former times to see Erasmus, it would have been hard for me not to find adages and apothegms in every thing he might say to his servant or the hostess of his inn. We can much more fitly imagine an artisan upon his stool or on his wife than a great President, of venerable demeanour and sufficiency. We imagine that from those lofty thrones they will not even condescend to live. As vicious souls are often incited to do well by some foreign impulsion, so are virtuous souls to do ill. We must therefore judge them by their settled condition, when they are alone with themselves, if sometimes they are so; or, at least, when they are nearest repose and in their true position. Natural inclinations are assisted and strengthened by education; but they are rarely altered and overcome. A thousand characters, in my time, have slipped away toward virtue or toward vice, despite contrary instruction.

> So when wild beasts become unhabituated to the forest, and tamed by captivity, and, having lost their fierce look and learned to endure control by men, if a little blood touches their hot lips, their madness and fury return, their throat swells, excited by the taste of blood; they burn with anger, and hardly refrain from attacking their frightened master.

These original qualities are not extirpated: they are covered up, they are hidden. The Latin language is to me as my own; I understand it better than French, but for forty years past I have not used it at all in speaking and scarcely in writing; none the less, in the extreme and sudden emotions into which I have fallen two or three times in my life,—one was when I saw my father, who was in perfect health, fall over upon me in a swoon,—my first ejaculations, from the bottom of my heart, have always been Latin words, Nature coming to the surface and expressing herself forcibly in spite of such long habits; and this same thing is told of many others.

They who have tried to correct the morals of the world in my time, by new ideas, reform the manifest vices; the essential ones they let alone if they do not increase them; and increase in these is to be feared; we readily linger from all other well-doing on these arbitrary external reforms, of less cost and greater honour, and thus we cheaply provide for the other natural vices, consubstantial and intestinal. Consider a little what our experience warrants: no one, if he listens to himself, does not discover in himself a personal nature, a dominant nature, which is at strife with rules of life and with the storm of passions opposed to it. For my own part, I feel myself hardly aroused by sudden impulses; I am, as it were, always in my place, as unwieldy as heavy bodies are. When I am not entirely myself, I am never far from being so; my wanderings do not carry me very far; there is nothing extreme and strange in them; and, besides, my second thoughts are sound and vigorous. The real condemnation, and that which concerns the common manner of men of our day, is that their very retirement is full of corruption and filth; their idea of amendment blurred; their repentance diseased, and almost as much at fault as their sin. Some, either because they are fast bound to vice by a natural tie, or from long familiarity, do not perceive its ugliness. To others, in whose ranks I am, vice is a burden; but they counterbalance it with pleasure or other circumstance, and suffer it, and lend themselves to it for a certain reward, albeit viciously and basely. Yet it might be possible, perhaps, to conceive so great a disproportion of degree that the pleasure would justly excuse the sin, as we say of utility; not only if it were accidental and apart from the sin itself, as in theft, but if it existed in the very act of committing the sin, as in intercourse with women, where the provocation is violent, and, they say, sometimes invincible.

The other day, when I was in Armaignac, I saw, on the estate of a kinsman of mine, a peasant whom every one calls "the thief." He told the story of his life thus: being born in poverty, and finding that, gaining his bread by the work of his hands, he would never succeed in sufficiently protecting himself against want, he resolved to become a thief; and by means of his bodily strength, he had safely given his whole youth to that occupation; for he made his harvest and vintage in other men's fields; but it was at a distance, and in such huge bundles that it was inconceivable that any man could carry away so much on his shoulders in one night; and he had taken pains, moreover, to equalise and distribute the loss he caused, so that the burden was less intolerable to each individual. He is now, in his old age, rich for a man of his condition, thanks to this business, of which he makes open confession; and to reconcile God to his gettings, he says that he is daily in the way of giving satisfaction by benefits to the successors of those whom he robbed; and that, if he does not finish the task,—for accomplish it all at once he can not,—he will leave it in charge to his heirs, according to the knowledge that he alone has of the injury he has done to each one. This statement, be it true or false, shows that he regards theft as a shameful act and loathes it, but less than poverty; he repents of it in itself, but, in so far as it is thus counterbalanced and compensated, he does not repent of it. This is not that habit which makes us of one body with vice and conforms to it our very understanding; nor is it that impetuous blast which by gusts confuses and blinds our soul and casts us headlong for the time, judgement and all, into the power of vice.

I do ordinarily with my whole being what I do, and all of me is in the action; I have few movements which are hidden and secret from my reason, and which are not guided almost entirely by the concurrence of all my faculties, without division, without intestinal dissension; my judgement has the whole blame or praise for them; and the blame which once it has, it has always; for almost from its birth it is unchanged: the same character, the same course, the same strength. And in the matter of general beliefs, I established myself in my youth at the point where I was to remain.

There are impetuous, hasty, and sudden sins: let us leave them at one side; but in those other sins, so often repeated, meditated, and considered, whether they be sins belonging to the temperament or to the profession and vocation, I can not conceive that they should be so long rooted in the same heart, unless the reason and the conscience of him who has them constantly so wills and so knows; and the repentance of them that he boasts of as coming to him at a certain appointed moment is somewhat hard for me to imagine and shape. I do not follow the school of Pythagoras, which believes that men take on a new soul when they approach the images of the gods to receive their oracles, unless he meant just this— that it must needs be a soul unfamiliar, new, and possessed only for the occasion, since our own shows so little sign of purification and cleanliness suitable for that office. They do just contrary to the precepts of the Stoics, which bid us, indeed, to correct the imperfections and vices which we recognise in ourselves, but order us not to disturb the quiet of our souls therewith. They give us to believe that they have great inward grief and remorse for their vices; but of amendment and correction, or of discontinuance, they show us nothing. Yet it is not a cure if the malady is not got rid of. If repentance were laid in the scale, it would outweigh the sin. I find no quality so easy to counterfeit as godliness, where one's morals and life do not conform to it; its essence is abstruse and hidden; the externals easy and ostentatious.

As for me, I may desire, in general, to be other than I am; I may condemn, and be displeased by, my character as a whole, and beseech God to change me completely, and to excuse my natural weakness; but that, it seems to me, I ought not to call repentance, any more than my discontent in being neither an angel nor Cato. My actions are controlled and fashioned by what I am and by my condition of life. I can do no better; and repentance does not properly concern things that are not in our power, but regret, in truth, does. I can imagine numberless loftier and better ordered natures than mine; but I do not thereby amend my faculties; just as neither my arm nor my mind can become more vigorous by conceiving another that is so. If to imagine and to desire a conduct nobler than our own caused repentance for our own, we should have to repent of our most innocent doings, inasmuch as we rightly judge that in a more excellent nature they would have been performed with greater perfection and nobility and we should wish to do the like. When I take counsel with my old age concerning my conduct in my youth, I find that I usually behaved myself fittingly, in my opinion; that is all that my power to withstand the facts can do. I do not flatter myself: under like circumstances I should be always the same man. It is not being smutched; it is rather a general stain that blackens me. I have no knowledge of a superficial, half-way, formal repentance: it must touch me in every part before I call it so, and must wring my heart and affect it as deeply as God sees me, and as thoroughly.

As for business affairs, many good chances have escaped me for lack of fortunate management; yet my judgement made an excellent choice according to the matters presented to it; its habit is to take always the easiest and safest course. I find that in my past deliberations I have, in my way, proceeded wisely in respect to the state of the subject that was brought before me and I should do the same a thousand years hence under like circumstances. I do not regard what its state is now, but what it was when I was considering it. The weight of all opinions depends upon the hour; circumstances and matters change and revolve constantly. I have made some foolish and important mistakes in my life, not for lack of good judgement, but for lack of good-fortune. There are, in the matters we deal with, hidden paths, not discoverable, notably in the nature of man; mute conditions that make, no show, unknown sometimes even to their possessor, which are produced and aroused by supervening circumstances. If my foresight has been unable to fathom and predict them, I bear it no ill-will therefor; its function is limited to its compass. If the event goes against me, and if it approves the determination that I have rejected, there is no remedy; I do not blame myself for this; I blame my fortune, not what I have done; this is not to be called repentance.

Phocion had given the Athenians certain advice which was not followed. The affair, however, having been carried on prosperously, in opposition to his opinion, some one said to him: "Well, Phocion, are you glad that things are going so well?" "Indeed I am glad," he replied, "that this has happened, but I do not repent having advised the other." When my friends come to me for counsel, I give it freely and dearly, without hesitating as almost every one does because, the thing being a matter of chance, it may turn out contrary to my thought, whereby they may have reason to reproach me for my advice; for which I care not. For they will be in the wrong, since it was not for me to refuse them that service.

I seldom have ground to blame anyone but myself for my errors or mishaps; for, in truth, I rarely avail myself of others' advice,—unless it be byway of courtesy,—save when I have need of information, of learning, or of knowledge of the facts; but, in matters in which I have to employ only judgement, outside arguments may serve to confirm me, but rarely to dissuade. I listen graciously and beseemingly to all their reasonings; but, so far as I remember, I have never to this hour trusted any but my own. For me, these others are but flitting trifles that buzz about my will. I value little my own opinion, but I value as little those of others. Fortune requires me fittingly: if I do not accept advice, I give it still less. I am seldom asked for it, but I am still more seldom believed; and I know of no undertaking, public or private, which my advice has bettered or hindered. Even they whom fortune has in some sort bound to follow it have allowed themselves more readily to be guided by any other brain than mine. As one who is quite as jealous of the rights of his ease as of the rights of his authority, I prefer it to be so; in putting me aside, they act according to my open profession, which is, to be wholly set forth and comprehended in myself; it is agreeable to me to forgo all interest in the affairs of others, and to be freed from responsibility about them.

About all matters that are gone by, in whatsoever fashion, I have little regret; for this reflection prevents vexation, namely, that they must needs so pass; I see them as in the great movement of the universe, and in the chain of the Stoic causes. The mind can not, in desire and imagination, do away with the smallest part without subverting the whole order of things, both the past and the future. Furthermore, I hate that chance repentance which old age brings. The man who said of old that he was obliged to his years for having rid him of sensuality was not of my opinion; I can never be beholden to impotence for any good it can do me. *Providence will never be seen so hostile to its own work that weakness will rank among the best things.* Our passions are seldom excited in old age; we are seized with an extreme satiety after the act. In that I can see no sign of conscience; vexation and weakness imprint upon us a mean-spirited, rheumatic virtue. We must not allow ourselves to be so wholly carried away by our natural alterations as to warp our judgement. Youth and pleasure did not in former years so overpower me that I did not recognize the face of vice in sensual pleasure; nor does the distaste that years bring with it so overpower me now, that I do not recognize the face of sensual pleasure in vice. Now that I am no longer in it I judge as if I were still in it.

If I rudely shake up my reason and examine it attentively, I find it to be the same as in my most licentious years, except perhaps in so far as it has become enfeebled and impaired by age. And I find that the pleasure it refuses me in the interest of my bodily health, it would not refuse me, any more than formerly, for my spiritual health. I do not esteem her to be any more valiant for being *hors de combat*. My temptations are so broken and mortified that they are not worth being resisted by her. I exorcize them by merely spreading out my hands in front of me. Should she be face to face with that old lust, I fear she would have less power to resist it than she once had. I cannot see that she thinks any differently about it than she did then, or that she has acquired any new light. Wherefore. if there is any convalescence, it is a broken-down convalescence.

A miserable kind of cure to owe one's health to disease! It is not the part of our misfortune, but of the good fortune of our judgement, to do this office.

No one can make me do any thing by insults and grievances, except curse them; that is for those who rouse themselves only under the lash.

My judgement pursues its course more freely in prosperity; it is much more distraught and absorbed when digesting ills than pleasures. I am much more clear-sighted in pleasant weather; health admonishes me not only more gaily, but more effectively, than sickness. I progressed as far as I was able toward reformation and discipline when I was in a position to enjoy them. I should be ashamed and despiteful if I should have reason to prefer the wretchedness and ill-fortune of my old age to my happy, healthy, lusty, and vigorous youth; and if men should have to value me, not by what I have been, but by what I have ceased to be. In my opinion, it is the living happily, not, as Antisthenes said, the dying happily, which makes human felicity. I have not proposed to append, contrary to nature, the tail of a philosopher to the head and body of a graceless man; nor that a base ending should renounce and belie the best, most complete, and longest part of my life. I propose to present and exhibit myself uniformly, in every part. Had I to live again, I should live as I have lived; I neither lament the past, nor fear the future; and if I am not mistaken, it has been with me inwardly about as it has outwardly. One of my chief obligations to my fortune is that the course of my bodily existence has been so conducted that every thing has come in its season. I have seen the leaves and the flowers and the fruit; and now I see the withering—fortunately, since it has come naturally. I bear much more easily the ills that I have, because they have come at their time, and because they make me remember the more pleasantly the long-continued felicity of my past life. In like manner, my wisdom may well be of the same degree in one and the other period; but it was greater in performance, and of better grace, when lusty, joyous, ingenuous, than it is now—broken, peevish, toilsome. I renounce, therefore, these fortuitous and painful reformations.

It needs be that God touches our hearts; it needs be that our conscience be reformed by the enforcement of our reason, not by the enfeeblement of our appetites. Bodily pleasure is not in itself either pale or colourless because it is viewed by dull and dim eyes. Temperance should be loved for itself and from respect to God, who has enjoined it and chastity upon us; that which fevers bring us, and which I owe to the good offices of my colic, is neither chastity nor temperance. No man can pride himself upon despising and combatting sensuality, if he has no perception of it; if he knows nothing of it, either its charm, or its power, or its most alluring beauty. I know them all; it is I who can say this; but it seems to me that in old age our souls are subject to more troublesome maladies and weaknesses than in youth. I said this when I was young, when my beardlessness was looked down upon; I say it still at this hour, when my gray hair gives me authority. We call the fastidiousness of our tastes, our disrelish for things at hand, wisdom; but the truth is that we do not so much depart from vices as change them, and, in my opinion, for the worse. Besides a foolish and perishable pride, a tiresome love of talk, fault-finding and unsociable humours and superstition, and an absurd care about wealth when the use of it is lost, I find in old age more envy, injustice, and malignity. It imprints more wrinkles in our mind than on our face; and there are to be seen few souls which, as they grow old, do not become sour and peevish. Man in completeness moves toward his increase and toward his decrease.

In considering the wisdom of Socrates and many circumstances of his condemnation, I could venture to believe that he lent himself to it, in some degree, by prevarication, designedly, having so soon—he was seventy years of age—to suffer the benumbing of the rich activity of his mind and the bedimming of its wonted clearness. What metamorphoses do I daily see old age cause in many of my acquaintances! It is a potent malady and one that comes upon us naturally and imperceptibly; there is need of a great store of study and great precaution, to avoid the imperfections which it burdens us with, or at least to retard their progress. I feel that, in spite of all I can do to diminish its power, it is gaining upon me step by step; I resist as much as I can, but I know not where, at last, it will take me. Whatever may happen, I am glad that it should be known from what height I have fallen.

WILLIAM CORNWALLIS

OF ESSAYS AND BOOKS [1610]

I hold neither Plutarch's, nor none of these ancient short manner of writ-ings, nor Montaigne's, nor such of this latter time to be rightly termed essays, for though they be short, yet they are strong, and able to endure the sharpest trial: but mine are essays, who am but newly bound prentice to the inquisition of knowledge, and use these papers as a painter's boy a board, who is trying to bring his hand and his fancy acquainted. It is a manner of writing well befitting undigested motions, or a head not know-ing his strength like a circumspect runner trying for a start, or providence that tastes before she buys: for it is easier to think well than to do well; and no trial to have handsome dapper conceits run invisibly in a brain, but to put them out, and then look upon them: if they prove nothing but words, yet they break not promise with the world; for they say but an essay, like a scrivener trying his pen before he engrosses his work; nor to speak plainly, are they more to blame then many other that promise more: for the most that I have yet touched, have millions of words to the bringing forth one reason, and when a reason is gotten, there is such bor-rowing it one of another, that in a multitude of books, still that conceit, or some issued out of that, appears so belabored, and worn, as in the end it is good for nothing but for a proverb. When I think of the abilities of man, I promise myself much out of my reading, but it proves not so. Time goes, and I turn pages yet still find myself in the state of ignorance; wherefore I have thought better of honesty, then of knowledge: what I may know I will convert to that use, and what I write, I mean so; for I will choose rather to be an honest man than a good logician. There was never art yet that laid so fast hold on me, that she might justly call me her servant. I never knew them but superficially, nor indeed will not, though I might; for they swal-low their subject, and make him as Ovid said of himself:

Quinquid conabar dicere, versus erat
["Everything I tried to say came out as poetry"]

I would earn none of these so dearly, as to tie up the mind to think only of one thing: her best power by this means is taken from her; for so her circuit is limited to a distance, which should walk universally. Moreover there grows pride, and a self opinion out of this, which devours wisdom.

Mark but a grammarian, whose occupation well examined, is but a single-soled trade; for his subject is but words, and yet his construction is of great matters resting in himself. Socrates was the wisest man of his time, and his ground for that, was his turning all his acquired knowledge into morality; of whom one said, he fetched philosophy from heaven, and placed her in cities. Plato laughs at those commonwealth men, who intend only the enlarging, and enriching of their countries, and in the mean time they suffer the enjoyers of their labors to be vicious, and dishonest: even so of these thirsters after knowledge, for has he all that men possibly may have, and then enclose it in the chest of a dishonest breast, it but corrupts him, and makes the poison of his viciousness more forcible.

Non rebus me sed mihi res submittere conor
["I try to submit the things to myself,
not myself to the things"]

I live not to illustrate the excellence of any art, but to use arts as bridles, to rear up the headstrong willfulness of my natural corruption. Thus I see all things, and take example as well by a vicious prodigal fellow, as by one upon the gallows, and desire his part no more that is able, and doth nourish excess, than I do the others, and if I would believe Plato, he holds this state the better: for the one is now surfeiting, the other taking physic. I have heard of the effects of great reading, joined to an understanding able to digest, and carry it: of high acting spirits, whose ambitions have been fed by fortune and power: these make a great noise in the ears of men, and like a swaggerer seem to drown more humble spirits: but equally examined, the gifts of morality are more excellent, and virtuous. When Alexander thirsting threw the water offered him upon the ground, and would not add to the thirst of his companions with his own private affections, he did much more nobly than in winning all his victories: for those rightly determined take away marvel, and admiration; for they were for his own sake: but here, compassion, regard of others, and temperance, plead for an eternal applause; this was morality, and the inward discourse of an honest mind; this was no bloodshed, nor blows, but the preservation of his friends: here blood spotted not his arm, but purity so embellished it, that no eye loving virtue can see this peace without due praising it.

Nor of these searchers into the drifts of nature can I think so well, as of a mind observing his affections, moderating or spurring his will, as it flies, or strays from the right way of virtue. Thus do I think of Seneca, and Aristotle, the first's morality is easy to be understood, and easily digested to the nourishment of virtue; the others more high, and to the readers more questionable, whether it will make him curious, or honest.

Xenophon though his Cyrus be so good, as plainly showed it a life, rather imagined, than acted; yet he so plainly discovered the way of virtue, as the easiest understanding cannot go astray, nor the worst abuse him with interpretation. I hold these much more safe, than those works which stand upon allegories, for every head has not fire enough to distill them, nor every understanding patience enough to find out the good meaning; and many are so ill, as when they have found out an interpretation meet to nourish their sensuality, they stay there, and are the worse for their reading.

Thus offend, most poets, who larding their writings with fictions, feed the ignorant and vicious with as much poison as preservative. This one of them confesses speaking to his muse.

> e tu perdona
> s'intesso fregi al ver, s'adorno in parte
> d'altri diletti che de' tuoi, le carte

> ["Grant me pardon if
> with the truth I interweave embroiderings, if partly with
> pleasures other than yours I ornament my pages"
> —Tasso, *Gerusalemme Liberata*]

And he adds this reason.

> Sai che là corre il mondo ove più versi
> di sue dolcezze il lusinghier Parnaso,
> e che 'l vero, condito in molli versi,
> i più schivi allettando ha persuaso

> ["Thither thou know'st the world is best inclined Where
> luring Parnass most his sweet imparts,
> And truth conveyed in verse of gentle kind
> To read perhaps will move the dullest hearts"]

Though rightly he touches the tenderness of human conceits, which willingly admit nothing that represents not pleasure, and flatters not sensuality; yet should it be far from the gravity of a writer, to run with the stream of unbridled affections. He should rank with the constitutors of commonwealths: lawmakers, and wise authors ought to intend both one thing, they no way differ, but that only these last compel not, but entreat their countrymen to be virtuous. But should a lawmaker instead of punishing malefactors widen his laws, and make them soft upon the complaints of men, no state could stand: for the cause of commonwealths mankind would destroy themselves; and this world by laws made beautiful, by being without, would become a spectacle of ruin, and desolation. Though in this kind poetry hath most offended, yet intending well, it is not to be rejected. It is a short and sweet tuned eloquence; it stirs up noble desires, and good intentions, when, according to Plato, it performs its office which is *Divinos hymnos canere, et leges patrias, magnorumque gesta virorum graviter recensere.* Thus it is not basely employed, nor were it reason, for it is a divine issue of understandings, and dresses the subjects of her pen full of witty delight, and is the wings of the soul with which she seems to fly to the highest part of imagination. Among poets, Seneca's Tragedies fit well the hands of a statesman, for upon that supposed stage are brought many actions, and fitting the stage of life, as when he says.

Ars prima regni est posse in inuidia pati
["The first art of the ruler is to be able to endure envy"
—Seneca]

History would have carried you through many regions, into many battles and many changes, and you should have little more for your pains, as in the life of Sylla, and many others of all times. A truly disposed mind must meditate of this, even at his entering into this life, so shall it be no stranger to him, nor drown his well performed actions with tears, and exclamations. In another place he draws the excellency of virtue, and that her strength passes all strengths.

Vertutis est domare quae cuncti pavent
["It is a virtue of courage to tame what it fears"]

For so doth virtue prepare her subject, that nothing but herself is seen of them with love, and affection, all other things being by her caught to be transitory, and mortal, even part of himself, knowing which, he neither fears nor longs for, the time of his dissolution. So is Virgil's *Aeneid* a book meet for a prince, and his nearest instruments: for it being agreed by the most judicial censures, that in matters of state many things fall out both beyond expectation and natural reason, which we therefore call the acts of fortune: he says,

Superanda omnis fortuna ferendo est
["Every misfortune is to be subdued by patience"—Virgil]

For patience keeps the reputation unspotted; though outward forces be destroyed, this makes the mind invincible, which not only gives graces and preservation of the best parts of man, but enforces more commiseration from the victor, than baseness, entreaty, and supplications, which Aemilius the utter ruin of the Macedonian glory explained, when Perseus the last of their kings being vanquished, prostrated himself at his feet, from which sight he turned his eyes, and called him the robber of his glory, for his power, and name made his victory glorious, which the vileness of his person brought back to contempt, as if he had overcome a boy, or a woman, the poorness of whose strength makes tears and supplications readier then resistance. At what time England remained unpolished and unmannered by the sweetness of letters, there was found one Caractatus, whose name Tacitus celebrates with as great praises, as if a Roman, and a conqueror; which last I name as the spur of commendations, for more faintly do all men, as well as historians mention the vanquished than conqueror: for many actions are brought forth by the haste of occasion, to whom a long discourse is not midwife, yet done, the world makes someone accessory of many plots, which he never thought of, and another guilty of imputations, because overcome. But Caractatus betrayed, and brought in triumph to Rome, was neither dejected with thinking of his captivity, nor amazed at the Romans' splendor, but then taught Claudius how it became him to use his fortune, and in spite of fortune with the magnanimity of his own mind made the action of those times confess, that Caesar

dum suum decus extollit, addidit gloriam victo
["The emperor, while he exalted his own glory,
enhanced the renown of the
vanquished" —Tacitus].

How slowly and unwillingly praises are bestowed upon the vanquished, Tacitus relates, speaking of a king of Suiones,

Digressus castellis Vannius funditur praelio : quamquam rebus adversis, laudatus quod et pugnam manu capescit, et corpore adverso vulnera excepit
["So Vannius came down out of his fortresses, and though he was defeated in battle, notwithstanding his reverse, he won some credit by having fought with his own hand, and received wounds on his breast."].

He fought valiantly, and received wounds, but was not valiant, because fortune gave him not the victory. In another, Virgil teaches that no noble minds are fearful,

degeneres animos timor argui—
["Fear betrays ignoble souls"]

Who ought better to think of this than a statesman, the height of whose actions brings him to handle things to an unprepared mind dangerous, and fearful, to eschew which binds him in a strong band, he foretells his honor, which is the most precious jewel of greatness, without which he becomes as unprofitable as a bee without a sting, for whatsoever he is, be he never so great, or good, yet,

magis fama quam vi stare res suas
["His empire was supported by reputation"
—Tacitus on Emperor Tiberius],

The reputation of a statesman, the credit of a merchant, and the modesty of a woman, prevailing more, than their powers, riches, or beauty. In another place,

Mens immota manet, lachrimae volvuntur inanes
["Though tears flow, the mind remains unmoved" —Virgil]

How feeble the succors of the body are, every understanding observing those creatures that either have no soul, or having, use it not, may easily know: for the grossness of the body's nature prevailing but by strength, when that is vanquished Lachrimae voluntur Inanes ["though tears flow"]: but a mind made strong by use and exercise Immota manet ["the mind remains unmoved"]; it looks not upon fortune with a dejected spirit, but not puffed up with the vain allurements of the body, is then plotting how to recover, not how to desire pardon: he looks upon his present state, not with tears, but upon it, because upon that groundwork he must build the course of his freedom, as he says afterward,

Tu ne cede malis sed contra audentior ito
Quatua te Fortuna sinet
["Do not yield to misfortunes; on the contrary, go more
boldly to meet them, the way your fortunes allow you"
—Virgil]

Howsoever that Scythian fellow esteemed music basely by preferring the neighing of horses before it, yet no question both music, and letters, and especially verses, which participate both with music and letters, is a brave raiser of the spirits: and I think arms disable not themselves with taking assistance from Poesie, for doubtless it makes valor beautiful, and well becoming, for taking away part of his fierceness, and adding, instead thereof, reason, makes it true fortitude. Of poets for this purpose, some learned, talk much of Homer, but though they are learned, yet I dare not speak of him, because as near as I can, I will not build upon others. Of those whom I understand, Lucan, and Tasso, the one of which is ancient, and the other as worthy, if seasoned by so much time, but I will not chide the world for that, for the reverencing of age, and times past moderately is a good fault of a good nature. But this life of arms which custom has taught to put on a gallant jolliness in his outward behavior, thereby to show, danger and distress cannot in their course mourn, or be fearful, giving leave to the mind in these outward semblances to play the braggart, and lay open what she thinks of her own resolution, which fashion of a soldier binds him to entertain all fortunes alike. For the high words and big, that use has made tolerable in this life, would add deformity to his yielding tears or complaints, but especially here.

—*Crescit on aduersis Virtus*—
["Virtue is born in hardship"]

There is the alteration which the frowns of fortune should breed in him, being rather an alarm for the summoning of his spirits, than a terror draining them away, which power, nature hath given to the elements by instinct, but a more excellent power has she given to man, namely reason, with which if he does not more than those more meanly endowed, it is his fault, not nature's, for in reason and discourse, the abilities of man, there is more than an Antipaerist aticall virtue.

> *sua quisque pericula nescit*
> *attonitus maiore metu—*
> ["Everyone's danger needs attention" —Lucan]

So fear ought every way to be remote from the life of a soldier, for neither is it handsome, nor safe, so stupefying his understanding, that neither the danger, his honor, his country, or his life is in, are either defended or regarded. But this banished makes not valor, but fury, for justice must be matched with daring, or else it is not fortitude; the cause must reconcile the effect to upright truth, or else;

> *hen quantum poena misero, mens conscia donat?*
> ["Conscience is a source of pain"]

Were guiltiness removed from punishment, yet to wrest the understanding against justice, is full of terror, the conscience being an inseparable companion, which neither corruption nor fear can make silent. In no course is it more behooving than in the life of a soldier, for arms takes upon it to correct the disorder of peace; it is the Physitian of a state, the justicer of a state, the divine of a state, for his enforcement is the Physick, the execution, the counsel administered to those obstinacies intractable, but by computation. Tasso does also yield many plentiful rules leading to the preservation of life, and after that of honor.

> *e par lieto morir, poscia che 'l crudo*
> *Totila è vinto e salvo il caro scudo*
> ["That smiling seemed to cruel death to yield,
> When Totila was fled, and safe his shield." —Tasso]

Cowards feel not death, but the meditation of death, for that concluder of mortality is no more cruel to the coward, than to the valiant, the difference rests only in their opinions, as it is in many other things of this

world. What by some imaginations are called jewels, are by others determined trifles: as these outward things, so the choosers of these, the affections, are according to their possessor: for a coward's fear, is in a wise man
providence; lavish joy, solid contentment: appetite made choice, wishes
intents, making hope fruition. Thus certain do wisdom's resolution perform his journey without halting, tiring, or straying. *E par lieto morir* ["a
cruel death"]. No doubt but to a mind that can inwardly relate a well-run
course, it cannot but be joy to be taken up, for with glory he ends, and
remaining longer he could not end better, therefore longer life could have
been but superfluous, perhaps dangerous: for many years well followed
have doted before their ends, and so corrupted their work fairly begun. *E
salvo il caro scudo* ["safe his shield"]. In this shield I hold the preservation
of honor, care of his country, and honest life, for detraction cannot be kept
out without such a triple-leaved shield: but this shield embraced, envy
itself cannot wound, but death appears like a grateful master releasing his
servant from travel.

> *E tempo è ben che qualche nobil opra*
> *De la nostra virtute omai si scopra*
> ["And time requires . . . that by some noble feat
> I should make known my strength and power great."]

So lazy, and sluggish are our natural inclinations, that I wish these
verses the perpetual object of my eyes, and if I should wish all men the
same medicine being sick of the same disease, I should do them no harm.
Who thinks of the infinite capacity of man, of his admirable invention, of
his immortalizing the whole volume of abstract, and most forms: of the
fertileness of his brain, where things are continually in conceiving, and
bringing forth new, and they new, I cannot think of any thing which he
hath done that might not be excelled, considering his abilities, his works
are mean and slight, and their perfections so imperfect, as they are not
worthy to be called the children of his loins.

> *E tempo ben*
> ["And time requires"]

It is time, so soon as our breathing hath set a scotch upon time: what
can I speak of this time, but as of the light given us to live by, which who
spends idly, or (as ill) luxuriously, is worthy to go to bed darkling, which is,

to die without being able to produce any matter worthy of his life, which vacuity of virtue at that time will breed more terror to him, then darkness to children. It is time to do that we came for; for those employed to be vigilant, to the flourishing of their country: to those private to be an example to others, and safety to themselves, in taking the direct way of right.

che qualche nobil opra
["That by some noble feat"]

I am not so precise to call no actions noble, that carry not with them a rumor, or a glittering to my meaning nobility and honesty mean all one, and thus may a painful artisan be noble, if he follow his vocation painfully and constantly, he is honest, and so noble, being a limb of a state, though no main organ, and his being in right temper, so far as his strength goes, a preservative to the whole. To know this he ought to temper the hotness of ambition, for it is not the greatness, but the goodness of an action that makes it worthy, which who so knows, and yet prosecutes the violence of that humor, ought to be cut off, for nothing is more fatal to a state than innovation, neither is there any thing so fast drawing to innovation as ambition, it being innovation's minority, like a pimple the child's age of a sore.

de la nostra virtute omai si scopra
["I should make known my strength and power great" —Tasso]

Here is the whole power of man taught, the right use, which we have a common speech no less illustrates when we call the quality of things their virtue, by which we enforce the strength of each thing to work by the line of virtue: to this center should all the diametrical parts of man tend, for they are but like the rays of the sun, which borrow their beauty from the sun, for without virtue all the abilities of man are in darkness, performing all things doubtfully, and perniciously:

si scopra
["great power"]

I do not think there can be concealed virtues, for though I hate ostentation, yet virtue aiming at nothing but the transforming her self into goodness, and the excellence of goodness resting in her communicating power, virtue is not come to her perfection, until come to the perfection of goodness.

Duce sei tu, non semplice guerriero
Publico fora, e non privato il lutto.
["No private soldier thou, thou are our guide,
If thou miscarry, all our hope were lost"]

Here doth he show the office of a general, whose judgment, not body, ought to be employed: nature has taught this to every man, for she has made his arms to give blows, and defend, his head to teach his arms; and to be sure we should not use it out of the right kind, she hath given it neither nimbleness, nor strength, but direction to teach the other parts that use. More need not be said of this, for common experience makes it every man's. I will speak now of no more poets, though there be more of use; only thus much of the ancient satirists, I hold them not meet for every man's reading, for they chide vice, and show it both together, besides their darkness, and personal meanings, take up more time, than known, they are worth: of other books though I have already commended Plato, yet speaking of books, I must again mention him for his commenter's sake, who does excellently illustrate him, which he performs with as little delay, and as few idle speeches, as the understanding receives knowledge from the sight of things which deliver themselves truly and simply unto her. I know not whether I should speak of philosophical books more, since if the reader be not a physician, or a Hebraist, they breed in him curiosity rather then use, for I account these words of Plato, *Peritia enim efficit ut via nostra per artem incedat, imperitia vero ut per fortunam temere circumvagetur*, to tend rather to the knowledges pertinent to an intended life, than to her universal body: for should a judge talk of the observations of an urn, when he is about matters of life and death, who would not determine his skill unnecessary and ridiculous, since his art cures the mind, Physick the body?

nam medici curant corpora, Poene Animam
["doctors cure the body, poetry the spirit"]

What books, or art meddles with a doctrine remote from the use of life, is a busy idleness, and a cover of an unprofitable mind, like fiddlers undertaking the use of an instrument to keep them from a more laborious trade. Less astronomy than will make a calendar, will serve my turn:

only so much is sufficient in a gentleman, as seeing the revolutions of the heavens, he may see them without dismayedness, and use his knowledge to the comfort of his ignorant charge: as Dion going against Dionysius the tyrant, an eclipse happened, which astonished the multitude, but he converted it to the eclipse of their enemies' height which fortified, and persuaded the fear, and blindness of his soldiers: the eclipse (I think) would have fallen out, though Dion had been at home quietly in his chamber, and I doubt not but this friend of Plato thought so to, but yet the minds not able to judge of truths, must be held with the exposition of these celestial appearances, and be persuaded that the heavens work thus, only to encourage, and hearten them on.

For that coupler, and combiner of words, grammar, to be much longer than it is in the arms of our nurse, is naught. I account it a pitiful sight to see a fellow at sixty years old, learning to speak: to know the names of things without the things is unprofitable, as a power to repeat the alphabet by a fellow altogether illiterate. I like well to speak, rather than to make signs, and to be careful of joining the nominative case to the verb, as my servants and friends may understand what I would; but to be prentice of Tonus and Sonus for a life time, is as needless as to make new clothes when one lies dying, for words are but clothes, matters substance. Rhetoric cookery, is the vomit of a pedant, which to make saleable, he imitated the dyer, whose fat working ill, he makes amends by giving those ill colors new names: so this venting his infinity of words with calling it eloquence, and fortifying eloquence with methodical divisions. *Rhetorica suadet, non docet* ["rhetoric to recommend, not to instruct"]. If she could persuade what were worthy to be taught, and bring that worthy with her, it were better: but the slippery glibness of the tongue gives such a facility to speak, as commonly it runs without reason, and so is as fruitless as a messenger without an errand. I might say of those remaining, that they hold more conclusions than are needful for every man, but I will go no farther than this taste. Again of books, morality hath very ill luck nowadays, for many have meddled with her with ill success: I not will name, for they are unhappy enough to be destined to waste paper. Those of commonwealths, came as much short, but it is no marvel, for commonly they are scholars that never knew more of government, than it pleased Aristotle's Politics, or some such, rich only in the names of Economics, Despoticus, and Politics, and then to define the three several governments, but they were to blame; for the theory, and practice of no art nor subject differ so much, as that of commonwealths, and state business.

Seneca of morality is the best, Petrarch's *De Remediis Utriusque Fortunae* [*Remedies of Fortune*—a popular "self-help" book], does well; but he was a sharper poet than a philosopher, there being a more excellent quickness in his sonnets than dialogues. There is now left history, which resembles counselors that advise nothing but what they themselves have done, which study is not without danger, for it is so bound to truth, that it must relate falsehood, and continue rather in relation, than in advice: of these, the truest reflecting glasses, are those that present particular men's lives. Among those I have seen none are worthy but Plutarch, and Diogenes Laertius, which two being diligently read, and rightly used, cannot but recompense the reader's pains, for the temperance of these philosophers mingled with the valor of Plutarch's captains cannot choose but make an exact man. Tacitus already has received his sentence from me, but I must again say, he is more wise than safe, but that is not his fault: for the painter is not to be blamed, though his picture be ill-favored if his pattern were so, nor Tacitus thought ill, because Tiberius was a tyrant, Claudius a fool, Nero vicious. But never was there so wise an author so ill-handled by commenter, for where, as I am sure he meant still wisely, some of them have so powdered him with morality, that they convert his juice into as little variety of good use, as beware by me good people; or if more gently, like Aesop's talking creatures, that have morals tied to their tails. The rest have left him as they found him, without making him confess anything; so that all of them have done no more than to try who loves gold so well as to pull it out of the dirt, for he that fetches his sentences out of their pages, adventures a bemiring. Comines is a good historian, he knew much of the practical part of state learning; but I hold Guicciardini a better scholar, and more sententious, as when he says,

in tutte le azioni umane, e nelle guerre massimamente,
bisogna spesso accomodare il consiglio alla necessityà.
["It was necessary to have woven fabric to
transfer the body of a saint from the Lower World"]

For the marshaling advice more cannot be said, for it teaches an adviser to take his mark so sure as he cannot miss: for respects appearing weighty in the time of the health of a state, must not be redeemed in her sickness, for preservation is to be preferred before comeliness. There are many books by me omitted, precious enough, if time will give us leave to digest these: for I am of Seneca's mind concerning this variety of books, who compares an unsettled reader, to a traveler, who has many hosts, and few friends. There are more, but mine is but an essay, not a catalogue, I think well of these books named, and the better, because they teach me how to manage myself: where any of them grow subtle, or intend high matters, I give my memory leave to lose them.

There are none that I scratch with my pen that do not fatherly counsel me to the way of virtue. I like much better to do well, than to talk well, choosing to be beloved rather than admired, aspiring to no more height than the comfort of a good conscience, and doing good to some, harm to none. If my essays speak thus, they speak as I would have them, for I think not of making morality full of embroidery, cutworks, but to clothe her in truth, and plainness: nor if they stray do I seek to amend them, for I profess not method, neither will I chain myself to the head of my chapter. If there be any yet so ignorant as may profit by them, I am content: if understandings of a higher reach despise them, not discontent, for I moderate things pleasing upon that condition, not to be touched with things displeasing; who accounts them dark and obscure, let them not blame me, for perhaps they go about to read them in darkness without a light, and then the fault is not mine, but the dimness of their own understanding: if there be any such, let them snuff their light, and look where the fault of their failing rests.

THOMAS CULPEPER
······························

OF ESSAYES [1671]

The word *essay* we have from the French, in which tongue it signifies a
trial or probation. As it is applied to things, it admits of no positive definition, which might be the reason that neither the great essayist Montaigne
nor the Lord Bacon, our more incomparable writer in the same kind, hath
thought it requisite to define the word, because it hath so little to do with
the matter it handles, rather expressing a generality of knowledge than
obliged to any particular science. As we see in building, there are many
artists that may own the completing of some parts of the fabric, yet not
claim the perfecting of the whole structure, so in essays there is required
instructions from philosophy, history, and what else can be usefully expressed for other observations and moralities of life, that in them a man
may read an epitome of himself, and the world together. Neither is it wit
and eloquence (the ornaments of the pen and thought) more lively to be
expressed in any kind of writing than in this of essays, which as they treat
of men and manners (the most natural employment of our best conceptions) there ought to be in them such a pertinent ingenuity, as tends most
to application and benefit. Histories may discover the actions of some
particular times and men, whilst essays have more familiarity with ourselves and business, giving us besides a useful acquaintance both of the
dead and living together.

Nor are they to be termed descants upon such or such particular objects
(like the wit or clinch of an epigram), or the smart sayings in characters
and satyrs (though handling much of the same argument), nor the sweet
and elegant insinuations of poets and orators, that can contain the business of essays. Though they may gather some honey from the best flowers of wit and learning, they have a limitation from none, and yet come
nearer ourselves than these can make them, which as it is a just dignity
appearing to this kind of writing, so it needed not to have been instanced
to the judicious reader, who cannot be unknowing thereof. Besides I am
not to forget that in extolling the subject which I handle, I do in some sort
prompt a greater expectation in point of performance than I desire the
reader should have from my abilities, since howsoever this book comes

now to be published, it was but the result of private thoughts, by which I endeavoured to take some prospect of the opinions, business, and manners of the world (being indeed the chief accomplishments of human life), though not without hopes that if these papers at any time were made so bold as to be seen by the world in print, it would not be altogether without that profit which I have reaped from them myself.

CHARLES COLTON
....

ON WRITING [1685]

The awkwardness and embarrassment which all feel on beginning to
write, when they *themselves* are the theme, ought to serve as a hint to authors, that *self* is a subject they ought very rarely to descant upon. It is
extremely easy to be as egotistical as Montaigne, and as conceited as Rousseau; but it is extremely difficult to be as entertaining as the one, or as
eloquent as the other.

Men whose reputation stands deservedly high as writers, have often
miserably failed as speakers: their pens seem to have been enriched at the
expense of their tongues. Addison and Gibbon attempted oratory in the
senate, only to fail. "*The good speakers,*" says Gibbon, "*filled me with despair,
the bad ones with apprehension.*" And in more modern times, the powerful
depicter of Harold, and the elegant biographer of Leo, have both failed in
oratory; the capital of the former is so great in many things, that he can
afford to fail in one. But to return, many reasons might be offered to reconcile that contradiction which my subject seems to involve. In the first
place, those talents that constitute a fine writer, are more distinct from
those that constitute an orator, than might be at first supposed; I admit
that they may be sometimes accidentally, but never necessarily combined.
—That the qualifications for writing and those for eloquence, are in many
points distinct, would appear from the converse of the proposition, for
there have been many fine speakers, who have proved themselves bad
writers. There is good ground for believing that Mr. Pitt would not have
shone as an author; and the attempt of Mr. Fox in that arena, has added
nothing to his celebrity. Abstraction of thought, seclusion from popular
tumult, occasional retirement to the study, a diffidence in our own opinions, a deference to those of other men, a sensibility that feels every thing,
a humility that arrogates nothing, are necessary qualifications for a writer;
but their very opposites would perhaps be preferred by an orator. He that
has spent much of his time in a study, will seldom be collected enough
to think in a crowd, or confident enough to talk in one. We may also add;
that mistakes of the pen in the study, may be committed without publicity;
and rectified without humiliation. But mistakes of the tongue, commit-

ted in the senate, never escape with impunity. *Fugit irrevocabile verbum.* Eloquence, to produce her full effect, should start from the head of the orator, as Pallas from the brain of Jove, completely armed and equipped. Diffidence, therefore, which is so able a mentor to the writer, would prove a dangerous counsellor for the orator. As writers, the most timid may boggle twenty times in a day with their pen, and it is their own fault if it be known even to their valet; but, as orators, if they chance to boggle once with their tongue, the detection is as public as the delinquency; the punishment is irremissible, and immediately follows the offence. It is the knowledge and the fear of this, that destroys their eloquence as orators, who have sensibility and taste for writing, but neither collectedness nor confidence for speaking; for fear not only magnifies difficulties, but diminishes our power to overcome them, and thus doubly debilitates her victims. But another cause of their deficiency as orators, who have shone as writers, is this, *mole runt sua;* they know they have a character to support by their tongue, which they have previously gained by their pen, They rise, determined to attempt more than other men, and for that very reason they effect less, and doubly disappoint their hearers. They miss of that which is clear, obvious, and appropriate, in a laboured search after that which is far-fetched, recondite, and refined; like him that would fain give us better bread than can be made of wheat. Affectation is the cause of this error, disgust its consequence, and disgrace its punishment.

JOSEPH ADDISON
....

ON THE ESSAY FORM [1711]

Méga Biblion, méga kakón
["A great book is a great evil."]

A Man who publishes his Works in a Volume, has an infinite Advantage over one who communicates his Writings to the World in loose Tracts and single Pieces. We do not expect to meet with any thing in a bulky Volume, till after some heavy Preamble, and several Words of Course, to prepare the Reader for what follows: Nay, Authors have established it as a kind of Rule, that a Man ought to be dull sometimes; as the most severe Reader makes Allowances for many Rests and Nodding-places in a Voluminous Writer. This gave Occasion to the famous Greek Proverb which I have chosen for my Motto, *That a great Book is a great Evil.*

On the contrary, those who publish their Thoughts in distinct Sheets, and as it were by Piece-meal, have none of these Advantages. We must immediately fall into our Subject, and treat every Part of it in a lively Manner, or our Papers are thrown by as dull and insipid: Our Matter must lie close together, and either be wholly new in itself, or in the Turn it receives from our Expressions. Were the Books of our best Authors thus to be retailed to the Publick, and every Page submitted to the Taste of forty or fifty thousand Readers, I am afraid we should complain of many flat Expressions, trivial Observations, beaten Topicks, and common Thoughts, which go off very well in the Lump. At the same Time, notwithstanding some Papers may be made up of broken Hints and irregular Sketches, it is often expected that every Sheet should be a kind of Treatise, and make out in Thought what it wants in Bulk: That a Point of Humour should be worked up in all its Parts; and a Subject touched upon in its most essential Articles, without the Repetitions, Tautologies and Enlargements, that are indulged to longer Labours. The ordinary Writers of Morality prescribe to their Readers after the Galenick way; their Medicines are made up in large Quantities. An Essay-Writer must practise in the Chymical Method, and give the Virtue of a full Draught in a few Drops. Were all Books reduced thus to their Quintessence, many a bulky Author would make his Appearance in a Penny-Paper: There would be scarce such a thing in Nature as a Folio. The Works of an Age would be contained on a few Shelves; not to mention millions of Volumes that would be utterly annihilated.

I cannot think that the Difficulty of furnishing out separate Papers of this Nature, has hindered Authors from communicating their Thoughts to the World after such a Manner: Though I must confess I am amazed that the Press should be only made use of in this Way by News-Writers, and the Zealots of Parties; as if it were not more advantageous to Mankind to be instructed in Wisdom and Virtue, than in Politicks; and to be made good Fathers, Husbands and Sons, than Counsellors and Statesmen. Had the Philosophers and great Men of Antiquity, who took so much Pains in order to instruct Mankind, and leave the World wiser and better than they found it; had they, I say, been possessed of the Art of Printing, there is no question but they would have made such an Advantage of it, in dealing out their Lectures to the Publick. Our common Prints would be of great Use were they thus calculated to diffuse good Sense through the Bulk of a People, to clear up their Understandings, animate their Minds with Virtue, dissipate the Sorrows of a heavy Heart, or unbend the Mind from its more severe Employments with innocent Amusements. When Knowledge, instead of being bound up in Books and kept in Libraries and Retirements, is thus obtruded upon the Publick; when it is canvassed in every Assembly, and exposed upon every Table, I cannot forbear reflecting upon that Passage in the Proverbs:

Wisdom crieth without, she uttereth her Voice in the Streets: she crieth in the chief Place of Concourse, in the Openings of the Gates. In the City she uttereth her Words, saying, How long, ye simple ones, will ye love Simplicity? and the Scorners delight in their Scorning? and Fools hate Knowledge?

The many Letters which come to me from Persons of the best Sense in both Sexes, (for I may pronounce their Characters from their Way of Writing) do not at a little encourage me in the Prosecution of this my Undertaking: Besides that my Book-seller tells me, the Demand for these my Papers increases daily. It is at his Instance that I shall continue my rural Speculations to the End of this Month; several having made up separate Sets of them, as they have done before of those relating to Wit, to Operas, to Points of Morality, or Subjects of Humour.

I am not at all mortified, when sometimes I see my Works thrown aside by Men of no Taste nor Learning. There is a kind of Heaviness and Ignorance that hangs upon the Minds of ordinary Men, which is too thick for Knowledge to break through. Their Souls are not to be enlightened.

Nox atra cava circumvolat umbra.
["Black night surrounded [us] with its enfolding shadows."
—Virgil. *Aeneid* 2.360]

To these I must apply the Fable of the Mole, That after having consulted many Oculists for the bettering of his Sight, was at last provided with a good Pair of Spectacles; but upon his endeavouring to make use of them, his Mother told him very prudently, "That Spectacles, though they might help the Eye of a Man, could be of no use to a Mole." It is not therefore for the Benefit of Moles that I publish these my daily Essays.

But besides such as are Moles through Ignorance, there are others who are Moles through Envy. As it is said in the Latin Proverb, 'That one Man is a Wolf to another;' so generally speaking, one Author is a Mole to another Author. It is impossible for them to discover Beauties in one another's Works; they have Eyes only for Spots and Blemishes: They can indeed see the Light as it is said of the Animals which are their Namesakes, but the Idea of it is painful to them; they immediately shut their Eyes upon it, and withdraw themselves into a willful Obscurity. I have already caught two or three of these dark undermining Vermin, and intend to make a String of them, in order to hang them up in one of my Papers, as an Example to all such voluntary Moles.

OF ESSAY WRITING [1742]

The elegant Part of Mankind, who are not immersed in the animal Life, but employ themselves in the Operations of the Mind, may be divided into the learned and conversible. The Learned are such as have chosen for their Portion the higher and more difficult Operations of the Mind, which require Leisure and Solitude, and cannot be brought to Perfection, without long Preparation and severe Labor. The conversible World join to a sociable Disposition, and a Taste of Pleasure, an Inclination to the easier and more gentle Exercises of the Understanding, to obvious Reflections on human Affairs, and the Duties of common Life, and to the Observation of the Blemishes or Perfections of the particular Objects, that surround them. Such Subjects of Thought furnish not sufficient Employment in Solitude, but require the Company and Conversation of our Fellow-Creatures, to render them a proper Exercise for the Mind: And this brings Mankind together in Society, where every one displays his Thoughts and Observations in the best Manner he is able, and mutually gives and receives Information, as well as Pleasure.

The Separation of the Learned from the conversible World seems to have been the great Defect of the last Age, and must have had a very bad Influence both on Books and Company: For what Possibility is there of finding Topics of Conversation fit for the Entertainment of rational Creatures, without having Recourse sometimes to History, Poetry, Politics, and the more obvious Principles, at least, of Philosophy? Must our whole Discourse be a continued Series of gossiping Stories and idle Remarks? Must the Mind never rise higher, but be perpetually

> Stun'd and worn out with endless Chat
> Of WILL did this, and NAN said that.

This would be to render the Time spent in Company the most unentertaining, as well as the most unprofitable Part of our Lives.

On the other Hand, Learning has been as great a Loser by being shut up in Colleges and Cells, and secluded from the World and good Company. By that Means, every Thing of what we call *Belles Lettres* became totally barbarous, being cultivated by Men without any Taste of Life or Manners, and without that Liberty and Facility of Thought and Expression, which can only be acquired by Conversation. Even Philosophy went to Wrack by this moping recluse Method of Study, and became as chimerical in her Conclusions as she was unintelligible in her Stile and Manner of Delivery. And indeed, what could be expected from Men who never consulted Experience in any of their Reasonings, or who never searched for that Experience, where alone it is to be found, in common Life and Conversation?

'Tis with great Pleasure I observe, That Men of Letters, in this Age, have lost, in a great Measure, that Shyness and Bashfulness of Temper, which kept them at a Distance from Mankind; and, at the same Time, That Men of the World are proud of borrowing from Books their most agreeable Topics of Conversation.

'Tis to be hoped, that this League betwixt the learned and conversible Worlds, which is so happily begun, will be still farther improved to their mutual Advantage; and to that End, I know nothing more advantageous than such *Essays* as these with which I endeavor to entertain the Public. In this View, I cannot but consider myself as a Kind of Resident or Ambassador from the Dominions of Learning to those of Conversation; and shall think it my constant Duty to promote a good Correspondence betwixt these two States, which have so great a Dependence on each other. I shall give Intelligence to the Learned of whatever passes in Company, and shall endeavor to import into Company whatever Commodities I find in my native Country proper for their Use and Entertainment. The Balance of Trade we need not be jealous of, nor will there be any Difficulty to preserve it on both Sides. The Materials of this Commerce must chiefly be furnished by Conversation and common Life: The manufacturing of them alone belongs to Learning.

As 'twould be an unpardonable Negligence in an Ambassador not to pay his Respects to the Sovereign of the State where he is commissioned to reside; so it would be altogether inexcusable in me not to address myself, with a particular Respect, to the Fair Sex, who are the Sovereigns of the Empire of Conversation. I approach them with Reverence; and were not my Countrymen, the Learned, a stubborn independent Race of Mortals, extremely jealous of their Liberty, and unaccustomed to Subjection, I should resign into their fair Hands the sovereign Authority over the Republic of Letters. As the Case stands, my Commission extends no farther, than to desire a League, offensive and defensive, against our common Enemies, against the Enemies of Reason and Beauty, People of dull Heads and cold Hearts. From this Moment let us pursue them with the severest Vengeance: Let no Quarter be given, but to those of sound Understandings and delicate Affections; and these Characters, 'tis to be presumed, we shall always find inseparable.

To be serious, and to quit the Allusion before it be worn thread-bare, I am of Opinion, that Women, that is, Women of Sense and Education (for to such alone I address myself) are much better Judges of all polite Writing than Men of the same Degree of Understanding; and that 'tis a vain Panic, if they be so far terrified with the common Ridicule that is leveled against learned Ladies, as utterly to abandon every Kind of Books and Study to our Sex. Let the Dread of that Ridicule have no other Effect, than to make them conceal their Knowledge before Fools, who are not worthy of it, nor of them. Such will still presume upon the vain Title of the Male Sex to affect a Superiority above them: But my fair Readers may be assured, that all Men of Sense, who know the World, have a great Deference for their Judgment of such Books as lie within the Compass of their Knowledge, and repose more Confidence in the Delicacy of their Taste, though unguided by Rules, than in all the dull Labors of Pedants and Commentators. In a neighboring Nation, equally famous for good Taste, and for Gallantry, the Ladies are, in a Manner, the Sovereigns of the *learned* World, as well as of the *conversible*; and no polite Writer pretends to venture upon the Public, without the Approbation of some celebrated Judges of that Sex. Their Verdict is, indeed, sometimes complained of; and, in particular, I find, that the Admirers of *Corneille*, to save that great Poet's Honor upon the Ascendant that *Racine* began to take over him, always said, That it was not to be expected, that so old a Man could dispute the Prize, before such Judges, with so young a Man as his Rival. But this Observation has been found unjust, since Posterity seems to have ratified the Verdict of that Tribunal: And *Racine*, tho' dead, is still the Favorite of the Fair Sex, as well as of the best Judges among the Men.

There is only one Subject, on which I am apt to distrust the Judgment of Females, and that is, concerning Books of Gallantry and Devotion, which they commonly affect as high flown as possible; and most of them seem more delighted with the Warmth, than with the justness of the Passion. I mention Gallantry and Devotion as the same Subject, because, in Reality, they become the same when treated in this Manner; and we may observe that they both depend upon the very same Complexion. As the Fair Sex have a great Share of the tender and amorous Disposition, it perverts their Judgment on this Occasion, and makes them be easily affected, even by what has no Propriety in the Expression nor Nature in the Sentiment. Mr. *Addison's* elegant Discourses of Religion have no Relish with them, in Comparison of Books of mystic Devotion: And *Otway's* Tragedies are rejected for the Rants of Mr. *Dryden*.

Would the Ladies correct their false Taste in this Particular; Let them accustom themselves a little more to Books of all Kinds: Let them give Encouragement to Men of Sense and Knowledge to frequent their Company: And finally, let them concur heartily in that Union I have projected betwixt the learned and conversible Worlds. They may, perhaps, meet with more Complaisance from their usual Followers than from Men of Learning; but they cannot reasonably expect so sincere an Affection: And, I hope, they will never be guilty of so wrong a Choice, as to sacrifice the Substance to the Shadow.

SAMUEL JOHNSON

....

THE RAMBLER, TUESDAY, MARCH 20, 1750

FIRST ADDRESS

> Cur tamen hoc libeat potius decurrere campo
> Per quem magnus equos auruncæ flexit alumnus,
> Si vacat, et placidi rationem admittitis, edam.
> —Juvenal

> Why to expatiate in this beaten field,
> Why arms, oft us'd in vain, I mean to wield:
> If time permit, and candour will attend,
> Some satisfaction this essay may lend.
> —Elphinston

The difficulty of the first address on any new occasion, is felt by every man in his transactions with the world, and confessed by the settled and regular forms of salutation which necessity has introduced into all languages. Judgment was wearied with the perplexity of being forced upon choice, where there was no motive to preference; and it was found convenient that some easy method of introduction should be established, which, if it wanted the allurement of novelty, might enjoy the security of prescription.

Perhaps few authors have presented themselves before the publick, without wishing that such ceremonial modes of entrance had been anciently established, as might have freed them from those dangers which the desire of pleasing is certain to produce, and precluded the vain expedients of softening censure by apologies, or rousing attention by abruptness.

The epick writers have found the proemial part of the poem such an addition to their undertaking, that they have almost unanimously adopted the first lines of Homer, and the reader needs only be informed of the subject, to know in what manner the poem will begin.

But this solemn repetition is hitherto the peculiar distinction of heroick poetry; it has never been legally extended to the lower orders of literature, but seems to be considered as an hereditary privilege, to be enjoyed only by those who claim it from their alliance to the genius of Homer.

The rules which the injudicious use of this prerogative suggested to Horace, may indeed be applied to the direction of candidates for inferior fame; it may be proper for all to remember, that they ought not to raise expectation which it is not in their power to satisfy, and that it is more pleasing to see smoke brightening into flame, than flame sinking into smoke.

This precept has been long received, both from regard to the authority of Horace, and its conformity to the general opinion of the world; yet there have been always some, that thought it no deviation from modesty to recommend their own labours, and imagined themselves entitled by indisputable merit to an exemption from general restraints, and to elevations not allowed in common life. They perhaps believed, that when, like Thucydides, they bequeathed to mankind, 'χλημα ἐς ἀδί—*an estate for ever,*' it was an additional favour to inform them of its value.

It may, indeed, be no less dangerous to claim, on certain occasions, too little than too much. There is something captivating in spirit and intrepidity, to which we often yield, as to a resistless power; nor can he reasonably expect the confidence of others, who too apparently distrusts himself.

Plutarch, in his enumeration of the various occasions on which a man may without just offence proclaim his own excellencies, has omitted the case of an author entering the world, unless it may be comprehended under his general position, that a man may lawfully praise himself for those qualities which cannot be known but from his own mouth; as when he is among strangers, and can have no opportunity of an actual exertion of his powers. That the case of an author is parallel will scarcely be granted, because he necessarily discovers the degree of his merit to his judges when he appears at his trial. But it should be remembered, that unless his judges are inclined to favour him, they will hardly be persuaded to hear the cause.

In love, the state which fills the heart with a degree of solicitude next that of an author, it has been held a maxim, that success is most easily obtained by indirect and unperceived approaches; he who too soon professes himself a lover, raises obstacles to his own wishes, and those whom disappointments have taught experience, endeavour to conceal their passion till they believe their mistress wishes for the discovery. The same method, if it were practicable to writers, would save many complaints of the severity of the age, and the caprices of criticism. If a man could glide imperceptibly into the favour of the publick, and only proclaim his pretensions to literary honours when he is sure of not being rejected, he might commence author with better hopes, as his failings might escape contempt, though he shall never attain much regard.

But since the world supposes every man that writes ambitious of applause, as some ladies have taught themselves to believe that every man intends love, who expresses civility, the miscarriage of any endeavour in learning raises an unbounded contempt, indulged by most minds, without scruple, as an honest triumph over unjust claims and exorbitant expectations. The artifices of those who put themselves in this hazardous state, have therefore been multiplied in proportion to their fear as well as their ambition; and are to be looked upon with more indulgence, as they are incited at once by the two great movers of the human mind—the desire of good, and the fear of evil. For who can wonder that, allured on one side, and frightened on the other, some should endeavour to gain favour by bribing the judge with an appearance of respect which they do not feel, to excite compassion by confessing weakness of which they are not convinced; and others to attract regard by a show of openness and magnanimity, by a daring profession of their own deserts, and a publick challenge of honours and rewards?

The ostentatious and haughty display of themselves has been the usual refuge of diurnal writers, in vindication of whose practice it may be said, that what it wants in prudence is supplied by sincerity, and who at least may plead, that if their boasts deceive any into the perusal of their performances, they defraud them of but little time.

Quid enim? Concurritur horæ
Memento cita mors venit, aut victoria læta.
—Horace.

The battle join, and in a moment's flight,
Death, or a joyful conquest, ends the fight.
—Francis.

The question concerning the merit of the day is soon decided, and we are not condemned to toil through half a folio, to be convinced that the writer has broke his promise.

It is one among many reasons for which I purpose to endeavour the entertainment of my countrymen by a short essay on Tuesday and Saturday, that I hope not much to tire those whom I shall not happen to please;

and if I am not commended for the beauty of my works, to be at least pardoned for their brevity. But whether my expectations are most fixed on pardon or praise, I think it not necessary to discover; for having accurately weighed the reasons for arrogance and submission, I find them so nearly equiponderant, that my impatience to try the event of my first performance will not suffer me to attend any longer the trepidations of the balance.

There are, indeed, many conveniences almost peculiar to this method of publication, which may naturally flatter the author, whether he be confident or timorous. The man to whom the extent of his knowledge, or the sprightliness of his imagination has, in his own opinion, already secured the praises of the world, willingly takes that way of displaying his abilities which will soonest give him an opportunity of hearing the voice of fame; it heightens his alacrity to think in how many places he shall hear what he is now writing, read with ecstasies to-morrow. He will often please himself with reflecting, that the author of a large treatise must proceed with anxiety, lest, before the completion of his work, the attention of the publick may have changed its object; but that he who is confined to no single topic may follow the national taste through all its variations, and catch the aura *popularis*, the gale of favour, from what point soever it shall blow.

Nor is the prospect less likely to ease the doubts of the cautious, and the terrors of the fearful; for to such the shortness of every single paper is a powerful encouragement. He that questions his abilities to arrange the dissimilar parts of an extensive plan, or fears to be lost in a complicated system, may yet hope to adjust a few pages without perplexity; and if, when he turns over the repositories of his memory, he finds his collection too small for a volume, he may yet have enough to furnish out an essay. He that would fear to lay out too much time upon an experiment of which he knows not the event, persuades himself that a few days will show him what he is to expect from his learning and his genius. If he thinks his own judgment not sufficiently enlightened, he may, by attending the remarks which every paper will produce, rectify his opinions. If he should with too little premeditation encumber himself by an unwieldy subject, he can quit it without confessing his ignorance, and pass to other topics less dangerous, or more tractable. And if he finds, with all his industry, and all his artifices, that he cannot deserve regard, or cannot attain it, he may let the design fall at once, and, without injury to others or himself, retire to amusements of greater pleasure, or to studies of better prospect.

SAMUEL JOHNSON

....

THE RAMBLER, SATURDAY, MARCH 14, 1752

THE RAMBLER'S FAREWELL

Ἡράκλειτος ἐγώ· τί μ' ἄνω κάτω ἕλκετ' ἄμουσοι;
οὐχ ὑμῖν ἐπόνουν, τοῖς δ' ἔμ' ἐπισταμένοις.
εἷς ἐμοὶ ἄνθρωπος τρισμύριοι, οἱ δ' ἀνάριθμοι
οὐδείς. ταῦτ' αὐδῶ καὶ παρὰ Φερσεφόνῃ.
—Diogenes Laertius

Begone, ye blockheads, Heraclitus cries,
And leave my labours to the learn'd and wise;
By wit, by knowledge, studious to be read,
I scorn the multitude, alive and dead.

Time, which puts an end to all human pleasures and sorrows, has likewise concluded the labours of the Rambler. Having supported, for two years, the anxious employment of a periodical writer, and multiplied my essays to upwards of two hundred, I have now determined to desist.

The reasons of this resolution it is of little importance to declare, since justification is unnecessary when no objection is made. I am far from supposing, that the cessation of my performances will raise any inquiry, for I have never been much a favourite of the publick, nor can boast that, in the progress of my undertaking, I have been animated by the rewards of the liberal, the caresses of the great, or the praises of the eminent.

But I have no design to gratify pride by submission, or malice by lamentation; nor think it reasonable to complain of neglect from those whose regard I never solicited. If I have not been distinguished by the distributors of literary honours, I have seldom descended to the arts by which favour is obtained. I have seen the meteors of fashions rise and fall, without any attempt to add a moment to their duration. I have never complied with temporary curiosity, nor enabled my readers to discuss the topick of the day; I have rarely exemplified my assertions by living characters; in my papers, no man could look for censures of his enemies, or praises of himself; and they only were expected to peruse them, whose passions left them leisure for abstracted truth, and whom virtue could please by its naked dignity.

To some, however, I am indebted for encouragement, and to others for assistance. The number of my friends was never great, but they have been such as would not suffer me to think that I was writing in vain, and I did not feel much dejection from the want of popularity.

My obligations having not been frequent, my acknowledgments may be soon despatched. I can restore to all my correspondents their productions, with little diminution of the bulk of my volumes, though not without the loss of some pieces to which particular honours have been paid.

The parts from which I claim no other praise than that of having given them an opportunity of appearing, are the four billets in the tenth paper, the second letter in the fifteenth, the thirtieth, the forty-fourth, the ninety-seventh, and the hundredth papers, and the second letter in the hundred and seventh.

Having thus deprived myself of many excuses which candour might have admitted for the inequality of my compositions, being no longer able to allege the necessity of gratifying correspondents, the importunity with which publication was solicited, or obstinacy with which correction was rejected, I must remain accountable for all my faults, and submit, without subterfuge, to the censures of criticism, which, however, I shall not endeavour to soften by a formal deprecation, or to overbear by the influence of a patron. The supplications of an author never yet reprieved him a moment from oblivion; and, though greatness has sometimes sheltered guilt, it can afford no protection to ignorance or dullness. Having hitherto attempted only the propagation of truth, I will not at last violate it by the confession of terrors which I do not feel; having laboured to maintain the dignity of virtue, I will not now degrade it by the meanness of dedication.

The seeming vanity with which I have sometimes spoken of myself, would perhaps require an apology, were it not extenuated by the example of those who have published essays before me, and by the privilege which every nameless writer has been hitherto allowed. "A mask," says Castiglione, "confers a right of acting and speaking with less restraint, even when the wearer happens to be known." He that is discovered without his own consent, may claim some indulgence, and cannot be rigorously called to justify those sallies or frolics which his disguise must prove him desirous to conceal.

But I have been cautious lest this offense should be frequently or grossly committed; for, as one of the philosophers directs us to live with a friend, as with one that is some time to become an enemy, I have always thought it the duty of an anonymous author to write, as if he expected to be hereafter known.

I am willing to flatter myself with hopes, that, by collecting these papers, I am not preparing, for my future life, either shame or repentance. That all are happily imagined, or accurately polished, that the same sentiments have not sometimes recurred, or the same expressions been too frequently repeated, I have not confidence in my abilities sufficient to warrant. He that condemns himself to compose on a stated day, will often bring to his task an attention dissipated, a memory embarrassed, an imagination overwhelmed, a mind distracted with anxieties, a body languishing with disease: he will labour on a barren topic, till it is too late to change it; or, in the ardour of invention, diffuse his thoughts into wild exuberance, which the pressing hour of publication cannot suffer judgment to examine or reduce.

Whatever shall be the final sentence of mankind, I have at least endeavoured to deserve their kindness. I have laboured to refine our language to grammatical purity, and to clear it from colloquial barbarisms, licentious idioms, and irregular combinations. Something, perhaps, I have added to the elegance of its construction, and something to the harmony of its cadence. When common words were less pleasing to the ear, or less distinct in their signification, I have familiarized the terms of philosophy, by applying them to popular ideas, but have rarely admitted any words not authorized by former writers; for I believe that whoever knows the English tongue in its present extent, will be able to express his thoughts without further help from other nations.

As it has been my principal design to inculcate wisdom or piety, I have allotted few papers to the idle sports of imagination. Some, perhaps, may be found, of which the highest excellence is harmless merriment; but scarcely any man is so steadily serious as not to complain, that the severity of dictatorial instruction has been too seldom relieved, and that he is driven by the sternness of the Rambler's philosophy to more cheerful and airy companions.

Next to the excursions of fancy are the disquisitions of criticism, which, in my opinion, is only to be ranked among the subordinate and instrumental arts. Arbitrary decision and general exclamation I have carefully avoided, by asserting nothing without a reason, and establishing all my principles of judgment on unalterable and evident truth.

In the pictures of life I have never been so studious of novelty or surprise, as to depart wholly from all resemblance; a fault which writers deservedly celebrated frequently commit, that they may raise, as the occasion requires, either mirth or abhorrence. Some enlargement may be allowed to declamation, and some exaggeration to burlesque, but as they deviate farther from reality, they become less useful, because their lessons will fail of application. The mind of the reader is carried away from the contemplation of his own manner; he finds in himself no likeness to the phantom before him; and though he laughs or rages, is not reformed.

The essays professedly serious, if I have been able to execute my own intentions, will be found exactly conformable to the precepts of Christianity, without any accommodation to the licentiousness and levity of the present age. I therefore look back on this part of my work with pleasure, which no blame or praise of man shall diminish or augment. I shall never envy the honours which wit and learning obtain in any other cause, if I can be numbered among the writers who have given ardour to virtue, and confidence to truth.

Αὐτῶν ἐκ μακάρων ἀντάξιος εἴη ἀμοιβή.

Celestial pow'rs! that piety regard,
From you my labours wait their last reward.

ON PERIODICAL ESSAYS [1808]

I look upon a periodical essayist as a writer who claims a peculiar intimacy with the public. He does not come upon them at once in all the
majesty of a quarto or all the gaiety of a *beau duodecimo,*' smooth and well
dressed: but his acquaintance is likely to be more lasting, because it is
more gradual and because you see him in a greater variety of subject and
opinion. If you do not like him at first you may give up his conversation;
but the author of a book is fixed upon you forever, and if he cannot entertain you beyond the moment, you must even give him sleeping room
in your library. But how many pleasant modes are there of getting rid of
a periodical essay? It may assist your meditation by lighting your pipe, it
may give steadiness to your candle, it may curl the tresses of your daughter or your sister, or lastly, if you are not rich enough to possess an urn or a
cloth-holder, it may save you a world of opodeldoc by wrapping the handle
of your tea-kettle. These are advantages.

The title of my essays may perhaps alarm some of my friends with
its magnificence, and the repetition of the name Examiner may annoy
others with its monotony. But with respect to the later objection, I regard
the various departments of this paper as children of the same family, and
therefore though of different professions they all have the same surname:
A gentleman of the name of Simkins for instance has three sons, one a
politician, another a theatrical critic, and the third a philosopher; a person
sees these three honest men and points them out to his friend, That is Mr.
Simkins the politician, with the black hair; the next to him, a thin man,
Mr. Simkins the critic; the other, pale-faced gentleman, is Mr. Simkins the
philosopher. Just so I have my Political Examiner, my Theatrical Examiner, and my Literary and Philosophical Examiner. As to the epithet *literary*, it is no very boastful title when every editor of a newspaper claims the
palm of authorship; and with respect to the title of philosopher, it means
nothing more in its original sense than a Lover of Wisdom, and my readers must confess, that it would be a most unpardonable rudeness in any
person to come with his objections between me and my mistress. (I put
the lady last for the sake of climax.)

A Philosopher in fact, or in other words a Lover of Wisdom, claims
no more merit to himself for his title than is claimed by the lover of any
other lady; all his praise consists in having discovered her beauty and
good sense. He is, like any other submissive swain, a mere machine in
her hands. It is his business to echo and to praise every word she says, to
doat upon her charms, and to insist to every body he meets that the world
would want its sunshine without her.

The age of periodical philosophy is perhaps gone by, but Wisdom is an
ever-lasting beauty; and I have the advantage of all the lessons in philosophic gallantry which my predecessors have left behind them. Perhaps I
may avoid some of the inelegancies, though I may be hopeless of attaining
the general charm of these celebrated men. I shall always endeavor to recollect the consummate ease and gentility with which Addison approached
his divine fair one and the passionate earnestness with which he would
gaze upon her in the intervals of the most graceful familiarity; but then I
must not forget his occasional incorrectness of language and his want of
depth, when he attempted to display the critic. Goldsmith, next to Addison, was the favorite who approached Wisdom with the happiest mixture
of seriousness and pleasantry; the instant he began to speak, you were
prepared for elegance, solidity; and a most natural manner of expression:
it must be confessed indeed, that he was infinitely more correct in his
general manner than Addison, but it must also be recollected that the latter spoke first and was more original.

Johnson paid his devoirs like one who claimed rather than entreated
notice, for he knew his desert; it becomes me to be more humble, and I
hope it will be my good fortune to see Wisdom in her cheerful moments a
little oftener than the melancholy Rambler; at the same time I must confess that I have not the slightest hope of viewing her so clearly or of venturing half so far within the sphere of her approach. There was a coldness
in the obeisance of Hawkesworth, but there was also a thoughtfulness
and a dignity: what he spoke was always acknowledged by the circle, but it
seldom reached their feelings. Colman and Thornton did not profess sensibility, they were content with a jauntiness and a pleasantry, that ought to
have been their ornament rather than their sole merit.

Mackenzie felt the beauty more than the mind of his goddess; he stood
rather bashfully behind, and could never venture into her presence without an introduction by some other admirer; but he was full of sensibility,
and Wisdom never smiled upon him with such complacency as when his
eyes were filled with tears.

If I can persuade the public to hear me after these celebrated men, I shall think myself extremely fortunate; if I can amuse them with any originality, I shall think myself deserving; if I procure them any moral benefit, I shall think myself most happy. It will be my endeavor to avoid those subjects which have been already handled in periodical works, or at any rate if I should be tempted to use them, I will exert myself to give them a new air and recommendation.

If I begin with promises however, my reader will begin with suspicion. I wish to make an acquaintance with him, and I know that it is not customary on your first introduction to a person to tell him how you mean to enchant him in your future connexion. My new acquaintance and I therefore will sit still a little and reconnoitre each other with true English civility.

William Hazlitt
·······················

ON THE PERIODICAL ESSAYISTS [1819]

THE PROPER STUDY OF MANKIND IS MAN

I now come to speak of that sort of writing which has been so successfully
cultivated in this country by our periodical Essayists, and which consists
in applying the talents and resources of the mind to all that mixed mass of
human affairs, which, though not included under the head of any regular
art, science, or profession, falls under the cognizance of the writer, and
comes home to the business and bosoms of men.

Quicquid agunt homines nostri farrago libelli,
["All the doings of mankind shall form the motley subject of my page."]

is the general motto of this department of literature. It does not treat of
minerals or fossils, of the virtues of plants, or the influence of planets;
it does not meddle with forms of belief, or systems of philosophy, nor
launch into the world of spiritual existences; but it makes familiar with
the world of men and women, records their actions, assigns their motives,
exhibits their whims, characterises their pursuits in all their singular and
endless variety, ridicules their absurdities, exposes their inconsistencies,
"holds the mirror up to nature, and shews the very age and body of the
time its form and pressure;" takes minutes of our dress, air, looks, words,
thoughts, and actions; shews us what we are, and what we are not; plays
the whole game of human life over before us, and by making us enlightened Spectators of its many-coloured scenes, enables us (if possible) to
become tolerably reasonable agents in the one in which we have to perform a part. "The act and practice part of life is thus made the mistress
of our theorique." It is the best and most natural course of study. It is in
morals and manners what the experimental is in natural philosophy, as
opposed to the dogmatical method. It does not deal in sweeping clauses of
proscription and anathema, but in nice distinctions and liberal constructions. It makes up its general accounts from details, its few theories from
many facts. It does not try to prove all black or all white as it wishes, but

lays on the intermediate colors, (and most of them not unpleasing ones,) as it finds them blended with "the web of our life, which is of a mingled yarn, good and ill together." It inquires what human life is and has been, to shew what it ought to be. It follows it into courts and camps, into town and country, into rustic sports or learned disputations, into the various shades of prejudice or ignorance, of refinement or barbarism, into its private haunts or public pageants, into its weaknesses and littlenesses, its professions and its practices—before it pretends to distinguish right from wrong, or one thing from another. How, indeed, should it do so otherwise?

> Quid sit pulchrum, quid turpe, quid
> utile, quid non, Plenius et melius
> Chrysippo et Crantore dicit.

The writers I speak of are, if not moral philosophers, moral historians, and that's better: or if they are both, they found the one character upon the other; their premises precede their conclusions; and we put faith in their testimony, for we know that it is true.

Montaigne was the first person who in his Essays led the way to this kind of writing among the moderns. The great merit of Montaigne then was, that he may be said to have been the first who had the courage to say as an author what he felt as a man. And as courage is generally the effect of conscious strength, he was probably led to do so by the richness, truth, and force of his own observations on books and men. He was, in the truest sense, a man of original mind, that is, he had the power of looking at things for himself, or as they really were, instead of blindly trusting to, and fondly repeating what others told him that they were. He got rid of the go-cart of prejudice and affectation, with the learned lumber that follows at their heels, because he could do without them. In taking up his pen he did not set up for a philosopher, wit, orator, or moralist, but he became all these by merely daring to tell us whatever passed through his mind, in its naked simplicity and force, that he thought any ways worth communicating. He did not, in the abstract character of an author, undertake to say all that could be said upon a subject, but what in his capacity as an inquirer after truth he happened to know about it. He was neither a pedant nor a bigot. He neither supposed that he was bound to know all things, nor that all things were bound to conform to what he had fancied or would have them to be. In treating of men and manners, he spoke of them as he found them, not according to preconceived notions and abstract dogmas; and he began by teaching us what he himself was. In criticizing books he did not compare them with "rules and systems," but told us what he saw to like or dislike in them. He did not take his standard of excellence "according to an exact scale" of Aristotle, or fall out with a work that was good for any thing, because "not one of the angles at the four corners was a right one." He was, in a word, the first author who was not a book-maker, and who wrote not to make converts of others to established creeds and prejudices, but to satisfy his own mind of the truth of things. In this respect we know not which to be most charmed with, the author or the man. There is an inexpressible frankness and sincerity, as well as power, in what he writes. There is no attempt at imposition or concealment, no juggling tricks or solemn mouthing, no labored attempts at proving himself always in the right, and everybody else in the wrong; he says what is uppermost, lays open what floats at the top or the bottom of his mind, and deserves Pope's character of him, where he professes to

pour out all as plain
As downright Shippen, or as old Montaigne.

He does not converse with us like a pedagogue with his pupil, whom he wishes to make as great a blockhead as himself, but like a philosopher and friend who has passed through life with thought and observation, and is willing to enable others to pass through it with pleasure and profit. A writer of this stamp, I confess, appears to me as much superior to a common bookworm, as a library of real books is superior to a mere book-case, painted and lettered on the outside with the names of celebrated works. As he was the first to attempt this new way of writing, so the same strong natural impulse which prompted the undertaking, carried him to the end of his career. The same force and honesty of mind which urged him to throw off the shackles of custom and prejudice, would enable him to complete his triumph over them. He has left little for his successors to achieve in the way of just and original speculation on human life. Nearly all the thinking of the two last centuries of that kind which the French denominate *morale observatrice*, is to be found in Montaigne's *Essays*: there is the germ, at least, and generally much more. He sowed the seed and cleared away the rubbish, even where others have reaped the fruit, or cultivated and decorated the soil to a greater degree of nicety and perfection.

There is no one to whom the old Latin adage is more applicable than to Montaigne, *Pereant isti qui ante nos nostra dixerunt*. There has been no new impulse given to thought since his time. Among the specimens of criticisms on authors which he has left us, are those on Virgil, Ovid, and Boccaccio, in the account of books which he thinks worth reading, or (which is the same thing) which he finds he can read in his old age, and which may be reckoned among the few criticisms which are worth reading at any age.*

Montaigne's Essays were translated into English by Charles Cotton, who was one of the wits and poets of the age of Charles II; and Lord Halifax, one of the noble critics of that day, declared it to be 'the book in the world he was the best pleased with.' This mode of familiar Essay-writing, free from the trammels of the schools, and the airs of professed authorship, was successfully imitated, about the same time, by Cowley and Sir William Temple, in their miscellaneous Essays, which are very agreeable and

---

*Note: As an instance of his general power of reasoning, I shall give his chapter entitled "One Man's Profit is another's Loss," in which he has nearly anticipated Mandeville's celebrated paradox of private vices being public benefits: [From: "One Man's Profit is another's Loss"]: Demades, the Athenian, condemned a fellow-citizen, who furnished out funerals, for demanding too great a price for his goods: and if he got an estate, it must be by the death of a great many people: but I think it a sentence ill grounded, forasmuch as no profit can be made, but at the expense of some other person, and that every kind of gain is by that rule liable to be condemned. The tradesman thrives by the debauchery of youth, and the farmer by the dearness of corn; the architect by the ruin of buildings, the officers of justice by quarrels and law-suits; nay, even the honour and function of divines is owing to our mortality and vices. No physician takes pleasure in the health even of his best friends, said the ancient Greek comedian, nor soldier in the peace of his country; and so of the rest. And, what is yet worse, let every one but examine his own heart, and he will find that his private wishes spring and grow up at the expense of some other person. Upon which consideration this thought came into my head, that nature does not hereby deviate from her general policy; for the naturalists hold, that the birth, nourishment, and increase of any one thing is the decay and corruption of another:
Nam quodcunque suit mutatumfinibus exit,
Continuo hoc mors est illius, quod fuit ante.
—Vol. I. Chap. Xxi.

learned talking upon paper. Lord Shaftesbury, on the contrary, who aimed at the same easy, *degagé* mode of communicating his thoughts to the world, has quite spoiled his matter, which is sometimes valuable, by his manner, in which he carries a certain flaunting, flowery, figurative, flirting style of amicable condescension to the reader, to an excess more tantalizing than the most starched and ridiculous formality of the age of James I. There is nothing so tormenting as the affectation of ease and freedom from affectation.

The ice being thus thawed, and the barrier that kept authors at a distance from common sense and feeling broken through, the transition was not difficult from Montaigne and his imitators, to our Periodical Essayists. These last applied the same unrestrained expression of their thoughts to the more immediate and passing scenes of life, to temporary and local matters; and in order to discharge the invidious office of *Censor Morum* more freely, and with less responsibility, assumed some fictitious and humorous disguise, which, however, in a great degree corresponded to their own peculiar habits and character. By thus concealing their own name and person under the title of the *Tatler*, *Spectator*, &c. they were enabled to inform us more fully of what was passing in the world, while the dramatic contrast and ironical point of view to which the whole is subjected, added a greater liveliness and *piquancy* to the descriptions. The philosopher and wit here commences news-monger, makes himself master of 'the perfect spy o' tie time,' and from his various walks and turns through life, brings home little curious specimens of the humors, opinions, and manners of his contemporaries, as the botanist brings home different plants and weeds, or the mineralogist different shells and fossils, to illustrate their several theories, and be useful to mankind.

The first of these papers that was attempted in this country was set up by Steele in the beginning of the last century; and of all our periodical Essayists, the *Tatler* (for that was the name he assumed) has always appeared to me the most amusing and agreeable. Montaigne, whom I have proposed to consider as the father of this kind of personal authorship among the moderns, in which the reader is admitted behind the curtain, and sits down with the writer in his gown and slippers, was a most magnanimous and undisguised egotist; but Isaac Bickerstaff, Esq. was the more disinterested gossip of the two. The French author is contented to describe the peculiarities of his own mind and constitution, which he does with a copious and unsparing hand. The English journalist good-naturedly lets you into the secret both of his own affairs and those of others. A young lady, on the other side Temple Bar, cannot be seen at her glass for half a day together, but Mr. Bickerstaff takes due notice of it; and he has the first intelligence of the symptoms of the *belle* passion appearing in any young gentleman at the West-end of the town. The departures and arrivals of widows with handsome jointures, either to bury their grief in the country, or to procure a second husband in town, are punctually recorded in his pages. He is well acquainted with the celebrated beauties of the preceding age at the court of Charles II; and the old gentleman (as he feigns himself) often grows romantic in recounting 'the disastrous strokes which his youth suffered' from the glances of their bright eyes, and their unaccountable caprices. In particular, he dwells with a secret satisfaction on the recollection of one of his mistresses, who left him for a richer rival, and whose constant reproach to her husband, on occasion of any quarrel between them, was 'I, that might have married the famous Mr. Bickerstaff, to be treated in this manner!' The club at the Trumpet consists of a set of persons almost as well worth knowing as himself. The cavalcade of the justice of the peace, the knight of the shire, the country squire, and the young gentleman, his nephew, who came to wait on him at his chambers, in such form and ceremony, seem not to have settled the order of their precedence to this hour; and I should hope that the upholsterer and his companions, who used to sun themselves in the Green Park, and who broke their rest and fortunes to maintain the balance of power in Europe, stand as fair a chance for immortality as some modern politicians. Mr. Bickerstaff himself is a gentleman and a scholar, a humorist, and a man of the world; with a great deal of nice easy *naiveté* about him. If he walks out and is caught in a shower of rain, he makes amends for this unlucky accident by a criticism on the shower in Virgil, and concludes with a burlesque copy of verses on a city-shower. He entertains us, when he dates from his own apartment, with a quotation from Plutarch, or a moral reflection; from the Grecian coffee-house with politics; and from Wills', or the Temple, with the poets and players, the beaux and men of wit and pleasure about town. In reading the pages of the *Tatler*, we seem as if suddenly carried back to the age of Queen Anne, of toupees and full-bottomed periwigs. The whole appearance of our dress and manners undergoes a delightful metamorphosis. The beaux and the belles are of a quite different species from what they are at present; we distinguish the dappers, the smarts, and the pretty fellows, as they pass by Mr. Lilly's shop-windows in the Strand; we are introduced to Betterton and Mrs. Old-field behind the scenes; are made familiar with the persons and perfor-mances of Will Estcourt or Tom Durfey; we listen to a dispute at a tavern, on the merits of the Duke of Marlborough, or Marshal Turenne; or are present at the first rehearsal of a play by Vanbrugh, or the reading of a new poem by Mr. Pope. The privilege of thus virtually transporting ourselves to past times, is even greater than that of visiting distant places in reality. London, a hundred years ago, would be much better worth seeing than Paris at the present moment.

It will be said, that all this is to be found, in the same or a greater de-gree, in the *Spectator*. For myself, I do not think so; or at least, there is in the last work a much greater proportion of common-place matter. I have, on this account, always preferred the *Tatler* to the *Spectator*. Whether it is owing to my having been earlier or better acquainted with the one than the other, my pleasure in reading these two admirable works is not in proportion to their comparative reputation. The *Tatler* contains only half the number of volumes, and, I will venture to say, nearly an equal quan-tity of sterling wit and sense. The first sprightly runnings are there; it has more of the original spirit, more of the freshness and stamp of nature. The indications of character and strokes of humour are more true and fre-quent; the reflections that suggest themselves arise more from the occa-sion, and are less spun out into regular dissertations. They are more like the remarks which occur in sensible conversation, and less like a lecture. Something is left to the understanding of the reader. Steele seems to have gone into his closet chiefly to set down what he observed out of doors. Addison seems to have spent most of his time in his study, and to have spun out and wire-drawn the hints, which he borrowed from Steele, or took from nature, to the utmost. I am far from wishing to depreciate Ad-dison's talents, but I am anxious to do justice to Steele, who was, I think, upon the whole, a less artificial and more original writer. The humorous descriptions of Steele resemble loose sketches, or fragments of a comedy; those of Addison are rather comments or ingenious paraphrases on the genuine text. The characters of the club not only in the *Tatler*, but in the *Spectator*, were drawn by Steele. That of Sir Roger de Coverley is among the number. Addison has, however, gained himself immortal honor by his manner of filling up this last character. Who is there that can forget, or be insensible to, the inimitable nameless graces and varied traits of na-ture and of old English character in it—to his unpretending virtues and amiable weaknesses—to his modesty, generosity, hospitality, and eccentric whims—to the respect of his neighbours, and the affection of his domestics—to his wayward, hopeless, secret passion for his fair enemy, the widow, in which there is more of real romance and true delicacy, than in a thousand tales of knight-errantry—(we perceive the hectic flush of his cheek, the faltering of his tongue in speaking of her bewitching airs and the whiteness of her hand)—to the havoc he makes among the game in his neighbourhood—to his speech from the bench, to shew the *Spectator* what is thought of him in the country—to his unwillingness to be put up as a sign-post, and his having his own likeness turned into the Saracen's head—to his gentle reproof of the baggage of a gipsy that tells him he has a widow in his line of life—to his doubts as to the existence of witchcraft, and protection of reputed witches—to his account of the family pictures, and his choice of a chaplain—to his falling asleep at church, and his reproof of John Williams, as soon as he recovered from his nap, for talking in sermon-time. The characters of Will. Wimble, and Will. Honeycomb are not a whit behind their friend, Sir Roger, in delicacy and felicity. The delightful simplicity and good-humored officiousness in the one, are set off by the graceful affectation and courtly pretension in the other. How long since I first became acquainted with these two characters in the *Spectator*! What old-fashioned friends they seem, and yet I am not tired of them, like so many other friends, nor they of me! How airy these abstractions of the poet's pen stream over the dawn of our acquaintance with human life! how they glance their fairest colours on the prospect before us! how pure they remain in it to the last, like the rainbow in the evening-cloud, which the rude hand of time and experience can neither soil nor dissipate! What a pity that we cannot find the reality, and yet if we did, the dream would be over. I once thought I knew a Will. Wimble, and a Will. Honeycomb, but they turned out but indifferently; the originals in the *Spectator* still read, word for word, the same that they always did. We have only to turn to the page, and find them where we left them!

Many of the most exquisite pieces in the *Tatler*, it is to be observed, are Addison's, as the Court of Honour, and the Personification of Musical Instruments, with almost all those papers that form regular sets or series. I do not know whether the picture of the family of an old college acquaintance, in the *Tatler*, where the children run to let Mr. Bickerstaff in at the door, and where the one that loses the race that way, turns back to tell the father that he is come; with the nice gradation of incredulity in the little boy, who is got into Guy of Warwick, and the Seven Champions, and who shakes his head at the improbability of Æsop's Fables, is Steele's or Addison's, though

I believe it belongs to the former. The account of the two sisters, one of whom held up her head higher than ordinary, from having on a pair of flowered garters, and that of the married lady who complained to the *Tatler* of the neglect of her husband, with her answers to some home questions that were put to her, are unquestionably Steele's. If the *Tatler* is not inferior to the *Spectator* as a record of manners and character, it is superior to it in the interest of many of the stories. Several of the incidents related there by Steele have never been surpassed in the heart-rending pathos of private distress. I might refer to those of the lover and his mistress, when the theatre, in which they were, caught fire; of the bridegroom, who by accident kills his bride on the day of their marriage; the story of Mr. Eustace and his wife; and the fine dream about his own mistress when a youth. What has given its superior reputation to the *Spectator*, is the greater gravity of its pretensions, its moral dissertations and critical reasonings, by which I confess myself less edified than by other things, which are thought more lightly of. Systems and opinions change, but nature is always true. It is the moral and didactic tone of the *Spectator* which makes us apt to think of Addison (according to Mandeville's sarcasm) as a parson in a tie-wig. Many of his moral Essays are, however, exquisitely beautiful and quite happy. Such are the reflections on cheerfulness, those in Westminster Abbey, on the Royal Exchange, and particularly some very affecting ones on the death of a young lady in the fourth volume. These, it must be allowed, are the perfection of elegant sermonising. His critical Essays are not so good. I prefer Steele's occasional selection of beautiful poetical passages, without any affectation of analysing their beauties, to Addison's finer-spun theories. The best criticism in the *Spectator*, that on the Cartoons of Raphael, of which Mr. Fuseli has availed himself with great spirit in his Lectures, is by Steele.*

I owed this acknowledgment to a writer who has so often put me in good humour with myself, and every thing about me, when few things else could, and when the tomes of casuistry and ecclesiastical history, with which the little duodecimo volumes of the *Tatler* were overwhelmed and surrounded, in the only library to which I had access when a boy, had tried their tranquillizing effects upon me in vain. I had not long ago in my hands,

*Note: The antithetical style and verbal paradoxes which Burke was so fond of, in which the epithet is a seeming contradiction to the substantive, such as proud submission and dignified obedience, are, I think, first to be found in the *Tatler*.

by favour of a friend, an original copy of the quarto edition of the *Tatler*, with a list of the subscribers. It is curious to see some names there which we should hardly think of, (that of Sir Isaac Newton is among them,) and also to observe the degree of interest excited by those of the different persons, which is not determined according to the rules of the Herald's College. One literary name lasts as long as a whole race of heroes and their descendants! The *Guardian*, which followed the *Spectator*, was, as may be supposed, inferior to it.

The dramatic and conversational turn which forms the distinguishing feature and greatest charm of the *Spectator* and *Tatler*, is quite lost in the *Rambler* by Dr. Johnson. There is no reflected light thrown on human life from an assumed character, nor any direct one from a display of the author's own. The *Tatler* and *Spectator* are, as it were, made up of notes and memorandums of the events and incidents of the day, with finished studies after nature, and characters fresh from the life, which the writer moralizes upon, and turns to account as they come before him: the *Rambler* is a collection of moral Essays, or scholastic theses, written on set subjects, and of which the individual characters and incidents are merely artificial illustrations, brought in to give a pretended relief to the dryness of didactic discussion. The *Rambler* is a splendid and imposing commonplace-book of general topics, and rhetorical declamation on the conduct and business of human life. In this sense, there is hardly a reflection that had been suggested on such subjects which is not to be found in this celebrated work, and there is, perhaps, hardly a reflection to be found in it which had not been already suggested and developed by some other author, or in the common course of conversation. The mass of intellectual wealth here heaped together is immense, but it is rather the result of gradual accumulation, the produce of the general intellect, labouring in the mine of knowledge and reflection, than dug out of the quarry, and dragged into the light by the industry and sagacity of a single mind. I am not here saying that Dr. Johnson was a man without originality, compared with the ordinary run of men's minds, but he was not a man of original thought or genius, in the sense in which Montaigne or Lord Bacon was. He opened no new vein of precious ore, nor did he light upon any single pebbles of uncommon size and unrivalled lustre. We seldom meet with any thing to give us pause; he does not set us thinking for the first time. His reflections present themselves like reminiscences; do not disturb the ordinary march of our thoughts; arrest our attention by the stateliness of their appearance, and the costliness of their garb, but pass on and mingle with the throng of our impressions. After closing the volumes of the *Rambler*, there is nothing that we remember as a new truth gained to the mind, nothing indelibly stamped upon the memory; nor is there any passage that we wish to turn to as embodying any known principle or observation, with such force and beauty that justice can only be done to the idea in the author's own words. Such, for instance, are many of the passages to be found in Burke, which shine by their own light, belong to no class, have neither equal nor counterpart, and of which we say that no one, but the author could have written them! There is neither the same boldness of design, nor mastery of execution in Johnson. In the one, the spark of genius seems to have met with its congenial matter: the shaft is sped; the forked lightning dresses up the face of nature in ghastly smiles, and the loud thunder rolls far away from the ruin that is made. Dr. Johnson's style, on the contrary, resembles rather the rumbling of mimic thunder at one of our theatres; and the light he throws upon a subject is like the dazzling effect of phosphorus, or an *ignis fatuus* of words. There is a wide difference, however, between perfect originality and perfect common-place: neither ideas nor expressions are trite or vulgar because they are not quite new. They are valuable, and ought to be repeated, if they have not become quite common; and Johnson's style both of reasoning and imagery holds the middle rank between startling novelty and vapid commonplace. Johnson has as much originality of thinking as Addison; but then he wants his familiarity of illustration, knowledge of character, and delightful humour.— What most distinguishes Dr. Johnson from other writers is the pomp and uniformity of his style.

All his periods are cast in the same mould, are of the same size and shape, and consequently have little fitness to the variety of things he professes to treat of. His subjects are familiar, but the author is always upon stilts. He has neither ease nor simplicity, and his efforts at playfulness, in part, remind one of the lines in Milton:

The elephant
To make them sport wreath'd his proboscis lithe.

His *Letters from Correspondents*, in particular, are more pompous and unwieldy than what he writes in his own person. This want of relaxation and variety of manner has, I think, after the first effects of novelty and surprise were over, been prejudicial to the matter. It takes from the general power, not only to please, but to instruct. The monotony of style produces an apparent monotony of ideas. What is really striking and valuable, is lost in the vain ostentation and circumlocution of the expression; for when we find the same pains and pomp of diction bestowed upon the most trifling as upon the most important parts of a sentence or discourse, we grow tired of distinguishing between pretension and reality, and are disposed to confound the tinsel and bombast of the phraseology with want of weight in the thoughts. Thus, from the imposing and oracular nature of the style, people are tempted at first to imagine that our author's speculations are all wisdom and profundity: till having found out their mistake in some instances, they suppose that there is nothing but common-place in them, concealed under verbiage and pedantry; and in both they are wrong. The fault of Dr. Johnson's style is, that it reduces all things to the same artificial and unmeaning level. It destroys all shades of difference, the association between words and things. It is a perpetual paradox and innovation. He condescends to the familiar till we are ashamed of our interest in it: he expands the little till it looks big. 'If he were to write a fable of little fishes,' as Goldsmith said of him, 'he would make them speak like great whales.' We can no more distinguish the most familiar objects in his descriptions of them, than we can a well-known face under a huge painted mask. The structure of his sentences, which was his own invention, and which has been generally imitated since his time, is a species of rhyming in prose, where one clause answers to another in measure and quantity, like the tagging of syllables at the end of a verse; the close of the period follows as mechanically as the oscillation of a pendulum, the sense is balanced with the sound; each sentence, revolving round its centre of gravity, is contained with itself like a couplet, and each paragraph forms itself into a stanza. Dr. Johnson is also a complete balance-master in the topics of morality. He never encourages hope, but he counteracts it by fear; he never elicits a truth, but he suggests some objection in answer to it. He seizes and alternately quits the clue of reason, lest it should involve him in the labyrinths of endless error: he wants confidence in himself and his fellows. He dares not trust himself with the immediate impressions of things, for fear of compromising his dignity; or follow them into their consequences, for fear of committing his prejudices. His timidity is the result, not of ignorance, but of morbid apprehension. 'He runs the great circle, and is still at home.' No advance is made by his writings in any sentiment, or mode of reasoning. Out of the pale of established authority and received dogmas, all is skeptical, loose, and desultory: he seems in imagination to strengthen the dominion of prejudice, as he weakens and dissipates that of reason; and round the rock of faith and power, on the edge of which he slumbers blindfold and uneasy, the waves and billows of uncertain and dangerous opinion roar and heave for evermore. His Rasselas is the most melancholy and debilitating moral speculation that ever was put forth. Doubtful of the faculties of his mind, as of his organs of vision, Johnson trusted only to his feelings and his fears. He cultivated a belief in witches as an out-guard to the evidences of religion; and abused Milton, and patronized Lauder, in spite of his aversion to his countrymen, as a step to secure the existing establishment in church and state. This was neither right feeling nor sound logic.

The most triumphant record of the talents and character of Johnson is to be found in Boswell's Life of him. The man was superior to the author. When he threw aside his pen, which he regarded as an encumbrance, he became not only learned and thoughtful, but acute, witty, humorous, natural, honest; hearty and determined, 'the king of good fellows and wale of old men.' There are as many smart repartees, profound remarks, and keen invectives to be found in Boswell's inventory of all he said, 'as are recorded of any celebrated man. The life and dramatic play of his conversation forms a contrast to his written works. His natural powers and undisguised opinions were called out in convivial intercourse. In public, he practiced with the foils on: in private, he unsheathed the sword of controversy, and it was the Ebro's temper.' The eagerness of opposition roused him from his natural sluggishness and acquired timidity; he returned blow for blow; and whether the trial were of argument or wit, none of his rivals could boast much of the encounter. Burke seems to have been the only person who had a chance with him: and it is the unpardonable sin of Boswell's work, that he has purposely omitted their combats of strength and skill. Goldsmith asked, Does he wind into a subject like a serpent, as Burke does? And when exhausted with sickness, he himself said, If that fellow Burke were here now, he would kill me. It is to be observed, that Johnson's colloquial style was as blunt, direct, and downright, as his style of studied composition was involved and circuitous. As when Topham Beauclerc and Langton knocked him up at his chambers, at three in the morning, and he came to the door with the poker in his hand, but seeing them, exclaimed, What, is it you, my lads? Then I'll have a frisk with you!' and he afterwards reproaches Langton, who was a literary milksop, for leaving them to go to an engagement "with some un-idead girls." What words to come from the mouth of the great moralist and lexicographer! His good deeds were as many as his good sayings. His domestic habits, his tenderness to servants, and readiness to oblige his friends; the quantity of strong tea that he drank to keep down sad thoughts; his many labours reluctantly begun, and irresolutely laid aside; his honest acknowledgement of his own, and indulgence to the weaknesses of others; his throwing himself back in the post-chaise with Boswell, and saying, 'Now I think I am a good-humoured fellow,' though nobody thought him so, and yet he was; his quitting the society of Garrick and his actresses, and his reason for it; his dining with Wilkes, and his kindness to Goldsmith; his sitting with the young ladies on his knee at the Mitre, to give them good advice, in which situation, if not explained, he might be taken for Falstaff; and last and noblest, his carrying the unfortunate victim of disease and dissipation on his back up through Fleet Street, (an act which realizes the parable of the good Samaritan)—all these, and innumerable others, endear him to the reader, and must be remembered to his lasting honour. He had faults, but they lie buried with him. He had his prejudices and his intolerant feelings; but he suffered enough in the conflict of his own mind with them. For if no man can be happy in the free exercise of his reason, no wise man can be happy without it. His were not time-serving, heartless, hypocritical prejudices; but deep, inwoven, not to be rooted out but with life and hope, which he found from old habit necessary to his own peace of mind, and thought so to the peace of mankind. I do not hate, but love him for them. They were between himself and his conscience; and should be left to that higher tribunal, where they in trembling hope repose, the bosom of his Father and his God. In a word, he has left behind him few wiser or better men.

The herd of his imitators shewed what he was by their disproportionate effects. The Periodical Essayists, that succeeded the *Rambler*, are, and deserve to be, little read at present. *The Adventurer*, by Hawksworth, is completely trite and vapid, aping all the faults of Johnson's style, without any thing to atone for them. The sentences are often absolutely unmeaning; and one half of each might regularly be left blank. *The World*, and *Connoisseur*, which followed, are a little better; and in the last of these there is one good idea, that of a man in indifferent health, who judges of every one's title to respect from their possession of this blessing, and bows to a sturdy beggar with sound limbs and a florid complexion, while he turns his back upon a lord who is a valetudinarian.

Goldsmith's *Citizen of the World*, like all his works, bears the stamp of the author's mind. It does not go about to cozen reputation without the stamp of merit. He is more observing, more original, more natural and picturesque than Johnson. His work is written on the model of the *Persian Letters*; and contrives to give an abstracted and somewhat perplexing view of things, by opposing foreign prepossessions to our own, and thus stripping objects of their customary disguises. Whether truth is elicited in this collision of contrary absurdities, I do not know; but I confess the process is too ambiguous and full of intricacy to be very amusing to my plain understanding. For light summer reading, it is like walking in a garden full of traps and pitfalls. It necessarily gives rise to paradoxes, and there are some very bold ones in the Essays, which would subject an author less established to no very agreeable sort of censura keraria. Thus the Chinese philosopher exclaims very unadvisedly, "The bonzes and priests of all religions keep up superstition and imposture: all reformations begin with the laity." Goldsmith, however, was staunch in his practical creed, and might bolt speculative extravagances with impunity. There is a striking difference in this respect between him and Addison, who, if he attacked authority, took care to have common sense on his side, and never hazarded any thing offensive to the feelings of others, or on the strength of his own discretional opinion. There is another inconvenience in this assumption of an exotic character and tone of sentiment, that it produces an inconsistency between the knowledge which the individual has time to acquire, and which the author is bound to communicate. Thus the Chinese has not been in England three days before he is acquainted with the characters of the three countries which compose this kingdom, and describes them to his friend at Canton, by extracts from the newspapers of each metropolis. The nationality of Scotchmen is thus ridiculed:—"Edinburgh. We are positive when we say, that Sanders Macgregor, lately executed for horse-stealing, is not a native of Scotland, but born at Carrickfergus." Now this is very good; but how should our Chinese philosopher find it out by instinct? Beau Tibbs, a prominent character in this little work, is the best comic sketch since the time of Addison; unrivalled in his finery, his vanity, and his poverty.

I have only to mention the names of the Lounger and the Mirror, which are ranked by the author's admirers with Sterne for sentiment, and with Addison for humor. I shall not enter into that: but I know that the story of La Roche is not like the story of Le Fevre, nor one hundredth part so good. Do I say this from prejudice to the author? No: for I have read his novels. Of the *Man of the World* I cannot think so favourably as some others; nor shall I here dwell on the picturesque and romantic beauties of Julia de

Roubigné, the early favorite of the author of Rosamond Gray; but of the *Man of Feeling* I would speak with grateful recollections: nor is it possible to forget the sensitive, irresolute, interesting Harley: and that lone figure of Miss Walton in it, that floats in the horizon, dim and ethereal, the day-dream of her lover's youthful fancy—better, far better than all the realities of life!

WILLIAM HAZLITT
....

ON FAMILIAR STYLE [1821]

It is not easy to write a familiar style. Many people mistake a familiar for
a vulgar style, and suppose that to write without affectation is to write at
random. On the contrary, there is nothing that requires more precision,
and, if I may so say, purity of expression, than the style I am speaking of.
It utterly rejects not only all unmeaning pomp, but all low, cant phrases,
and loose, unconnected, slipshod allusions. It is not to take the first word
that offers, but the best word in common use; it is not to throw words
together in any combinations we please, but to follow and avail ourselves
of the true idiom of the language. To write a genuine familiar or truly
English style, is to write as any one would speak in common conversation who had a thorough command and choice of words, or who could
discourse with ease, force, and perspicuity, setting aside all pedantic and
oratorical flourishes. Or, to give another illustration, to write naturally is
the same thing in regard to common conversation as to read naturally is
in regard to common speech. It does not follow that it is an easy thing to
give the true accent and inflection to the words you utter, because you do
not attempt to rise above the level of ordinary life and colloquial speaking. You do not assume, indeed, the solemnity of the pulpit, or the tone
of stage declamation; neither are you at liberty to gabble on at a venture,
without emphasis or discretion, or to resort to a vulgar dialect or clown-
ish pronunciation. You must steer a middle course. You are tied down to
a given and appropriate articulation, which is determined by the habitual
associations between sense and sound, and which you can only hit by entering into the author's meaning, as you must find the proper words and
style to express yourself by fixing your thoughts on the subject you have to
write about. Any one may mouth out a passage with a theatrical cadence,
or get upon stilts to tell his thoughts; but to write or speak with propriety
and simplicity is a more difficult task. Thus it is easy to affect a pompous
style, to use a word twice as big as the thing you want to express: it is
not so easy to pitch upon the very word that exactly fits it. Out of eight or
ten words equally common, equally intelligible, with nearly equal pretensions, it is a matter of some nicety and discrimination to pick out the very

one the preferableness of which is scarcely perceptible, but decisive. The reason why I object to Dr. Johnson's style is that there is no discrimination, no selection, no variety in it. He uses none but "tall, opaque words, "taken from the "first row of the rubric"—words with the greatest number of syllables, or Latin phrases with merely English terminations. If a fine style depended on this sort of arbitrary pretension, it would be fair to judge of an author's elegance by the measurement of his words and the substitution of foreign circumlocutions (with no precise associations) for the mother-tongue.*

How simple is it to be dignified without ease, to be pompous without meaning! Surely, it is but a mechanical rule for avoiding what is low, to be always pedantic and affected. It is clear you cannot use a vulgar English word if you never use a common English word at all. A fine tact is shown in adhering to those which are perfectly common, and yet never falling into any expressions which are debased by disgusting circumstances, or which owe their signification and point to technical or professional allusions. A truly natural or familiar style can never be quaint or vulgar, for this reason, that it is of universal force and applicability, and that quaintness and vulgarity arise out of the immediate connection of certain words with coarse and disagreeable, or with confined ideas. The last form what we understand by cant or slang phrases.—To give an example of what is not very clear in the general statement. I should say that the phrase "To cut with a knife," or "To cut a piece of wood," is perfectly free from vulgarity, because it is perfectly common; but to cut an acquaintance is not quite unexceptionable, because it is not perfectly common or intelligible, and has hardly yet escaped out of the limits of slang phraseology. I should hardly, therefore, use the word in this sense without putting it in italics as a license of expression, to be received *com grano salis*. All provincial or bye-phrases come under the same mark of reprobation—all such as the writer transfers to the page from his fireside or a particular coterie, or that he invents for his own sole use and convenience. I conceive that words are like money, not the worse for being common, but that it is the stamp of custom alone that gives them circulation or value. I am fastidious in

*Note: (I have heard of such a thing as an author who makes it a rule never to admit a monosyllable into his vapid verse. Yet the charm and sweetness of Marlow's lines depended often on their being made up almost entirely of monosyllables.)

this respect, and would almost as soon coin the currency of the realm as counterfeit the King's English. I never invented or gave a new and unauthorized meaning to any words but one single one (the term impersonal applied to feelings), and that was in an abstruse metaphysical discussion to express a very difficult distinction. I have been (I know) loudly accused of reveling in vulgarisms and broken English. I cannot speak to that point; but so far I plead guilty to the determined use of acknowledged idioms and common elliptical expressions. I am not sure that the critics in question know the one from the other, that is can distinguish any medium between formal pedantry and the most barbarous solecism. As an author I endeavor to employ plain words and popular modes of construction, as, were I a chapman and dealer, I should common weights and measures.

The proper force of words lies not in the words themselves, but in their application. A word may be a find-sounding word, of an unusual length, and very imposing from its learning and novelty, and yet in the connection in which it is introduced may be quite pointless and irrelevant. It is not pomp or pretension, but the adaptation of the expression to the idea, that clinches a writer's meaning :—as it is not the size or glossiness of the materials, but their being fitted each to its place, that gives strength to the arch; or as the pegs and nails are as necessary to the support of the building as the larger timber, and more so than the mere showy, unsubstantial ornaments. I hate anything that occupies more space than it is worth. I hate to see a load of band-boxes go along the street, and I hate to see a parcel of big words without anything in them. A person who does not deliberately dispose of all his thoughts alike in cumbrous draperies and flimsy disguises, may strike out twenty varieties of familiar every-day language, each coming somewhat nearer to the feeling he wants to convey, and at last not hit upon that particular and only one which may be said to be identical with the exact impression in his mind. This would seem to show that Mr. Cobbet is hardly right in saying that the first word that occurs is always the best. It may be a very good one; and yet a better may present itself on reflection or from time to time. It should be suggested naturally, however, and spontaneously, from a fresh and lively conception of the subject. We seldom succeed by trying at improvement, or by merely substituting one word for another that we are not satisfied with, as we cannot recollect the name of a place or person by merely plaguing ourselves about it. We wander farther from the point by persisting in a wrong scent; but it starts up accidentally in the memory when we least expect it, by touching some link in the chain of previous association.

There are those who hoard up and make a cautious display of nothing but *rich and rare phraseology*—ancient medals, obscure coins, and Spanish pieces of eight. They are very curious to inspect, but I myself would neither offer nor take them in the course of exchange. A sprinkling of archaisms is not amiss, but a tissue of obsolete expressions is more fit for keep than wear. I do not say I would not use any phrase that had been brought into fashion before the middle or the end of the last century, but I should be shy of using any that had not been employed by any approved author during the whole of that time. Words, like clothes, get old-fashioned, or mean and ridiculous, when they have been for some time laid aside. Mr. Lamb is the only imitator of old English style I can read with pleasure; and he is so thoroughly imbued with the spirit of his authors that the idea of imitation is almost done away. There is an inward unction, a marrowy vein, both in the thought and feeling, an intuition, deep and lively, of his subject, that carries off any quaintness or awkwardness arising from an antiquated style and dress. The matter is completely his own, though the manner is assumed. Perhaps his ideas are altogether so marked and individual as to require their point and pungency to be neutralized by the affectation of a singular but traditional form of conveyance. Tricked out in the prevailing costume, they would probably seem more startling and out of the way. The old English authors, Burton, Fuller, Coryate, Sir Thomas Browne, are a kind of mediators between us and the more eccentric and whimsical modern, reconciling us to his peculiarities. I do not, however, know how far this is the case or not, till he condescends to write like one of us. I must confess that what I like best of his papers under the signature of Elia (still I do no presume amidst such excellence, to decide what is most excellent) is the account of "Mrs. Battle's Opinions on Whist," which is also the most free from obsolete allusions and turns of expression—

"A well of native English undefiled."

To those acquainted with his admired prototypes, these Essays of the ingenious and highly gifted author have the same sort of charm and relish that Erasmus's Colloquies or a fine piece of modern Latin have to the classical scholar. Certainly, I do not know any borrowed pencil that has more power or felicity of execution than the one of which I have here been speaking.

It is as easy to write a gaudy style without ideas as it is to spread a pallet of showy colors or to smear in a flaunting transparency. "What do you

[handwritten top margin:] Othello?

read?" "Words, words, words."— What is the matter? "Nothing," it might
be answered. The florid style is the reverse of the familiar. The last is employed as an unvarnished medium to convey ideas; the first is resorted to
as a spangled veil to conceal the want of them. When there is nothing to
be set down but words, it costs little to have them fine. Look through the
dictionary and cull out a *florilegium*, rival the *tulippomania*. *Rouge* high
enough, and never mind the natural complexion. The vulgar, who are not
in the secret, will admire the look of preternatural health and vigor; and
the fashionable, who regard only appearances, will be delighted with the
imposition. Keep to your sounding generalities, your tinkling phrases,
and all will be well. Swell out an unmeaning truism to a perfect tympany
of style. A thought, a distinction is the rock on which all this brittle cargo
of verbiage splits at once. Such writers have merely verbal imaginations,
that retain nothing but words. Or their puny thoughts have dragon-wings,
all green and gold. They soar far above the vulgar failing of the *Sermo
humi obrepens*—their most ordinary speech is never short of an hyperbole,
splendid, imposing, vague, incomprehensible, magniloquent, a cento of
sounding common-places. If some of us, whose "ambition is more lowly,"
pry a little too narrowly into nooks and corners to pick up a number of
"unconsidered trifles," they never once direct their eyes or lift their hands
to seize on any but the most gorgeous, tarnished, thread-bare, patchwork
set of phrases, the left-off finery of poetic extravagance, transmitted down
through successive generations of barren pretenders. If they criticize ac-
tors and actresses, a huddled phantasmagoria of feathers, spangles, floods
of light, and oceans of sounds float before their morbid sense, which they
paint in the style of Ancient Pistol. Not a glimpse can you get of the merits
or defects of the performers: they are hidden in a profusion of barbarous
epithets and willful rodomontade. Our hypercritics are not thinking of
these little fantoccini beings—

That strut and fret their hour upon the stage—

but of tall phantoms of words, abstractions, genera and species, sweeping clauses, periods that unite the Poles, forced alliterations, astounding
antitheses—

And on their pens Fustian sits plumed.

If they describe kings and queens, it is an Eastern pageant. The Coronation at either House is nothing to it. We get at four repeated images, a curtain, a throne, a sceptre, and a foot-stool. These are with them the wardrobe of a lofty imagination; and they turn their servile strains to servile uses. Do we read a description of pictures? It is not a reflection of tones and hues which "nature's own sweet and cunning hand laid on," but piles of precious stones, rubies, pearls, emeralds, Golconda's mines, and all the blazonry of art. Such persons are in fact besotted with words, and their brains are turned with the glittering but empty and sterile phantoms of things. Personifications, capital letters, seas of sunbeams, visions of glory, shining inscriptions the figures of a transparency, Britannia with her shield, or Hope leaning on an anchor, make up their stock-in-trade. They may be considered *hieroglyphical* writers. Images stand out in their minds isolated and important merely in themselves, without any groundwork of feeling— there is no context in their imaginations. Words affect them in the same way, by the mere sound, that is, by their possible not by their actual application to the subject in hand. They are fascinated by first appearances, and have no sense of consequences. Nothing more is meant by them than meets the ear: they understand or feel nothing more than meets their eye. The web and texture of the universe, and of the heart of man, is a mystery to them: they have no faculty that strikes a chord in unison with it. They cannot get beyond the daubings of fancy, the varnish of sentiment. Objects are not linked to feelings, words to things, but images revolve in splendid mockery, words represent themselves in their strange rhapsodies. The categories of such a mind are pride and ignorance— pride in outside show, to which they sacrifice everything, and ignorance of the true worth and hidden structure both of words and things. With a sovereign contempt for what is familiar and natural, they are the slaves of vulgar affectation—of a routine of high-flown phrases. Scorning to imitate realities, they are unable to invent anything, to strike out one original idea. They are not copyists of nature, it is true; but they are the poorest of all plagiarists, the plagiarists of words. All is far-fetched, dear bought, artificial, oriental in subject and allusion; all is mechanical, conventional, vapid, formal, pedantic in style and execution. They startle and confound the understanding of the reader by the remoteness and obscurity to their illustrations; they soothe the ear by the monotony of the same everlasting round of circuitous metaphors. They are the mock-school in poetry and prose. They flounder about between fustian in expression and bathos in sentiment. They tantalize the fancy, but never reach the head nor touch the heart. Their Temple of Fame is like a shadow structure raised by Dulness to Vanity, or like Cowper's description of the Empress of Russia's palace of ice, "as worthless as in show 'twas glittering"—

"It smiled, and it was cold!"

"Words represent themselves"
(→this an interesting thing
about words in ayans.
which build upon the "nontol."
nature of the world (often
outside of the lexical items
/significant/ aspect)

MR LAMB [1825]

Mr Lamb has a distaste to new faces, to new books, to new buildings, to new customs. He is shy of all imposing appearances, of all assumptions of self-importance, of all adventitious ornaments, of all mechanical advantages, even to a nervous excess. It is not merely that he does not rely upon, or ordinarily avail himself of them; he holds them in abhorrence, he utterly abjures and discards them, and places a great gulph between him and them. He disdains all the vulgar artifices of authorship, all the cant of criticism, and helps to notoriety. He has no grand swelling theories to attract the visionary and the enthusiast, no passing topics to allure the thoughtless and the vain. He evades the present, he mocks the future. His affections revert to, and settle on the past, but then, even this must have something personal and local in it to interest him deeply and thoroughly; he pitches his tent in the suburbs of existing manners; brings down the account of character to the few straggling remains of the last generation; seldom ventures beyond the bills of mortality, and occupies that nice point between egotism and disinterested humanity. No one makes the tour of our southern metropolis, or describes the manners of the last age, so well as Mr Lamb!—with so fine, and yet so formal an air—with such vivid obscurity, with such arch piquancy, such picturesque quaintness, such smiling pathos. How admirably he has sketched the former inmates of the South Sea House; what "fine fretwork he makes of their double and single entries!" With what a firm, yet subtle pencil he has embodied *Mrs Battle's Opinions on Whist*! How notably he embalms a battered *beau*; how delightfully an amour, that was cold forty years ago, revives in his pages! With what well-disguised humour, he introduces us to his relations, and how freely he serves up his friends! Certainly, some of his portraits are *fixtures*, and will do to hang up as lasting and lively emblems of human infirmity. Then there is no one who has so sure an ear for 'the chimes at midnight; not even excepting Mr Justice Shallow; nor could Master Silence himself take his 'cheese and pippins' with a more significant and satisfactory air. With what a gusto Mr Lamb describes the inns and courts of law, the Temple and Gray's-Inn, as if he had been a student there for the last two hundred years, and had been as well acquainted with the person of Sir Francis Bacon as he is with his portrait or writings! It is hard to say whether St John's Gate is connected with more intense and authentic associations in his mind, as a part of old London Wall, or as the frontispiece (time out of mind) of the *Gentleman's Magazine*. He haunts Watling-street like a gentle spirit; the avenues to the playhouses are thick with panting recollections, and Christ's Hospital still breathes the balmy breath of infancy in his description of it! Whittington and his Cat are a fine hallucination for Mr Lamb's historic Muse, and we believe he never heartily forgave a certain writer who took the subject of Guy Faux out of his hands. The streets of London are his fairy-land, teeming with wonder, with life and interest to his retrospective glance, as it did to the eager eye of childhood; he has contrived to weave its tritest traditions into a bright and endless romance!

Mr Lamb's taste in books is also fine, and it is peculiar. It is not the worse for a little *idiosyncrasy*. He does not go deep into the Scotch novels, but he is at home in Smollet or Fielding. He is little read in Junius or Gibbon, but no man can give a better account of Burton's Anatomy of Melancholy, or Sir Thomas Brown's "Urn-Burial," or Fuller's "Worthies," or John Bunyan's "Holy War." No one is more unimpressible to a specious declamation; no one relishes a recondite beauty more. His admiration of Shakespeare and Milton does not make him despise Pope; and he can read Parnell with patience, and Gay with delight. His taste in French and German literature is somewhat defective; nor has he made much progress in the science of Political Economy or other abstruse studies, though he has read vast folios of controversial divinity, merely for the sake of the intricacy of style, and to save himself the pain of thinking. Mr Lamb is a good judge of prints and pictures. His admiration of Hogarth does credit to both, particularly when it is considered that Leonardo da Vinci is his next greatest favourite, and that his love of the actual does not proceed from a want of taste for the ideal. His worst fault is an over-eagerness of enthusiasm, which occasionally makes him take a surfeit of his highest favourites.— Mr Lamb excels in familiar conversation almost as much as in writing, when his modesty does not overpower his self-possession. He is as little of a prosper as possible; but he blurts out the finest wit and sense in the world. He keeps a good deal in the background at first, till some excellent conceit pushes him forward, and then he abounds in whim and pleasantry. There is a primitive simplicity and self-denial about his manners; and a Quakerism in his personal appearance, which is, however, relieved by a fine Titian head, full of dumb eloquence! Mr Lamb is a general favourite with those who know him. His character is equally singular and amiable. He is endeared to his friends no less by his foibles than his virtues; he insures their esteem by the one, and does not wound their self-love by the other. He gains ground in the opinion of others, by making no advances in his own. We easily admire genius where the diffidence of the possessor makes our acknowledgment of merit seem like a sort of patronage, or act of condescension, as we willingly extend our good offices where they are not exacted as obligations, or repaid with sullen indifference.— The style of the *Essays of Elia* is liable to the charge of a certain *mannerism*. His sentences are cast in the mould of old authors; his expressions are borrowed from them; but his feelings and observations are genuine and original, taken from actual life, or from his own breast; and he may be said (if anyone can) "to have coined his heart for *jests*," and to have split his brain for fine distinctions! Mr Lamb, from the peculiarity of his exterior and address as an author, would probably never have made his way by detached and independent efforts; but, fortunately for himself and others, he has taken advantage of the Periodical Press, where he has been stuck into notice, and the texture of his compositions is assuredly fine enough to bear the broadest glare of popularity that has hitherto shone upon them. Mr Lamb's literary efforts have procured him civic honours (a thing unheard of in our times), and he has been invited, in his character of Elia, to dine at a select party with the Lord Mayor. We should prefer this distinction to that of being poet-laureat. We would recommend to Mr Waithman's perusal (if Mr Lamb has not anticipated us) the *Rosamond Gray* and the *John Woodvil* of the same author, as an agreeable relief to the noise of a City feast, and the heat of City elections. A friend, a short time ago, quoted some lines* from the last-mentioned of these works, which meeting Mr Godwin's eye, he was so struck with the beauty of the passage, and with a consciousness of having seen it before, that he was uneasy till he could recollect where, and after hunting in vain for it in Ben Jonson, Beaumont and Fletcher, and other not unlikely places, sent to Mr Lamb to know if he could help him to the author!

FROM "LETTER TO ROBERT SOUTHEY"

ON WILLIAM HAZLITT [1823]

From the other gentleman I neither expect nor desire (as he is well as-sured) any such concessions as Leigh Hunt made to Coleridge. What hath soured him, and made him to suspect his friends of infidelity towards him, when there was no such matter, I know not. I stood well with him for fifteen years (the proudest of my life), and have ever spoken my full mind of him to some, to whom his panegyric must naturally be least tasteful. I never in thought swerved from him, I never betrayed him, I never slack-ened in my admiration of him; I was the same to him (neither better nor worse), though he could not see it, as in the days when he thought fit to trust me. At this instant he may be preparing for me some compliment, above my deserts, as he has sprinkled many such among his admirable books, for which I rest his debtor; or, for anything I know, or can guess to the contrary, he may be about to read a lecture on my weaknesses. He is welcome to them (as he was to my humble hearth), if they can divert a spleen or ventilate a fit of sullenness.

I wish he would not quarrel with the world at the rate he does; but the reconciliation must be effected by himself, and I despair of living to see that day. But protesting against much that he has written, and some things which he chooses to do; judging him by his conversation which I enjoyed so long, and relished so deeply; or by his books, in those places where no clouding passion intervenes—I should belie my own conscience, if I said less, than that I think William Hazlitt to be, in his natural and healthy state, one of the wisest and finest spirits breathing. So far from being ashamed of that intimacy, which was betwixt us, it is my boast that I was able for so many years to have preserved it entire; and I think I shall go to my grave without finding, or expecting to find, such another companion.

MONTAIGNE; OR, THE SKEPTIC [1850]

Every fact is related on one side to sensation and, on the other, to morals. The game of thought is, on the appearance of one of these two sides, to find the other; given the upper, to find the under side. Nothing so thin, but has these two faces; and, when the observer has seen the obverse, he turns it over to see the reverse.

Life is a pitching of this penny,—heads or tails. We never tire of this game, because there is still a slight shudder of astonishment at the exhibition of the other face, at the contrast of the two faces. A man is flushed with success, and bethinks himself what this good luck signifies. He drives his bargain in the street; but it occurs that he also is bought and sold. He sees the beauty of a human face, and searches the cause of that beauty, which must be more beautiful. He builds his fortunes, maintains the laws, cherishes his children; but he asks himself, why? and whereto? This head and this tail are called, in the language of philosophy, Infinite and Finite; Relative and Absolute; Apparent and Real; and many fine names beside.

Each man is born with a predisposition to one or the other of these sides of nature; and it will easily happen that men will be found devoted to one or the other. One class has the perception of difference, and is conversant with facts and surfaces; cities and persons; and the bringing certain things to pass;—the men of talent and action. Another class have the perception of identity, and are men of faith and philosophy, men of genius.

Each of these riders drives too fast. Plotinus believes only in philosophers; Fenelon, in saints; Pindar and Byron, in poets. Read the haughty language in which Plato and the Platonists speak of all men who are not devoted to their own shining abstractions: other men are rats and mice. The literary class is usually proud and exclusive. The correspondence of Pope and Swift describes mankind around them as monsters; and that of Goethe and Schiller, in our own time, is scarcely more kind.

It is easy to see how this arrogance comes. The genius is a genius by the first look he casts on any object. Is his eye creative? Does he not rest in angles and colors, but beholds the design—he will presently undervalue the actual object. In powerful moments, his thought has dissolved the

works of art and nature into their causes, so that the works appear heavy
and faulty. He has a conception of beauty which the sculptor cannot embody. Picture, statue, temple, railroad, steam-engine, existed first in an
artist's mind, without flaw, mistake, or friction, which impair the executed
models. So did the church, the state, college, court, social circle, and all
the institutions. It is not strange that these men, remembering what they
have seen and hoped of ideas, should affirm disdainfully the superiority
of ideas. Having at some time seen that the happy soul will carry all the
arts in power, they say, Why cumber ourselves with superfluous realiza-
tions? and, like dreaming beggars, they assume to speak and act as if
these values were already substantiated.

On the other part, the men of toil and trade and luxury,—the animal
world, including the animal in the philosopher and poet also,—and the
practical world, including the painful drudgeries which are never excused
to philosopher or poet any more than to the rest,—weigh heavily on the
other side. The trade in our streets believes in no metaphysical causes,
thinks nothing of the force which necessitated traders and a trading planet
to exist; no, but sticks to cotton, sugar, wool, and salt. The ward meetings,
on election days, are not softened by any misgivings of the value of these
ballotings. Hot life is streaming in a single direction. To the men of this
world, to the animal strength and spirits, to the men of practical power,
whilst immersed in it, the man of ideas appears out of his reason. They
alone have reason.

Things always bring their own philosophy with them, that is, prudence.
No man acquires property without acquiring with it a little arithmetic,
also. In England, the richest country that ever existed, property stands for
more, compared with personal ability, than in any other. After dinner, a
man believes less, denies more; verities have lost some charm. After dinner, arithmetic is the only science; ideas are disturbing, incendiary, follies
of young men, repudiated by the solid portion of society; and a man comes
to be valued by his athletic and animal qualities. Spence relates, that Mr.
Pope was with Sir Godfrey Kneller one day, when his nephew, a Guinea
trader, came in. "Nephew," said Sir Godfrey, "you have the honor of seeing the two greatest men in the world." "I don't know how great men you
may be," said the Guinea man, "but I don't like your looks. I have often
bought a man much better than both of you, all muscles and bones, for
ten guineas." Thus, the men of the senses revenge themselves on the
professors, and repay scorn for scorn. The first had leaped to conclusions
not yet ripe, and say more than is true; the others make themselves merry

with the philosopher, and weigh man by the pound.—They believe that mustard bites the tongue, that pepper is hot, friction-matches are incendiary, revolvers to be avoided, and suspenders hold up pantaloons; that there is much sentiment in a chest of tea; and a man will be eloquent, if you give him good wine. Are you tender and scrupulous,—you must eat more mince-pie. They hold that Luther had milk in him when he said,

"Wer nicht liebt Wein, Weib, und Gesang Der bleibt ein Narr sein Leben lang,"

one must be a fool to not enjoy life's novelties

and when he advised a young scholar perplexed with fore-ordination and free-will, to get well drunk. "The nerves," says Cabanis, "they are the man." My neighbor, a jolly farmer, in the tavern bar-room, thinks that the use of money is sure and speedy spending. "For his part," he says, "he puts his down his neck, and gets the good of it."

Avoiding the feeling of pain of insincerity doesn't set the question answered

The inconvenience of this way of thinking is, that it runs into indifferentism, and then into disgust. Life is eating us up. We shall be fables presently. Keep cool: it will be all one a hundred years hence. Life's well enough; but we shall be glad to get out of it, and they will all be glad to have us. Why should we fret and drudge? Our meat will taste to-morrow as it did yesterday, and we may at last have had enough of it. "Ah," said my languid gentleman at Oxford, "there's nothing new or true,—and no matter."

driven to the end chasing what is out of reach ignoring all the beauty free for one to admire

With a little more bitterness, the cynic moans: our life is like an ass led to market by a bundle of hay being carried before him: he sees nothing but the bundle of hay. "There is so much trouble in coming into the world," said Lord Bolingbroke, "and so much more, as well as meanness, in going out of it, that 'tis hardly worth while to be here at all." I knew a philosopher of this kidney, who was accustomed briefly to sum up his experience of human nature in saying, "Mankind is a damned rascal"—and the natural corollary is pretty sure to follow,—"The world lives by humbug, and so will I."

This is so negative and off-putting

The abstractionist and the materialist thus mutually exasperating each other, and the scoffer expressing the worst of materialism, there arises a third party to occupy the middle ground between these two, the skeptic, namely. He finds both wrong by being in extremes. He labors to plant his

abstractionist ← ——————— → materialist

Skeptic

feet, to be the beam of the balance. He will not go beyond his card. He sees the one-sidedness of these men of the street; he will not be a Gibeonite; he stands for the intellectual faculties, a cool head, and whatever serves to keep it cool; no unadvised industry, no unrewarded self-devotion, no loss of the brains in toil. Am I an ox, or a dray?—You are both in extremes, he says. You that will have all solid, and a world of pig-lead, deceive yourselves grossly. You believe yourselves rooted and grounded on adamant; and, yet, if we uncover the last facts of our knowledge, you are spinning like bubbles in a river, you know not whither or whence, and you are bottomed and capped and wrapped in delusions.

Academics must be skeptics, "I'll say", but Extremists' help expand discourse

Neither will he be betrayed to a book, and wrapped in a gown. The studious class are their own victims; they are thin and pale, their feet are cold, their heads are hot, the night is without sleep, the day a fear of interruption,—pallor, squalor, hunger, and egotism. If you come near them, and see what conceits they entertain,—they are abstractionists, and spend their days and nights in dreaming some dreams; in expecting the homage of society to some precious scheme built on a truth, but destitute of proportion in its presentment, of justness in its application, and of all energy of will in the schemer to embody and vitalize it.

But I see plainly, he says, that I cannot see. I know that human strength is not in extremes, but in avoiding extremes. I, at least, will shun the weakness of philosophizing beyond my depth. What is the use of pretending to powers we have not? What is the use of pretending to assurances we have not, respecting the other life? Why exaggerate the power of virtue? Why be an angel before your time? These strings, wound up too high, will snap. If there is a wish for immortality, and no evidence, why not say just that? If there are conflicting evidences, why not state them? If there is not ground for a candid thinker to make up his mind, yea or nay,—why not suspend the judgment? I weary of these dogmatizers. I tire of these hacks of routine, who deny the dogmas. I neither affirm nor deny. I stand here to try the case. I am here to consider,—to consider how it is. I will try to keep the balance true. Of what use to take the chair, and glibly rattle off theories of societies, religion, and nature, when I know that practical objections lie in the way, insurmountable by me and by my mates? Why so talkative in public, when each of my neighbors can pin me to my seat by arguments I cannot refute? Why pretend that life is so simple a game, when we know how subtle and elusive the Proteus is? Why think to shut up all things in

Absts. Q's

your narrow coop, when we know there are not one or two only, but ten, twenty, a thousand things, and unlike? Why fancy that you have all the truth in your keeping? There is much to say on all sides.

Who shall forbid a wise skepticism, seeing that there is no practical question on which anything more than an approximate solution can be had? Is not marriage an open question when it is alleged, from the beginning of the world, that such as are in the institution wish to get out, and such as are out wish to get in? And the reply of Socrates, to him who asked whether he should choose a wife, still remains reasonable, "that, whether he should choose one or not, he would repent it." Is not the state a question? All society is divided in opinion on the subject of the state. Nobody loves it; great numbers dislike it, and suffer conscientious scruples to allegiance: and the only defense set up, is, the fear of doing worse in disorganizing. Is it otherwise with the church? Or, to put any of the questions

which touch mankind nearest,—shall the young man aim at a leading part in law, in politics, in trade? It will not be pretended that a success in either of these kinds is quite coincident with what is best and inmost in his mind. Shall he, then, cutting the stays that hold him fast to the social state, be put out to sea with no guidance but his genius? There is much to say on both sides. Remember the open question between the present order of "competition," and the friends of "attractive and associated labor." The generous minds embrace the proposition of labor shared by all; it is the only honesty; nothing else is safe. It is from the poor man's hut alone, that strength and virtue come; and yet, on the other side, it is alleged that labor impairs the form, and breaks the spirit of man, and the laborers cry unanimously, "We have no thoughts." Culture, how indispensable! I cannot forgive you the want of accomplishment; and yet, culture will instantly destroy that chiefest beauty of spontaneousness. Excellent is culture for a savage; but once let him read in the book, and he is no longer able not to think of Plutarch's heroes. In short, since true fortitude of understanding consists "in not letting what we know be embarrassed by what we do not know," we ought to secure those advantages which we can command, and not risk them by clutching after the airy and unattainable. Come, no chimeras! Let us go abroad; let us mix in affairs; let us learn, and get, and have, and climb. "Men are a sort of moving plants, and, like trees, receive a great part of their nourishment from the air. If they keep too much at home, they pine." Let us have a robust, manly life; let us know what we know, for certain; what we have, let it be solid, and seasonable, and our own. A world in the hand is worth two in the bush. Let us have to do with real men and women, and not with skipping ghosts.

This, then, is the right ground of the skeptic,—this of consideration, of self-containing; not at all of unbelief; not at all of universal denying, nor of universal doubting,—doubting even that he doubts; least of all, of scoffing and profligate jeering at all that is stable and good. These are no more his moods than are those of religion and philosophy. He is the considerer, the prudent, taking in sail, counting stock, husbanding his means, believing that a man has too many enemies, than that he can afford to be his own; that we cannot give ourselves too many advantages, in this unequal conflict, with powers so vast and unweariable ranged on one side, and this little, conceited, vulnerable popinjay that a man is, bobbing up and down into every danger, on the other. It is a position taken up for better defense, as of more safety, and one that can be maintained; and it is one of more opportunity and range; as, when we build a house, the rule is, to set it not too high nor too low, under the wind, but out of the dirt.

The philosophy we want is one of fluxions and mobility. The Spartan and Stoic schemes are too stark and stiff for our occasion. A theory of Saint John, and of non-resistance, seems, on the other hand, too thin and aerial. We want some coat woven of elastic steel, stout as the first, and limber as the second. We want a ship in these billows we inhabit. An angular, dogmatic house would be rent to chips and splinters, in this storm of many elements. No, it must be tight, and fit to the form of man, to live at all; as a shell is the architecture of a house founded on the sea. The soul of man must be the type of our scheme, just as the body of man is the type after which a dwelling-house is built. Adaptiveness is the peculiarity of human nature. We are golden averages, volitant stabilities, compensated or periodic errors, houses founded on the sea. The wise skeptic wishes to have a near view of the best game, and the chief players; what is best in the planet; art and nature, places and events, but mainly men. Everything that is excellent in mankind,—a form of grace, an arm of iron, lips of persuasion, a brain of resources, every one skilful to play and win,—he will see and judge.

The terms of admission to this spectacle are, that he have a certain solid and intelligible way of living of his own; some method of answering the inevitable needs of human life; proof that he has played with skill and success; that he has evinced the temper, stoutness, and the range of qualities which, among his contemporaries and countrymen, entitle him to fellowship and trust. For, the secrets of life are not shown except to sympathy and likeness. Men do not confide themselves to boys, or coxcombs, or pedants, but to their peers. Some wise limitation, as the modern phrase is; some condition between the extremes, and having itself a positive quality; some stark and sufficient man, who is not salt or sugar, but sufficiently related to the world to do justice to Paris or London, and, at the same time, a vigorous and original thinker, whom cities cannot overawe, but who uses them,—is the fit person to occupy this ground of speculation.

These qualities meet in the character of Montaigne. And yet, since the personal regard which I entertain for Montaigne may be unduly great, I will, under the shield of this prince of egotists, offer, as an apology for electing him as the representative of skepticism, a word or two to explain how my love began and grew for this admirable gossip.

A single odd volume of Cotton's translation of the Essays remained to me from my father's library, when a boy. It lay long neglected, until, after many years, when I was newly escaped from college, I read the book, and procured the remaining volumes. I remember the delight and wonder in which I lived with it. It seemed to me as if I had myself written the book, in some former life, so sincerely it spoke to my thought and experience. It happened, when in Paris, in 1833, that, in the cemetery of Pere Lachaise, I came to a tomb of Augustus Collignon, who died in 1830, aged sixty-eight years, and who, said the monument, "lived to do right, and had formed himself to virtue on the Essays of Montaigne." Some years later, I became acquainted with an accomplished English poet, John Sterling; and, in prosecuting my correspondence, I found that, from a love of Montaigne, he had made a pilgrimage to his chateau, still standing near Castellan, in Perigord, and, after two hundred and fifty years, had copied from the walls of his library the inscriptions which Montaigne had written there. That Journal of Mr. Sterling's, published in the *Westminster Review*, Mr. Hazlitt has reprinted in the Prolegomenae to his edition of the *Essays*. I heard with pleasure that one of the newly-discovered autographs of William Shakspeare was in a copy of Florio's translation of Montaigne. It is the only book which we certainly know to have been in the poet's library. And, oddly enough, the duplicate copy of Florio, which the British Museum purchased, with a view of protecting the Shakspeare autograph (as

I was informed in the Museum), turned out to have the autograph of Ben Jonson in the fly-leaf. Leigh Hunt relates of Lord Byron, that Montaigne was the only great writer of past times whom he read with avowed satisfaction. Other coincidences, not needful to be mentioned here, concurred to make this old Gascon still new and immortal for me.

In 1571, on the death of his father, Montaigne, then thirty-eight years old, retired from the practice of law, at Bordeaux, and settled himself on his estate. Though he had been a man of pleasure, and sometimes a courtier, his studious habits now grew on him, and he loved the compass, staidness, and independence of the country gentleman's life. He took up his economy in good earnest, and made his farms yield the most. Downright and plain-dealing, and abhorring to be deceived or to deceive, he was esteemed in the country for his sense and probity. In the civil wars of the League, which converted every house into a fort, Montaigne kept his gates open, and his house without defense. All parties freely came and went, his courage and honor being universally esteemed. The neighboring lords and gentry brought jewels and papers to him for safekeeping. Gibbon reckons, in these bigoted times, but two men of liberality in France,— Henry IV and Montaigne.

Montaigne is the frankest and honestest of all writers. His French freedom runs into grossness; but he has anticipated all censures by the bounty of his own confessions. In his times, books were written to one sex only, and almost all were written in Latin; so that, in a humorist, a certain nakedness of statement was permitted, which our manners, of a literature addressed equally to both sexes, do not allow. But, though a biblical plainness, coupled with a most uncanonical levity, may shut his pages to many sensitive readers, yet the offence is superficial. He parades it: he makes the most of it; nobody can think or say worse of him than he does. He pretends to most of the vices; and, if there be any virtue in him, he says, it got in by stealth. There is no man, in his opinion, who has not deserved hanging five or six times; and he pretends no exception in his own behalf. "Five or six as ridiculous stories," too, he says, "can be told of me, as of any man living." But, with all this really superfluous frankness, the opinion of an invincible probity grows into every reader's mind.

"When I the most strictly and religiously confess myself, I find that the best virtue I have has in it some tincture of vice; and I am afraid that

Plato, in his purest virtue (I, who am as sincere and perfect a lover of virtue of that stamp as any other whatever), if he had listened, and laid his ear close to himself, would have heard some jarring sound of human mixture; but faint and remote, and only to be perceived by himself."

Here is an impatience and fastidiousness at color or pretense of any kind. He has been in courts so long as to have conceived a furious disgust at appearances; he will indulge himself with a little cursing and swearing; he will talk with sailors and gypsies, use flash and street ballads; he has stayed indoors till he is deadly sick; he will to the open air, though it rain bullets. He has seen too much of gentlemen of the long robe, until he wishes for cannibals; and is so nervous, by factitious life, that he thinks, the more barbarous man is, the better he is. He likes his saddle. You may read theology, and grammar, and metaphysics elsewhere. Whatever you get here, shall smack of the earth and of real life, sweet, or smart, or stinging. He makes no hesitation to entertain you with the records of his disease; and his journey to Italy is quite full of that matter. He took and kept this position of equilibrium. Over his name, he drew an emblematic pair of scales, and wrote, *Que sais-je?* under it. As I look at his effigy opposite the title-page, I seem to hear him say, "You may play old Poz, if you will; you may rail and exaggerate,—I stand here for truth, and will not, for all the states, and churches, and revenues, and personal reputations of Europe, overstate the dry fact, as I see it; I will rather mumble and prose about what I certainly know,—my house and barns; my father, my wife, and my tenants; my old lean bald pate; my knives and forks; what meats I eat, and what drinks I prefer; and a hundred straws just as ridiculous,— than I will write, with a fine crow-quill, a fine romance. I like gray days, and autumn and winter weather. I am gray and autumnal myself, and think an undress, and old shoes that do not pinch my feet, and old friends who do not constrain me, and plain topics where I do not need to strain myself and pump my brains, the most suitable. Our condition as men is risky and ticklish enough. One cannot be sure of himself and his fortune an hour, but he may be whisked off into some pitiable or ridiculous plight. Why should I vapor and play the philosopher, instead of ballasting, the best I can, this dancing balloon? So, at least, I live within compass, keep myself ready for action, and can shoot the gulf, at last, with decency. If there be anything farcical in such a life, the blame is not mine; let it lie at fate's and nature's door."

The Essays, therefore, are an entertaining soliloquy on every random topic that comes into his head; treating everything without ceremony, yet with masculine sense. There have been men with deeper insight; but, one would say, never a man with such abundance of thoughts; he is never dull, never insincere, and has the genius to make the reader care for all that he cares for.

The sincerity and marrow of the man reaches to his sentences. I know not anywhere the book that seems less written. It is the language of conversation transferred to a book. Cut these words, and they would bleed; they are vascular and alive. One has the same pleasure in it that we have in listening to the necessary speech of men about their work, when any unusual circumstance give momentary importance to the dialogue. For blacksmiths and teamsters do not trip in their speech; it is a shower of bullets. It is Cambridge men who correct themselves, and begin again at every half-sentence, and, moreover, will pun, and refine too much, and swerve from the matter to the expression. Montaigne talks with shrewdness, knows the world, and books, and himself, and uses the positive degree; never shrieks, or protests, or prays; no weakness, no convulsion, no superlative; does not wish to jump out of his skin, or play any antics, or annihilate space or time; but is stout and solid; tastes every moment of the day; likes pain, because it makes him feel himself, and realize things; as we pinch ourselves to know that we are awake. He keeps the plain; he rarely mounts or sinks; likes to feel solid ground, and the stones underneath. His writing has no enthusiasms, no aspiration; contented, self-respecting, and keeping the middle of the road. There is but one exception,—in his love for Socrates. In speaking of him, for once his cheek flushes, and his style rises to passion.

Montaigne died of a quinsy, at the age of sixty, in 1592. When he came to die, he caused the mass to be celebrated in his chamber. At the age of thirty-three, he had been married. "But," he says, "might I have had my own will, I would not have married Wisdom herself, if she would have had me; but 'tis to much purpose to evade it, the common custom and use of life will have it so. Most of my actions are guided by example, not choice." In the hour of death he gave the same weight to custom. *Que sais-je?* What do I know?

This book of Montaigne the world has endorsed, by translating it into all tongues, and printing seventy-five editions of it in Europe; and that, too, a circulation somewhat chosen, namely, among courtiers, soldiers, princes, men of the world, and men of wit and generosity.

Shall we say that Montaigne has spoken wisely, and given the right and permanent expression of the human mind, on the conduct of life?

We are natural believers. Truth, or the connection between cause and effect, alone interests us. We are persuaded that a thread runs through all things; all worlds are strung on it, as beads; and men, and events, and life, come to us, only because of that thread; they pass and repass, only that we may know the direction and continuity of that line. A book or statement which goes to show that there is no line, but random and chaos, a calamity out of nothing, a prosperity and no account of it, a hero born from a fool, a fool from a hero,—dispirits us. Seen or unseen, we believe the tie exists. Talent makes counterfeit ties; genius finds the real ones. We hearken to the man of science, because we anticipate the sequence in natural phenomena which he uncovers. We love whatever affirms, connects, preserves; and dislike what scatters or pulls down. One man appears whose nature is to all men's eyes conserving and constructive; his presence supposes a well-ordered society, agriculture, trade, large institutions, and empire. If these did not exist, they would begin to exist through his endeavors. Therefore, he cheers and comforts men, who feel all this in him very readily. The nonconformist and the rebel say all manner of unanswerable things against the existing republic, but discover to our sense no plan of house or state of their own. Therefore, though the town, and state, and way of living, which our counselor contemplated, might be a very modest or musty prosperity, yet men rightly go for him, and reject the reformer, so long as he comes only with axe and crowbar.

But though we are natural conservers and causationists, and reject a sour, dumpish unbelief, the skeptical class, which Montaigne represents, have reason, and every man, at some time, belongs to it. Every superior mind will pass through this domain of equilibration,—I should rather say, will know how to avail himself of the checks and balances in nature, as a natural weapon against the exaggeration and formalism of bigots and blockheads.

Skepticism is the attitude assumed by the student in relation to the particulars which society adores, but which he sees to be reverent only in their tendency and spirit. The ground occupied by the skeptic is the vestibule of the temple. Society does not like to have any breath of question blown on the existing order. But the interrogation of custom at all points is an inevitable stage in the growth of every superior mind, and is the evidence of its perception of the flowing power which remains itself in all changes.

The superior mind will find itself equally at odds with the evils of society, and with the projects that are offered to relieve them. The wise skeptic is a bad citizen; no conservative; he sees the selfishness of property, and the drowsiness of institutions. But neither is he fit to work with any democratic party that ever was constituted; for parties wish every one committed, and he penetrates the popular patriotism. His politics are those of the "Soul's Errand" of Sir Walter Raleigh; or of Krishna, in the *Bhagavat*, "There is none who is worthy of my love or hatred;" while he sentences law, physic, divinity, commerce, and custom. He is a reformer: yet he is no better member of the philanthropic association. It turns out that he is not the champion of the operative, the pauper, the prisoner, the slave. It stands in his mind, that our life in this world is not of quite so easy interpretation as churches and school-books say. He does not wish to take ground against these benevolences, to play the part of devil's attorney, and blazon every doubt and sneer that darkens the sun for him. But he says, There are doubts.

I mean to use the occasion, and celebrate the calendar-day of our Saint Michel de Montaigne, by counting and describing these doubts or negations. I wish to ferret them out of their holes, and sun them a little. We must do with them as the police do with old rogues, who are shown up to the public at the marshal's office. They will never be so formidable, when once they have been identified and registered. But I mean honestly by them—that justice shall be done to their terrors. I shall not take Sunday objections, made up on purpose to be put down. I shall take the worst I can find, whether I can dispose of them, or they of me.

I do not press the skepticism of the materialist. I know the quadruped opinion will not prevail. 'Tis of no importance what bats and oxen think. The first dangerous symptom I report is, the levity of intellect; as if it were fatal to earnestness to know much. Knowledge is the knowing that we cannot know. The dull pray; the geniuses are light mockers. How respectable is earnestness on every platform! but intellect kills it. Nay, San Carlo, my subtle and admirable friend, one of the most penetrating of men, finds that all direct ascension, even of lofty piety, leads to this ghastly insight, and sends back the votary orphaned. My astonishing San Carlo thought the lawgivers and saints infected. They found the ark empty; saw, and would not tell; and tried to choke off their approaching followers, by saying, "Action, action, my dear fellows, is for you!" Bad as was to me this detection by San Carlo, this frost in July, this blow from a brick, there was still a worse, namely, the cloy or satiety of the saints. In the mount of vision, ere they have yet risen from their knees, they say, "We discover that this our homage and beatitude is partial and deformed; we must fly for relief to the suspected and reviled Intellect, to the Understanding, the Mephistopheles, to the gymnastics of latent."

This is hobgoblin the first; and, though it has been the subject of much elegy, in our nineteenth century, from Byron, Goethe, and other poets of less fame, not to mention many distinguished private observers,—I confess it is not very affecting to my imagination; for it seems to concern the shattering of baby-houses and crockery-shops. What flutters the church of Rome, or of England, or of Geneva, or of Boston, may yet be very far from touching any principle of faith. I think that the intellect and moral sentiment are unanimous; and that, though philosophy extirpates bugbears, yet it supplies the natural checks of vice, and polarity to the soul. I think that the wiser a man is, the more stupendous he finds the natural and moral economy, and lifts himself to a more absolute reliance.

There is the power of moods, each setting at nought all but its own tissue of facts and beliefs. There is the power of complexions, obviously modifying the dispositions and sentiments. The beliefs and unbeliefs appear to be structural; and, as soon as each man attains the poise and vivacity which allow the whole machinery to play, he will not need extreme examples, but will rapidly alternate all opinions in his own life. Our life is March weather, savage and serene in one hour. We go forth austere, dedicated, believing in the iron links of Destiny, and will not turn on our heel to save our life; but a book, or a bust, or only the sound of a name, shoots a spark through the nerves, and we suddenly believe in will: my finger-ring shall be the seal of Solomon: fate is for imbeciles: all is possible to the resolved mind. Presently, a new experience gives a new turn to our thoughts: common sense resumes its tyranny: we say, "Well, the army, after all, is the gate to fame, manners, and poetry: and, look you,—on the whole, selfishness plants best, prunes best, makes the best commerce, and the best citizen." Are the opinions of a man on right and wrong, on fate and causation, at the mercy of a broken sleep or an indigestion? Is his belief in God and Duty no deeper than a stomach evidence? And what guaranty for the permanence of his opinions? I like not the French celerity,—a new church and state once a week.—This is the second negation; and I shall let it pass for what it will. As far as it asserts rotation of states of mind, I suppose it suggests its own remedy, namely, in the record of larger periods. What is the mean of many states; of all the states? Does the general voice of ages affirm any principle, or is no community of sentiment discoverable in distant times and places? And when it shows the power of self-interest, I accept that as a part of the divine law, and must reconcile it with aspiration the best I can.

The word Fate, or Destiny, expresses the sense of mankind, in all ages,—that the laws of the world do not always befriend, but often hurt and crush us. Fate, in the shape of Kinde or nature, grows over us like grass. We paint Time with a scythe; Love and Fortune, blind; and Destiny, deaf. We have too little power of resistance against this ferocity which champs us up. What front can we make against these unavoidable, victorious, maleficent forces? What can I do against the influence of Race, in my history? What can I do against hereditary and constitutional habits, against scrofula, lymph, impotence? against climate, against barbarism, in my country? I can reason down or deny everything, except this perpetual Belly; feed he must and will, and I cannot make him respectable.

But the main resistance which the affirmative impulse finds, and one including all others, is in the doctrine of the Illusionists. There is a painful rumor in circulation, that we have been practiced upon in all the principal performances of life, and free agency is the emptiest name. We have been sopped and drugged with the air, with food, with woman, with children, with sciences, with events which leave us exactly where they found us. The mathematics, 'tis complained, leave the mind where they find it: so do all sciences; and so do all events and actions. I find a man who has passed through all the sciences, the churl he was; and, through all the offices, learned, civil, and social, can detect the child. We are not the less necessitated to dedicate life to them. In fact, we may come to accept it as the fixed rule and theory of our state of education, that God is a substance, and his method is illusion. The eastern sages owned the goddess Yogani-dra, the great illusory energy of Vishnu, by whom, as utter ignorance, the whole world is beguiled.

Or, shall I state it thus?—The astonishment of life, is, the absence of any appearance of reconciliation between the theory and practice of life. Reason, the prized reality, the Law, is apprehended, now and then, for a serene and profound moment, amidst the hubbub of cares and works which have no direct bearing on it;—is then lost, for months or years, and again found, for an interval, to be lost again. If we compute it in time, we may, in fifty years, have half a dozen reasonable hours. But what are these cares and works the better? A method in the world we do not see, but this parallelism of great and little, which never react on each other, nor discover the smallest tendency to converge. Experiences, fortunes, governings, readings, writings are nothing to the purpose; as when a man comes into the room, it does not appear whether he has been fed on yams or buffalo,—he has contrived to get so much bone and fibre as he wants, out of rice or out of snow. So vast is the disproportion between the sky of law and the pismire of performance under it, that, whether he is a man of worth or a sot, is not so great a matter as we say. Shall I add, as one juggle of this enchantment, the stunning non-intercourse law which makes co-operation impossible? The young spirit pants to enter society. But all the ways of culture and greatness lead to solitary imprisonment. He has been often baulked. He did not expect a sympathy with his thought from the village, but he went with it to the chosen and intelligent, and found no entertainment for it, but mere misapprehension, distaste, and scoffing. Men are strangely mistimed and misapplied; and the excellence of each is an inflamed individualism which separates him more.

There are these, and more than these diseases of thought, which our or-dinary teachers do not attempt to remove. Now shall we, because a good nature inclines us to virtue's side, say, There are no doubts,—and lie for the right? Is life to be led in a brave or in a cowardly manner? and is not the satisfaction of the doubts essential to all manliness? Is the name of virtue to be a barrier to that which is virtue? Can you not believe that a man of earnest and burly habit may find small good in tea, essays, and cat-echism, and want a rougher instruction, want men, labor, trade, farming, war, hunger, plenty, love, hatred, doubt, and terror, to make things plain to him; and has he not a right to insist on being convinced in his own way?

When he is convinced, he will be worth the pains.

Belief consists in accepting the affirmations of the soul; unbelief in denying them. Some minds are incapable of skepticism. The doubts they profess to entertain are rather a civility or accommodation to the common discourse of their company. They may well give themselves leave to speculate, for they are secure of a return. Once admitted to the heaven of thought, they see no relapse into night, but infinite invitation on the other side. Heaven is within heaven, and sky over sky, and they are encompassed with divinities. Others there are, to whom the heaven is brass, and it shuts down to the surface of the earth. It is a question of temperament, or of more or less immersion in nature. The last class must needs have a reflex or parasite faith; not a sight of realities, but an instinctive reliance on the seers and believers of realities. The manners and thoughts of believers astonish them, and convince them that these have seen something which is hid from themselves. But their sensual habit would fix the believer to his last position, whilst he as inevitably advances; and presently the unbeliever, for love of belief, burns the believer.

Great believers are always reckoned infidels, impracticable, fantastic, atheistic, and really men of no account. The spiritualist finds himself driven to express his faith by a series of skepticisms. Charitable souls come with their projects, and ask his cooperation. How can he hesitate? It is the rule of mere comity and courtesy to agree where you can, and to turn your sentence with something auspicious, and not freezing and sinister. But he is forced to say, "O, these things will be as they must be: what can you do? These particular griefs and crimes are the foliage and fruit of such trees as we see growing. It is vain to complain of the leaf or the berry: cut it off; it will bear another just as bad. You must begin your cure lower down." The generosities of the day prove an intractable element for him. The people's questions are not his; their methods are not his; and, against all the dictates of good nature, he is driven to say, he has no pleasure in them.

Even the doctrines dear to the hope of man, of the divine Providence, and of the immortality of the soul, his neighbors cannot put the statement so that he shall affirm it. But he denies out of more faith, and not less. He denies out of honesty. He had rather stand charged with the imbecility of skepticism, than with untruth. I believe, he says, in the moral design of the universe; it exists hospitably for the weal of the souls; but your dogmas seem to me caricatures; why should I make believe them? Will any say, this is cold and infidel? The wise and magnanimous will not say so. They will exult in his far-sighted good-will, that can abandon to the adversary all the ground of tradition and common belief, without losing a jot of strength. It sees to the end of all transgression. George Fox saw "that there was an ocean of darkness and death; but withal, an infinite ocean of light and love which flowed over that of darkness."

The final solution in which skepticism is lost is in the moral sentiment, which never forfeits its supremacy. All moods may be safely tried, and their weight allowed to all objections: the moral sentiment as easily outweighs them all, as any one. This is the drop which balances the sea. I play with the miscellany of facts, and take those superficial views which we call skepticism; but I know that they will presently appear to me in that order which makes skepticism impossible. A man of thought must feel the thought that is parent of the universe, that the masses of nature do undulate and flow.

This faith avails to the whole emergency of life and objects. The world is saturated with deity and with law. He is content with just and unjust, with sots and fools, with the triumph of folly and fraud. He can behold with serenity the yawning gulf between the ambition of man and his power of performance, between the demand and supply of power, which makes the tragedy of all souls.

Charles Fourier announced that "the attractions of man are proportioned to his destinies;" in other words, that every desire predicts its own satisfaction. Yet, all experience exhibits the reverse of this; the incompetency of power is the universal grief of young and ardent minds. They accuse the divine Providence of a certain parsimony. It has shown the heaven and earth to every child, and filled him with a desire for the whole; a desire raging, infinite; a hunger, as of space to be filled with planets; a cry of famine, as of devils for souls. Then for the satisfaction,—to each man is administered a single drop, a bead of dew of vital power per day,—a cup as large as space, and one drop of the water of life in it. Each man woke in the morning, with an appetite that could eat the solar system like a cake; a spirit for action and passion without bounds; he could lay his hand on the morning star; he could try conclusions with gravitation or chemistry; but, on the first motion to prove his strength—hands, feet, senses, gave way, and would not serve him. He was an emperor deserted by his states, and left to whistle by himself, or thrust into a mob of emperors, all whistling: and still the sirens sang, "The attractions are proportioned to the destinies." In every house, in the heart of each maiden, and of each boy, in the soul of the soaring saint, this chasm is found,— between the largest promise of ideal power, and the shabby experience.

The expansive nature of truth comes to our succor, elastic, not to be surrounded. Man helps himself by larger generalizations. The lesson of life is practically to generalize; to believe what the years and the centuries say against the hours; to resist the usurpation of particulars; to penetrate to their catholic sense. Things seem to say one thing, and say the reverse. The appearance is immoral; the result is moral. Things seem to tend downward, to justify despondency, to promote rogues, to defeat the just; and, by knaves, as by martyrs, the just cause is carried forward. Although knaves win in every political struggle, although society seems to be delivered over from the hands of one set of criminals into the hands of another set of criminals, as fast as the government is changed, and the march of civilization is a train of felonies, yet, general ends are somehow answered. We see, now, events forced on, which seem to retard or retrograde the civility of ages. But the world-spirit is a good swimmer, and storms and waves cannot drown him. He snaps his finger at laws; and so, throughout history, heaven seems to affect low and poor means. Through the years and the centuries, through evil agents, through toys and atoms, a great and beneficent tendency irresistibly streams.

Let a man learn to look for the permanent in the mutable and fleeting; let him learn to bear the disappearance of things he was wont to reverence, without losing his reverence; let him learn that he is here, not to work, but to be worked upon; and that, though abyss open under abyss, and opinion displace opinion, all are at last contained in the Eternal Cause.

"If my bark sink, 'tis to another sea."

ALEXANDER SMITH
....

ON THE WRITING OF ESSAYS [1863]

I have already described my environments and my mode of life, and out of both I contrive to extract a very tolerable amount of satisfaction. Love in a cottage, with a broken window to let in the rain, is not my idea of comfort; no more is Dignity, walking forth richly clad, to whom every head uncovers, every knee grows supple. Bruin in winter-time fondly sucking his own paws, loses flesh; and love, feeding upon itself, dies of inanition. Take the candle of death in your hand, and walk through the stately galleries of the world, and their splendid furniture and array are as the tinsel armour and pasteboard goblets of a penny theatre; fame is but an inscription on a grave, and glory the melancholy blazon on a coffin lid. We argue fiercely about happiness. One insists that she is found in the cottage which the hawthorn shades. Another that she is a lady of fashion, and treads on cloth of gold. Wisdom, listening to both, shakes a white head, and considers that "a good deal may be said on both sides."

There is a wise saying to the effect that "a man can eat no more than he can hold." Every man gets about the same satisfaction out of life. Mr. Suddlechops, the barber of Seven Dials, is as happy as Alexander at the head of his legions. The business of the one is to depopulate kingdoms, the business of the other to reap beards seven days old; but their relative positions do not affect the question. The one works with razors and soap-lather, the other with battle-cries and well-greaved Greeks. The one of a Saturday night counts up his shabby gains and grumbles; the other on his Saturday night sits down and weeps for other worlds to conquer. The pence to Mr. Suddlechops are as important as are the worlds to Alexander. Every condition of life has its peculiar advantages, and wisdom points these out and is contented with them. The varlet who sang—

A king cannot swagger
Or get drunk like a beggar,
Nor be half so happy as I—

had the soul of a philosopher in him. The harshness of the parlour is revenged at night in the servants' hall. The coarse rich man rates his domestic, but there is a thought in the domestic's brain, docile and respectful as he looks, which makes the matter equal, which would madden the rich man if he knew it—make him wince as with a shrewdest twinge of hereditary gout. For insult and degradation are not without their peculiar solaces. You may spit upon Shylock's gaberdine, but the day comes when he demands his pound of flesh; every blow, every insult, not without a certain satisfaction, he adds to the account running up against you in the day-book and ledger of his hate—which at the proper time he will ask you to discharge. Every way we look we see even-handed nature administering her laws of compensation. Grandeur has a heavy tax to pay. The usurper rolls along like a god, surrounded by his guards. He dazzles the crowd—all very fine; but look beneath his splendid trappings and you see a shirt of mail, and beneath that a heart cowering in terror of an air-drawn dagger. Whom did the memory of Austerlitz most keenly sting? The beaten emperor? or the mighty Napoleon, dying like an untended watch-fire on St. Helena?

Giddy people may think the life I lead here staid and humdrum, but they are mistaken. It is true, I hear no concerts, save those in which the thrushes are performers in the spring mornings. I see no pictures, save those painted on the wide sky-canvas with the colours of sunrise and sunset. I attend neither rout nor ball; I have no deeper dissipation than the tea-table; I hear no more exciting scandal than quiet village gossip. Yet I enjoy my concerts more than I would the great London ones. I like the pictures I see, and think them better painted, too, than those which adorn the walls of the Royal Academy; and the village gossip is more after my turn of mind than the scandals that convulse the clubs. It is wonderful how the whole world reflects itself in the simple village life. The people around me are full of their own affairs and interests; were they of imperial magnitude, they could not be excited more strongly. Farmer Worthy is anxious about the next market; the likelihood of a fall in the price of butter and eggs hardly allows him to sleep o' nights. The village doctor—happily we have only one—skirrs hither and thither in his gig, as if man could neither die nor be born without his assistance. He is continually standing on the confines of existence, welcoming the new-comer, bidding farewell to the goer-away. And the robustious fellow who sits at the head of the table when the Jolly Swillers meet at the Blue Lion on Wednesday evenings is a great politician, sound of lung metal, and wields the village in

Margin notes (handwritten): gout as a disease or "penalesc" · Reflects the standard · why is seeing a real landscape not as good or better than a museum · Everyone has his or her thing to worry about — life is only dull from the outside

the taproom, as my Lord Palmerston wields the nation in the House. His listeners think him a wiser personage than the Premier, and he is inclined to lean to that opinion himself. I find everything here that other men find in the big world. London is but a magnified Dreamthorp.

And just as the Rev. Mr. White took note of the ongoings of the seasons in and around Hampshire Selborne, watched the colonies of the rooks in the tall elms, looked after the swallows in the cottage and rectory eaves, played the affectionate spy on the private lives of chaffinch and hedge-sparrow, was eaves-dropper to the solitary cuckoo; so here I keep eye and ear open; take note of man, woman, and child; find many a pregnant text imbedded in the commonplace of village life; and, out of what I see and hear, weave in my own room my essays as solitary as the spider weaves his web in the darkened corner. The essay, as a literary form, resembles the lyric, in so far as it is moulded by some central mood—whimsical, serious, or satirical. Give the mood, and the essay, from the first sentence to the last, grows around it as the cocoon grows around the silkworm. The essay-writer is a chartered libertine, and a law unto himself. A quick ear and eye, an ability to discern the infinite suggestiveness of common things, a brooding meditative spirit, are all that the essayist requires to start business with. Jacques, in "As You Like It," had the makings of a charming essayist. It is not the essayist's duty to inform, to build pathways through metaphysical morasses, to cancel abuses, any more than it is the duty of the poet to do these things. Incidentally he may do something in that way, just as the poet may, but it is not his duty, and should not be expected of him. Skylarks are primarily created to sing, although a whole choir of them may be baked in pies and brought to table; they were born to make music, although they may incidentally stay the pangs of vulgar hunger. The essayist is a kind of poet in prose, and if questioned harshly as to his uses, he might be unable to render a better apology for his existence than a flower might. The essay should be pure literature as the poem is pure literature. The essayist wears a lance, but he cares more for the sharpness of its point than for the pennon that flutters on it, than for the banner of the captain under whom he serves. He plays with death as Hamlet plays with Yorick's skull, and he reads the morals—strangely stern, often, for such fragrant lodging—which are folded up in the bosoms of roses. He has no pride, and is deficient in a sense of the congruity and fitness of things. He lifts a pebble from the ground, and puts it aside more carefully than any gem; and on a nail in a cottage-door he will hang the mantle of his thought, heavily brocaded with the gold of rhetoric. He

[handwritten marginalia, left margin middle:] One can do something outside his scope but it is not fundamental definition

[handwritten marginalia, lower left:] Doesn't make the purpose of what something cur07y could be

finds his way into the Elysian fields through portals the most shabby and commonplace. ——> TOPOS

The essayist plays with his subject, now whimsical, now in grave, now in melancholy mood. He lies upon the idle grassy bank, like Jacques, letting the world flow past him, and from this thing and the other he extracts his mirth and his moralities. His main gift is an eye to discover the suggestiveness of common things; to find a sermon in the most unpromising texts. Beyond the vital hint, the first step, his discourses are not beholden to their titles. Let him take up the most trivial subject, and it will lead him away to the great questions over which the serious imagination loves to brood,—fortune, mutability, death,—just as inevitably as the runnel, trickling among the summer hills, on which sheep are bleating, leads you to the sea; or as, turning down the first street you come to in the city, you are led finally, albeit by many an intricacy, out into the open country, with its waste places and its woods, where you are lost in a sense of strangeness and solitariness. The world is to the meditative man what the mulberry plant is to the silkworm. The essay-writer has no lack of subject-matter. He has the day that is passing over his head; and, if unsatisfied with that, he has the world's six thousand years to depasture his gay or serious humour upon. I idle away my time here, and I am finding new subjects every hour. Everything I see or hear is an essay in bud. The world is everywhere whispering essays, and one need only be the world's amanuensis. The proverbial expression which last evening the clown dropped as he trudged homeward to supper, the light of the setting sun on his face, expands before me to a dozen pages. The coffin of the pauper, which to-day I saw carried carelessly along, is as good a subject as the funeral procession of an emperor. Craped drum and banner add nothing to death; penury and disrespect take nothing away. Incontinently my thought moves like a slow-paced hearse with sable nodding plumes. Two rustic lovers, whispering between the darkening hedges, is as potent to project my mind into the tender passion as if I had seen Romeo touch the cheek of Juliet in the moon-light garden. Seeing a curly-headed child asleep in the sunshine before a cottage door is sufficient excuse for a discourse on childhood; quite as good as if I had seen infant Cain asleep in the lap of Eve with Adam looking on. A lark cannot rise to heaven without raising as many thoughts as there are notes in its song. Dawn cannot pour its white light on my village without starting from their dim lair a hundred reminiscences; nor can sunset burn above yonder trees in the west without attracting to itself the melancholy of a lifetime. When spring unfolds her green leaves I would be provoked to indite an essay on hope and youth, were it not that it is already writ in the carols of the birds; and I might be tempted in autumn to improve the occasion, were it not for the rustle of the withered leaves as I walk through the woods. Compared with that simple music, the saddest-cadenced words have but a shallow meaning.

The essayist who feeds his thoughts upon the segment of the world which surrounds him cannot avoid being an egotist; but then his egotism is not unpleasing. If he be without taint of boastfulness, of self-sufficiency, of hungry vanity, the world will not press the charge home. If a man discourses continually of his wines, his plate, his titled acquaintances, the number and quality of his horses, his men-servants and maid-servants, he must discourse very skilfully indeed if he escapes being called a coxcomb. If a man speaks of death—tells you that the idea of it continually haunts him, that he has the most insatiable curiosity as to death and dying, that his thought mines in churchyards like a "demon-mole"—no one is specially offended, and that this is a dull fellow is the hardest thing likely to be said of him. Only, the egotism that overcrows you is offensive, that exalts trifles and takes pleasure in them, that suggests superiority in matters of equipage and furniture; and the egotism is offensive, because it runs counter to and jostles your self-complacency. The egotism which rises no higher than the grave is of a solitary and a hermit kind—it crosses no man's path, it disturbs no man's *amour propre*. You may offend a man if you say you are as rich as he, as wise as he, as handsome as he. You offend no man if you tell him that, like him, you have to die. The king, in his crown and coronation robes, will allow the beggar to claim that relationship with him. To have to die is a distinction of which no man is proud. The speaking about one's self is not necessarily offensive. A modest, truthful man speaks better about himself than about anything else, and on that subject his speech is likely to be most profitable to his hearers. Certainly, there is no subject with which he is better acquainted, and on which he has a better title to be heard. And it is this egotism, this perpetual reference to self, in which the charm of the essayist resides. If a man is worth knowing at all, he is worth knowing well. The essayist gives you his thoughts, and lets you know, in addition, how he came by them. He has nothing to conceal; he throws open his doors and windows, and lets him enter who will. You like to walk round peculiar or important men as you like to walk round a building, to view it from different points, and in different lights. Of the essayist, when his mood is communicative, you obtain a full picture. You are made his contemporary and familiar friend. You enter into his humours and his seriousness. You are made heir of his whims, prejudices, and playfulness. You walk through the whole nature of him, as you walk through the streets of Pompeii, looking into the interior of stately mansions, reading the satirical scribblings on the walls. And the essayist's habit of not only giving you his thoughts, but telling you how he came by them, is interesting, because it shows you by what alchemy the ruder world becomes transmuted into the finer. We like to know the lineage of ideas, just as we like to know the lineage of great earls and swift race-horses. We like to know that the discovery of the law of gravitation was born of the fall of an apple in an English garden on a summer afternoon. Essays written after this fashion are racy of the soil in which they grow, as you taste the larva in the vines grown on the slopes of Etna, they say. There is a healthy Gascon flavour in Montaigne's *Essays*; and Charles Lamb's are scented with the primroses of Covent Garden.

The essayist does not usually appear early in the literary history of a country: he comes naturally after the poet and the chronicler. His habit of mind is leisurely; he does not write from any special stress of passionate impulse; he does not create material so much as he comments upon material already existing. It is essential for him that books should have been written, and that they should, at least to some extent, have been read and digested. He is usually full of allusions and references, and these his reader must be able to follow and understand. And in this literary walk, as in most others, the giants came first: Montaigne and Lord Bacon were our earliest essayists, and, as yet, they are our best. In point of style, these essays are different from anything that could now be produced. Not only is the thinking different—the manner of setting forth the thinking is different also. We despair of reaching the thought, we despair equally of reaching the language. We can no more bring back their turns of sentence than we can bring back their tournaments. Montaigne, in his serious moods, has a curiously rich and intricate eloquence; and Bacon's sentence bends beneath the weight of his thought, like a branch beneath the weight of its fruit. Bacon seems to have written his essays with Shakspeare's pen. There is a certain want of ease about the old writers which has an irresistible charm. The language flows like a stream over a pebbled bed, with propulsion, eddy, and sweet recoil—the pebbles, if retarding movement, giving ring and dimple to the surface, and breaking the whole into babbling music. There is a ceremoniousness in the mental habits of these ancients. Their intellectual garniture is picturesque, like the garniture of their bodies. Their thoughts are courtly and high mannered. A singular analogy exists between the personal attire of a period and its written style. The peaked beard, the starched collar, the quilted doublet, have their correspondences in the high sentence and elaborate ornament (worked upon the thought like figures upon tapestry) of Sidney and Spenser. In Pope's day men wore rapiers, and their weapons they carried with them into literature, and frequently unsheathed them too. They knew how to stab to the heart with an epigram. Style went out with the men who wore knee-breeches and buckles in their shoes. We write more easily now; but in our easy writing there is ever a taint of flippancy: our writing is to theirs, what shooting-coat and wide-awake are to doublet and plumed hat.

Montaigne and Bacon are our earliest and greatest essayists, and likeness and unlikeness exist between the men. Bacon was constitutionally the graver nature. He writes like one on whom presses the weight of affairs, and he approaches a subject always on its serious side. He does not play with it fantastically. He lives amongst great ideas, as with great nobles, with whom he dare not be too familiar. In the tone of his mind there is ever something imperial. When he writes on building, he speaks of a palace with spacious entrances, and courts, and banqueting-halls; when he writes on gardens, he speaks of alleys and mounts, waste places and fountains, of a garden "which is indeed prince-like." To read over his table of contents, is like reading over a roll of peers' names. We have, taking them as they stand, essays treating Of Great Place, Of Boldness, Of Goodness, and Goodness of Nature, Of Nobility, Of Seditions and Troubles, Of Atheism, Of Superstition, Of Travel, Of Empire, Of Counsel,—a book plainly to lie in the closets of statesmen and princes, and designed to nurture the noblest natures. Bacon always seems to write with his ermine on. Montaigne was different from all this. His table of contents reads, in comparison, like a medley, or a catalogue of an auction. He was quite as wise as Bacon; he could look through men quite as clearly, and search them quite as narrowly; certain of his moods were quite as serious, and in one corner of his heart he kept a yet profounder melancholy; but he was volatile, a humourist, and a gossip. He could be dignified enough on great occasions, but dignity and great occasions bored him. He could stand in the presence with propriety enough, but then he got out of the presence as rapidly as possible. When, in the thirty-eighth year of his age, he—somewhat world-weary, and with more scars on his heart than he cared to discover—retired to his chateau, he placed his library "in the great tower overlooking the entrance to the court," and over the central rafter he inscribed in large letters the device—"I DO NOT UNDERSTAND; I PAUSE; I EXAMINE." When he began to write his Essays he had no great desire to shine as an author; he wrote simply to relieve teeming heart and brain. The best method to lay the spectres of the mind is to commit them to paper. Speaking of the Essays, he says, "This book has a domestic and private object. It is intended for the use of my relations and friends; so that, when they have lost me, which they will soon do, they may find in it some features of my condition and humours; and by this means keep up more completely, and in a more lively manner, the knowledge they have of me." In his Essays he meant to portray himself, his habits, his modes of thought, his opinions, what fruit of wisdom he had gathered from experience sweet and bitter; and the task he has executed with wonderful fidelity. He does not make himself a hero. Cromwell would have his warts painted; and Montaigne paints his, and paints them too with a certain fondness. He is perfectly tolerant of himself and of everybody else. Whatever be the subject, the writing flows on easy, equable, self-satisfied, almost always with a personal anecdote floating on the surface. Each event of his past life he considers a fact of nature; creditable or the reverse, there it is; sometimes to be speculated upon, not in the least to be regretted. If it is worth nothing else, it may be made the subject of an essay, or, at least, be useful as an illustration. We have not only his thoughts, we see also how and from what they arose. When he presents you with a bouquet, you notice that the flowers have been plucked up by the roots, and to the roots a portion of the soil still adheres. On his daily life his Essays grew like lichens upon rocks. If a thing is useful to him, he is not squeamish as to where he picks it up. In his eye there is nothing common or unclean; and he accepts a favour as willingly from a beggar as from a prince. When it serves his purpose, he quotes a tavern catch, or the smart saying of a kitchen wench, with as much relish as the fine sentiment of a classical poet, or the gallant *bon mot* of a king. Everything is important which relates to himself. That his mustache, if stroked with his perfumed glove, or handkerchief, will retain the odour a whole day, is related with as much gravity as the loss of a battle, or the march of a desolating plague. Montaigne, in his grave passages, reaches an eloquence intricate and highly wrought; but then his moods are Protean, and he is constantly alternating his stateliness with familiarity, anecdote, humour, coarseness. His Essays are like a mythological landscape—you hear the pipe of Pan in the distance, the naked goddess moves past, the satyr leers from the thicket. At the core of him profoundly melancholy, and consumed by a hunger for truth, he stands like Prospero in the enchanted island, and he has Ariel and Caliban to do his behests and run his errands. Sudden alternations are very characteristic of him. Whatever he says suggests its opposite. He laughs at himself and his reader. He builds his castle of cards for the mere pleasure of knocking it down again. He is ever unexpected and surprising. And with this curious mental activity, this play and linked dance of discordant elements, his page is alive and restless, like the constant flicker of light and shadow in a mass of foliage which the wind is stirring.

Montaigne is avowedly an egotist; and by those who are inclined to make this a matter of reproach, it should be remembered that the value of egotism depends entirely on the egotist. If the egotist is weak, his egotism is worthless. If the egotist is strong, acute, full of distinctive character, his egotism is precious, and remains a possession of the race. If Shakspeare had left personal revelations, how we should value them; if, indeed, he has not in some sense left them—if the tragedies and comedies are not personal revelations altogether—the multiform nature of the man rushing towards the sun at once in Falstaff, Hamlet, and Romeo. But calling Montaigne an egotist does not go a great way to decipher him. No writer takes the reader so much into his confidence, and no one so entirely escapes the penalty of confidence. He tells us everything about himself, we think; and when all is told, it is astonishing how little we really know. The esplanades of Montaigne's palace are thoroughfares, men from every European country rub clothes there, but somewhere in the building there is a secret room in which the master sits, of which no one but himself wears the key. We read in the Essays about his wife, his daughter, his daughter's governess, of his cook, of his page, "who was never found guilty of telling the truth," of his library, the Gascon harvest outside his chateau, his habits of composition, his favourite speculations; but somehow the man himself is constantly eluding us. His daughter's governess, his page, the ripening Gascon fields, are never introduced for their own sakes; they are employed to illustrate and set off the subject on which he happens to be writing. A brawl in his own kitchen he does not consider worthy of being specially set down, but he has seen and heard everything: it comes in his way when travelling in some remote region, and accordingly it finds a place. He is the frankest, most outspoken of writers; and that very frankness and outspokenness puts the reader off his guard. If you wish to preserve your secret, wrap it up in frankness. The Essays are full of this trick.

The frankness is as well simulated as the grape-branches of the Grecian artist which the birds flew towards and pecked. When Montaigne retreats, he does so like a skilful general, leaving his fires burning. In other ways, too, he is an adept in putting his reader out. He discourses with the utmost gravity, but you suspect mockery or banter in his tones. He is serious with the most trifling subjects, and he trifles with the most serious. "He broods eternally over his own thought," but who can tell what his thought may be for the nonce? He is of all writers the most vagrant, surprising, and, to many minds, illogical. His sequences are not the sequences of other men. His writings are as full of transformations as a pantomime or a fairy tale. His arid wastes lead up to glittering palaces, his banqueting-halls end in a dog-hutch. He begins an essay about trivialities, and the conclusion is in the other world. And the peculiar character of his writing, like the peculiar character of all writing which is worth anything, arises from constitutional turn of mind. He is constantly playing at fast and loose with himself and his reader. He mocks and scorns his deeper nature; and, like Shakspeare in Hamlet, says his deepest things in a jesting way. When he is gayest, be sure there is a serious design in his gaiety. Singularly shrewd and penetrating—sad, not only from sensibility of exquisite nerve and tissue, but from meditation, and an eye that pierced the surfaces of things—fond of pleasure, yet strangely fascinated by death—sceptical, yet clinging to what the Church taught and believed—lazily possessed by a high ideal of life, yet unable to reach it, careless perhaps often to strive after it, and with no very high opinion of his own goodness, or of the goodness of his fellows—and with all these serious elements, an element of humour mobile as flame, which assumed a variety of forms, now pure fun, now mischievous banter, now blistering scorn—humour in all its shapes, carelessly exercised on himself and his readers—with all this variety, complexity, riot, and contradiction almost of intellectual forces within, Montaigne wrote his bewildering Essays—with the exception of Rabelais, the greatest Modern Frenchman—the creator of a distinct literary form, and to whom, down even to our own day, even in point of subject-matter, every essayist has been more or less indebted.

Bacon is the greatest of the serious and stately essayists,—Montaigne the greatest of the garrulous and communicative. The one gives you his thoughts on Death, Travel, Government, and the like, and lets you make the best of them; the other gives you his on the same subjects, but he wraps them up in personal gossip and reminiscence. With the last it is never Death or Travel alone: it is always Death one-fourth, and Montaigne three-fourths; or Travel one-fourth, and Montaigne three-fourths. He pours his thought into the water of gossip, and gives you to drink. He gilds his pill always, and he always gilds it with himself. The general characteristics of his Essays have been indicated, and it is worth while inquiring what they teach, what positive good they have done, and why for three centuries they have charmed, and still continue to charm.

The Essays contain a philosophy of life, which is not specially high, yet which is certain to find acceptance more or less with men who have passed out beyond the glow of youth, and who have made trial of the actual world. The essence of his philosophy is a kind of cynical common-sense. He will risk nothing in life; he will keep to the beaten track; he will not let passion blind or enslave him; he will gather round him what good he can, and will therewith endeavour to be content. He will be, as far as possible, self-sustained; he will not risk his happiness in the hands of man, or of woman either. He is shy of friendship, he fears love, for he knows that both are dangerous. He knows that life is full of bitters, and he holds it wisdom that a man should console himself, as far as possible, with its sweets, the principal of which are peace, travel, leisure, and the writing of essays. He values obtainable Gascon bread and cheese more than the unobtainable stars. He thinks crying for the moon the foolishest thing in the world. He will remain where he is. He will not deny that a new world may exist beyond the sunset, but he knows that to reach the new world there is a troublesome Atlantic to cross; and he is not in the least certain that, putting aside the chance of being drowned on the way, he will be one whit happier in the new world than he is in the old. For his part he will embark with no Columbus. He feels that life is but a sad thing at best; but as he has little hope of making it better, he accepts it, and will not make it worse by murmuring. When the chain galls him, he can at least revenge himself by making jests on it. He will temper the despotism of nature by epigrams. He has read Aesop's fable, and is the last man in the world to relinquish the shabbiest substance to grasp at the finest shadow.

Of nothing under the sun was Montaigne quite certain, except that every man—whatever his station—might travel farther and fare worse; and that the playing with his own thoughts, in the shape of essay-writing, was the most harmless of amusements. His practical acquiescence in things does not promise much fruit, save to himself; yet in virtue of it he became one of the forces of the world—a very visible agent in bringing about the Europe which surrounds us today. He lived in the midst of the French religious wars. The rulers of his country were execrable Christians, but most orthodox Catholics. The burning of heretics was a public amusement, and the court ladies sat out the play. On the queen-mother and on her miserable son lay all the blood of the St. Bartholomew. The country was torn asunder; everywhere was battle, murder, pillage, and such woeful partings as Mr. Millais has represented in his incomparable picture. To the solitary humourous essayist this state of things was hateful. He was a good Catholic in his easy way; he attended divine service regularly; he crossed himself when he yawned. He conformed in practice to every rule of the Church; but if orthodox in these matters, he was daring in speculation. There was nothing he was not bold enough to question. He waged war after his peculiar fashion with every form of superstition. He worked under the foundations of priestcraft. But while serving the Reformed cause, he had no sympathy with Reformers. If they would but remain quiet, but keep their peculiar notions to themselves, France would rest! That a man should go to the stake for an opinion, was as incomprehensible to him as that a priest or king should send him there for an opinion. He thought the persecuted and the persecutors fools about equally matched. He was easy-tempered and humane—in the hunting-field he could not bear the cry of a dying hare with composure—martyr-burning had consequently no attraction for such a man. His scepticism came into play, his melancholy humour, his sense of the illimitable which surrounds man's life, and which mocks, defeats, flings back his thought upon himself. Man is here, he said, with bounded powers, with limited knowledge, with an unknown behind, an unknown in front, assured of nothing but that he was born, and that he must die; why, then, in Heaven's name should he burn his fellow for a difference of opinion in the matter of surplices, or as to the proper fashion of conducting devotion? Out of his scepticism and his merciful disposition grew, in that fiercely intolerant age, the idea of toleration, of which he was the apostle. Widely read, charming every one by his wit and wisdom, his influence spread from mind to mind, and assisted in bringing about the change which has taken place in European thought. His ideas, perhaps, did not spring from the highest sources. He was no ascetic, he loved pleasure, he was tolerant of everything except cruelty; but on that account we should not grudge him his meed. It is in this indirect way that great writers take their place among the forces of the world. In the long run, genius and wit side with the right cause. And the man fighting against wrong to-day is assisted, in a greater degree than perhaps he is himself aware, by the sarcasm of this writer, the metaphor of that, the song of the other, although the writers themselves professed indifference, or were even counted as belonging to the enemy.

Montaigne's hold on his readers arises from many causes. There is his frank and curious self-delineation; that interests, because it is the revelation of a very peculiar nature. Then there is the positive value of separate thoughts imbedded in his strange whimsicality and humour. Lastly, there is the perennial charm of style, which is never a separate quality, but rather the amalgam and issue of all the mental and moral qualities in a man's possession, and which bears the same relation to these that light bears to the mingled elements that make up the orb of the sun. And style, after all, rather than thought, is the immortal thing in literature. In literature, the charm of style is indefinable, yet all-subduing, just as fine manners are in social life. In reality, it is not of so much consequence what you say, as how you say it. Memorable sentences are memorable on account of some single irradiating word. "But Shadwell never deviates into sense," for instance. Young Roscius, in his provincial barn, will repeat you the great soliloquy of Hamlet, and although every word may be given with tolerable correctness, you find it just as commonplace as himself; the great actor speaks it, and you "read Shakspeare as by a flash of lightning." And it is in Montaigne's style, in the strange freaks and turnings of his thought, his constant surprises, his curious alternations of humour and melancholy, his careless, familiar form of address, and the grace with which everything is done, that his charm lies, and which makes the hundredth perusal of him as pleasant as the first.

And on style depends the success of the essayist. Montaigne said the most familiar things in the finest way. Goldsmith could not be termed a thinker; but everything he touched he brightened, as after a month of dry weather, the shower brightens the dusty shrubbery of a suburban villa. The world is not so much in need of new thoughts as that when thought grows old and worn with usage it should, like current coin, be called in, and, from the mint of genius, reissued fresh and new. Love is an old story enough, but in every generation it is re-born, in the downcast eyes and blushes of young maidens. And so, although he fluttered in Eden, Cupid is young to-day. If Montaigne had lived in Dreamthorp, as I am now living, had he written essays as I am now writing them, his English Essays would have been as good as his Gascon ones. Looking on, the country cart would not for nothing have passed him on the road to market, the setting sun would be arrested in its splendid colours, the idle chimes of the church would be translated into a thoughtful music. As it is, the village life goes on, and there is no result. My sentences are not much more brilliant than the speeches of the clowns; in my book there is little more life than there is in the market-place on the days when there is no market.

VIRGINIA WOOLF
....

THE DECAY OF ESSAY-WRITING [1905]

The spread of education and the necessity which haunts us to impart what we have acquired have led, and will lead still further, to some startling results. We read of the over-burdened British Museum—how even as appetite for printed matter flags, and the monster pleads that it can swallow no more.[1] This public crisis has long been familiar in private houses. One member of the household is almost officially deputed to stand at the hall door with flaming sword and do battle with the invading armies. Tracts, pamphlets, advertisements, gratuitous copies of magazines, and the literary productions of friends come by post, by van, by messenger—come at all hours of the day and fall in the night, so that the morning breakfast-table is fairly snowed up with them.

This age has painted itself more faithfully than any other in a myriad of clever and conscientious though not supremely great works of fiction; it has tried seriously to liven the faded colours of bygone ages; it has delved industriously with spade and axe in the rubbish-heaps and ruins; and, so far, we can only applaud our use of pen and ink. But if you have a Monster like the British public to feed, you will try to tickle its stale palate in new ways; fresh and amusing shapes must be given to the old commodities—for we really have nothing so new to say that it will not fit into one of the familiar forms. So we confine ourselves to no one literary medium; we try to be new by being old; we revive mystery-plays and effect an archaic accent; we deck ourselves in the fine raiment of an embroidered style; we cast off all clothing and disport ourselves nakedly. In short, there is no end to our devices, and at this very moment probably some ingenious youth is concocting a fresh one which, be it ever so new, will grow stale in its turn. If there are thus an infinite variety of fashions in the external shapes of our wares, there are a certain number—naturally not so many—of wares that are new in substance and in form which we have either invented or very much developed. Perhaps the most significant of these literary inventions is the invention of the personal essay. It is true that it is at least as old as Montaigne, but we may count him the first of the moderns. It has been used with considerable frequency since his day, but its popularity with us is so immense and so peculiar that we are justified in looking upon it as something of our own—typical, characteristic, a sign of the times which will strike the eye of our great-great-grandchildren. Its significance, indeed, lies not so much in the fact that we have attained any brilliant success in essay-writing—no one has approached the essays of Elia—but in the undoubted facility with which we write essays as though this were beyond all others our natural way of speaking. The peculiar form of an essay implies a peculiar substance; you can say in this shape what you cannot with equal fitness say in any other. A very wide definition obviously must be that which will include all the varieties of thought which are suitably enshrined in essays; but perhaps if you say that an essay is essentially egoistical you will not exclude many essays and you will certainly include a portentous number. Almost all essays begin with a capital—"I think", "I feel"—and when you have said that, it is clear that you are not writing history or philosophy or biography or anything but an essay, which may be brilliant or profound, which may deal with the immortality of the soul, or the rheumatism in your left shoulder, but is primarily an expression of personal opinion.

We are not—there is, alas! no need to prove it—more subject to ideas than our ancestors; we are not, I hope, in the main more egoistical; but there is one thing in which we are more highly skilled than they are; and that is in manual dexterity with a pen. There can be no doubt that it is to the art of penmanship that we owe our present literature of essays. The very great of old—Homer and Aeschylus—could dispense with a pen; they were not inspired by sheets of paper and gallons of ink; no fear that their harmonies, passed from lip to lip, should lose their cadence and die. But our essayists write because the gift of writing has been bestowed on them. Had they lacked writing-masters we should have lacked essayists. There are, of course, certain distinguished people who use this medium from genuine inspiration because it best embodies the soul of their thought. But, on the other hand, there is a very large number who make the fatal pause, and the mechanical act of writing is allowed to set the brain in motion which should only be accessible to a higher inspiration.

The essay, then, owes its popularity to the fact that its proper use is to express one's personal peculiarities, so that under the decent veil of print one can indulge one's egoism to the full. You need know nothing of music, art, or literature to have a certain interest in their productions, and the great burden of modern criticism is simply the expression of such individual likes and dislikes—the amiable garrulity of the tea-table—cast into the form of essays. If men and women must write, let them leave the great mysteries of art and literature unassailed; if they told us frankly not of the books that we can all read and the pictures which hang for us all to see, but of that single book to which they alone have the key and of that solitary picture whose face is shrouded to all but one gaze—if they would write of themselves—such writing would have its own permanent value. The simple words "I was born" have somehow a charm beside which all the splendours of romance and fairy-tale turn to moonshine and tinsel. But though it seems thus easy enough to write of one's self, it is, as we know, a feat but seldom accomplished. Of the multitude of autobiographies that are written, one or two alone are what they pretend to be. Confronted with the terrible spectre of themselves, the bravest are inclined to run away or shade their eyes. And thus, instead of the honest truth which we should all respect, we are given timid side-glances in the shape of essays, which, for the most part, fail in the cardinal virtue of sincerity. And those who do not sacrifice their beliefs to the turn of a phrase or the glitter of paradox think it beneath the dignity of the printed word to say simply what it means; in print they must pretend to an oracular and infallible nature. To say simply "I have a garden, and I will tell you what plants do best in my garden" possibly justified its egoism; but to say "I have no sons, though I have six daughters, all unmarried, but I will tell you how I should have brought up my sons had I had any" is not interesting, cannot be useful, and is a specimen of the amazing and unclothed egoism for which first the art of penmanship and then the invention of essay-writing are responsible.

NOTES

1   An essay in *Academy & Literature*, 15 February 1905, (Kp c07). Submitted as "A Plague of Essays," it appeared (cut by "a good half") under the present editorially imposed title ('which means nothing') above the reviewer's name ("to which I do object"); see *I VW Letters*, no. 1 r 9, to Violet Dickinson. See also "The Modern Essay," *IV VW Essays* and *CR I*.
2   Montaigne's *Essais* were first published in 1580 and 1588. See also "Montaigne," *IV VW Essays* and *CR I*.
3   Charles Lamb, *Elia* (1813 and 1828) and the *The Last Essays of Elia* (1833).

portrait is alway

One cannot force another to see somethng

VIRGINIA WOOLF
....

MONTAIGNE [1925]

Once at Bar-le-Duc Montaigne saw a portrait which Rene, King of Sicily, had painted of himself, and asked, 'Why is it not, in like manner, lawful for every one to draw himself with a pen, as he did with a crayon?' Off-hand one might reply, Not only is it lawful, but nothing could be easier. Other people may evade us, but our own features are almost too familiar. Let us begin. And then, when we attempt the task, the pen falls from our fingers; it is a matter of profound, mysterious, and overwhelming difficulty.

After all, in the whole of literature, how many people have succeeded in drawing themselves with a pen? Only Montaigne and Pepys and Rousseau perhaps. The *Religio Medici* is a coloured glass through which darkly one sees racing stars and a strange and turbulent soul. A bright polished mirror reflects the face of Boswell peeping between other people's shoulders in the famous biography. But this talking of oneself, following one's own vagaries, giving the whole map, weight, colour, and circumference of the soul in its confusion, its variety, its imperfection—this art belonged to one man only: to Montaigne. As the centuries go by, there is always a crowd before that picture, gazing into its depths, seeing their own faces reflected in it, seeing more the longer they look, never being able to say quite what it is that they see. New editions testify to the perennial fas- *(continued sign)* cination. Here is the Navarre Society in England reprinting in five fine volumes Cotton's translation; while in France the firm of Louis Conard is issuing the complete works of Montaigne with the various readings in an edition to which Dr Armaingaud has devoted a long lifetime of research.

To tell the truth about oneself, to discover oneself near at hand, is not easy.

We hear of but two or three of the ancients who have beaten this road [said Montaigne]. No one since has followed the track; 'tis a rugged road, more so than it seems, to follow a pace so rambling and uncertain, as that of the soul; to penetrate the dark profundities of its intricate internal windings; to choose and lay hold of so many little nimble motions; 'tis a new and extraordinary undertaking, and that withdraws us from the common and most recommended employments of the world.

There is, in the first place, the difficulty of expression. We all indulge in the strange, pleasant process called thinking, but when it comes to saying, even to some one opposite, what we think, then how little we are able to convey! The phantom is through the mind and out of the window before we can lay salt on its tail, or slowly sinking and returning to the profound darkness which it has lit up momentarily with a wandering light. Face, voice, and accent eke out our words and impress their feebleness with character in speech. But the pen is a rigid instrument; it can say very little; it has all kinds of habits and ceremonies of its own. It is dictatorial too: it is always making ordinary men into prophets, and changing the natural stumbling trip of human speech into the solemn and stately march of pens. It is for this reason that Montaigne stands out from the legions of the dead with such irrepressible vivacity. We can never doubt for an instant that his book was himself. He refused to teach; he refused to preach; he kept on saying that he was just like other people. All his effort was to write himself down, to communicate, to tell the truth, and that is a "rugged road, more than it seems."

For beyond the difficulty of communicating oneself, there is the supreme difficulty of being oneself. This soul, or life within us, by no means agrees with the life outside us. If one has the courage to ask her what she thinks, she is always saying the very opposite to what other people say. Other people, for instance long ago made up their minds that old invalidish gentlemen ought to stay at home and edify the rest of us by the spectacle their connubial fidelity. The soul of Montaigne said, on the contrary, that it is in old age that one ought to travel, and marriage, which, rightly, is very seldom founded on love, is apt to become, towards the end of life, a formal tie better broken up. Again with politics, statesmen are always praising the greatness of Empire, and preaching the moral duty of civilising the savage. But look at the Spanish in Mexico, cried Montaigne in a burst of rage. 'So many cities levelled with the ground, so many nations exterminated . . . and the richest and most beautiful part of the world turned upside down for the traffic of pearl and pepper! Mechanic victories!' And then when the peasants came and told him that they had found a man dying of wounds and deserted him for fear lest justice might incriminate them, Montaigne asked:

What could I have said to these people? 'Tis certain that this office of

he couldn't assuage them with words

humanity would have brought them into trouble. . . . There is nothing so much, nor so grossly, nor so ordinarily faulty as the laws?

Here the soul, getting restive, is lashing out at the more palpable forms of Montaigne's great bug-bears, convention and ceremony. But watch her as she broods over the fire in the inner room of that tower which, though detached from the main building, has so wide a view over the estate. Really she is the strangest creature in the world, far from heroic, variable as a weathercock, "bashful, insolent; chaste, lustful; prating, silent; laborious, delicate; ingenious, heavy; melancholic, pleasant; lying, true; knowing, ignorant; liberal, covetous, and prodigal"—in short, so complex, so indefinite, corresponding so little to the version which does duty for her in public, that a man might spend his life merely in trying to run her to earth. The pleasure of the pursuit more than rewards one for any damage that it may inflict upon one's worldly prospects. The man who is aware of himself is henceforward independent; and he is never bored, and life is only too short, and he is steeped through and through with a profound yet temperate happiness. He alone lives, while other people, slaves of ceremony, let life slip past them in a kind of dream. Once conform, once do what other people do because they do it, and a lethargy steals over all the finer nerves and faculties of the soul. She becomes all outer show and inward emptiness; dull, callous, and indifferent.

Surely then, if we ask this great master of the art of life to tell us his secret, he will advise us to withdraw to the inner room of our tower and there turn the pages of books, pursue fancy after fancy as they chase each other up the chimney, and leave the government of the world to others. Retirement and contemplation—these must be the main elements of his prescription. But no; Montaigne is by no means explicit. It is impossible to extract a plain answer from that subtle, half smiling, half melancholy man, with the heavy-lidded eyes and the dreamy, quizzical expression. The truth is that life in the country, with one's books and vegetables and flowers, is often extremely dull. He could never see that his own green peas were so much better than other people's. Paris was the place he loved best in the whole world—"jusques á ses verrues et á ses taches." As for reading, he could seldom read any book for more than an hour at a time, and his memory was so bad that he forgot what was in his mind as he walked from one room to another. Book learning is nothing to be proud of, and as for the achievements of science, what do they amount to? He had always mixed with clever men, and his father had a positive veneration for them, but he had observed that, though they have their fine moments, their rhapsodies, their visions, the cleverest tremble on the verge of folly. Observe yourself: one moment you are exalted; the next a broken glass puts your nerves on edge. All extremes are dangerous. It is best to keep in the middle of the road, in the common ruts, however muddy. In writing choose the common words; avoid rhapsody and eloquence—yet, it is true, poetry is delicious; the best pro, is that which is most full of poetry.

It appears, then, that we are to aim at a democratic simplicity. We may enjoy our room in the tower, with the painted wall and the commodious bookcases, but down in the garden there is a man digging who buried his father this morning, and it is he and his like who live the real life and speak the real language. There is certainly an element of truth in that. Things are said very finely at the lower end of the table. There are perhaps more of the qualities that matter among the ignorant than among the learned. But again, what a vile thing the rabble is! "the mother of ignorance, injustice, and inconstancy. Is it reasonable that the life of a wise man should depend upon the judgment of fools?" Their minds are weak, soft and without power of resistance. They must be told what it is expedient for them to know. It is not for them to face facts as they are. The truth can only be known by the well-born soul—Time "l'âme bien née." Who, then, are these well-born souls, whom we would imitate if only Montaigne would enlighten us more precisely?

But no. "Je n'enseigne poinct; je raconte." After all, how could he explain other people's souls when he could say nothing 'entirely simply and solidly, without confusion or mixture, in one word', about his own, when indeed it became daily more and more in the dark to him? One quality or principle there is perhaps—that one must not lay down rules. The souls whom one would wish to resemble, like Etienne de La Boétie, for example, are always the supplest. "C'est estre, mais ce n'est pas vivre, que de se tenir attaché et obligé par necessité a un seul train." The laws are mere conventions, utterly unable to keep touch with the vast variety and turmoil of human impulses; habits and customs are a convenience devised for the support of timid natures who dare not allow their souls free play. But we, who have a private life and hold it infinitely the dearest of our possessions, suspect nothing so much as an attitude. Directly we begin to protest, to attitudinise, to lay down laws, we perish. We are living for others, not for ourselves. We must respect those who sacrifice themselves in the public service, load them with honours, and pity them for allowing, as they must, the inevitable compromise; but for ourselves let us fly fame, honour, and all offices that put us under an obligation to others. Let us simmer over our incalculable cauldron, our enthralling confusion, our hotch-potch of impulses, our perpetual miracle—for the soul throws up wonders every second. Movement and change are the essence of our being; rigidity is death; conformity is death: let us say what comes into our heads, repeat ourselves, contradict ourselves, fling out the wildest nonsense, and follow the most fantastic fancies without caring what the world does or thinks or says. For nothing matters except life; and, of course, order.

This freedom, then, which is the essence of our being, has to be controlled. But it is difficult to see what power we are to invoke to help us, since every restraint of private opinion or public law has been derided, and Montaigne never ceases to pour scorn upon the misery, the weakness, the vanity of human nature. Perhaps, then, it will be well to turn to religion to guide us? 'Perhaps' is one of his favourite expressions; 'perhaps' and 'I think' and all those words which qualify the rash assumptions of human ignorance. Such words help one to muffle up opinions which it would be highly impolitic to speak outright. For one does not say everything; there are some things which at present it is advisable only to hint. One writes for a very few people, who understand. Certainly, seek the Divine guidance by all means, but meanwhile there is, for those who live a private life, another monitor, an invisible censor within, "tin patron au dedans," whose blame is much more to be dreaded than any other because he knows the truth; nor is there anything sweeter than the chime of his approval. This is the judge to whom we must submit; this is the censor who will help us to achieve that order which is the grace of a well-born soul. For "C'est une vie exquise, tale qui se maintient en ordre jusques en son prive." But he will act by his own light; by some internal balance will achieve that precarious and everchanging poise which, while it controls, in no way impedes the soul's freedom to explore and experiment. Without other guide, and without precedent, undoubtedly it is far more difficult to live well the private life than the public. It is an art which each must learn separately, though there are, perhaps, two or three men, like Homer, Alexander the Great, and Epaminondas among the ancients, and Etienne de La Boétie among the moderns, whose example may help us. But it is an art; and the very material in which it works is variable and complex and infinitely mysterious—human nature. To human nature we must keep close. ". . . il faut vivre entre les vivants." We must dread any eccentricity or refinement which cuts us off from our fellow-beings. Blessed are those who chat easily with their neighbours about their sport or their buildings or their quarrels, and honestly enjoy the talk of carpenters and gardeners. To communicate is our chief business; society and friendship our chief delights; and reading, not to acquire knowledge, not to earn a living, but to extend our intercourse beyond our own time and province. Such wonders there are in the world; halcyon and undiscovered lands, men with dogs' heads and eyes in their chests, and laws and customs, it may well be, far superior to our own. Possibly we are asleep in this world; possibly there is some other which is apparent to beings with a sense which we now lack.

Here then, in spite of all contradictions and all qualifications, is something definite. These essays are an attempt to communicate a soul. On this point at least he is explicit. It is not fame that he wants; it is not that men shall quote him in years to come; he is setting up no statue in the market-place; he wishes only to communicate his soul. Communication is health; communication is truth; communication is happiness. To share is our duty; to go down boldly and bring to light those hidden thoughts which are the most diseased; to conceal nothing; to pretend nothing; if we are ignorant to say so; if we love our friends to let them know it.

> . . . car, comme je scay par une trop certaine experience, il n'est aucune si douce consolation en la perte de nos amis que cello que nous aporte la science de n'avoir rien oublié a leur dire et d'avoir eu avec eux tine parfaite et entiere communication."

There are people who, when they travel, wrap themselves up, 'se défendans de la contagion d'un air incogneu' in silence and suspicion. When they dine they must have the same food they get at home. Every sight and custom is bad unless it resembles those of their own village. They travel only to return. That is entirely the wrong way to set about it. We should start without any fixed idea where we are going to spend the night, or when we propose to come back; the journey is everything. Most necessary of all, but rarest good fortune, we should try to find before we start some man of our own sort who will go with us and to whom we can say the first thing that comes into our heads. For pleasure has no relish unless we share it. As for the risks—that we may catch cold or get a headache—it is always worth while to risk a little illness for the sake of pleasure. "Le plaisir est des principales espêces du profit." Besides if we do what we like, we always do what is good for us. Doctors and wise men may object, but let us leave doctors and wise men to their own dismal philosophy. For ourselves, who are ordinary men and women, let us return thanks to Nature for her bounty by using every one of the senses she has given us; vary our state as much as possible; turn now this side, now that, to the warmth, and relish to the full before the sun goes down the kisses of youth and the echoes of a beautiful voice singing Catullus. Every season is likeable, and wet days and fine, red wine and white, company and solitude. Even sleep, that deplorable curtailment of the joy of life, can be full of dreams; and the most common actions—a walk, a talk, solitude in one's own orchard can be enhanced and lit up by the association of the mind. Beauty is everywhere, and beauty only two fingers'-breadth from goodness. So, in the name of health and sanity, let us not dwell on the end of the journey. Let death come upon us planting our cabbages, or on horseback, or let us steal away to some cottage and there let strangers closeout eyes, for a servant sobbing or the touch of a hand would break in down. Best of all, let death find us at our usual occupations, among girls and good fellows who make no protests, no lamentations; let him find us "parmy les jeux, les festins, faceties, entretiens communs et populaires, et la musique, et des vers amoureux." But enough of death; it is life that matters.

It is life that emerges more and more clearly as these essays reach not their end, but their suspension in full career. It is life that becomes more and more absorbing as death draws near, one's self, one's soul, every fact of existence: that one wears silk stockings summer and winter; puts water in one's wine; has one's hair cut after dinner; must have glass to drink from; has never worn spectacles; has a loud voice; carries a switch in one's hand; bites one's tongue; fidgets with one's feet; is apt to scratch one's ears; likes meat to be high; rubs one's teeth with a napkin (thank God, they are good!); must have curtains to one's bed; and, what is rather curious, began by liking radishes, then disliked them, and now likes them again. No fact is too little to let it slip through one's fingers, and besides the interest of facts themselves there is the strange power we have of changing facts by the force of the imagination. Observe how the soul is always casting her own lights and shadows; makes the substantial hollow and the frail substantial; fills broad daylight with dreams; is as much excited by phantoms as by reality; and in the moment of death sports with a trifle. Observe, too, her duplicity, her complexity. She hears of a friend's loss and sympathises, and yet has a bitter-sweet malicious pleasure in the sorrows of others. She believes; at the same time she does not believe. Observe her extraordinary susceptibility to impressions, especially in youth. A rich man steals because his father kept him short of money as a boy. This wall one builds not for oneself, but because one's father loved building. In short, the soul is all laced about with nerves and sympathies which affect her every action, and yet, even now in 1580, no one has any clear knowledge—such cowards we are, such lovers of the smooth conventional ways—how she works or what she is except that of all things she is the most mysterious, and one's self the greatest monster and miracle in the world. ". . . plus je me hante et connois, plus ma difformité m'estonne, moins je m'entens en moy." Observe, observe perpetually, and, so long as ink and paper exist, "sans cesse et sans travail" Montaigne will write.

But there remains one final question which, if we could make him look up from his enthralling occupation, we should like to put to this great master of the art of life. In these extraordinary volumes of short and broken, long and learned, logical and contradictory statements, we have heard the very pulse and rhythm of the soul, beating day after day, year after year, through a veil which, as time goes on, fines itself almost to transparency. Here is some one who succeeded in the hazardous enterprise of living; who served his country and lived retired; was landlord, husband, father; entertained kings, loved women, and mused for hours alone over old books. By means of perpetual experiment and observation of the subtlest he achieved at last a miraculous adjustment of all these wayward parts that constitute the human soul. He laid hold of the beauty of the world with all his fingers. He achieved happiness. If he had had to live again, he said, he would have lived the same life over. But, as we watch with absorbed interest the enthralling spectacle of a soul living openly beneath our eyes, the question frames itself, Is pleasure the end of all? Whence this overwhelming interest in the nature of the soul? Why this overmastering desire to communicate with others? Is the beauty of this world enough, or is there, elsewhere, some explanation of the mystery? To this what answer can there be? There is none. There is only one more question: "Que sais-je?"

VIRGINIA WOOLF
....

THE MODERN ESSAY [1925]

As Mr Rhys truly says, it is unnecessary to go profoundly into the history and origin of the essay—whether it derives from Socrates or Siranney the Persian—since, like all living things, its present is more important than its past. Moreover, the family is widely spread; and while some of its representatives have risen in the world and wear their coronets with the best, others pick up a precarious living in the gutter near Fleet Street. The form, too, admits variety. The essay can be short or long, serious or trifling, about God and Spinoza, or about turtles and Cheapside. But as we turn over the pages of these five little volumes, containing essays written between 1870 and 1920, certain principles appear to control the chaos, and we detect in the short period under review something like the progress of history.

Of all forms of literature, however, the essay is the one which least calls for the use of long words. The principle which controls it is simply that it should give pleasure; the desire which impels us when we take it from the shelf is simply to receive pleasure. Everything in an essay must be subdued to that end. It should lay us under a spell with its first word, and we should only wake, refreshed, with its last. In the interval we may pass through the most various experiences of amusement, surprise, interest, indignation; we may soar to the heights of fantasy with Lamb or plunge to the depths of wisdom with Bacon, but we must never be roused. The essay must lap us about and draw its curtain across the world.

So great a feat is seldom accomplished, though the fault may well be as much on the reader's side as on the writer's. Habit and lethargy have dulled his palate. A novel has a story, a poem rhyme; but what art can the essayist use in these short lengths of prose to sting us wide awake and fix us in a trance which is not sleep but rather an intensification of life—a basking, with every faculty alert, in the sun of pleasure? He must know—that is the first essential—how to write. His learning may be as profound as Mark Pattison's, but in an essay it must be so fused by the magic of writing that not a fact juts out, not a dogma tears the surface of the texture. Macaulay in one way, Froude in another, did this superbly over

THE MODERN ESSAY 139

and over again. They have blown more knowledge into us in the course of one essay than the innumerable chapters of a hundred text-books. But when Mark Mattison has to tell us, in the space of thirty-five little pages, about Montaigne, we feel that he had not previously assimilated M. Grün. M. Grün was a gentleman who once wrote a bad book. M. Grün and his book should have been embalmed for our perpetual delight in amber. But the process is fatiguing; it requires more time and perhaps more temper than Mattison had at his command. He served M. Grün up raw, and he remains a crude berry among the cooked meats, upon which our teeth must grate for ever. Something of the sort applies to Matthew Arnold and a certain translator of Spinoza. Literal truth-telling and finding fault with a culprit for his good are out of place in an essay, where everything should be for our good and rather for eternity than for the March number of the *Fortnightly Review*. But if the voice of the scold should never be heard in this narrow plot, there is another voice which is as a plague of locusts— the voice of a man stumbling drowsily among loose words, clutching aimlessly at vague ideas, the voice, for example, of Mr. Hutton in the following passage:

> Add to this that his married life was brief, only seven years and a half, being unexpectedly cut short, and that his passionate reverence for his wife's memory and genius—in his own words, "a religion"—was one which, as he must have been perfectly sensible, he could not make to appear otherwise than extravagant, not to say an hallucination, in eyes of the rest of mankind, and yet that he was possessed by an irresistible yearning to attempt to embody it in all the tender and enthusiastic hyperbole of which it is so pathetic to find a man who gained his fame by his "dry-light" a master, and it is impossible not to feel that the human incidents in Mr Mill's career are very sad.

A book could take that blow, but it sinks an essay. A biography in two volumes is indeed the proper depository; for there, where the license is so much wider, and hints and glimpses of outside things make part of the feast (we refer to the old type of Victorian volume), these yawns and stretches hardly matter, and have indeed some positive value of their own. But that value, which is contributed by the reader, perhaps illicitly, in his desire to get as much into the book from all possible sources as he can, must be ruled out here.

There is no room for the impurities of literature in an essay. Somehow or other, by dint of labour or bounty of nature, or both combined, the essay must be pure—pure like water or pure like wine, but pure from dullness, deadness, and deposits of extraneous matter. Of all writers in the first volume, Walter Mater best achieves this arduous task, because before setting out to write his essay (Notes on Leonardo da Vinci) he has somehow contrived to get his material fused. He is a learned man, but it is not knowledge of Leonardo that remains with us, but a vision, such as we get in a good novel where everything contributes to bring the writer's conception as a whole before us. Only here, in the essay, where the bounds are so strict and facts have to be used in their nakedness, the true writer like Walter Pater makes these limitations yield their own quality. Truth will give it authority; from its narrow limits he will get shape and intensity; and then there is no more fitting place for some of those ornaments which the old writers loved and we, by calling them ornaments, presumably despise. Nowadays nobody would have the courage to embark on the once famous description of Leonardo's lady who has

> learned the secrets of the grave; and has been a diver in deep seas and keeps their fallen day about her; and trafficked for strange webs with Eastern merchants; and, as Leda, was the mother of Helen of Troy, and, as Saint Anne, the mother of Mary . . .

The passage is too thumb-marked to slip naturally into the context. But when we come unexpectedly upon "the smiling of women and the motion of great waters," or upon "full of the refinement of the dead, in sad, earth-coloured raiment, set with pale stones," we suddenly remember that we have ears and we have eyes, and that the English language fills a long array of stout volumes with innumerable words, many of which are of more than one syllable. The only living Englishman who ever looks into these volumes is, of course, a gentleman of Polish extraction. But doubtless our abstention saves as much gush, much rhetoric, much high-stepping and cloud-prancing, and for the sake of the prevailing sobriety and hard-headedness we should be willing to barter the splendour of Sir Thomas Browne and the vigour of Swift.

Yet, if the essay admits more properly than biography or fiction of sudden boldness and metaphor, and can be polished till every atom of its surface shines, there are dangers in that too. We are soon in sight of ornament. Soon the current, which is the life-blood of literature, runs slow; and instead of sparkling and flashing or moving with a quieter impulse which has a deeper excitement, words coagulate together in frozen sprays which, like the grapes on a Christmas-tree, glitter for a single night, but are dusty and garish the day after. The temptation to decorate is great where the theme may be of the slightest. What is there to interest another in the fact that one has enjoyed a walking tour, or has amused oneself by rambling down Cheapside and looking at the turtles in Mr Sweeting's shop window? Stevenson and Samuel Butler chose very different methods of exciting our interest in these domestic themes. Stevenson, of course, trimmed and polished and set out his matter in the traditional eighteenth-century form. It is admirably done, but we cannot help feeling anxious, as the essay proceeds, lest the material may give out under the craftsman's fingers. The ingot is so small, the manipulation so incessant. And perhaps that is why the peroration—

> To sit still and contemplate—to remember the faces of women without desire, to be pleased by the great deeds of men without envy, to be everything and everywhere in sympathy and yet content to remain where and what you are—

has the sort of insubstantiality which suggests that by the time he got to the end he had left himself nothing solid to work with. Butler adopted the very opposite method. Think your own thoughts, he seems to say, and speak them as plainly as you can. These turtles in the shop window which appear to leak out of their shells through heads and feet suggest a fatal faithfulness to a fixed idea. And so, striding unconcernedly from one idea to the next, we traverse a large stretch of ground; observe that a wound in the solicitor is a very serious thing; that Mary Queen of Scots wears surgical boots and is subject to fits near the Horse Shoe in Tottenham Court Road; take it for granted that no one really cares about Aeschylus; and so, with many amusing anecdotes and some profound reflections, reach the peroration, which is that, as he had been told not to see more in Cheapside than he could get into twelve pages of the Universal Review, he had better stop. And yet obviously Butler is at least as careful of our pleasure as Stevenson; and to write like oneself and call it not writing is a much harder exercise in style than to write like Addison and call it writing well.

But, however much they differ individually, the Victorian essayists yet had something in common. They wrote at greater length than is now usual, and they wrote for a public which had not only time to sit down to its magazine seriously, but a high, if peculiarly Victorian, standard of culture by which to judge it. It was worth while to speak out upon serious matters in an essay; and there was nothing absurd in writing as well as one possibly could when, in a month or two, the same public which had welcomed the essay in a magazine would carefully read it once more in a book. But a change came from a small audience of cultivated people to a larger audience of people who were not quite so cultivated. The change was not altogether for the worse. In volume iii, we find Mr Birrell and Mr Beerbohm. It might even be said that there was a reversion to the classic type, and that the essay by losing its size and something of its sonority was approaching more nearly the essay of Addison and Lamb. At any rate, there is a great gulf between Mr Birrell on Carlyle and the essay which one may suppose that Carlyle would have written upon Mr Birrell. There is little similarity between *A Cloud of Pinafores*, by Max Beerbohm, and *A Cynic's Apology*, by Leslie Stephen. But the essay is alive; there is no reason to despair. As the conditions change so the essayist, most sensitive of all plants to public opinion, adapts himself, and if he is good makes the best of the change, and if he is bad the worst. Mr Birrell is certainly good; and so we find that, though he has dropped a considerable amount of weight, his attack is much more direct and his movement more supple. But what did Mr Beerbohm give to the essay and what did he take from it? That is a much more complicated question, for here we have an essayist who has concentrated on the work and is without doubt the prince of his profession.

What Mr Beerbohm gave was, of course, himself. This presence, which has haunted the essay fitfully from the time of Montaigne, had been in exile since the death of Charles Lamb. Matthew Arnold was never to his readers Matt, nor Walter Pater affectionately abbreviated in a thousand homes to Wat. They gave us much, but that they did not give. Thus, some time in the nineties, it must have surprised readers accustomed to exhortation, information, and denunciation to find themselves familiarly addressed by a voice which seemed to belong to a man no larger than themselves. He was affected by private joys and sorrows, and had no gospel to preach and no learning to impart. He was himself, simply and directly, and himself he has remained. So we look back upon essay after essay by Mr Beerbohm, knowing that, come September or May, we shall sit down with them and talk. Yet it is true that the essayist is the most sensitive of all writers to public opinion. The drawing-room is the place where a great deal of reading is done nowadays, and the essays of Mr Beerbohm lie, with an exquisite appreciation of all that the position exacts, upon the drawing-room table. There is no gin about; no strong tobacco, no puns, drunkenness, or insanity. Ladies and gentlemen talk together, and some things, of course, are not said.

But if it would be foolish to attempt to confine Mr Beerbohm to one room, it would be still more foolish, unhappily, to make him, the artist, the man who gives us only his best, the representative of our age. There are no essays by Mr Beerbohm in the fourth or fifth volumes of the present collection. His age seems already a little distant, and the drawing-room table, as it recedes, begins to look rather like an altar where, once upon a time, people deposited offerings—fruit from their own orchards, gifts carved with their own hands. Now once more the conditions have changed. The public needs essays as much as ever, and perhaps even more. The demand for the light middle not exceeding fifteen hundred words, or in special cases seventeen hundred and fifty, much exceeds the supply. Where Lamb wrote one essay and Max perhaps writes two, Mr Belloc at a rough computation produces three hundred and sixty-five. They are very short, it is true. Yet with what dexterity the practised essayist will utilise his space—beginning as close to the top of the sheet as possible, judging precisely how far to go, when to turn, and how, without sacrificing a hair's-breadth of paper, to wheel about and alight accurately upon the last word his editor allows! As a feat of skill it is well worth watching. But the personality upon which Mr Belloc, like Mr Beerbohm, depends suffers in the process. It comes to us not with the natural richness of the speaking voice, but strained and thin and familiarly addressed by a voice which seemed to belong to a man no larger than themselves. He was affected by private joys and sorrows, and had no gospel to preach and no learning to impart. He was himself, simply and directly, and himself he has remained. Once again we have an essayist capable of using the essayist's most proper but most dangerous and delicate tool. He has brought personality into literature, not unconsciously and impurely, but so consciously and purely that we do not know whether there is any relation between Max the essayist and Mr Beerbohm the man. We only know that the spirit of personality permeates every word that he writes. The triumph is the triumph of style. For it is only by knowing how to write that you can make use in literature of your self; that self which, while it is essential to literature, is also its most dangerous antagonist. Never to be yourself and yet always—that is the problem. Some of the essayists in Mr Rhys' collection, to be frank, have not altogether succeeded in solving it. We are nauseated by the sight of trivial personalities decomposing in the eternity of print. As talk, no doubt, it was charming, and certainly the writer is a good fellow to meet over a bottle of beer. But literature is stern; it is no use being charming, virtuous, or even learned and brilliant into the bargain, unless, she seems to reiterate, you fulfil her first condition—to know how to write.

This art is possessed to perfection by Mr Beerbohm. But he has not searched the dictionary for polysyllables. He has not moulded firm periods or seduced our ears with intricate cadences and strange melodies. Some of his companions—Henley and Stevenson, for example—are momentarily more impressive. But *A Cloud of Pinafores* has in it that indescribable inequality, stir, and final expressiveness which belong to life and to life alone. You have not finished with it because you have read it, any more than friendship is ended because it is time to part. Life wells up and alters and adds. Even things in a book-case change if they are alive; we find ourselves wanting to meet them again; full of mannerisms and affectations, like the voice of a man shouting through a megaphone to a crowd on a windy day. "Little friends, my readers," he says in the essay called "An Unknown Country," and he goes on to tell us how—

> There was a shepherd the other day at Findon Fair who had come from the cast by Lewes with sheep, and who had in his eyes that reminiscence of horizons which makes the eyes of shepherds and of mountaineers different from the eyes of other men. . . . I went with him to hear what he had to say, for shepherds talk quite differently from other men.

Happily this shepherd had little to say, even under the stimulus of the inevitable mug of beer, about the Unknown Country, for the only remark that he did make proves him either a minor poet, unfit for the care of sheep, or Mr Belloc himself masquerading with a fountain pen. That is the penalty which the habitual essayist must now be prepared to face. He must masquerade. He cannot afford the time either to be himself or to be other people. He must skim the surface of thought and dilute the strength of personality. He must give us a worn weekly halfpenny instead of a solid sovereign once a year.

But it is not Mr Belloc only who has suffered from the prevailing conditions. The essays which bring the collection to the year 1920 may not be the best of their authors' work, but, if we except writers like Mr Conrad and Mr Hudson, I who have strayed into essay writing accidentally, and concentrate upon those who write essays habitually, we shall find them a good deal affected by the change in their circumstances. To write weekly, to write daily, to write shortly, to write for busy people catching trains in the morning or for tired people coming home in the evening, is a heart-breaking task for men who know good writing from bad. They do it, but instinctively draw out of harm's way anything precious that might be damaged by contact with the public, or anything sharp that might irritate its skin. And so, if one reads Mr Lucas, Mr Lynd, or Mr Squire in the bulk, one feels that a common greyness silvers everything. They are as far removed from the extravagant beauty of Walter Pater as they are from the intemperate candour of Leslie Stephen. Beauty and courage are dangerous spirits to bottle in a column and a half; and thought, like a brown paper parcel in a waistcoat pocket, has a way of spoiling the symmetry of an article. It is a kind, tired, apathetic world for which they write, and the marvel is that they never cease to attempt, at least, to write well.

But there is no need to pity Mr Clutton Brock for this change in the essayist's conditions. He has clearly made the best of his circumstances and not the worst. One hesitates even to say that he has had to make any conscious effort in the matter, so naturally has he effected the transition from the private essayist to the public, from the drawing-room to the Albert Hall. Paradoxically enough, the shrinkage in size has brought about a corresponding expansion of individuality. We have no longer the "I" of Max and of Lamb, but the 'we' of public bodies and other sublime personages. It is "we" who go to hear the *Magic Flute*; "we" who ought to profit by it; "we," in some mysterious way, who, in our corporate capacity, once upon a time actually wrote it. For music and literature and art must submit to the same generalisation or they will not carry to the farthest recesses of the Albert Hall. That the voice of Mr Clutton Brock, so sincere and so disinterested, carries such a distance and reaches so many without pandering to the weakness of the mass or its passions must be a matter of legitimate satisfaction to us all. But while "we" are gratified, "I," that unruly partner in the human fellowship, is reduced to despair. "I" must always think things for himself, and feel things for himself. To share them in a diluted form with the majority of well-educated and well-intentioned men and women is for him sheer agony; and while the rest of us listen intently and profit profoundly, slips off to the woods and the fields and rejoices in a single blade of grass or a solitary potato.

In the fifth volume of modern essays, it seems, we have got some way from pleasure and the art of writing. But in justice to the essayists of

1920 we must be sure that we are not praising the famous because they have been praised already and the dead because we shall never meet them wearing spats in Piccadilly. We must know what we mean when we say that they can write and give us pleasure. We must compare them; we must bring out the quality. We must point to this and say it is good because it is exact, truthful, and imaginative:

> Nay, retire men cannot when they would; neither will they, when it were Reason; but are impatient of Privateness, even in age and sickness, which require the shadow: like old Townsmen: that will still be sitting at their street door, though therby they offer Age to Scorn. . .

and to this, and say it is bad because it is loose, plausible, and commonplace:

> With courteous and precise cynicism on his lips, he thought of quiet virginal chambers, of waters singing under the moon, of terraces where taintless music sobbed into the open night, of pure maternal mistresses with protecting arms and vigilant eyes, of fields slumbering in the sunlight, of leagues of ocean heaving under warm tremulous heavens, of hot ports, gorgeous and perfumed. . .

It goes on, but already we are bemused with sound and neither feel nor hear. The comparison makes us suspect that the art of writing has for backbone some fierce attachment to an idea. It is on the back of an idea, something believed in with conviction or seen with precision and thus compelling words to its shape, that the diverse company which includes Lamb and Bacon, and Mr Beerbohm and Hudson, and Vernon Lee and Mr Conrad, and Leslie Stephen and Butler and Walter Mater reaches the farther shore. Very various talents have helped or hindered the passage of the idea into words. Some scrape through painfully; others fir with every wind favouring. But Mr Belloc and Mr Lucas and Mr Squire are not fiercely attached to anything in itself. They share the contemporary dilemma—that lack of an obstinate, conviction which lifts ephemeral sounds through the misty sphere of anybody's language to the land where there is a perpetual marriage, a perpetual union. Vague as all definitions are, a good essay must have this permanent quality about it; it must draw its curtain round us, but it must be a curtain that shuts us in, not out.

GEORG LUKÁCS
....

ON THE NATURE AND FORM
OF THE ESSAY [1910]

A LETTER TO LEO POPPER

My friend,

The essays intended for inclusion in this book lie before me and I ask myself whether one is entitled to publish such works—whether such works
can give rise to a new unity, a book. For the point at issue for us now is
not what these essays can offer as "studies in literary history," but whether
there is something in them that makes them a new literary form of its
own, and whether the principle that makes them such is the same in each
one. What is this unity—if unity there is? I make no attempt to formulate
it because it is not I nor my book that should be the subject cession here.
The question before us is a more important, general one. It is the question whether such a unity is possible. To what extent have the really great
writings which belong to this category been given literary form, and to
what extent is of theirs an independent one? To what extent do the standpoint of such a work and the form given to this standpoint lift it out of
the sphere of science and place it at the side of the arts, yet blurring the
frontiers of either? To what extent do they endow the work with the force
necessary for a conceptual re-ordering of life and yet distinguish it from
the icy, final perfection of philosophy? That is the only profound apology
to be made for such writings, as well as the only profound criticism to be
addressed to them; for they are measured first and foremost by the yard-
stick of these questions, and the determining of such an objective will be
the first step towards showing how far they fall short of attaining it.

The critique, the essay—call it provisionally what you will—as a work
of art, a genre? I know you think the question tedious; you feel that all
the arguments for and against have been exhausted long ago. Wilde and
Kerr merely made familiar to everyone a truth whose ultimate meaning
the Greeks and Romans felt, quite unconsciously, to be self-evident: that
criticism is an art and not a science. Yet I believe—and it is for this reason

alone that I venture to importune you with these observations—that all the discussions have barely touched upon the essence of the real question: what is an essay? What is its intended form of expression, and what are the ways and means whereby this expression is accomplished? I believe that the aspect of "being well written" has been too one-sidedly emphasized in this context. It has been argued that the essay can be stylistically of equal value to a work of the imagination, and that, for this reason, it is unjust to speak of value differences at all. Yet what does that mean? Even if we consider criticism to be a work of art in this sense, we have not yet said anything at all about its essential nature. 'Whatever is well written is a work of art." Is a well-written advertisement or news item a work of art? Here I can see what so disturbs you about such a view of criticism: it is anarchy, the denial of form in order that an intellect which believes itself to be sovereign may have free play with possibilities of every kind. But if I speak here of criticism as a form of art, I do so in the name of order (i.e. almost purely symbolically and non-essentially), and solely on the strength of my feeling that the essay has a form which separates it, with the rigour of a law, from all other art forms. I want to try and define the essay as strictly as is possible, precisely by describing it as an art form.

Let us not, therefore, speak of the essay's similarities with works of literary imagination, but of what divides it from them. Let any resemblance serve here merely as a background against which the differences stand out all the more sharply; the purpose of mentioning these resemblances at all will be to limit our attention to genuine essays, leaving aside those writings which, useful though they are, do not deserve to be described as essays because they can never give us anything more than information, facts and "relationships." Why, after all, do we read essays? Many are read as a source of instruction, but there are others whose attraction is to be found in something quite different. It is not difficult to identify these. Our view, our appreciation of classical tragedy is quite different today, is it not, from Lessing's in the *Dramaturgy*; Winckelmann's Greeks seem strange, almost incomprehensible to us, and soon we may feel the same about Burckhardt's Renaissance. And yet we read them: why? On the other hand there are critical writings which, like a hypothesis in natural science, like a design for a machine part, lose all value at the precise moment when a new and better one becomes available. But if—as I hope and expect—someone were to write a new *Dramaturgy*, a *Dramaturgy* in favour of Corneille and against Shakespeare—how could it damage Lessing's? And what did Burckhardt and Pater, Rhode and Nietzsche do to change the effect upon us of Winckelmann's dreams of Greece?

"Of course, if criticism were a science . . ." writes Kerr. "But the im-
ponderables are too strong. Criticism is, at the very best, an art." And if
it were a science—it is not so impossible that it will become one—how
would that change our problem? We are not concerned here with replac-
ing something by something else, but with something essentially new,
something that remains untouched by the complete or approximate at-
tainment of scientific goals. Science affects us by its contents, art by its
forms; science offers us facts and the relationships between facts, but art
offers us souls and destinies. Here the ways part; here there is no replacement and no transition. In primitive, as yet undifferentiated epochs,
science and art (and religion and ethics and politics) are integrated, they
form a single whole; but as soon as science has become separate and
independent, everything that has led up to it loses its value. Only when
something has dissolved all its content in form, and thus become pure
art, can it no longer become superfluous; but then its previous scientific
nature is altogether forgotten and emptied of meaning.

There is, then, a science of the arts; but there is also an entirely different kind of expression of the human temperament, which usually takes
the form of writing about the arts. Usually, I say, for there are many writings which are engendered by such feelings without ever touching upon
literature or art—writings in which the same life-problems are raised as
in the writings which call themselves criticism, but with the difference
that here the questions are addressed directly to life itself: they do not
need the mediation of literature or art. And it is precisely the writings of
the greatest essayists which belong to this category: Plato's *Dialogues*, the
texts of the mystics, Montaigne's Essays, Kierkegaard's imaginary diaries
and short stories.

An endless series of almost imperceptible, subtle transitions leads
from here to imaginative writing. Think of the last scene in the *Heracles*
of Euripides: the tragedy is already over when Theseus appears and discovers everything that has happened—Hera's terrible vengeance on Heracles. Then begins the dialogue about life between the mourning Heracles
and his friend; questions akin to those of the Socratic dialogues are asked,
but the questioners are stiffer and less human, and their questions more
conceptual, less related to direct experience than in Plato. Think of the last
act of Michael Kramer, of the *Confessions of a Beautiful Soul*, of Dante, of
Everyman, of Bunyan—must I quote further examples?

Doubtless you will say that the end of *Heracles* is undramatic and Bu-

nyan is. . . . Certainly, certainly, but why? The *Heracles* is undramatic because every dramatic style has this natural corollary, that whatever happens within human souls is projected into human actions, movements
and gestures and is thus made visible and palpable to the senses. Here
you see Hera's vengeance overtaking Heracles, you see Heracles in the
blissful enjoyment of victory before vengeance is upon him, you see his
frenzied gestures in the madness which Hera has dealt to him and his
wild despair after the storm, when he sees what has happened to him.
But of what comes after you see nothing at all. Theseus comes—and you
try in vain to determine by other than conceptual means what happens
next: what you see and hear is no longer a true means of expression of
the real event, and that the event occurs at all is deep down a matter of
indifference to you. You see no more than that Theseus and Heracles
leave the stage together. Prior to that some questions are asked: what is
the true nature of the gods? Which gods may we believe in, and which
not? What is life and what is the best way of bearing one's sufferings
manfully? The concrete experience which has led up to these questions
is lost in an infinite distance. And when the answers return once more
into the world of facts, they are no longer answers to questions posed by
real life—questions of what these men must do or refrain from doing
in this particular situation. These answers cast a stranger's eye upon all
facts, for they have come from life and from the gods and know scarcely
anything of Heracles' pain or of its cause in Hera's vengeance. Drama,
I know, also addresses questions to life, and in drama, too, the answer
comes from destiny—and in the last analysis the questions and answers,
even in drama, are tied to certain definite facts. But the true dramatist (so
long as he is a true poet, a genuine representative of the poetic principle)
will see *a life* as being so rich and so intense that almost imperceptibly
it becomes *life*. Here, however, everything becomes undramatic because
here the other principle comes into effect: for the life that here poses the
question loses all its corporeality at the moment when the first word of
the question is uttered.

There are, then, two types of reality of the soul: one is *life* and the other
living; both are equally effective, but they can never be effective at the
same time. Elements of both are contained in the lived experience of every
human being, even if in always varying degrees of intensity and depth; in
memory too, there is now one, now the other, but at any one moment we
can only feel one of these two forms. Ever since there has been life and
men have sought to understand and order life, there has been this duality

in their lived experience. But the struggle for priority and pre-eminence between the two has mostly been fought out in philosophy, so that the battle-cries have always had a different sound, and for this reason have gone unrecognized by most men and have been unrecognizable to them. It would seem that the question was posed most clearly in the Middle Ages, when thinkers divided into two camps, the ones maintaining that the universalia—concepts, or Plato's Ideas if you will—were the sole true realities, while the others acknowledged them only as words, as names summarizing the sole true and distinct things.

The same duality also separates means of expression: the opposition here is between image and "significance." One principle is an image-creating one, the other a significance—supposing one. For one there exist only things, for the other only the relationships between them, only concepts and values. Poetry in itself knows of nothing beyond things; for it, every thing is serious and unique and incomparable. That is also why poetry knows no questions: you do not address questions to pure *things*, only to their relationships, for—as in fairy-tales—every question here turns again into a thing resembling the one that called it into being. The hero stands at the crossroads or in the midst of the struggle, but the crossroads and the struggle are not destinies about which questions may be asked and answers given; they are simply and literally struggles and crossroads. And the hero blows his miraculous horn and the expected miracle occurs: a thing which once more orders life. But in really profound criticism there is no life of things, no image, only transparency, only something that no image would be capable of expressing completely. An "imagelessness of all images" is the aim of all mystics, and Socrates speaks mockingly and contemptuously to Phaedrus of poets, who never have nor ever could worthily celebrate the true life of the soul. "For the great existence which the immortal part of the soul once lived is colourless and without form and impalpable, and only the soul's guide, the mind, can behold it."

You may perhaps reply that my poet is an empty abstraction and so, too, is my critic. You are right—both are abstractions, but not, perhaps, quite empty ones. They are abstractions because even Socrates must speak in images of his "world without form," his world on the far side of form, and even the German mystic's "imagelessness" is a metaphor. Nor is there any poetry without some ordering of things. Matthew Arnold once called it *criticism of life*. It represents the ultimate relationships between man and destiny and world, and without doubt it has its origin in those profound regions, even if, often, it is unaware of it. If poetry often refuses all questioning, all taking up of positions, is not the denial of all questions in itself an asking of questions, and is not the conscious rejection of any position in itself a position? I shall go further: the separation of image and signifi-cance is itself an abstraction, for the significance is always wrapped in im-ages and the reflection of a glow from beyond the image shines through every image. Every image belongs to our world and the joy of being in the world shines in its countenance; yet it also reminds us of something that was once there, at some time or another, a somewhere, its home, the only thing that, in the last analysis, has meaning and significance for the soul. Yes, in their naked purity they are merely abstractions, those two limits of human feeling, but only with the help of such abstractions can I define the two poles of possible literary expression. And the writings which most resolutely reject the image, which reach out most passionately for what lies behind the image, are the writings of the critics, the Platonists and the mystics.

But in saying this I have already explained why this kind of feeling calls for an art form of its own—why every expression of this kind of feeling must always disturb us when we find it in other forms, in poetry. It was you who once formulated the great demand which everything that has been given form must satisfy, the only absolutely universal demand, per-haps, but one that is inexorable and allows of no exception: the demand that everything in a work must be fashioned from the same material, that each of its parts must be visibly ordered from one single point. And be-cause all writing aspires to both unity and multiplicity, this is the univer-sal problem of style: to achieve equilibrium in a welter of disparate things, richness and articulation in a mass of uniform matter. Something that is viable in one art form is dead in another: here is practical, palpable proof of the inner divorce of forms. Do you remember how you explained to me the living quality of human figures in certain heavily stylized mural paint-ings? You said: these frescoes are painted between pillars, and even if the gestures of the men depicted in them are stiff like those of puppets and every facial expression is only a mask, still all this is more alive than the columns which frame the pictures and form a decorative unity with them. Only a little more alive, for the unity must be preserved; but more alive all the same, so that there may be an illusion of life. Here, however, the problem of equilibrium is posed in this way: the world and the beyond, image and transparency, idea and emanation lie in the two cups of a scale which is to remain balanced. The deeper down the question reaches—you need only compare the tragedy with the fairy-tale—the more linear the images become, the smaller the number of planes into which everything is compressed, the paler and more matte the radiance of the colours, the simpler the richness and multiplicity of the world, the more mask-like the expressions of the characters. But there are other experiences, for the expression of which even the simplest and most measured gesture would be too much—and too little; there are questions which are asked so softly that beside them the sound of the most toneless of events would be crude noise, not musical accompaniment; there are destiny-relationships which are so exclusively relationships between destinies as such that anything human would merely disturb their abstract purity and grandeur. I am not speaking here of subtlety or depth: those are value categories and are therefore valid only within a particular form. We are speaking of the fundamental principles which separate forms from one another—of the material from which the whole is constructed, of the standpoint, the world-view which gives unity to the entire work. Let me put it briefly: were one to compare the forms of literature with sunlight refracted in a prism, the writings of the essayists would be the ultra-violet rays.

There are experiences, then, which cannot be expressed by any gesture and which yet long for expression. From all that has been said you will know what experiences I mean and of what kind they are. I mean intellectuality, conceptuality as sensed experience, as immediate reality, as spontaneous principle of existence the world-view in its undisguised purity as an event of the soul, as the motive force of life. The question is posed immediately: what is life, what is man, what is destiny? But posed as a question only: for the answer, here, does not supply a "solution" like one of the answers of science or, at purer heights, those of philosophy. Rather, as in poetry of every kind, it is symbol, destiny and tragedy. When a man experiences such things, then everything that is outward about him awaits in rigid immobility the outcome of the struggle between invisible forces to which the senses have no access. Any gesture with which such a man might wish to express something of his experience would falsify that experience, unless it ironically emphasized its own inadequacy and thus cancelled itself out. A man who experiences such things cannot be characterized by any outward feature—how then can he be given form in a work of literature? All writings represent the world in the symbolic terms of a destiny-relationship; everywhere, the problem of destiny determines the problem of form. This unity, this coexistence is so strong that neither element ever occurs without the other; here again a separation is possible only by way of abstraction. Therefore the separation which I am trying to accomplish here appears, in practice, merely as a shift of emphasis: poetry receives its profile and its form from destiny, and form in poetry appears always only as destiny; but in the works of the essayists form becomes destiny, it is the destiny-creating principle. This difference means the following: destiny lifts things up outside the world of things, accentuating the essential ones and eliminating the inessential; but form sets limits round a substance which otherwise would dissolve like air in the All. In other words, destiny comes from the same source as everything else, it is a thing among things, whereas form—seen as something finished, i.e. seen from outside—defines the limits of the immaterial. Because the destiny which orders things is flesh of their flesh and blood of their blood, destiny is not to be found in the writings of the essayists. For destiny, once stripped of its uniqueness and accidentality, is just as airy and immaterial as all the rest of the incorporeal matter of these writings, and is no more capable of giving them form than they themselves possess any natural inclination or possibility of condensing themselves into form.

That is why such writings speak of forms. The critic is one who glimpses destiny in forms: whose most profound experience is the soul-content which forms indirectly and unconsciously conceal within themselves. Form is his great experience, form—as immediate reality—is the image-element, the really living content of his writings. This form, which springs from a symbolic contemplation of life-symbols, acquires a life of its own through the power of that experience. It becomes a world-view, a standpoint, an attitude vis-á-vis the life from which it sprang: a possibility of reshaping it, of creating it anew. The critic's moment of destiny, therefore, is that moment at which things become forms—the moment when all feelings and experiences on the near or the far side of form receive form, are melted down and condensed into form. It is the mystical moment of union between the outer and the inner, between soul and form. It is as mystical as the moment of destiny in tragedy when the hero meets his destiny, in the short story when accident and cosmic necessity converge, in poetry when the soul and its world meet and coalesce into a new unity that can no more be divided, either in the past or in the future. Form is reality in the writings of critics; it is the voice with which they address their questions to life. That is the true and most profound reason why literature and art are the typical, natural subject-matter of criticism. For here the end-point of poetry can become a starting-point and a beginning; here form appears, even in its abstract conceptuality, as something surely and concretely real. But this is only the typical subject-matter of the essay, not the sole one. For the essayist needs form only as lived experience and he needs only its life, only the living soul-reality it contains. But this reality is to be found in every immediate sensual expression of life, it can be read out of and read into every such experience; life itself can be lived and given form through such a scheme of lived experience. Because literature, art and philosophy pursue forms openly and directly, whereas in life they are no more than the ideal demand of a certain kind of men and experiences, a lesser intensity of critical capacity is needed to experience something formed than to experience something lived; and that is why the reality of form-vision appears, at the first and most superficial glance, less problematic in the sphere of art than in life. But this only seems to be so at the first and most superficial glance, for the form of life is no more abstract than the form of a poem. Here as there, form becomes perceptible only through abstraction, and there as here the reality of form is no stronger than the force with which it is experienced. It would be superficial to distinguish between poems according to whether they take their subject-matter from life or elsewhere; for in any case the form-creating power of poetry breaks and scatters whatever is old, whatever has already been formed, and everything becomes unformed raw material in its hands. To draw such a distinction here seems to me just as superficial, for both ways of contemplating the world are merely standpoints taken up in relation to things, and each is applicable everywhere, although it is true that for both there exist certain things which, with a naturalness decreed by nature, submit themselves to one particular standpoint and others which can only be forced to do so by violent struggles and profound experiences.

As in every really essential relationship, natural effect and immediate usefulness coincide here: the experiences which the writings of the essayists were written to express become conscious in the minds of most people only when they look at the pictures or read the poem discussed and even then they rarely have a force that could move life itself. That is why most people have to believe that the writings of the essayists are produced only in order to explain books and pictures, to facilitate their understanding. Yet this relationship is profound and necessary, and it is precisely the indivisible and organic quality of this mixture of being-accidental and being-necessary which is at the root of that humour and that irony which we find in the writings of every truly great essayist—that peculiar humour which is so strong that to speak of it is almost indecent, for there is no use in pointing it out to someone who does not spontaneously feel it.

And the irony I mean consists in the critic always speaking about the ultimate problems of life, but in a tone which implies that he is only discussing pictures and books, only the inessential and pretty ornaments of real life—and even then not their innermost substance but only their beautiful and useless surface. Thus each essay appears to be removed as far as possible from life, and the distance between them seems the greater, the more burningly and painfully we sense the actual closeness of the true essence of both. Perhaps the great Sieur de Montaigne felt something like this when he gave his writings the wonderfully elegant and apt title of "Essays." The simple modesty of this word is an arrogant courtesy. The essayist dismisses his own proud hopes which sometimes lead him to believe that he has come close to the ultimate: he has, after all, no more to offer than explanations of the poems of others, or at best of his own ideas. But he ironically adapts himself to this smallness—the eternal smallness of the most profound work of the intellect in face of life—and even emphasizes it with ironic modesty. In Plato, conceptuality is underlined by the irony of the small realities of life. Eryximachos cures Aristophanes of hiccups by making him sneeze before he can begin his deeply meaningful hymn to Eros. And Hippothales watches with anxious attention while Socrates questions his beloved Lysis—and little Lysis, with childish malice, asks Socrates to torment his friend Menexenos with questions just as he has tormented him. Rough guardians come and break up the gently scintillating dialogue, and drag the boys off home. Socrates, however, is more amused than anything else: "Socrates and the two boys wanted to be friends, yet were not even able to say what a friend really is." I see a similar irony in the vast scientific apparatus of certain modern essayists (think only of Weininger), and only a different expression of it in the discreetly reserved manner of a Dilthey. We can always find the same irony in every text by every great essayist, though admittedly always in a different form. The mystics of the Middle Ages are the only ones without inner irony—I surely need not tell you why.

We see, then, that criticism and the essay generally speak of pictures, books and ideas. What is their attitude towards the matter which is represented? People say that the critic must always speak the truth, whereas the poet is not obliged to tell the truth about his subject-matter. It is not our intention here to ask Pilate's question nor to enquire whether the poet, too, is not impelled towards an inner truthfulness and whether the truth of any criticism can be stronger or greater than this. I do not propose to ask these questions because I really do see a difference here, but once again a difference which is altogether pure, sharp and without transitions only at its abstract poles. When I wrote about Kassner I pointed out that the essay always speaks of something that has already been given form, or at least something that has already been there at some time in the past; hence it is part of the nature of the essay that it does not create new things from an empty nothingness but only orders those which were once alive. And because it orders them anew and does not form something new out of formlessness, it is bound to them and must always speak "the truth" about them, must find expression for their essential nature. Perhaps the difference can be most briefly formulated thus: poetry takes its motifs from life (and art); the essay has its models in art (and life). Perhaps this is enough to define the difference: the paradox of the essay is almost the same as that of the portrait. You see why, do you not? In front of a landscape we never ask ourselves whether this mountain or that river really is as it is painted there; but in front of every portrait the question of likeness always forces itself willy-nilly upon us. Give a little more thought, therefore, to this problem of likeness—this problem which, foolish and superficial as it is, drives true artists to despair. You stand in front of a Velasquez portrait and you say: "What a marvellous likeness." and you feel that you have really said something about the painting. Likeness? Of whom? Of no one, of course. You have no idea whom it represents, perhaps you can never find out; and if you could, you would care very little. Yet you feel that it is a likeness. Other portraits produce their effect only by colour and line, and so you do not have this feeling. In other words, the really significant portraits give us, besides all other artistic sensations, also this: the life of a human being who once was really alive, forcing us to feel that his life was exactly as shown by the lines and colours of the painting. Only because we see painters in front of their models fight such a hard battle for this ideal expression—because the look and the battle-cry of this battle are such that it cannot be anything else than a battle for likeness—only for this reason do we give this name to the portrait's suggestion of real life, even though there is no one in the world whom the portrait could be like. For even if we know the person represented, whose portrait we may call "like" or "unlike"—is it not an abstraction to say of an arbitrarily chosen moment or expression that this is that person's likeness? And even if we know thousands of such moments or expressions, what do we know of the immeasurably large part of his life when we do not see him, what do we know of the inner light which burns within this "known" person, what of the way this inner light is reflected in others? And that, you see, is more or less how I imagine the truth of the essay to be. Here too there is a struggle for truth, for the incarnation of a life which someone has seen in a man, an epoch or a form; but it depends only on the intensity of the work and its vision whether the written text conveys to us this suggestion of that particular life.

The great difference, then, is this: poetry gives us the illusion of life of the person it represents; nowhere is there a conceivable someone or something against which the created work can be measured. The hero of the essay was once alive, and so his life must be given form; but this life, too, is as much inside the work as everything is in poetry. The essay has to create from within itself all the preconditions for the effectiveness and validity of its vision. Therefore two essays can never contradict one another: each creates a different world, and even when, in order to achieve a higher universality, it goes beyond that created world, it still remains inside it by its tone, colour and accent; that is to say, it leaves that world only in the inessential sense. It is simply not true that there exists an ob-jective, external criterion of life and truth, e.g. that the truth of Grimm's, Dilthey's or Schlegel's Goethe can be tested against the "real" Goethe. It is not true because many Goethes, different from one another and each profoundly different from our Goethe, may convince us of their life: and, conversely, we are disappointed if our own visions are presented by oth-ers, yet without that vital breath which would give them autonomous life. It is true that the essay strives for truth: but just as Saul went out to look for his father's she-asses and found a kingdom, so the essayist who is re-ally capable of looking for the truth will find at the end of his road the goal he was looking for: life.

The illusion of truth! Do not forget how slowly and with how much difficulty poetry abandoned that ideal. It happened not so very long ago, and it is highly questionable whether the disappearance of the illusion was entirely advantageous. It is highly questionable whether man should want the precise thing he sets out to attain, whether he has the right to walk towards his goal along straight and simple paths. Think of the chiv-alresque epics of the Middle Ages, think of the Greek tragedies, think of Giotto and you will see what I am trying to say. We are not speaking here of ordinary truth, the truth of naturalism which it would be more accurate to call the triviality of everyday life, but of the truth of the myth by whose power ancient tales and legends are kept alive for thousands of years. The true poets of myths looked only for the true meaning of their themes; they neither could nor wished to check their pragmatic reality. They saw these myths as sacred, mysterious hieroglyphics which it was their mission to read. But do you not see that both worlds can have a mythology of their own? It was Friedrich Schlegel who said long ago that the national gods of the Germans were not Hermann or Wotan but science and the arts. Admittedly, that is not true of the *whole* life of Germany, but it is all the more apt as a description of *part* of the life of every nation in every epoch—that part, precisely, of which we are speaking. That life, too, has its golden ages and its lost paradises; we find in it rich lives full of strange adventures and enigmatic punishments of dark sins; heroes of the sun appear and fight out their harsh feuds with the forces of darkness; here, too, the magic words of wise magicians and the tempting songs of beautiful sirens lead weaklings into perdition; here too there is original sin and redemption. All the struggles of life are present here, but the stuff of which everything is made is different from the stuff of the "other" life.

We want poets and critics to give us life-symbols and to mould the still-living myths and legends in the form of our questions. It is a subtle and poignant irony, is it not, when a great critic dreams our longing into early Florentine paintings or Greek torsos and, in that way, gets something out of them for us that we would have sought in vain everywhere else— and then speaks of the latest achievements of scientific research, of new methods and new facts? Facts are always there and everything is always contained in facts, but every epoch needs its own Greece, its own Middle Ages and its own Renaissance. Every age creates the age it needs, and only the next generation believes that its fathers' dreams were lies which must be fought with its own new "truths". The history of the effect of poetry follows the same course, and in criticism, too, the continuing life of the grandfather's dreams—not to mention those of earlier generations—is barely touched by the dreams of men alive today. Consequently the most varied "conceptions" of the Renaissance can live peacefully side by side with one another, just as a new poet's new *Phèdre*, *Siegfried* or *Tristan* must always leave intact the *Phèdre*, *Siegfried* or *Tristan* of his predecessors.

Of course there is a science of the arts; there has to be one. The greatest essayists are precisely those who can least well do without it: what they create must be science, even when their vision of life has transcended the sphere of science. Sometimes its free flight is constrained by the unassailable facts of dry matter; sometimes it loses all scientific value because it is, after all, a vision, because it precedes facts and therefore handles them freely and arbitrarily. The essay form has not yet, today, travelled the road to independence which its sister, poetry, covered long ago—the road of development from a primitive, undifferentiated unity with science, ethics and art. Yet the beginning of that road was so tremendous that subsequent developments have rarely equalled it. I speak, of course, of Plato, the greatest essayist who ever lived or wrote, the one who wrested everything from life as it unfolded before his eyes and who therefore needed no mediating medium; the one who was able to connect his questions, the most profound questions ever asked, with life as lived. This greatest master of the form was also the happiest of all creators: man lived in his immediate proximity, man whose essence and destiny constituted the paradigmatic essence and destiny of his form. Perhaps they would have become paradigmatic in this way even if Plato's writing had consisted of the driest notations—not just because of his glorious form-giving—so strong was the concordance of life and form in this particular case. But Plato met Socrates and was able to give form to the myth of Socrates, to use Socrates' destiny as the vehicle for the questions he, Plato, wanted to address to life about destiny. The life of Socrates is the typical life for the essay form, as typical as hardly any other life is for any literary form—with the whole exception of Oedipus' life for tragedy. Socrates always lived in the ultimate questions; every other living reality was as little alive for him as his questions are alive for ordinary people. The concepts into which he poured the whole of his life were lived by him with the most direct and immediate life energy; everything else was but a parable of that sole true reality, useful only as a means of expressing those experiences. His life rings with the sound of the deepest, the most hidden longing and is full of the most violent struggles; but that longing is—simply—longing, and the form in which it appears is the attempt to comprehend the nature of longing and to capture it in concepts, while the struggles are simply verbal battles fought solely in order to give more definite limits to a few concepts. Yet the longing fills that life completely and the struggles are always, quite literally, a matter of life and death. But despite everything the longing which seems to fill that life is not the essential thing about life, and neither Socrates' life nor his death was able to express those life-and-death struggles. If this had been possible, the death of Socrates would have been a martyrdom or a tragedy—which means that it could be represented in epic or dramatic form. But Plato knew exactly why he burned the tragedy he wrote in his youth. For a tragic life is crowned only by its end, only the end gives meaning, sense and form to the whole, and it is precisely the end which is always arbitrary and ironic here, in every dialogue and in Socrates' whole life. A question is thrown up and extended so far in depth that it becomes the question of all questions, but after that everything remains open; something comes from outside—from a reality which has no connection with the question nor with that which, as the possibility of an answer, brings forth a new question to meet it—and interrupts everything. This interruption is not an end, because it does not come from within, and yet it is the most profound ending because a conclusion from within would have been impossible. For Socrates every event was only an occasion for seeing concepts more clearly, his defence in front of the judges only a way of leading weak logicians *ad absurdum*—and his death? Death does not count here, it cannot be grasped by concepts, it interrupts the great dialogue—the only true reality—just as brutally, and merely from the outside, as those rough tutors who interrupted the conversation with Lysis. Such an interruption, however, can only be viewed humoristically, it has so little connection with that which it interrupts. But it is also a profound life-symbol—and, for that reason, still more profoundly humorous—that the essential is always interrupted by such things in such a way.

The Greeks felt each of the forms available to them as a reality, as a living thing and not as an abstraction. Alcibiades already saw clearly what Nietzsche was to emphasize centuries later—that Socrates was a new kind of man, profoundly different in his elusive essence from all other Greeks who lived before him. But Socrates, in the same dialogue, expressed the eternal ideal of men of his kind, an ideal which neither those whose way of feeling remains tied to the purely human nor those who are poets in their innermost being will ever understand: that tragedies and comedies should be written by the same man; that "tragic" and "comic" is entirely a matter of the chosen standpoint. In saying this, the critic expressed his deepest life-sense: the primacy of the standpoint, the concept, over feeling; and in saying it he formulated the profoundest anti-Greek thought.

Plato himself, as you see, was a "critic," although criticism, like everything else, was for him only an occasion, an ironic means of expressing himself. Later on, criticism became its own content; critics spoke only of poetry and art, and they never had the fortune to meet a Socrates whose life might have served them as a springboard to the ultimate. But Socrates was the first to condemn such critics. "It seems to me," he said to Protagoras, "that to make a poem the subject of a conversation is too reminiscent of those banquets which uneducated and vulgar people give in their houses. . . . Conversations like the one we are now enjoying—conversations among men such as most of us would claim to be—do not need outside voices or the presence of a poet. . ."

Fortunately for us, the modern essay does not always have to speak of books or poets; but this freedom makes the essay even more problematic. It stands too high, it sees and connects too many things to be the simple exposition or explanation of a work; the tide of every essay is preceded in invisible letters, by the words "Thoughts occasioned by . . . ." The essay has become too rich and independent for dedicated service, yet it is too intellectual and too multiform to acquire form out of its own self. Has it perhaps become even more problematic, even further removed from life-values than if it had continued to report faithfully on books?

When something has once become problematic—and the way of think-ing that we speak of, and its way of expression, have not become problem-atic but have always been so—then salvation can only come from accen-tuating the problems to the maximum degree, from going radically to its root. The modern essay has lost that backdrop of life which gave Plato and the mystics their strength; nor does it any longer possess a naive faith in the value of books and what can be said about them. The problematic of the situation has become accentuated almost to the point of demanding a certain frivolity of thought and expression, and this, for most critics, has become their life-mood. This has shown, however, that salvation is neces-sary and is therefore becoming possible and real The essayist must now become conscious of his own self, must find himself and build something of his own out of himself. The essayist speaks of a picture or a book, but leaves it again at once—why? Because, I think, the idea of the picture or book has become predominant in his mind, because he has forgotten all that is concretely incidental about it, because he has used it only as a starting-point, a springboard. Poetry is older and greater—a larger, more important thing—than all the works of poetry: that was once the mood with which critics approached literature, but in our time it has had to be-come a conscious attitude. The critic has been snit into the world in order to bring to light this *a priori* primacy over great and small, to proclaim it, to judge every phenomenon by the scale of values glimpsed and grasped through this recognition. The idea is there before any of its expressions, it is a soul-value, a world-moving and life-forming force in itself: and that is why such criticism will always speak of life where it is most alive. The idea is the measure of everything that exists, and that is why the critic whose thinking is "occasioned by" something already created, and who reveals its idea, is the one who will write the truest and most profound criticism. Only something that is great and true can live in the proximity of the idea.

When this magic word has been spoken, then everything that is brittle, small and unfinished falls apart, loses its usurped wisdom, its badly fitting essence. It does not have to be "criticism": the atmosphere of the idea is enough to judge and condemn it.

Yet it is now that the essayist's possibility of existence becomes profoundly problematic. He is delivered from the relative, the inessential, by the force of judgement of the idea he has glimpsed; but who gives him the right to judge? It would be almost true to say that he seizes that right, that he creates his judgement-values from within himself. But nothing is separated from true judgement by a deeper abyss than its approximation, the squint-eyed category of complacent and self-satisfied knowledge. The criteria of the essayist's judgement are indeed created within him, but it is not he who awakens them to life and action: the one who whispers them into his ear is the great value-definer of aesthetics, the one who is always about to arrive, the one who is never quite yet there, the only one who has been called to judge. The essayist is a Schopenhauer who writes his *Parerga* while waiting for the arrival of his own (or another's) *The World as Will and Idea*, he is a John the Baptist who goes out to preach in the wilderness about another who is still to come, whose shoelace he is not worthy to untie. And if that other does not come—is not the essayist then without justification? And if the other does come, is he not made superfluous thereby? Has he not become entirely problematic by thus trying to himself? He is the pure type of the precursor, and it seems questionable whether, left to himself—i.e., independent from the fate of that other of whom he is the herald—he could lay claim to any value or validity. To stand fast against those who deny his fulfilment within the great, redeeming system is easy enough: a true longing always triumphs over those who lack the energy to rise above the vulgar level of given facts and experiences; the existence of the longing is enough to decide the outcome. For it tears the mask off everything that is only apparently positive and immediate, reveals it as petty longing and cheap fulfilment, points to the measure and order to which even they who vainly and contemptibly deny its existence—because measure and order seem inaccessible to them—unconsciously aspire. The essay can calmly and proudly set its fragmentariness against the petty completeness of scientific exactitude or impressionistic freshness; but its purest fulfilment, its most vigorous accomplishment becomes powerless once the great aesthetic comes. Then all its creations are only an application of the measure which at last has become undeniable, it is then something merely provisional and occasional, its results can no longer be justified purely from within themselves. Here the essay seems truly and completely a mere precursor, and no independent value can be attached to it. But this longing for value and form, for measure and order and purpose, does not simply lead to an end that must be reached so that it may be cancelled out and become a presumptuous tautology. Every true end is a real end, the end of a road, and although road and end do not make a unity and do not stand side by side as equals, they nevertheless coexist: the end is unthinkable and unrealizable without the road being travelled again and again; the end is not standing still but arriving there, not resting but conquering a summit. Thus the essay seems justified as a necessary means to the ultimate end, the penultimate step in this hierarchy. This, however, is only the value of what it does; the fact of what it is has yet another more independent value. For in the system of values yet to be found, the longing we spoke of would be satisfied and therefore abolished; but this longing is more than just something waiting for fulfilment, it is a fact of the soul with a value and existence of its own: an original and deep-rooted attitude towards the whole of life, a final, irreducible category of possibilities of experience. Therefore it needs not only to be satisfied (and thus abolished) but also to be given form which will redeem and release its most essential and now indivisible substance into eternal value. That is what the essay does. Think again of the example of the *Parerga*: whether they occurred before or after the system is not a matter simply of a time-sequence; the time-historical difference is only a symbol of the difference between their two natures. The *Parerga* written before the system create their pre-conditions from within themselves, create the whole world out of their longing for the system, so that—it seems—they can give an example, a hint; immanently and inexpressibly, they contain the system and its connection with lived life. Therefore they must always occur before the system; even if the system had already been created, they would not be a mere application but always a new creation, a coming-alive in real experience. This "application" creates both that which judges and that which is judged, it encompasses a whole world in order to raise to eternity, in all its uniqueness, something that was once there. The essay is a judgement, but the essential, the value-determining thing about it is not the verdict (as is the case with the system) but the process of judging.

Only now may we write down the opening words: the essay is an art form, an autonomous and integral giving-of-form to an autonomous and complete life. Only now would it not be contradictory, ambiguous and false to call it a work of art and yet insist on emphasizing the thing that differentiates it from art: it faces life with the same gesture as the work of art, but only the gesture, the sovereignty of its attitude is the same; otherwise there is no correspondence between them.

It was of this possibility of the essay that I wanted to speak to you here, of the nature and form of these "intellectual poems", as the older Schlegel called those of Hemsterhuys. This is not the place to discuss or decide whether the essayists' becoming conscious of their own nature, as they have been doing for some time past, has brought perfection or can bring it. The point at issue was only the possibility, only the question of whether the road upon which this book attempts to travel is really a road; it was not a question of who has already travelled it or how—nor, least of all, the distance this particular book has travelled along it. The critique of this book is contained, in all possible sharpness and entirety, in the very approach from which it sprang.

Florence, October 1910.

Translated by Anna Bostock

FROM "MODERN ESSAYS FOR SCHOOLS"

PREFACE [1921]

It had been my habit, I am now aware, to speak somewhat lightly of the labors of anthologists: to insinuate that they led lives of bland sedentary ease. I shall not do so again. When the publisher suggested a collection of representative contemporary essays, I thought it would be the most lenient of tasks. But experience is a fine aperitive to the mind.

Indeed the pangs of the anthologist, if he has conscience, are burdensome. There are so many considerations to be tenderly weighed; personal taste must sometimes be set aside in view of the general plan; for every item chosen half a dozen will have been affectionately conned and sifted; and perhaps some favorite pieces will be denied because the authors have reasons for withholding permission. It would be enjoyable (for me, at any rate) to write and essay on the things I have lingered over with intent to include them in this little book, but have finally sacrificed for one reason or another. How many times—twenty at least—have I taken down from my shelf Mr. Chesterton's *The Victorian Age in Literature* to reconsider whether his ten pages on Dickens, or his glorious summing-up of Decadents and Aesthetes, were not absolutely essential. How many times I have palpitated upon certain passages in *The Education of Henry Adams* and in Mr. Wells's *Outline of History*, which, I assured myself, would legitimately stand as essays if shrewdly excerpted.

But I usually concluded that would not be quite fair. I have not been overscrupulous in this matter, for the essay is a mood rather that a form; the frontier between the essay and the short story is as imperceptible as is at present the once famous Mason and Dixon line. Indeed, in that pleasant lowland country between the two empires lie (to my way of thinking) some of the most fertile fields of prose—fiction that expresses feeling and character and setting rather than action and plot; fiction beautifully ripened by the lingering mild sunshine of the essayist's mood. This is fiction, I might add, extremely unlikely to get into the movies. I think of short stories such as George Gissing's, in that too little known volume *The*

House of Cobwebs, which I read again and again at midnight with unfailing delight; fall asleep over; forget; and again re-read with undiminished satisfaction. They have no brilliance of phrase, no smart surprises, no worked-up 'situations' which have to be taken at high speed to pass without breakdown over their brittle bridgework of credibility. They have only the modest and faintly melancholy savor of life itself.

Yet it is a mere quibble to pretend that the essay does not have easily recognizable manners. It may be severely planned, or it may ramble in ungirdled mood, but it has its own point of view that marks it from the short story proper, or the merely personal memoir. That distinction, easily felt by the sensitive reader, is not readily expressible. Perhaps the true meaning of the word essay—an attempt—gives a clue. No matter how personal or trifling the topic may be, there is always a tendency to generalize, to walk round the subject or the experience, and view it from several vantages; instead of (as in the short story) cutting a carefully landscaped path through a chosen tract of human complication. So an essay can never be more than an attempt, for it is an excursion into the endless. Any student of fiction will admit that in the composition of a short story many entertaining and valuable elaborations may rise in the mind of the author which must be strictly rejected because they do not forward the essential motive. But in the essay (of an informal sort) we ask not relevance to plot, but relevance to mood. That is why there are so many essays that are mere marking time. The familiar essay is easier to write than the short story, but it imposes equal restraints on a scrupulous author. For in fiction the writer is controlled and limited and swept along by his material; but in the essay, the writer rides his pen. A good story, once clearly conceived, almost writes itself; but essays are written.

There also we find a pitfall of the personal essay—the temptation to become too ostentatiously quaint, too deliberately 'whimsical' (the word which, by loathsome repetition, has become emetic). The fine flavor and genius of the essay—as in Bacon and Montaigne, Lamb, Hazlitt, Thackeray, Thoreau; perhaps even in Stevenson—is the rich bouquet of personality. But soliloquy must not fall into monologue. One might put it thus: that the perfection of the familiar essay is a conscious revelation of self done inadvertently.

The art of the anthologist is the art of the host: his tact is exerted in choosing a congenial group; making them feel comfortable and at ease; keeping the wine and tobacco in circulation; while his eye is tenderly alert down the bright vista of tablecloth, for any lapse in the general cheer. It is well, also, for him to hold himself discreetly in the background, giving his guests the pleasure of clinching the jape, and seeking only, by innocent wiles, to draw each one into some characteristic and felicitous vein. I think I can offer you, in this parliament of philomaths, entertainment of the most genuine sort; and having said so much, I might well retire and be heard no more.

But I think it is well to state, as even the most bashful host may do, just why this particular company has been called together. My intention is not merely to please the amiable dilettante, though I hope to do that too. I made my choices, first and foremost, with a view to stimulating those who are themselves interested in the arts of writing. I have, to be frank, a secret ambition that a book of this sort may even be used as small but useful weapon in the classroom. I wanted to bring it home to the student that as brilliant and sincere work is being done to-day in the essay as in any period of our literature. Accordingly the pieces reprinted here are very diverse. There is the grand manner; there is foolery; there is straightforward literary criticism; there is pathos, politics, and the picturesque. But every selection is, in its own way, a work of art. And I would call the reader's attention to this: that the greater number of these essays were written not by retired aesthetes, but by practising journalists in the harness of the daily or weekly press. The names of some of the most widely bruited essayists of our day are absent from this roster, not by malice, but because I desired to include material less generally known.

I should apologize, I suppose, for the very informal tone of the introductory notes to each author. But I conceived the reader in the rôle of a friend spending the evening in happy gossip along the shelves. Pulling out one's favorites and talking about them, now and then reading a chosen extract aloud, and ending (some time after midnight) by choosing some special volume for the guest to take to bed with him—in the same spirit I have compiled this collection. Perhaps the editorial comments have too much the manner of dressing gown and slippers; but what a pleasant book this will be to read in bed!

And perhaps this collection may be regarded as a small contribution to Anglo-American friendliness. Of course when I say Anglo-, I mean Brito-, but that is such a hideous prefix. Journalists on this side are much better acquainted with what their professional colleagues are doing in Britain, than they with our concerns. But surely there should be a congenial fraternity of spirit among all who use the English tongue in print. There are some of us who even imagine a day when there may be regular international exchanges of journalists, as there have been of scholars and students. The contributions to this book are rather evenly divided between British and American hands; and perhaps it is not insignificant that two of the most pleasing items come from Canada, where they often combine the virtues of both sides.

It is a pleasant task to thank the authors and publishers who have assented to the reprinting of these pieces. To the authors themselves, and to the following publishers, I admit my sincere gratitude for the use of material copyrighted by them:—Doubleday Page and Company for the extracts from books by John Macy, Stewart Edward White and Pearsall Smith; Charles Scribner's Sons for Rupert Brooke's *Niagara Falls*; the New York *Sun* for Don Marquis's *Almost Perfect State*; the George H. Doran Company for the essays by Joyce Kilmer and Robert Cortes Holliday; Mr. James B. Pinker for permission to reprint Mr. Conrad's Preface to *A Personal Record*; Alfred A. Knopf, Inc., for the essays by H. M. Tomlinson, A. P. Herbert and Philip Guedalla; Lady Osler for the essay by the late Sir William Osler; Henry Holt and Company for Thomas Burke's *The Russian Quarter*; E. P. Dutton and Company for *A Word for Autumn*, by A. A. Milne; the New York *Evening Post* for the essays by Stuart P. Sherman and Harry Esty Dounce; Harper and Brothers for Marian Storm's *A Woodland Valentine*; Dodd, Mead and Company for Simeon Strunsky's *Nocturne*, from his volume *Post-Impressions*; the Macmillan Company for *Beer and Cider*, from Professor Saintsbury's *Notes on a Cellar Book*; Longmans Green and Company for Bertrand Russell's *A Free Man's Worship*, from *Mysticism and Logic*; Robert M. McBride and Company for the selection from James Branch Cabell; Harcourt, Brace and Company for the essay by Heywood Broun; *The Weekly Review* for the essays by O. W. Firkins, Harry Morgan Ayres and Robert Palfrey Utter. The present ownership of the copyright of the essay by Louise Imogen Guiney I have been unable to discover. It was published in *Patrins* (Copeland and Day, 1897), which has long been out of print. Knowing the purity of my motives I have used this essay, hoping that it might introduce Miss Guiney's exquisite work to the younger generation that knows her hardly at all.

G. K. CHESTERTON

ON ESSAYS [1930]

There are dark and morbid moods in which I am tempted to feel that Evil re-entered the world in the form of Essays. The Essay is like the Serpent, smooth and graceful and easy of movement, also wavering or wandering. Besides, I suppose that the very word Essay had the original meaning of 'trying it on'. The serpent was in every sense of the word tentative. The tempter is always feeling his way, and finding out how much other people will stand. That misleading air of irresponsibility about the Essay is very disarming through appearing to be disarmed. But the serpent can strike without claws, as it can run without legs. It is the emblem of all those arts which are elusive, evasive, impressionistic, and shading away from tint to tint. I suppose that the Essay, so far as England at least is concerned, was almost invented by Francis Bacon. I can well believe it. I always thought he was the villain of English history.

It may be well to explain that I do not really regard all Essayists as wicked men. I have myself been an essayist; or tried to be an essayist; or pretended to be an essayist. Nor do I in the least dislike essays. I take perhaps my greatest literary pleasure in reading them; after such really serious necessities of the intellect as detective stories and tracts written by madmen. There is no better reading in the world than some contemporary essays, like those of Mr. E. V. Lucas or Mr. Robert Lynd. And though, unlike Mr. Lucas and Mr. Lynd, I am quite incapable of writing a really good essay, the motive of my dark suggestion is not a diabolic jealousy or envy. It is merely a natural taste for exaggeration, when dealing with a point too subtle to permit of exactitude. If I may myself imitate the timid and tentative tone of the true essayist, I will confine myself to saying that there is something in what I say. There is really an element in modern letters which is at once indefinite and dangerous.

What I mean is this. The distinction between certain old forms and certain relatively recent forms of literature is that the old were limited by a logical purpose. The Drama and the Sonnet were of the old kind; the Essay and the Novel are of the new. If a sonnet breaks out of the sonnet form, it ceases to be a sonnet. It may become a wild and inspiring specimen of free verse; but you do not have to call it a sonnet because you have nothing else to call it. But in the case of the new sort of novel, you do very often have to call it a novel because you have nothing else to call it. It is sometimes called a novel when it is hardly even a narrative. There is nothing to test or define it, except that it is not spaced like an epic poem, and often has even less of a story. The same applies to the apparently attractive leisure and liberty of the essay. By its very nature it does not exactly explain what it is trying to do, and thus escapes a decisive judgment about whether it has really done it. But in the case of the essay there is a practical peril; precisely because it deals so often with theoretical matters. It is always dealing with theoretical matters without the responsibility of being theoretical, or of propounding a theory.

For instance, there is any amount of sense and nonsense talked both for and against what is called medievalism. There is also any amount of sense and nonsense talked for and against what is called modernism. I have occasionally tried to talk a little of the sense, with the result that I have been generally credited with all the nonsense. But if a man wanted one real and rational test, which really does distinguish the medieval from the modern mood, it might be stated thus. The medieval man thought in terms of the Thesis, where the modern man thinks in terms of the Essay. It would be unfair, perhaps, to say that the modern man only essays to think—or, in other words, makes a desperate attempt to think. But it would be true to say that the modern man often only essays, or attempts, to come to a conclusion. Whereas the medieval man hardly thought it worthwhile to think at all, unless he could Nano to a conclusion. That is why he took a definite thing called a Thesis, and proposed to prove it. That Is why Martin Luther, a very medieval man in most ways, nailed up on the door the theses he proposed to prove. Many people suppose that he was doing something revolutionary, and even modernist, in doing this. In fact, he was doing exactly what all the other medieval students and doctors had done ever since the twilight of the Dark Ages. If the really modern Modernist attempted to do it, he would probably find that he had never arranged his thoughts in the forms of theses at all. Well, it is quite an error to suppose, so far as I am concerned, that it is any question of restoring the rigid apparatus of the medieval system. But I do think that the Essay has wandered too far away from the Thesis. There is a sort of irrational and indefensible quality in many of the most brilliant phrases of the most beautiful essays. There is no essayist I enjoy more than Stevenson; there is probably no man now alive who admires Stevenson more than I. But if we take some favourite and frequently quoted sentence, such as, 'to travel hopefully is better than to arrive,' we shall see that it gives a loophole for every sort of sophistry and unreason. If it could be stated as a thesis, it could not be defended as a thought. A man would not travel hopefully at all, if he thought that the goal would be disappointing as compared with the travels. It is tenable that travel is the more enjoyable; but in that case it cannot be called hopeful. For the traveler is here presumed to hope for the end of travel, not merely for its continuance.

Now, of course, I do not mean that pleasant paradoxes of this sort have not a place in literature; and because of them the essay has a place in literature. There is room for the merely idle and wandering essayist, as for the merely idle and wandering traveller. The trouble is that the essayists have become the only ethical philosophers. The wandering thinkers have become the wandering preachers, and our only substitute for preaching friary. And whether our system is to be materialist or moralist, or sceptical or transcendental, we need more of a system than that. After a certain amount of wandering the mind wants either to get there or to go home. It is one thing to travel hopefully, and say half in jest that it is better than to arrive. It is another thing to travel hopelessly, because you know you will never arrive.

I was struck by the same tendency in re-reading some of the best essays ever written, which were especially enjoyed by Stevenson—the essays of Hazlitt. 'You can live like a gentleman on Hazlitt's Ideas,' as Mr. Augustine Birrell truly remarked; but even in these we see the beginning of this inconsistent and irresponsible temper. For instance, Hazlitt was a Radical and constantly railed at Tories for not trusting men or mobs. I think it was he who lectured Walter Scott for so small a matter as making the medieval mob in Ivanhoe jeer ungenerously at the retreat of the Templars. Anyhow, from any number of passages, one would infer that Hazlitt Offered himself as a friend of the people. But he offered himself most furiously as an enemy of the Public. When he began to write about the Public he described exactly the same many-headed monster of Ignorance and cowardice and cruelty which the worst Tories called the Mob. Now, if Hazlitt had been obliged to set forth his thoughts on Democracy in the theses of a medieval schoolman, he would have had to think much more clearly and make up his mind much more decisively. I will leave the last word with the essayist; and admit that I am not sure whether he would have written such good essays.

THEODOR W. ADORNO
··································

THE ESSAY AS FORM * [1958]

Destined, to see the illuminated, not the light.
—Goethe, *Pandora*

That in Germany the essay is decried as a hybrid; that it is lacking a convincing tradition; that its strenuous requirements have only rarely been met: all this has been often remarked upon and censured. "The essay form has not yet, today, traveled the road to independence which its sister, poetry, covered long ago; the road of development from a primitive, undifferentiated unity with science, ethics, and art."[1] But neither discontent with this situation, nor discontent with the mentality that reacts to the situation by fencing up art as a preserve for the irrational, identifying knowledge with organized science and excluding as impure anything that does not fit this antithesis: neither discontent has changed anything in the customary national prejudice. The bestowal of the garland "writer" still suffices to exclude from academia the person one is praising. Despite the weighty perspicacity that Simmel and the young Lukács, Kassner and Benjamin entrusted to the essay, to the speculative investigation of specific, culturally pre-determined objects,[2] the academic guild only has patience for philosophy that dresses itself up with the nobility of the universal, the everlasting, and today—when possible—with the primal; the cultural artifact is of interest only to the degree that it serves to exemplify universal categories, or at the very least allows them to shine through—however little the particular is thereby illuminated. The stubbornness with which this stereotypical thought survives would be as puzzling as its emotional rootedness if it were not fed by motives that are stronger than the painful recollection of how much cultivation is missing from a culture that historically scarcely recognizes the *homme de lettres*. In Germany

*Adorno's "Der Essay als Form" was written between 1954 and 1958 and first published as the Iead essay of *Noten zur Literatur I* in 1958. It is now contained in Adorno, *Gesammelte Schriften*, 11 (Frankfurt am Main: Suhrkamp, 1974). The essay is published here in English with the permission of Suhrkamp Verlag.

the essay provokes resistance because it is reminiscent of the intellectual freedom that, from the time of an unsuccessful and lukewarm Enlightenment, since Leibniz's day, all the way to the present has never really emerged, not even under the conditions of formal freedom; the German Enlightenment was always ready to proclaim, as its essential concern, subordination under whatever higher courts. The essay, however, does not permit its domain to be prescribed. Instead of achieving something scientifically, or creating something artistically, the effort of the essay reflects a childlike freedom that catches fire, without scruple, on what others have already clone. The essay mirrors what is loved and hated instead of presenting the intellect, on the model of a boundless work ethic, as *creatio ex nihilo*. Luck and play are essential to the essay. It does not begin with Adam and Eve but with what it wants to discuss; it says what is at issue and stops where it feels itself complete—not where nothing is left to say. Therefore it is classed among the oddities. Its concepts are neither deduced from any first principle nor do they come full circle and arrive at a final principle. Its interpretations are not philologically hardened and sober, rather—according to the predictable verdict of that vigilant calculating reason that hires itself out to stupidity as a guard against intelligence it over interprets. Due to a fear of negativity *per se*, the subject's effort to break through what masks itself as objectivity is branded as idleness. Everything is supposedly much simpler. The person who interprets instead of unquestioningly accepting and categorizing is slapped with the charge of intellectualizing as if with a yellow star; his misled and decadent intelligence is said to subtilize and project meaning where there is nothing to interpret. Technician or dreamer, those are the alternatives. Once one lets oneself be terrorized by the prohibition of going beyond the intended meaning of a certain text, one becomes the dupe of the false intentionality that men and things harbor of themselves. Understanding then amounts to nothing more than unwrapping what the author wanted to say, or, if need by, tracking down the individual psychological reactions that the phenomenon indicates. But just as it is scarcely possible to figure out what someone at a certain time and place felt and thought, such insights could not hope to gain anything essential. The author's impulses are extinguished in the objective substance they grasp. The objective abundance of significations encapsulated within each spiritual phenomenon, if it is to reveal itself, requires from the person receiving them precisely that spontaneity of subjective fantasy that is chastised in the name of objective discipline. Nothing can be interpreted out of a work without at the same time being interpreted into it. The criteria of this process are the compatibility of the interpretation with the text and with itself and its power to release the object's expression in the unity of its elements. The essay thereby acquires an aesthetic autonomy that is easily criticized as simply borrowed from art, though it distinguishes itself from art through its conceptual character and its claim to truth free from aesthetic semblance. Lukács failed to recognize this when he called the essay an art form in a letter to Leo Popper that serves as the introduction to *Soul and Form*.[3] Neither is the positivist maxim superior to Lukács' thesis, namely the maxim which maintains that what is written about art may claim nothing of art's mode of presentation, nothing, that is, of its autonomy of form. The positivist tendency to set up every possible examinable object in rigid opposition to the knowing subject remains—in this as in every other instance—caught up with the rigid separation of form and content: for it is scarcely possible to speak of the aesthetic unaesthetically, stripped of any similarity with its object, without becoming narrow-minded and *a priori* losing touch with the aesthetic object. According to a positivist procedure the content, once rigidly modelled on the protocol sentence, should be indifferent to its presentation. Presentation should be conventional, not demanded by the matter itself. Every impulse of expression—as far as the instinct of scientific purism is concerned—endangers an objectivity that is said to spring forth after the subtraction of the subject; such expression would thus endanger the authenticity of the material, which is said to prove itself all the better the less it relies on form, even though the measure of form is precisely its ability to render content purely and without addition. In its allergy to forms, as pure accidents, the scientific mind approaches the stupidly dogmatic mind. Positivism's irresponsibly bungled language fancies itself to be responsibly objective and adequate to the matter at hand; the reflection on the spiritual becomes the privilege of the spiritless.

None of these offspring of resentment are simply untruth. If the essay disdains to begin by deriving cultural products from something underlying them, it embroils itself only more intently in the culture industry and it falls for the conspicuousness, success and prestige of products designed for the market place. Fictional biographies and all the related commercial writing are no mere degeneration but the permanent temptation of a form whose suspicion toward false profundity is no defense against its own turning into skillful superficiality. The essay's capitulation is already evident in Sainte-Beuve, from whom the genre of the modern essay really stems. Such works—along with products like the biographical sketches of Herbert Eulenberg,[4] the German model for a flood of cultural trash-literature, all the way to the films about Rembrandt, Toulouse-Lautrec, and the Holy Bible—have promoted the neutralizing transformation of cultural artifacts into commodities, a transformation which, in recent cultural history, has irresistibly seized up all that which in the eastern bloc is shamelessly called "the cultural heritage." This process is perhaps most striking in the instance of Stefan Zweig, who in his youth wrote several discerning essays, and who finally, in his book on Balzac, stooped so low as to describe the psychology of the creative artist. Such writing does not criticize basic abstract concepts, mindless dates, worn-out clichés, but implicitly and thereby with the greater complicity, it presupposes them. The detritus of a hermeneutic psychology is fused with common categories drawn from the *Weltanschauung* of the cultural philistines, categories like those of personality and the irrational. Such essays mistake themselves for that kind of feuilleton journalism with which mistake themselves for that kind of feuilleton journalism with which the enemies of form confuse the form of the essay. Torn itself becomes unfree and sets itself to work in the service of the socially performed needs of its customers. The moment of irresponsibility, in itself an aspect of every truth that does not exhaust itself in responsibility toward the status qua, will account for itself when faced with the needs of the established consciousness; bad essays are no less conformist than bad dissertations. Responsibility, however, respects not only authorities and committees but the object itself.

The bad essay chats about people instead of opening up the matter at hand; in this the essay form is somewhat complicitous. The separation of knowledge from art is irreversible. Only the naivete of the literary entrepreneur takes no notice of this separation; he thinks of himself as at least an organizational genius, and simply chews up good art-works into bad ones. With the objectification of the world in the course of progressing demythologization, science and art have separated from each other. A consciousness in which perception and concept, image and sign would be one is not, if it ever existed, to be re-created with a wave of the wand; its restitution would be a return to chaos. Only as the completion of the mediating process would such a consciousness be thinkable, as a utopia just as that on which idealist philosophers since Kant had bestowed the name of creative intuition, and which failed them whenever actual knowledge appealed to it. When philosophy supposes that by borrowing from art it can do away with objectifying thought and its history—with what is usually termed the antithesis of subject and object—and indeed expects that being itself would speak out of a poetic montage of Parmenides and Jungnickel,[5] it only approximates a washed-out pseudo-culture. With peasant cunning legitimated as primordiality, it refuses to honor the obligation of conceptual thought to which it has subscribed as soon as it has employed concepts in statements and judgments. At the same time its aesthetic element remains a second-hand thinned-out cultural reminiscence of Hölderlin or Expressionism, or possibly of *art nouveau*, simply because no thought can entrust itself to language as boundlessly and blindly as the idea of a primal utterance deceptively suggests. Out of the violence that image and concept do to one another in such writings springs the jargon of authenticity in which words tremble as though possessed, while remaining secretive about that which possesses them. The ambitious transcendence of language beyond its meaning results in a meaninglessness that can easily be seized upon by a positivism to which one thinks oneself superior; and yet, one falls victim to positivism precisely through that meaninglessness that positivism criticizes and which one shares with it. The playing chips of both are the same. Under the spell of such developments, language, where in the sciences it still dares to stir, approximates pseudo-art; and only that scientist proves, negatively, his fidelity to the aesthetic who in general resists language and instead of degrading the word to a mere paraphrase of his calculations prefers the charts that uninhibitedly admit the reification of consciousness and so produces a sort of form for reification without resorting to any apologetic borrowing from art. Of course art was always so interwoven with the dominant tendency of the Enlightenment that it has, since antiquity, incorporated scientific discoveries in its technique. Yet quantity becomes quality. When technique is made absolute in the art-work; when construction becomes total, eliminating what motivates it and what resists it, expression; when art claims to be science and makes scientific criteria its standard, it sanctions a crude pre-artistic manipulation of raw material as devoid of meaning as all the talk about "Being" (*Seyn*) in philosophical seminars. It allies itself with that reification against which it is the function of functionless art, even today, to raise its own however mute and objectified protest. But although art and science have separated from each other in history, their opposition is not to be hypostatized. The disgust for anachronistic eclecticism does not sanctify a culture organized according to departmental specialization. In all of their necessity these divisions simply attest institutionally to the renunciation of the whole truth. The ideals of purity and cleanliness bear the marks of a repressive order; these ideals are shared by the bustle of authentic philosophy aiming at eternal values, a sealed and flawlessly organized science, and by a conceptless, intuitive art. Spirit must pass a competency test to assure that it will not overstep the official culture or cross its officially sanctioned borders. The presupposition is that all knowledge can potentially be converted into science. Theories of knowledge that distinguish pre-scientific from scientific consciousness have therefore grasped this distinction as one of degree only. The fact that this convertibility has remained a mere assertion and that living consciousness has never really been transformed into scientific consciousness, points to the precariousness of the transition itself, to a qualitative difference. The simplest reflection on the life of consciousness would reveal just how little acts of knowledge, which are not just arbitrary premonitions, can be completely caught by the net of science. The work of Marcel Proust, no more lacking than Bergson's in scientific-positivistic elements, is a single effort to express necessary and compelling perceptions about men and their social relations which science can simply not match, while at the same time the claim of these perceptions to objectivity would be neither lessened nor left up to vague plausibility. The measure of such objectivity is not the verification of asserted theses through repeated testing, but individual experience, unified in hope and disillusion. Experience, reminiscing, gives depth to its observations by confirming or refuting them. But their individually grasped unity, in which the whole surely appears, could not be divided up and re-organized under the separated *personae* and apparatuses of psychology and sociology. Under the pressure of the scientific spirit and of an ever-present desire latent in every artist, Proust attempted, by means of a scientifically modeled technique, a sort of experimentation, to save or reproduce a form of knowledge that was still considered valid in the days of bourgeois individualism when the individual consciousness still trusted itself and was not yet worried about organizational censure: the knowledge of an experienced man, that extinct *homme de lettres*, whom Proust once again conjures up as the highest form of the dilettante. No one would have thought to dismiss as unimportant, accidental or irrational the observations of an experienced man because they are only his own and as such do not lend themselves readily to scientific generalization. Those of his discoveries which slip through the meshes of science certainly elude science itself. Science, as cultural science (*Geisteswissenschaft*), negates what it promises to culture: to open up its artifacts from within. The young writer who wants to learn at college what an art-work is, what linguistic form, aesthetic quality, even aesthetic technique are, will only haphazardly learn anything at all about the matter; at best he will pick up information ready culled from whatever modish philosophy and more or less arbitrarily slapped on to the content of works currently under discussion. If he turns, how- ever, to philosophical aesthetics he is beleaguered with highly abstract propositions that have neither a connection with the works he wants to understand, nor with the content after which he is groping. The division of labor within the *kosmos-noetikos* (intelligible world) into art and science is not, however, altogether responsible for this situation; the internal boundaries between art and science will not be obviated by good will or over-arching planning. Rather, the spirit irretrievably modeled on the pattern of the control of nature and material production forgoes both recollection of any surpassed phase that would promise any other future and any transcendence vis-à-vis the frozen relations of production; this cripples the technical intelligence's own specialized procedure precisely with regard to its specific objects.

With regard to scientific procedure and its philosophic grounding as method, the essay, in accordance with its idea, draws the fullest consequences from the critique of the system. Even the empiricist doctrines that grant priority to open, unanticipated experience over firm, conceptual ordering remain systematic to the extent that they investigate what they hold to be the more or less constant pre-conditions of knowledge and develop them in as continuous a context as possible. Since the time of Bacon, who was himself an essayist, empiricism—no less than rationalism—has been "method." Doubt about the unconditional priority of method was raised, in the actual process of thought, almost exclusively by the essay. It does justice to the consciousness of non-identity, without needing to say so, radically un-radical in refraining from any reduction to a principle, in accentuating the fragmentary, the partial rather then the total. "Perhaps the great Sieur de Montaigne feit something like this when he gave his writings the wonderfully elegant and apt title of *Essays*. The simple modesty of this word is an arrogant courtesy. The essayist dismisses his own proud hopes which sometimes lead him to believe that he has come close to the ultimate: he has, after all, no more to offer than explanations of the poems of others, or at best of his own ideas. But he ironically adapts himself to this smallness—the eternal smallness of the most profound work of the intellect in face of life—and even emphasizes it with ironic modesty."[6] The essay does not obey the rules of the game of organized science and theory that, following Spinoza's principle, the order of things is identical with that of ideas. Since the airtight order of concepts is not identical with existence, the essay does not strive for closed, deductive or inductive, construction. It revolts above all against the doctrine—deeply rooted since Plato—that the changing and ephemeral is unworthy of philosophy; against that ancient injustice toward the transitory, by which it is once more anathematized, conceptually. The essay shies away from the violence of dogma, from the notion that the result of abstraction, the temporally invariable concept indifferent to the individual phenomenon grasped by it, deserves ontological dignity. The delusion that the *ordo idearum* (order of ideas) should be the *ordo rerum* (order of things) is based on the insinuation that the mediated is unmediated. Just as little as a simple fact can be thought without a concept, because to think it always already means to conceptualize it, it is equally impossible to think the purest concept without reference to the factual. Even the creations of phantasy that are supposedly independent of space and time, point toward individual existence—however far they may be removed from it. Therefore the essay is not intimidated by the depraved profundity which claims that truth and history are incompatible. If truth has in fact a temporal core, then the full historical content becomes an integral moment in truth; the *a posteriori* becomes concretely the *a priori*, as only generally stipulated by Fichte and his followers. The relation to experience—and from it the essay takes as much substance as does traditional theory from its categories—is a relation to all of history; merely individual experience, in which consciousness begins with what is nearest to it, is itself mediated by the all-encompassing experience of historical humanity; the claim that social-historical contents are nevertheless supposed to be only indirectly important compared with the immediate life of the individual is a simple self-delusion of an individualistic society and ideology. The depreciation of the historically produced, as an object of theory, is therefore corrected by the essay. There is no salvaging the distinction of a first philosophy from a mere philosophy of culture that assumes the former and builds on it, a distinction with which the taboo on the essay is rationalized theoretically. The intellectual process which canonizes a distinction between the temporal and the timeless is losing its authority. Higher levels of abstraction invest thought neither with a greater sanctity nor with metaphysical content; rather, the metaphysical content evaporates with the progress of abstraction, for which the essay attempts to make reparation. The usual reproach against the essay, that it is fragmentary and random, itself assumes the givenness of totality and thereby the identity of subject and object, and it suggests that man is in control of totality. But the desire of the essay is not to seek and filter the eternal out of the transitory; it wants, rather, to make the transitory eternal. Its weakness testifies to the non-identity that it has to express, as well as to that excess of intention over its object, and thereby it points to that utopia which is blocked out by the classification of the world into the eternal and the transitory. In the emphatic essay, thought gets rid of the traditional idea of truth.

The essay simultaneously suspends the traditional concept of method. Thought acquires its depth from penetrating deeply into a matter, not from referring it back to something else. In this the essay becomes polemical by treating what is normally held to be derived, without however pursuing its ultimate derivation. The essay freely associates what can be found associated in the freely chosen object. It does not insist stubbornly on a realm transcending all mediations—and they are the historical ones in which the whole of society is sedimented—rather the essay seeks truth contents as being historical in themselves. It does not concern itself with any supposed primeval condition in order to Contravene society's false sociality, which, just because it tolerates nothing not stamped by it, ultimately tolerates nothing indicative of it own omnipresence and necessarily cites, as its ideological complement, that nature which its own praxis eliminates. The essay silently abandons the illusion that thought can breakout of *thesis* into *physis*, out of culture into nature. Spellbound by what is fixed and admittedly deduced, by artifacts, the essay honors nature by confirming that it no longer exists for human beings. The essay's Alexandrianism replies to the fact that by their very existence the lilac and the nightingale, wherever the universal net allows them to survive, only want to delude us that life still lives. The essay abandons the main road to the origins, the road leading to the most derivative, to being, the ideology that simply doubles that which already exists; at the same time the essay does not allow the idea of immediacy, postulated by the very concept of mediation, to disappear entirely. All levels of the mediated are immediate to the essay, before its reflection begins.

As the essay denies any primeval givens, so it refuses any definition of its concepts. Philosophy has completed the fullest critique of definition from the most diverse perspectives, including those of Kant, Hegel and Nietzsche. But science has never adopted this critique. While the movement beginning with Kant, a movement against the scholastic residues in modern thought, replaces verbal definition with an understanding of concepts as part of the process in which they are temporally embodied, the individual sciences insist stubbornly on the pre-critical job of definition—and do so for the sake of the undisturbed security of their operation. In this regard the neopositivists, who identify philosophy with scientific method, agree with Scholasticism. The essay, in contrast, takes the anti-systematic impulse into its own procedure, and introduces concepts directly, "immediately," as it receives them. They gain their precision only through their relation to one another. In this, however, the essay gets some support from the concepts themselves. For it is a mere superstition of a science exclusively concerned with the appropriation of raw materials to believe that concepts are in themselves undetermined, that they are first determined by their definition. Science requires the image of the concept as a *tabula rasa*, in order to secure its claim to domination; the claim to be the sole power at the head of the table. Actually, all concepts are already implicitly concretized through the language in which they stand. The essay begins with such meanings and, itself being essentially language, it forces these meanings on farther; it wants to help language, in its relation to concepts, to grasp these concepts reflectively in the way that they are already unconsciously named in language. That effort is already envisaged by the procedure of meaning-analysis in phenomenology; only there the relation of concepts to language is fetishized. The essay remains as skeptical of this as it is of definition. Without apology the essay draws on itself the reproach that it does not know beyond a doubt just what is to be understood as the real content of concepts. For the essay perceives that the longing for strict definitions has long offered, through fixating manipulations of the meanings of concepts, to eliminate the irritating and dangerous elements of things that live within concepts. Yet the essay can neither do without general concepts—even language that does not fetishize the concept cannot do without concepts—nor does it treat them arbitrarily. It therefore takes the matter of presentation more seriously than do those procedures that separate out method from material and are indifferent to the way they represent their objectified contents. The how of expression should rescue, in precision, what the refusal to outline sacrifices, without, however, betraying the intended matter to the arbitrariness of previously decreed significations. In this Benjamin was an unequaled master. Such precision, however, cannot remain atomistic. Not less, but more than the process of defining, the essay urges the reciprocal interaction of its concepts in the process of intellectual experience. In the essay, concepts do not build a continuum of operations, thought does not advance in a single direction, rather the aspects of the argument interweave as in a carpet. The fruitfulness of the thoughts depends on the density of this texture.

Actually, the thinker does not think, but rather transforms himself into an arena of intellectual experience, without simplifying it. While even traditional thought draws its impulses from such experience, such thought by its form eliminates the remembrance of these impulses. The essay, on the other hand, takes them as its model, without simply imitating them as reflected form; it mediates them through its own conceptual organization; it proceeds, so to speak, methodically unmethodically.

The way in which the essay appropriates concepts is most easily comparable to the behavior of a man who is obliged, in a foreign country, to speak that country's language instead of patching it together from its elements, as he did in school. He will read without a dictionary. If he has looked at the same word thirty times, in constantly changing contexts, he has a clearer grasp of it than he would if he looked up all the word's meanings; meanings that are generally too narrow, considering they change depending on the context, and too vague in view of the nuances that the context establishes in every individual case. Just as such learning remains exposed to error, so does the essay as form; it must pay for its affinity with open intellectual experience by the lack of security, a lack which the norm of established thought fears like death. It is not so much that the essay ignores indisputable certainty, as that it abrogates the ideal. The essay becomes true in its progress, which drives it beyond itself, and not in a hoarding obsession with fundamentals. Its concepts receive their light from a *terminus ad quem* hidden to the essay itself, and not from an obvious *terminus a quo*. In this the very method of the essay expresses the utopian intention. All of its concepts are presentable in such a way that they support one another, that each one articulates itself according to the configuration that it forms with the others. In the essay discreetly separated elements enter into a readable context; it erects no scaffolding, no edifice. Through their own movement the elements crystallize into a configuration. It is a force field, just as under the essay's glance every intellectual artifact must transform itself into a force field.

The essay gently defies the ideals of *clara et distincta perceptio* and of absolute certainty. On the whole it could be interpreted as a protest against the four rules that Descartes' *Discourse on Method* sets up at the beginning of modern Western science and its theory. The second of these rules, the decomposition of the object into "as many parts as possible and as might be necessary for its adequate solution,"[7] formulates that analysis of elements under whose sign traditional theory equates a conceptual order with the structure of being. But the object of the essay, the artifact, refuses any analysis of its elements and can only be constructed from its specific idea; it is not accidental that Kant treated art-works and organisms analogously, although at the same time he insisted, against all romantic obscurantism, on distinguishing them. The whole is to be hypostatized into a first principle just as little as is the product of analysis, the elements. In opposition to both, the essay is informed by the idea of that interaction which in fact tolerates the question of elements as little as that of the elementary. Neither are the specific elements to be developed purely out of the whole, nor vice versa. The artifact is a monad, yet it is not; its elements, as such of a conceptual kind, point beyond the specific object in which they gather themselves. But the essay does not follow these elements to that point where they legitimize themselves, on the far side of the specific object; otherwise it would turn into a bad kind of infinity. Rather, the essay comes so close to the here and now of the object, up to the point where that object, instead of being simply an object, dissociates itself into those elements in which it has its life.

The third Cartesian rule, "to conduct my thoughts in such an order that, by commencing with the simplest and easiest to know, I might ascend little by little, step by step, to the knowledge of the more complex,"[8] is sharply contravened by the form of the essay in that it begins with the most complex, not the most simple, which is in every instance the habitual. The essay as form will be a good guide for the person who is beginning to study philosophy, and before whose eyes the idea of philosophy somehow stands. He will hardly begin by reading the easiest writers, whose common sense[9] will skim the surface where depth is called for; he will rather go for the allegedly difficult writers, who shed light on what is simple and illuminate it as a "stance of the mind toward objectivity." The naivete of the student, to whom the difficult and formidable seems good enough, is wiser than the adult pedantry that admonishes thought with a threatening finger to understand the simple before risking that complexity which alone entices it. Such a postponement of knowledge only prevents knowledge. In opposition to the cliche of the "understandable," the notion of truth as a network of causes and effects, the essay insists that a matter be considered, from the very first, in its whole complexity; it counteracts that hardened primitiveness that always allies itself with reason's current form. Whereas science treats the difficulties and complexities of an antagonistic and monadologically split reality according to the expectation of this society by reducing them to simplifying models and then belatedly differentiates them with fabricated material, the essay shakes off the illusion of a simple, basically logical world that so perfectly suits the defense of the status quo. Its differentiation is no supplement, but its medium. Established thought readily ascribes that differentiation to the mere psychology of the author and then thinks that it has adequately dealt with it. The pompous scientific objections to over-sophistication actually do not aim at the impertinently unreliable method but at the irritating aspects of the object which the essay reveals.

The fourth Cartesian rule that one "should in every case institute such exhaustive enumerations and such general surveys" that one "is sure of leaving nothing out"—this ultimate principle of systematic thought—reappears unchanged in Kant's polemic against Aristotle's "rhapsodic" thought. This rule corresponds to the particular objection to the essay that, in the words of the schoolmaster, it is not exhaustive, while it is clear that every object, and above all a cultural object, encloses endlessly many aspects, the choice among which can only be determined by the intention of the knower. The "general survey" would only be possible if it were determined in advance that the object in question can be fully grasped by the concepts which treat it; that nothing is left over that could not be anticipated by these concepts. Following that assumption, the rule requiring the exhaustive enumeration of the individual elements claims that the object can be presented in an airtight deductive system: a supposition of a philosophy of identity. As a practical technique of thought, as for example in its insistence on definition, the Cartesian rule has outlived the rationalistic theorem on which it was founded: a comprehensive general view and a continuity of presentation is urged even upon empirically open scientific procedure. In this fashion the intellectual conscience that should, in Descartes' philosophy, keep watch over the necessity of knowledge is transformed into the arbitrariness of a "frame of reference."[10] In order to satisfy a methodological need and to support the plausibility of the whole, it becomes an axiomatic doctrine that is being set up as the gateway to thought while no longer being able to demonstrate its own validity or proof. Or, in the German version, it becomes a "project"(*Entwurf*) that, with the pathos-laden claim of reaching into being, simply suppresses its subjective conditions. The insistence on the continuity of thought's process tends to prejudice the inner coherence of the object, its own harmony. A continuous presentation would contradict material that is full of antogonisms as long as it did not simultaneously define continuity as discontinuity. Unconsciously and far from theory, the need arises in the essay as form to annul the theoretically outmoded claims of docility and continuity, and to do so in the concrete procedure of the intellect. If the essay struggles aesthetically against that narrow-minded method that will leave nothing out, it is obeying an epistemological motive. The romantic conception of the fragment as an artifact that is not complete in itself but openly striding into infinity by way of self-reflection, advocates this anti-idealist motive even in the midst of idealism. Even in its manner of delivery the essay refuses to behave as though it had deduced its object and had exhausted the topic. Self-relativization is immanent in its form; it must be constructed in such a way that it could always, and at any point, break off. It thinks in fragments just as reality is fragmented and gains its unity only by moving through the fissures, rather than by smoothing them over. The unanimity of the logical order deceives us about the antagonistic nature of that on which it was jauntily imposed. Discontinuity is essential to the essay; its concern is always a conflict brought to a stand still. While the essay adjusts concepts to one another by virtue of their function in the parallelogram of the forces of the materials, it shrinks back from the over-arching concept under which particular concepts should be subordinated; what the over-arching concept merely pretends to accomplish, the essay's method recognizes as insoluble while nevertheless attempting to accomplish it. The word "essay"—in which thought's utopia of hitting the bull's eye unites with the consciousness of its own fallibility and provisional nature—indicates something, like most historically surviving terminologies, about the form, the importance of which is magnified by the fact that it results not programmatically but as a characteristic of the form's groping intention. The essay must let the totality light up in one of its chosen or haphazard features but without asserting that the whole is present. It corrects the isolated and accidental aspects of its insights by allowing them to multiply, confirm, and restrict themselves—whether in the essay's proper progress or in its mosaic-like relation to other essays; and it does so not by abstracting characteristic features from its insights. "Thus the essay distinguishes itself from a scientific treatise. He writes essayistically who writes while experimenting, who turns his object this way and that, who questions it, feels it, tests it, thoroughly reflects on it, attacks it from different angles, and in his mind's eye collects what he sees, and puts into words what the object allows to be seen under the conditions established in the course of writing."[11] The discontent with this procedure, the feeling that it could all go on indefinitely, has its truth and untruth. Its truth, because in fact the essay comes to no final conclusions and makes explicit its inability to do so by parodying its own *a priori*; it is then saddled with the guilt that is actually incurrered by those forms that erase every trace of arbitrariness. Yet that discontent with the essay is at the same time untrue because, as a constellation, the essay is not arbitrary in the way that it seems to a philosophical subjectivism which translates the exigencies of the object into those of its conceptual organization. The essay is determined by the unity of its object, together with that of theory and experience which have migrated into the object. The essay's openness is not vaguely one of feeling and mood, but obtains its contour from its content. It resists the idea of the masterwork that reflects the idea of creation and totality. Its form follows the critical thought that man is no creator, that nothing human is creation. The essay, always directed towards artifacts, does not present itself as a creation; nor does it long for something all-embracing, the totality of which would resemble creation. Its totality, the unity of a form thoroughly constructed in itself, is that of non-totality; one that even as form does not assert the thesis of the identity of thought and thing, the thesis which in its own content the essay rejects. Freedom from the pressure of identity occasionally provides the essay (and this is lacking in official thought) with an aspect of ineffaceability, of inextinguishable color. In Simmel certain foreign words—cachet, attitude—betray this intention, without it being treated theoretically as such.

The essay is both more open and more closer than traditional thought would like. It is more open in so far as, through its inner nature, it negates anything systematic and satisfies itself all the better the more strictly it excludes the systematic; residual of the systematic in the essay such as the infiltration of literary studies with ready-made, wide-spread philosophical commonplaces, by which these studies try to make themselves respectable, are of no more value than psychological banalities. On the other hand, the essay is more closer in that it labors emphatically on the form of its presentation. The consciousness of the non-identity between presentation and presenter material forces the form to make unlimited efforts. In that respect alone the essay resembles art; otherwise, on account of the concepts which appear in it and which import not only their meaning but also their theoretical aspects, the essay is necessarily related to theory. To be sure, the essay relates itself to theory as cautiously as to the concept. It neither deduces itself rigidly from theory—the cardinal fault of all Lukács' later essayistic work—nor is it a down-payment on future syntheses. Disaster threatens intellectual experience the more strenuously it ossifies into theory and acts as if it held the philosopher's stone in hand. And yet, intellectual experience itself strives by its own nature toward such objectification. This antinomy is mirrored by the essay. Just as it absorbs concepts and experiences, so it absorbs theories. However, its relation to them is not that of a standpoint. If this lack of a standpoint is no longer naive and dependent on the prominence of its objects; if the essay rather uses the relationship to its objects as a weapon against the spell of beginnings, it parodically practices the otherwise only feeble polemic of thought against mere standpoint philosophy. The essay swallows up the theories that are close by; its tendency is always toward the liquidation of opinion, even that from which it takes its own impulse. The essay remains what it always was, the critical form *par excellence*; specifically, it constructs the immanent criticism of cultural artifacts, and it confronts that which such artifacts are with their concept; it is the critique of ideology. "The essay is the form of the critical category of our mind. For whoever criticizes must necessarily experiment; he must create conditions under which an object is newly seen, and he must do so in a fashion different from that of a creative author. Above all the fragility of the object must be probed, tested; this is precisely the meaning of the small variation that an object undergoes in the hands of its critic."[12] If the essay is accused of lacking a Standpoint and of tending toward relativism because it recognizes no Standpoint lying outside of itself, then the accusation implicitly contains the conception of truth as something "ready-made," a hierarchy of concepts, an image of truth that Hegel destroyed in his dislike of standpoints: in this the essay touches its polar opposite, the philosophy of absolute knowledge. The essay would like to cure thought of its arbitrariness by taking arbitrariness reflectively into its own procedure instead of masking it as spontaneity.

Hegelian philosophy, to be sure, remained trapped in the inconsistency that it criticized the abstract, over-arching concept, the mere "result," in the name of an internally discontinuous process, while at the same time, in the idealist tradition, speaking about dialectical method. Therefore the essay is more dialectical than the dialectic as it articulates itself. The essay takes Hegelian logic at its word: neither may the truth of the totality be played off immediately against individual judgments, nor may truth be reduced to individual judgments; rather, the claim of the particular to truth is taken literally to the point where there is evidence of its untruth. The risked, anticipatory, and incompletely redeemed aspect of every essayistic detail draws in other details as negation; the untruth in which the essay knowingly entangles itself is the element of its truth. Untruth certainly also resides in the essay's basic form, in its relation to what is culturally preformed and derived as though it were something in-itself. But the more energetically the essay suspends the concept of some first principle, the more it refuses to spin culture out of nature, the more fundamentally it recognizes the unremittingly natural essence of culture itself. Up to the present day, a blind natural interconnectedness, myth, perpetuates itself in culture. It is precisely this upon which the essay reflects: its proper theme is interrelation of nature and culture. It is not by coincidence that rather than "reducing" the artifact, the essay immerses itself in cultural phenomena as in a second nature, a second immediacy, in order through persistence to remove the illusion of immediacy. The essay deceives itself as little as the philosophy of origins about the difference between culture and that which underlies it. Yet for the essay, culture is not some epiphenomenon superimposed on being that must be eliminated, but rather what lies underneath is itself artificial (*thesei*), false society. Thus, for the essay, origins have no priority over the super-structure. The essay owes its freedom in its choice of objects, its sovereignty vis-à-vis all priorities[13] of fact or theory to the circumstance that for it all objects are equally near the center, to the principle that casts a spell over everything. The essay refuses to glorify concern for the primal as something more primal than concern for the mediated, because to the essay primacy itself is an object of reflection, something negative. It corresponds to a situation in which the primal, as a Standpoint of the mind within the falsely socialized world, becomes a lie. It covers a wide territory from the enshrinement as primal words of historical concepts extracted from historical languages, to academic instruction in "creative writing;"[14] from craft-shop primitiveness to recorders and finger-painting:[15] in every instance the pedagogical necessity sets itself up as a metaphysical virtue. Thought is not exempt from Baudelaire's rebellion of poetry against nature as a social reservation. Even the paradises of thought are only artificial, and in them the essay indulges. Since, according to Hegel's dictum, there is nothing between heaven and earth that is not mediated, thought may only hold true to the idea of immediacy by way of the mediated, but it becomes the prey of the mediated the instant it grasps directly for the unmediated. Cunningly, the essay settles itself into texts, as though they were simply there and had authority; without the illusion of the primal, it gets under its feet a ground, however dubious, comparable to earlier theological exegesis of holy writings. The essay's impulse, however, is the exact opposite of the theological; it is critical: through confrontation of texts with their own emphatic concept, with the truth that each text intends even in spite of itself, to shatter the claim of culture and move it to remember its untruth—the untruth of that ideological moment which reveals culture's bondage to nature. Under the glance of the essay second nature becomes conscious of itself as first nature.

If the truth of the essay gains its momentum by way of its untruth, its truth is not to be sought in mere opposition to what is ignoble and proscribed in it, but in these very things: in its mobility, its lack of that solidity which science demands, transferring it, as it were, from property-relationships to the intellect. Those who believe they must defend the intellect against the charge of a lack of solidity are the enemies of intellect: intellect itself, once emancipated, is mobile. As soon as it wants more than simply the administrative repetition and manipulated presentation of what already exists, it is somehow exposed; truth abandoned by play would be nothing more than tautology. Thus historically the essay is related to rhetoric, which the scientific mentality, since Descartes and Bacon, has always wanted to do away with; that is, until, appropriately in the age of science, rhetoric decayed and became a science *sui generis*) the science of communication. Of course rhetoric has always been a form of thought which accommodated itself to communicative language. It directed itself to the unmediated: the substitute-satisfaction of its audience. Yet the essay preserves in the very autonomy of its presentation, through which it distinguishes itself from the scientific mode of communication, traces of the communicative with which science dispenses. The pleasures which rhetoric wants to provide to its audience are sublimated in the essay into the idea of the pleasure of freedom vis-à-vis the object, freedom that gives the object more of itself than if it were mercilessly incorporated into the order of ideas. The scientific consciousness, which is directed against any anthropomorphic idea whatsoever, was always closely bound up with the reality principle and similarly hostile to happiness. While happiness is supposedly the goal of all domination over nature, it always appears to the reality principle as regression to mere nature. This can be seen even in the highest philosophies, including Kant's and Hegel's. Reason, in whose absolute idea these philosophies have their pathos, is denounced by them as something both pert and disrespectful as soon as it challenges the established system of values. Against this inclination the essay rescues a sophistic element. The hostility to happiness of official critical thought can be felt particularly in Kant's transcendental dialectic: it wants to eternalize the boundary between understanding and speculation, and, according to its characteristic metaphor, to prevent any "roaming around in intelligible worlds." While self-critical reason should, according to Kant, keep both feet planted on the ground, indeed should ground itself, it follows its innermost principle and seals itself off against anything new as well as against curiosity, the pleasure principle of thought, that is also upbraided by existential ontology. What in the content of his thought Kant projects as the goal of reason, utopia, the production of humanity, is disbarred by the form of his thought, the theory of knowledge; it forbids reason to go beyond the realm of experience, which, caught in the machinery of mere material and unchangeable categories, is reduced to that which always was. But the object of the essay is the new as something genuinely new, as something not translatable back into the staleness of already existing forms. By reflecting the object without doing violence to it, the essay silently laments the fact that truth has betrayed happiness and thus itself; this lament incites the rage against the essay. In the essay the persuasive aspect of communication, analogously to the functional transformation of many traits in autonomous music, is alienated from its original goal and converted into the pure articulation of presentation in itself; it becomes a compelling construction that does not want to copy the object, but to reconstruct it out of its conceptual *membra disjecta*. But the objectionable transitions in rhetoric, in which association, ambiguity of words, neglect of logical synthesis all make it easy for the auditor, yoking him to the speaker's will: all these are fused in the essay with its truth-content. Its transitions disavow rigid deduction in the interest of establishing internal cross-connections, something for which discursive logic has no use. It uses equivocation neither out of slovenliness nor in ignorance of their proscription by science, but to clarify what usually remains obscure to the critique of equivocation and its mere discrimination of meanings: whenever a word means a variety of things, the differences are not entirely distinct, for the unity of the word points to some unity, no matter how hidden, in the thing itself; however, it is obviously not the case that this unity, as claimed by contemporary restorative philosophies, can itself be taken simply as a unity of linguistic affinities. Here as well the essay verges on the logic of music, the stringent and yet a conceptual art of transition; it aims at appropriating for expressive language something that it forfeited under the domination of a discursive logic which cannot be circumvented, but may be outwitted in its own form by the force of an intruding subjective expression. For the essay is not situated in simple opposition to discursive procedure. It is not unlogical; rather it obeys logical criteria in so far as the totality of its sentences must fit together coherently. Mere contradictions may not remain, unless they are grounded in the object itself. It is just that the essay develops thoughts differently from discursive logic. The essay neither makes deductions from a principle nor does it draw conclusions from coherent individual observations. It coordinates elements, rather than subordinating them; and only the essence of its content, not the manner of its presentation, is commensurable with logical criteria. If, thanks to the tension between presentation and what is presented, the essay—compared with forms which indifferently convey a ready-made content is more dynamic than traditional thought, it is at the same time, as a constructed juxtaposition of elements, more static than traditional thought. In that alone rests the essay's affinity to the visual image; except that the essay's static quality is itself composed of tensions which, as it were, have been brought to a standstill. The slightly yielding quality of the essayist's thought forces him to greater intensity than discursive thought can offer; for the essay, unlike discursive thought, does not proceed blindly, automatically, but at every moment it must reflect on itself. This reflection, however, does not only extend to the essay's relation to established thought, but also to its relation to rhetoric and communication. Otherwise the essay, while fancying itself meta-scientific, would become vainly pre-scientific.

The relevance of the essay is that of anachronism. The hour is more unfavorable to it than ever. It is being crushed between an organized science, on one side, in which everyone presumes to control everyone and everything else, and which excludes, with the sanctimonious praise of "intuitive" or "stimulating," anything that does not conform to the status quo; and, on the other side, by a philosophy that makes do with the empty and abstract residues left aside by the scientific apparatus, residues which then become, for philosophy, the objects of second-degree operations. The essay, however, has to do with that which is blind in its objects. Conceptually it wants to blow open what cannot be absorbed by concepts, or what, through contradictions in which concepts entangle themselves, betrays the fact that the network of their objectivity is a purely subjective rigging. It wants to polarize the opaque, to unbind the powers latent in it. It strives to concretize content as determined by space and time; it constructs the interwovenness of concepts in such a way that they can be imagined as themselves inter-woven in the object. It frees itself from the stipulation of those attributes which since the definition in the Symposium have been ascribed to ideas; the notion that ideas "exist eternally and neither come into being nor pass away, neither change nor wane;" "A being eternally created in itself and for itself;" and yet the essay remains idea, in that it does not capitulate under the burden of mere being, does not bow down before what merely is. It does not measure what is by some eternal standard, rather by an enthusiastic fragment from Nietzsche's later life: "If we affirm one single moment, we thus affirm not only ourselves but all existence. For nothing is self-sufficient, neither in ourselves nor in things: and if our soul has trembled with happiness and sounded like a harp string just once, all eternity was needed to produce this one event and in this single moment of affirmation all eternity was called good, redeemed, justified, and affirmed."[16] This with the exception that the essay mistrusts such justification and affirmation. For the happiness that Nietzsche found holy, the essay has no other name than the negative. Even the highest manifestations of the intellect that express happiness are always at the same time caught in the guilt of thwarting happiness as long as they remain mere intellect. Therefore the law of the innermost form of the essay is heresy. By transgressing the orthodoxy of thought, something becomes visible in the object which it is orthodoxy's secret purpose to keep invisible.

Translated by Bob Hullot-Kentor and Frederic Will

NOTES

1 George Lukács, *Soul and Form*, trans. Anna Bostock (Cambridge: MIT, 1974), p. 13.

2 *Ibid.*, p. 10. "The essay is always concerned with something already formed, at best, with something that has been; it is part of its essence that it does not draw something new out of an empty vacuum, but only gives a new order to such things as once lived. And because he only newly orders them, not forming something new out of the formless, he is bound to them; he must always speak "the truth" about them, find, that is, the expression for their essence."

3 Lukács, "On the Nature and Form of the Essay," in *Soul and Form*, pp. 1–18.

4 (Herben Eulenberg (1876–1949), author of *Schattenbilder* (*Silhouettes*), a collection of biographical miniatures of notables published in 1910. Translator's footnote.

5 [Ludwig Heinrich Jungnickel (b. 1881 in Vienna), painter and handicraft artist well-known for his animal woodcuts. This and the following passage refer to Heidegger. Translator's note.]

6 Lukács, p. 9.

7 René Descartes, *A Discourse On Method*, trans. John Veitch (NewYork: E. P.

Dutton, 1951), p. 15.

8 *Ibid.*

9 [In English]

10 [In English]

11 Max Bense, "Über den Essay und seine Prosa," *Merkur* 1:3 (1947), 418.

12 *Ibid.* 420.

13 [In English]

14 [In English]

15 [In English]

16 Friedrich Nietzsche, The Will to Power, trans. W. Kaufmann and R. J. Hollingdale (London: Weidenfeeld and Nicolson, 1968), pp. 532–533.

THE ESSAY—IS IT LITERATURE? [1987]

> *Genius laughs at all the boundary lines of criticism.*
> —G. E. Lessing

"Is literature a collection of individual poems and plays and novels which share a common name?" ask Rene Wellek and Austin Warren as they begin their chapter on genre in *Theory of Literature* (215). I find their question paradigmatic of most discussion of literary genre: the essay is either excluded or included only tangentially. To the academic and critical profession, literature means imaginative literature; and imaginative literature (no matter how thick or thin we slice it) is made up of fiction, poetry, and drama. One doesn't need Plato, Aristotle, Horace, or any modern genre theorist to confirm this. Any list of English department course offerings from any university in the country will easily demonstrate the dominance of fiction, poetry, and, increasingly less so, drama within the English curriculum.

This, of course, wasn't always the case: The novel only gradually acquired the academic eminence it has today, and throughout the first half of this century the curriculum was characterized by a strong belletristic emphasis. But by mid-century a rift began to widen between imaginative and (what I'll now for convenience call) "nonimaginative" literature. At one time it was common for undergraduates to read familiar essays as part of their literary education; but, as Cynthia Ozick notes, as the "print supremacy" that still reigned throughout the early twentieth century lost ground to a new, technological "aural" culture, the belles lettres that comprised much of literary study started to look "archaic and bizarre . . . the property of a segregated caste or the dissipated recollections of the very old" (Ozick 360). By the 1960s the terms *belles lettres* and *belletristic* had clearly taken on pejorative meanings, as prominent magazines and literary periodicals increasingly favored the informative and critical "article" over the informal essay. The English curriculum, in the process of being overhauled by a new academic caste of critically trained professionals, followed this cultural trend and made less and less room in the syllabus for the old-fashioned essay. Today, though genre courses on poetry or the novel are commonly taught, it is rare to find an undergraduate course devoted solely to the essay as a literary form. And if there happens to be a course still "on the books," it is rarely offered. Just about the only place within the curriculum that you will find the essay today is in the freshman syllabus, where the genre for many years has found-or perhaps we should say has been "put in"—its place.

Yet even within composition programs, where it has occupied a comfortable niche for at least two decades, the essay is still far from being viewed as a legitimate literary form. In fact, most composition programs simply echo the literature department's decision of what is and what is not imaginative literature, and they frequently do so in terms not very different from Wellek and Warren's. A good example of this can be seen in a debate between Erika Lindemann and Gary Tate conducted in the March 1993 issue of *College English*. Each writer, a well-respected specialist in composition, addresses the question of whether there is a place for literature in first-year writing programs. Lindemann, who believes that the composition program is not the place to teach literature, acknowledges that some instructors regret that freshman English has been "stripped of the imaginative literature we love to teach." These instructors argue, she maintains, "that poetry, fiction, and drama offer essential training in the processes of reading" (311). Gary Tate, one of those teachers who believes that first-year writing courses should offer students a sampling of literature, begins his counter-argument by admitting that the "presence of literature-fiction, poetry, drama-in freshman composition courses in 1992 is minimal" (317).

Though they maintain contrary positions on the topic, Lindemann and Tate apparently do agree on a fundamental point: on what is and what is not literature. Though Tate concludes his eloquent plea for reinstating literature in the composition classroom by confessing that he is "a great fan of the personal essay," he then quickly changes direction and admits that he is "wrong" to teach essays because his fascination with them leads him "to ignore other forms of literature that might benefit" his students (321). It seems that Tate wants to view essays as literature after all, though perhaps he places them at the far end of the literary spectrum. The ambivalence of his final remark, I believe, is understandable and symptomatic of a larger and unresolved professional problem: Now that the essay has become the special province of composition programs, how should it be studied?

The role of the essay in the English curriculum over the past two decades, it may be argued, symbolizes the professional split between literature and composition studies. Though not my topic here, the implications of this division are serious and deserve far more attention than they've received. The identification of imaginative literature with Literature has resulted in the canonical dismissal of many exceptional, intelligent authors whose goals or genius turned them to the essay rather than to fiction, to disquisition rather than to poetry. There is no reason why such writers—William Hazlitt is a good example; Margaret Fuller another—should not be widely studied in literature courses. By systematically valuing works of fiction, poetry, and drama over essays and nonfiction, English departments exclude many exciting types of literature from critical attention and discussion—for example, autobiography and memoir. When such works or writers do gain admission through specialized courses (usually under the auspices of multiculturalist or feminist studies), they come to the student's attention more than slightly blemished; most students realize that they're reading such texts as part of a special agenda rather than as significant literary works in their own right. Writers who are only now being invited into the literature curriculum would have been there all along had departments not excluded most "nonimaginative" literature from serious study. In fact, a fair number of nonfiction writers currently surfacing in the undergraduate curriculum (such as Maxine Hong Kingston) were first introduced to students not in their literature but in their composition courses. This isn't because composition instructors were in closer touch than their literature colleagues with multicultural, feminist, or ethnic issues (though they perhaps were), but because many of them were in closer touch with essays, memoir, and autobiography. All one need do to confirm this fact is look at the table of contents of any recent freshman anthology.

Why did the essay enter the special domain of the composition program? One reason, of course, is that first-year college students are expected to be able to write nonimaginative—or should we say here "unimaginative"?—prose, and that English departments have long regarded the essay as offering suitable models of such prose for students to duplicate. No matter what theoretical basis a composition program subscribes to—whether it's oriented to the writing process, collaborative writing, critical thinking, etc.—the goal is always the same: the production of essays. And that single purpose presupposes and reinforces the nonliterary nature of the genre. The essay, in other words, is taught in composition precisely because it is not considered imaginative literature. First-year students are very rarely asked to read essays as literature and, even more rarely, asked to consider the essays they write as literature. Perhaps one unspoken reason essays are not taught as literature is that students might then logically infer that in composing their own essays, they too, would be writing literature. Such an inference could throw most of the country's composition programs into intellectual chaos.

How, then, are essays taught if not as literature? They are taught almost always within a rhetorical framework, studied, we might say, as the distinct embodiment of the art of rhetoric. As seen within this pedagogical context essays are not literary works in themselves but more or less effective examples of narration, exposition, argument, and persuasion. This almost symbiotic relationship between the essay and rhetoric, it should be added, has, especially stifled the reputation of the essay. Like *belletristic*, *rhetoric*, too, has become encrusted with pejorative connotations. While commenting on his linguistic approach to narrative discourse, Roland Barthes notes that both *rhetoric* and *belles lettres* are no longer serviceable terms: "This linguistics of discourse," he says in *The Semiotic Challenge*, "has for a very long time possessed a celebrated name: Rhetoric; but since Rhetoric, through a complex historical development, had become linked to belles lettres and since belles lettres had been separated from the study of language, it has seemed necessary, in recent years, to take up the question anew" (99). Since rhetoric is often viewed as antithetical to imaginative literature, composed as it is of all those persuasive and manipulative ingredients of discourse that literature must disassociate itself from in order to be truly "literary," the rhetorical density of the essay can only reinforce the genre's nonliterary status.

Readers were once far more comfortable with the rhetorical dimensions of literary language than they are today. This greater accommodation to rhetoric was accorded not only to the essay itself but to the essayistic elements that routinely appeared within the other genres. It was, it appears, only around the beginning of the twentieth century that sophisticated readers grew uneasy with such rhetorical features of imaginative literature as authorial commentary, interpolated essays, philosophical asides, encyclopedic digressions, exposition and argument, or whatever else "contaminated" the aesthetic integrity of a novel, poem, or play. Imagine what Moby Dick would be like if Melville had considered such essayistic elements to be literary impurities. The notion of rhetorical contamination finds perhaps its fullest expression in Paul Valéry, who, in both theory and practice, promoted the ideal of a "pure" literature. Valéry valued in a poem only those fragments or moments that he believed contained the work's literary essence: a poem "in practice" was "composed of fragments of pure poetry embedded in the substance of a discourse" (Valéry 185). For Valéry, the true poem did not exist in itself. It could never fully encompass or annul the entire discourse that contained it. It was wholly a literary ideal; the enveloping discourse was an inescapable presence that could not simply be peeled away. But this perceived tension between the poem and its surrounding discourse, a tension that can also be expressed as one of literature versus rhetoric or poetry versus abstract thought, had enormous critical and aesthetic consequences, especially for the methodology of the New Criticism that took root in American universities in the late 1930s. As critics began singling out the more genuine literary works—those that were organically whole and consistently dramatic—the traditional rhetorical aspects of imaginative literature were increasingly viewed as aesthetic violations, nonliterary contaminations. The New Criticism's inhospitality to the rhetorical uses of language resulted in a dismissal of prose discourse in general; it was often a sweeping dismissal that effectively denied aesthetic status to practically all forms of nonfiction, the essay included.

Of all the new critics, John Crowe Ransom carried out the most persistent and certainly the most influential assault on prose discourse. Ransom spent the greater part of an illustrious career arguing for the literary superiority of poetry over prose. He agreed with Valéry that the essence of prose is to perish, that prose vanished in the act of being understood. In one critical essay after another, Ransom passionately defended art against argument, the "iconic" against the "statemental." For Ransom, the southern agrarian, prose discourse was associated with such dubious social and cultural forces as science, technology, and progress. To risk an oversimplification, in Ransom's characteristic dualism prose represented the industrialized North, poetry the traditionalist South. Ransom's dichotomizing intelligence led to the construction of many intriguing polarizations, but perhaps none is so astonishing as the extended analogy he draws between prose and poetry in a 1941 essay, "Criticism as Pure Speculation":

A poem is, so to speak, a democratic state, whereas a prose discourse—mathematical, scientific, ethical, or practical and vernacular—is a totalitarian state. The intention of a democratic state is to perform the work of state as effectively as it can perform it, subject to one reservation of conscience: that it will not despoil its members, the citizens, of the free exercise of their own private and independent characters. But the totalitarian state is interested solely in being effective, and regards the citizens as no citizens at all; that is, regards them as functional members whose existence is totally defined by their alloted contributions to its ends; it has no use for their private characters, and therefore no provision for them. (137)

Ransom's value-laden trope, of course, persuasively reveals his literary agenda. Prose discourse as he sees it (and from his list of examples we can assume that he has not definitively exempted the essay) tends towards the efficient, the functional, the purposive—in other words, all of the features associated with a dialectical or rhetorical style. As one of America's first literary theoreticians and one of the earliest promoters of a university-oriented criticism, Ransom played a considerable role in establishing not only how literature should be read in our colleges but, perhaps more importantly, how it should be defined.

In his introduction to the essays of Paul Valéry, T. S. Eliot goes to the heart of this controversy, taking issue with Valéry's sharp distinction between poetry and prose (read: literature and essay), and especially with Valéry's famous analogy that poetry is to prose as dancing is to walking. Walking has as its purpose a destination; the "purpose of dance is the dance itself" (xv). For Valéry, Eliot claims, prose is *instrumental*—it is akin, to *purposive movement*—and its purpose is "to convey a meaning, to impart information, to convince of a truth, to direct action" (xv)—in other words, our familiar exposition, argument, persuasion. But is this attractive distinction valid? Only, says Eliot, if we ignore the fact that "dancing is sometimes purposive," for example, a war dance (xv). And, I would add, only if we ignore the fact that walking can be an end in itself; it is no coincidence that "walking" is one of the great themes and dominant tropes of the personal essay. Eliot correctly reminds us that Valery's distinction is entirely artificial: "I think," he says, "that much poetry will be found to have the instrumental value that Valéry reserves to prose, and that much prose gives us the kind of delight that Valéry holds to be solely within the province of poetry" (xv–xvi).

At least two other important critics reacted to the New Criticism's dismissal of prose discourse and rallied to the support of the rhetorical: Northrop Frye and Wayne Booth. Frye was especially concerned about the critical ascendency of the novel and the way it was rapidly becoming synonymous with fiction itself. In his *Anatomy of Criticism*, he complained that modern readers ignored the copious variety of literary prose and consequently judged many different types of works by a "novel-centered conception of fiction" (310). Frye attempted to counter this tendency by defining "fiction" so broadly that it included both novels and essays. He broke prose "fiction" down into four dominant forms: novels, romances, confessions, and anatomies, all of which could "cross-fertilize," resulting in six possible combinations, for example, the "romance anatomy" (*Moby Dick*) or the "confession-anatomy" (*Sartor Resartus*) (312). This is not the place to summarize the rationale behind Frye's nomenclature, but in general his distinctions make us aware of the many ways essayistic elements (arguments, ideas, erudition, catalogues, authorial commentary, etc.) have long been an integral part of imaginative literature.

One of the most important critical contributions of Frye's *Anatomy* is its bold attempt to broaden the range of works that fall under the name of "literature." In developing his rhetorical "theory of genres," Frye in effect expands the canon; he not only introduces into serious discussion previously neglected books but also encourages the reception of previously excluded literary types. Frye is especially attracted to certain marginalized texts, what he calls "the unclassified books lying on the boundary of 'nonfiction' and 'literature'" (303)—an invidious distinction he is keenly aware of. Frye's radically expanded definition of "fiction" has two powerful effects: first, in one stroke it eliminates the always troublesome dichotomy between imaginative and truthful works; and, second, since Fry realizes that "fiction" has become identified with literature itself, his definition automatically raises nonfiction prose to a literary level. He could not have made his intentions clearer. In arguing for the autobiographical "confession" as "a distinct prose form," Frye contends that it "gives several of our best prose works a definable place in fiction instead of keeping them in a vague limbo of books which are not quite literature because they are 'thought,' and not quite religion or philosophy because they are Examples of Prose Style" (307). In other words, unless we consider the essay as "fiction" it easily vanishes into that subliterary limbo of the unclassifiable. The familar essay, Frye maintains, is an offshoot ("the short form") of the confession: "Montaigne's *livre de bonne foy* is a confession made up of essays in which only the continuous narrative of the longer form is missing" (307).

In a rather circuitous fashion, Frye thus manages to elevate the literary status of the personal essay. But his behind-the-scenes reasoning is plain: If the essay is essentially autobiographical confession, and if confession is one of the forms of fiction, and fiction is literature, then the essay, too, must be classified as literature. Frye's remark about the "vague limbo" that some of the best prose works descend into also reminds us of the essay's uneasy position between literature and philosophy. Because of its long-standing association with rhetoric, the essay to a great extent remains banished from serious philosophy as well as serious literature. In the realm of literature, the essay is too philosophical to be considered literary, and in the realm of philosophy, too literary to be considered philosophical. The essay's peculiar identity conflict perhaps has its origins in Aristotle's still powerful triad of poetics, dialectic, and rhetoric, with the tools of imagination and truth often taking precedence over those of persuasion. In modern terms, poetics covers the domain of imaginative or creative writing, dialectics that of hard-nosed philosophical argument, and rhetoric, of course, covers that language which is neither-the essay. A recent manifestation of the essay's problematic identity can be found in Jurgen Habermas's "Excursus on Leveling the Genre Distinction between Philosophy and Literature," where Habermas argues for the antirhetorical nature of philosophy. He attacks Derrida for deliberately blurring the distinctions between the two disciplines and for refusing to tame the rhetorical dimensions of philosophical language (185–210). By "literature," Habermas means, ironically enough, not poetry or fiction but the essay. Just as literary critics have complained about rhetorical impurities infiltrating fiction and poetry, so, too, Habermas takes issue with Derrida's willingness to contaminate propositional thought with essayistic elements. Throughout much of his philosophical and critical writing Derrida has indirectly defended the essay. How seriously one respects the "genre distinction" between philosophy and literature, moreover, will determine how seriously one respects the intellectual reputations of certain writers whose subject was often the process of thinking itself—Emerson and Nietzsche are good examples.

One of the most comprehensive accounts of how literary impurities have affected the modern reader can be found in Wayne Booth's *Rhetoric of Fiction*. Booth, I believe correctly, criticizes Frye's classificatory system as unwieldy and insufficiently inductive (37). Yet Booth, too, recognizes the novel's emerging critical dominance, and his well-known study of fiction provides one of the most systematic attempts to identify and defend all those elements of fiction that were beginning to seem "intrusive" to the modern reader. His defense of the various rhetorical techniques (omniscience, commentary, etc.) found in even the "purest" forms of modern fiction is essentially a justification of rhetoric itself. "Is there any defense," Booth asks at the outset, "that can be offered, on aesthetic grounds, for an art full of rhetorical appeals?" (xiii). Like Frye, Booth hopes to demonstrate that rhetoric and aesthetics are not mutually incompatible; in other words, that fiction's essayistic elements are not necessarily artistic blemishes.

Booth makes us aware of how critically unproductive it is to expect some sort of aesthetic purity from most great works of fiction. And, since the essay, as I noted earlier, is almost always studied within a rhetorical framework, much of Booth's justification of fiction's rhetorical features can be read as a defense of the essay's imaginative and aesthetic potential, at least insofar as it is found embedded in other genres. It is this aspect of the essay—its active, creative presence within other works of literature—that I now want to examine. If we observe how inseparably connected the essay is to what we ordinarily call "imaginative" literature, we should be more suspicious of a generic classification system that routinely excludes the essay from serious literary study.

A BRIEF SURVEY OF "ESSAYISM"

Histories of the essay are usually constructed along two different lines. The most straightforward approach follows the development of the genre as it passes through the major practitioners—Montaigne, Bacon, Addison, Johnson, Emerson, Woolf, and so forth. The other studies the genre's evolving forms—familiar, formal, critical, journalistic, mosaic. I want here, however, to look at the essay in an altogether different way; not as a separate genre represented by a number of important writers that we call essayists or works that we call essays, but rather as a genre operating within the genres, one that has since the Renaissance continuously permeated and helped shape much of imaginative literature. In this alternate history of the essay, a novelist like Henry Fielding, who was proud of the way he had interlaced the periodical essay into his fiction, has as much to contribute to the genre as does Addison. There is no term that I know of that conveniently describes the pervasive presence of the essay within other genres, its intrageneric character. We might refer to the "interpolated" essay or the "embedded" essay, or, to borrow a term from M. M. Bakhtin, the "inserted" essay (263) as a way to describe the type of essay that appears as a freestanding chapter of a novel or that is sometimes so impacted within the fiction that we can't be sure whether we're reading an essay or a story.

Imaginative literature offers so many examples of such essays that I shall borrow a descriptive term from imaginative literature itself. The term is *essayism* and the source is Robert Musil's remarkable novel, *The Man Without Qualities*, which appeared in Germany between 1930 and 1933. In one of the novel's many digressive chapters, Musil's protagonist, Ulrich, "pays homage to the Utopian idea of Essayism," an intellectual attitude he associates "with the peculiar concept of the essay," which "in the sequence of its paragraphs, takes a thing from many sides without comprehending it wholly" (1:297). Though Musil employs the term specifically to describe the state of mind of a particular character, the chapter makes it clear that *essayism* also fittingly describes Musil's aesthetic intentions: "There was something in Ulrich's nature that worked in a haphazard, paralysing, disarming manner against logical systematisation, against the one-track will, against the definitely directed urges of ambition" (300). What would happen, Musil must have wondered, if I create a fictional hero whose unique mental equipment keeps him in a perpetual state of inaction and indirection, and if I then place him inside a busy, accelerating narrative that continually demands progressive movement and activity? What Musil achieved is one of the great modern books: a novel, like Proust's, with an essayist at its center, a fiction continually at odds with its own narrative process.

Musil was not the first to use the word *essayism*, though he appears to be the first to give it a theoretical significance. *Essayism* first appears in English (according to the OED) in 1821, where it is used pejoratively; but by 1887 the *Saturday Review* employs it in a context appropriate to Musil's: a reviewer writes of "that mysterious literary essence known as essayism that pervades all literature." A history of essayism—as opposed to that of the essay—would include a large number of imaginative works of literature in which the essay or various essayistic styles of discourse are wholly dominant or at least so pervasive that they are impossible to ignore. In these works the authors are, like Fielding in *Tom Jones*, either consciously writing essays that could more or less stand alone or they are, like Melville's narrators in "Bartleby, the Scrivener" or *Billy Budd, Sailor*, adopting a recognizable essayistic stance in relation to fictive material. In one of the very few studies of the term and concept, Thomas Harrison has recently examined the role of "essayism" (though largely in the context of moral philosophy) in the work of Joseph Conrad, Robert Musil, and Luigi Pirandello.

The history of essayism is, I've noted, inseparable from what we customarily think of as imaginative literature, I would further maintain that—for much of imaginative literature—an understanding of essayism is indispensable to a full critical assessment of the work. "[T]here is nothing either good or bad but thinking makes it so," argues Denmark's brooding Prince. And Melville aptly notes in the margin of his Shakespeare: "Here is forcibly ~own the great Montaigneism of Hamlet" (Pierre, "Notes" 1451). Though no one need consider Shakespeare's great tragedy as a dramatized essay, Hamlet's mind undeniably works in an essayistic fashion. In speech after speech, we can hear Shakespeare responding to Montaigne's newly formed genre; in more belletristic times, many of Hamlet's speeches were set into prose and separately printed as Baconian mini-essays, perhaps helping to reinforce the notion that only an essayist like Bacon could have written the plays. Even Polonius's adage-ridden language exemplifies the style of the Essais, especially in the way Shakespeare juxtaposes Hamlet's open and skeptical mental processes against the preformulated wisdom of an entrenched aphoristic reasoning.

Hamlet should remind us that many powerful works of literature do not merely illustrate or represent one particular genre but are usually made up of an uneasy combination of different genres. When, for example, Young Goodman Brown crosses the threshold of his new house and kisses his young wife good-bye, he not only steps across a border into a new zone of consciousness, but he also steps out of an allegory and into a short story. Melville's marginal comment suggests an interesting way of reading Hamlet—as Shakespeare's decision to pit a new essayistic sensibility against the furious confines of classical tragedy. From start to finish, the play provides an awesome inventory of the numerous ways language has entrapped human thought. Shakespeare, we might say, was essaying the essay within his tragedy, and in so doing he provided one of the earliest commentaries on Montaigne's literary creation.

Other imaginative works are far more explicit in their embrace of the essay. In Tom Jones, Fielding self-consciously included periodical-style essays in front of each book:

> Peradventure there may be no parts in this prodigious work which will give the reader less pleasure in the perusing, than those which have given the author the greatest pains in composing. Among these, probably, may be reckoned those initial essays which we have prefixed to the historical matter contained in every book; and which we have deter-

mined to be essentially necessary to this kind of writing. (460)

Fielding offers an interesting, though perhaps duplicitous, reason for these "initial essays." Since essays are more difficult to write than narrative fiction—requiring a "competent knowledge" of history and letters—he argues that their presence in his novel will prohibit lesser talents from slavish imitation. Fielding's prefatory essays were so popular that anthologists sometimes reprinted them (as my source demonstrates) separately in essay collections. Throughout the eighteenth century, novelists experimented with various ways of incorporating or assimilating the essay; *Tristram Shandy*, for example, foregrounds one of the essay's most characteristic features—the association of ideas-and does so, as Wolfgang Iser notes in *The Act of Reading*, by "linking up with Lockean empiricism" (74). Sterne's novel can thus be read as an imaginative response to one of the great seventeenth-century philosophical books, Locke's *An Essay Concerning Human Understanding*, a work that itself often moves nervously between the conversational or digressive essay and the rigorously argued treatise. Neoclassical verse also absorbed the essay as poets delighted in finding poetic outlets for description, exposition, and argument. A favorite Augustan form was the philosophical verse essay; with its roots in Lucretius, it is perhaps best typified by Pope's "Essay on Man."

Since the eighteenth century, many impressive works of literature have creatively assimilated various forms of the essay. A few landmarks of essayism are: Hawthorne's *The Scarlet Letter* (prefaced by one of American literature's most enigmatic autobiographical essays); Melville's "Bartleby" (an undoing of the conventional "character sketch"); Whitman's "Song of Myself" (which I have argued elsewhere audaciously scrambles the hierarchical categories of the philosophical verse essay); Baudelaire's *The Spleen of Paris* (the essay as "prose poem"); Proust's *Remembrance of Things Past* (whose narrator's mental processes are almost entirely essayistic); and Borges's *Ficciones* (with its borderless zones of prose). More recently, Milan Kundera has discussed in his *The Art of the Novel* the need for an "art of the specifically novelistic essay" (78), the kind of essay (reminiscent of Hermann Broch) he has interwoven into such novels as *The Unbearable Lightness of Being*. And in her introduction to *The Best American Poetry 1991*, Jorie Graham observed that a renewed "ambition to reclaim ground for eloquence and rhetoric is . . . starkly visible in the sharp, urgent poems of sheer argument—the lyric essay, which seems to be flourishing, stark offspring of the more classic meditation, also in vogue" (xii).

The essayistic elements contained in such works as these are not parasitical or excisable parts; instead, they represent compositional features wholly essential to the author's aesthetic purposes. Very often, the essay functions inside works of fiction in a conflictual manner that may be read, as in Hawthorne, Melville, or Kundera, as an analogue of other contentions (thematic, psychological, ideological) within the story. Melville, for example, expects us to hear the polite vein of Washington Irving's essays behind the voice of the well-intentioned Wall Street lawyer who reports the unhappy fate of Bartleby. Melville, in fact, set many of his novels and tales on the borderline of fiction and truth, where he explored the limits of imaginative literature. "Not long ago," he writes in the Preface to Mardi, "having published two narratives of voyages in the Pacific, which, in many quarters, were received with incredulity, the thought occured to me, of indeed writing a romance of Polynesian adventure, and publishing it as such; to see whether, the fiction might not, possibly, be received for a verity" (661). In "Bartleby," Melville may be writing fiction but his narrator is composing a biographical sketch. Much of the tale's fascination depends on the asymmetric relation of these two genres.

THE AESTHETICS OF ESSAYISM: "BIG TWO-HEARTED RIVER"

To illustrate how deeply submerged an essay can be within a work of imaginative literature, I want to turn to a well-known story whose essayistic qualities might at first seem invisible. Hemingway's "Big Two-Hearted River" appears to be a short story, pure and simple. Yet, what makes this piece of highly rhetorical prose a story? Only the use of third-person narration, perhaps. Put into the first person, the story would be practically indistinguishable from a familiar essay about a solitary fishing trip: The writer hops off a train, observes a burned-down town he once knew, hikes through the countryside, pitches camp, pan fries himself an appetizing meal of canned beans, spaghetti, and ketchup, crawls into his tent, gets a good night's sleep, and the next day wades into the river, catches two trout (after the proverbial big one gets away), and decides to return to camp. That is what "happens" in "Big Two-Hearted River." There is no cumulative action other than setting up camp and fishing, and no dialogue other than the few things Nick says to himself or to the blighted grasshoppers.

Whatever we might find conventionally fictional in "Big Two-Hearted River" is precisely what Hemingway leaves out—the details of how Seney became a wasteland, of why Nick returns to fish there, of why he feels a need for renewal (my terms, of course, are meant to echo T. S. Eliot's own mythopoetic response to the First World War). Hemingway's story offers little drama, no conclusive epiphany, and, though the world rendered is so insistently private, there is remarkably little reflection on the part of the one and only character. But the little reflection that does occur is crucial to the tale. As Nick makes himself a pot of coffee, he remembers an old friend with whom he used to argue about the proper way to brew coffee. He makes it the way Hopkins insisted and, as he drinks the coffee, it provokes in Proustian fashion a train of associations that take him back to an earlier fishing trip and happier days. "That was a long time ago," Nick recalls:

> Hopkins spoke without moving his lips. He had played polo. He made millions of dollars in Texas. He had borrowed carfare to go to Chicago, when the wire came that his first big well had come in. He could have wired for money. That would have been too slow. They called Hop's girl the Blonde Venus, Hop did not mind because she was not his real girl. Hopkins said very confidently that none of them would make fun of his real girl. He was right. Hopkins went away when the telegram came. That was on the Black River. It took eight days for the telegram to reach him. Hopkins gave away his .22 caliber Colt automatic pistol to Nick. He gave his camera to Bill. It was to remember him always by. They were all going fishing again next summer. The Hop Head was rich. He would get a yacht and they would all cruise along the north shore of Lake Superior. He was excited but serious. They said good-bye and all felt bad. It broke up the trip, They never saw Hopkins again. That was a long time ago on the Black River. (217)

This rushing stream of memories, despite its interrupted narrative sequence, represents—especially with its reverberations of the popular magazine "strike-it-rich" tale-the only conventional fiction in "Big Two-Hearted River." We even see the memories start to evolve as a short story: "Nick drank," the passage continues,

> the coffee according to Hopkins. The coffee was bitter. Nick laughed. It made a good ending to the story. His mind was starting to work. He knew he could choke it because he was tired enough. (218)

This reflective moment is pivotal. In "choking" the story taking shape in Nick's head, Hemingway effectively suppresses the impulse for fiction. Nick's short story is everything that "Big Two-Hearted River" is not. Hemingway's tale is essentially an anti-story; it depends upon a powerful resistance to fiction and its usual configurations. At the end of the story, Nick is permitted another flicker of literary consciousness. He contemplates heading into the swamp, where, he imagines, "fishing was a tragic adventure" (231); yet he stifles this impulse, as he did his story, and instead returns to camp. In restraining the narrative movements of fiction-a resistance wonderfully mirrored in the way the trout hold steady against the current—Hemingway simultaneously releases the countervailing movements of the familiar essay with its emphasis on exposition, its lack of suspense, its attention to ordinary processes, its curtailment of climax. In other words, Hemingway allows the story's essayistic, or nonimaginative, features to assume literary precedence. In so doing, he turns the genres inside out. Hemingway's compositional triumph in "Big Two-Hearted River" is precisely in the way he transforms the conventions of nonimaginative literature into a memorable work of the imagination.

Hemingway complicates matters by blurring the conventions of genre even further. Nick's flickering short story is told in a style of free association, a style that essayists since Montaigne have made a central feature of their genre. As Donald P. Spence argues in *Narrative Truth and Historical Truth*, a book on psychoanalytic interpretation that is nonetheless quite relevant to my topic, free association is inherently at odds with narration. Patients in psychotherapy will often try to shape their stories-and alter memories-so that they will possess a satisfying degree of narrative coherence. Associative thinking has little to do with such coherence and what Spence calls "narrative fit" (175ff). In looking for historical truth—what really happened—the analyst needs to be skeptical about narratives that appear too neatly shaped, too finished, too literary. Nick's miniature story in itself dramatizes a similar conflict. Though his memory proceeds by quirky associations, Nick eventually discovers (in a pun) some small degree of aesthetic closure or narrative fit: "a good ending to the story."

Essayism frequently appears in literary works as a resistance to the aesthetic satisfactions of narrative, a resistance which can generally be viewed as an opposition to the literary imagination itself. This type of oppositional essayism, for example, can often be seen running through the poetry of Wordsworth and Frost. A stubborn resistance to both narrative and imaginative constructs was, it should be recalled, at the core of Montaigne's literary agenda, In one of his earliest essays, "Of the Power of the Imagination" (an essay that, like Hemingway's story, confronts the issues of narrative truth, imaginative power, and sexual impotence), Montaigne claims that his "art" is an "escape" from imagination (68), This escape, he implies, is assisted by one of his many self-professed incapacities: "there is nothing," he adds, "so contrary to my style as an extended narration" (76).

A careful reading of Hemingway's story, especially in the context of Montaigne's "Of the Power of the Imagination," should persuade us that our convenient classification of literary genres has its limits. Many works of literature are compositionally impure, an amalgamation of genres, of genres often at odds with each other. Hemingway claimed, for instance, in a letter to Gertrude Stein, that in "Big Two-Hearted River" he was "trying to do the country like Cezanne" (*Selected Letters* 122), a comment that surely registers the extent of his aesthetic ambitions and, furthermore, when we consider what Cezanne achieved in his remarkable landscapes, suggests Hemingway's own juxtaposition of different conceptual frameworks. A story like "Big Two-Hearted River" should also make us hesitant in accepting the idea that some genres are inherently imaginative while others are not. Literary imagination is not a property of genre but of execution. Hemingway's essayistic sketch in which, as he himself put it, "nothing happens" (*Selected Letters* 122) is finally more imaginative than Nick's aborted story, and for the very reason that nothing happens.

For those who regularly read essays as literary works, I hope the question of my title does not seem merely rhetorical. I have not intended it as such; for once literature is defined exclusively in imaginative or fictional terms, the essay becomes a troublesome literary species. As a result, the essay has not fared well under the dominant assumptions of modern academic literary criticism, especially in the United States, where either (a) the essay is not defined as an imaginative genre, or (b) literature is not defined broadly enough to include the nonfictional. To cite Wellek and Warren's *Theory of Literature* once again: "The term 'literature' seems best if we limit it to the art of literature, that is, to imaginative literature" (10). For these critics, genuine literary works refer to "a world of fiction, of imagination. The statements in a novel, in a poem, or in a drama are not literally true; they are not logical propositions" (14). Though Wellek and Warren realize that by proposing "fictionality," "invention," or "imagination" as the "distinguishing trait of literature," they thereby create numerous "boundary cases," they nevertheless conclude that no "wrong is done to a great and influential work by relegating it to rhetoric, to philosophy, to political pamphleteering, all of which may pose problems of aesthetic analysis, of stylistics and composition, similar or identical to those presented by literature, but where the central quality of fictionality will be absent" (14–15). No wrong is done, say, to the essay, which they regard as a "transitional" form, except to ensure that it will not be taught in literature departments.

It is important to note that Wellek and Warren's theoretical position represents no aberrant viewpoint. Just how critically commonplace it has become is made clear in a recent study by Wolfgang Iser, *The Fictive and the Imaginary*. Iser maintains in his opening sentences that:

> It has long been a commonplace that literary texts are by definition fictional. Such a classification of the literary text clearly distinguishes it from those texts that, according to current terminology, are expository, meaning that they have a referent outside themselves. This opposition between reality and fiction is an elementary item in what the sociology of knowledge has come to call tacit knowledge—a term used to designate that storehouse of beliefs that seem so soundly based that their truth may be taken for granted. (1)

But Iser's question—"Are fictional texts truly fictions, and are nonfiction texts truly without fictions?"—challenges the dominant academic assumptions and opens up the possibility for a revaluation of the essay as a literary genre.

A definition of literature that esteems only the traditional triad of "imaginative" writing leads—as Frye tried to show—to a narrowing of the critical imagination. The persistent undervaluation of the essay and the essayistic underpinnings of much imaginative literature has resulted in a sharply skewed canon, the neglect of many important works, and it has helped create an unhealthy rift between literature and composition studies. Barthes writes of the essay as the generating principle behind the evolution of all genres, a kind of genre of genres (Hardison 12). Is the essay literature? Perhaps the question to ask is: can literature exist without it?

WORKS CITED

Atwan, Robert. "Observing a Spear of Summer Grass." *Kenyon Review* ns 12.2 (1990): 17–25.

Bakhtin, M. M. *The Dialogic Imagination*, Ed. Michael Holquist. Trans. Caryl Emerson and Michael Holquist. Austin: The U of Texas P, 1981.

Barthes, Roland. *The Semiotic Challenge*. Trans. Richard Howard. New York: Hill,

1988.

Baudelaire, Charles. *Le Spleen de Paris*. Paris: Brodard et Taupin, 1963.

Booth, Wayne C. *The Rhetoric of Fiction*. 2nd ed. Chicago: U of Chicago P, 1983.

Borges, Jorge Luis. *Ficciones*. Trans. Anthony Kerrigan et al. New York: Grove, 1962.

Broch, Hermann. *The Sleepwalkers: A Trilogy*. Trans. Willa and Edwin Muir. New York: Pantheon, 1947.

Eliot, T. S. Introduction, *The Art of Poetry*. By Paul Valéry. Trans. Denise Folliot. New York: Random, 1961. vii–xxiv.

"Essayism." *The Compact Edition of the Oxford English Dictionary*. Oxford: Oxford UP, 1971. 896.

Fielding, Henry. *Tom Jones*. 1749. Essays and Characters. Ed. Robert Withington. New York: Macmillan, 1933. 460–91.

Frye, Northrop. *Anatomy of Criticism: Four Essays*. Princeton: Princeton UP, 1971,

Graham, Jorie, ed. The Best American Poetry 1991. New York: Scribner's, 1991.

Habermas, Jurgen. The Philosophical Discourse of Modernity, Trans. Frederick G. Lawrence. Cambridge, MA: MIT P, 1987.

Hardison, O. B. "Binding Proteus: An Essay on the Essay," *Essays on the Essay: Redefining the Genre*. Ed. Alexander J. Butrym. Athens, GA: The U of Georgia P, 1989. 11–28.

Harrison, Thomas. *Essayism: Conrad, Musil, and Pirandello*. Baltimore: Johns Hopkins UP, 1992.

Hawthorne, Nathaniel. *The Scarlett Letter*. New York: Library of America, 1983.

————. "Young Goodman Brown." *Tales and Sketches*. New York: Library of America, 1982.

Hemingway, Ernest. "Big Two-Hearted River." *The Short Stories of Ernest Hemingway*. New York: Scribner's, 1938. 209–32,

————. "To Gertrude Stein and Alice B. Toklas." 15 Aug, 1924. Letter in *Ernest Hemingway: Selected Letters*. Ed. Carlos Baker. London: Granada, 1981. 122–23,

Iser, Wolfgang, *The Act of Reading*. Baltimore: Johns Hopkins UP, 1980.

————. *The Fictive and the Imaginary*. Baltimore: Johns Hopkins UP, 1993.

Kundera, Milan. *The Unbearable Lightness of Being*. Trans. Michael Henry Heim. New York: Harper, 1984.

————. *The Art of the Novel*, Trans. Linda Asher. New York: Grove, 1986.

Lindemann, Erika, "Freshman Composition: No Place for Literature." *College English* 55 (1993): 311–16.

Locke, John. *An Essay Concerning Human Understanding*. Ed. Peter H. Nidditch. Oxford: Oxford UP, 1979.

Melville, Herman. *Mardi*. New York: Library of America, 1982. 647–1316,

————. "Notes." *Pierre*. Ed. Harrison Hayford. New York: Library of America,

1984. 1450-78.

————. "Bartleby, the Scrivener" and *Billy Budd, Sailor*. New York: Library of America, 1984.

Montaigne, Michel de. *The Complete Essays of Montaigne*. Trans. Donald M. Frame. Stanford: Stanford UP, 1965.

Musil, Robert. *The Man Without Qualities*. Trans. Eithne Wilkins and Ernst Kaiser. Vol. 1. New York: Capricorn, 1965.

Ozick, Cynthia. "The Question of Our Speech: The Return to Aural Culture." *Ten on Ten: Major Essayists on Recurring Themes*. Ed. Robert Atwan. Boston: St. Martin's, 1992,

Pope, Alexander. The Complete Poetical Works of Alexander Pope. Ed. Henry W. Boynton. Boston: Houghton, 1903.

Proust, Marcel. *A la Recherche du Temps Perdu*. Ed. Pierre Clarac and Andre Ferre. 3 vols. Paris: Gallimard, 1954.

Ransom, John Crowe. "Criticism as Pure Speculation." *Selected Essays of John Crowe Ransom*. Ed. Thomas Daniel Young and John Hindle. Baton Rouge: Louisiana State UP, 1984. 128–46.

Spence, Donald P. *Narrative Truth and Historical Truth*. New York: Norton, 1982.

Sterne, Lawrence. *The Life and Opinions of Tristram Shandy, Gentleman*. 9 vols. London, 1760–67.

Tate, Gary. "A Place for Literature in Freshman Composition," *College English* 55 (1993): 317–21.

Valéry, Paul. *The Art of Poetry*. Trans. Denise Folliot. New York: Random, 1961.

Wellek, Rene, and Austin Warren. *Theory of Literature*. 2nd ed. New York: Harcourt, 1956.

Whitman, Walt. *Complete Poetry and Collected Prose*. New York: Library of America, 1982.

RÉDA BENSMAÏA

THE BARTHES EFFECT [1987]

1. THE LOGIC OF THE "SUFFICIENT WORD" IN THE MONTAIGNAN ESSAY

For a long time it was assumed that only with the *Essays* of *Book III* did Montaigne find his definitive style and pinpoint the specific strategy for which he is recognized. Nevertheless, because of Montaigne's continuous rewriting, *Book I* has at least one text where Montaigne proposes, together with a theory of reading, an explanation of the constitutive method of the Essays. The following is a fragment from "Consideration upon Cicero" in which Montaigne sets forth some rudiments of his poetics:

> In order to get more in, *I pile up only the headings of subjects*. Were I to add on their consequences, I *would multiply* this volume *many times over*. And how many stories have I spread around *which say nothing of themselves*, but from which anyone who *troubles to pluck them with a little ingenuity will produce numberless Essays*.
>
> Neither these stories nor my quotations serve always simply for *example, authority*, or *ornament*. I do not esteem them solely for the *use* I derive from them. They often bear, *outside of my subject*, the seeds of a richer and bolder material, and sound obliquely a subtler note, both for myself, who do not wish to express anything more, and for those who get my drift. (I, 40, 185, emphasis mine)

In this text dating from the *first* period of the *Essays*, Montaigne states a fundamental principle of his poetics: corresponding to the *scriptural actuality* of a given essay there is always a *lectural potentiality* irreducible to a "finite" mode of reading or reader. The particular structure of the essay permits the production of an *indefinite* number of developments from a finite set of elements. Therefore, there are always some pieces of story, some fragments of thought, some "bits" of quotation which, even if they do not come to anything in a given essay, even if they do not find the means to deploy their potentialities, will nevertheless continue to work in subterranean fashion. "Consequences" are lacking, there are only "headings" of certain ideas, thoughts, stories, etc. But this in no way precludes the essay from making them produce a maximum meaning. It is only in accordance with the principle of a closed system that a text can be said to be finite. Whoever wants to "pluck with a little ingenuity" a text not subject to any prior rhetorical norm will see that the essay appears positively: (a) as a potentially infinite and open text; (b) as a piling up—the metaphor is constant in Montaigne—or juxtaposition of n fragments. As Montaigne writes elsewhere, "I am likely to begin without a plan; the first remark leads to a second. . . . I would rather compose two letters than close and fold one."

When Montaigne specifies that his "quotations" do not serve as "examples," "authority," or "ornament," he clearly indicates their status as fragments: only insofar as they are taken into the general organization of the text—which they populate with a thousand potentialities—and not insofar as they focus on some "philosophical consideration" do fragments, bits, or pieces of stories produce their specific effects. They preserve throughout the mark of their original fragmentation: an arrangement of heterogeneous elements, a mélange or "mixture" of discussion with oneself, of free conversation, of letter or address, and also of sententiae and maxims. The unity of the essayistic text demands a new definition of the notion of text as well as a new position for reading. In fact, since the organizer of the text is no longer a principle of authority—Montaigne is neither the representative of a particular philosophical system nor the exponent of particular philosophical theses or questions—the reader will have to forge a path through the scattered fragments. This explains why the essayist can only reject the stereotyped usage of exemplum and quotation: in the essay, they no longer serve as illustration or confirmation of a thesis; rather, they are an element wholly constitutive of what traditionally tends to be hidden in the economy of classical texts: that is to say, their processive aspect—or, if you like, the rhetorical "artifices" that are constantly at work in them.

There is thus a "supernumerary" effect (I will consider this at greater length later) that is inextricably and essentially linked to the method of composition of the essay as text—"seeds of a richer and bolder material," as Montaigne says, that cannot be reduced. A classical point of view, invoking theories of "oblique vision" and "grotesques," would explain his accumulation of examples, stories, and the like as a horror of didacticism and a taste for suggestiveness. This is the sort of explanation found in Michel Butor's book on the *Essays* or in Michaël Baraz's study of the "images" in the *Essays*. Whatever their interest, such analyses do not throw a great deal of light on the nature of the genre, perhaps because they consider it only obliquely. These works lead us to believe that we are dealing still with a mode of composition and of writing in which the author's mastery over the text is the governing factor. But when Montaigne says that his stories and examples go outside his subject, everything points to another type of textual economy here, marginal effects and the overflow of meaning become the rule.

If we decide to follow Montaigne in renouncing the order, disposition, and canonical closure of the composed text, we can try to account for the mode of functioning of the essay as a "literary machine" (Deleuze) capable of producing, *at the same time*, supernumerary surface effects, subjects that are rash and bold oblique resonances and "infinite Essays" without *breaking down*. To do so, we must change our point of view and leave off studying the essays as if the form of their exposition and the mode of their functioning were extrinsic. "If I were a professional," Montaigne said, "I would naturalize art as much as they artialize nature."

When one studies the many texts in which Montaigne sets forth the "principles" of his poetics, the striking feature is his insistence on the intrinsic productivity of the form of each one of his *Essays*. This is readily apparent in the celebrated text in *Book III* where Montaigne puts on a dress rehearsal, as it were, of his poetics.

To the question of why he has just taken such a long "detour"—*quo diversibus abis*—on the "dismemberment" of France with its concomitant divisions and difficulties, Montaigne replies:

(1) This stuffing is a bit *outside of my subject*. I wander a little, but *rather by license than carelessness*. My fantasies follow one another, but sometimes it is from a distance, and *look at each other*, but *obliquely*, with a sidelong glance.
(2) I have run my eyes over a certain dialogue of Plato, a fantastic motley in two parts, the beginning part about love, all the rest about rhetoric. The ancients do not fear these changes, and with wonderful grace *they let themselves thus be tossed in the wind, or seem to*. The titles of my chapters do not always embrace their matter; often *they only denote it by some mark*, like those other titles, *The Maid of Andros*, *The Eunuch*, or

those other names, Sulla, Cicero, Torquatus. I love the poetic gait, by leaps and gambols. It is an art, as Plato says, light, flighty, daemonic. There are works of Plutarch's in which *he forgets his theme*, in which the treatment of *his subject is found only incidentally*, quite smothered in foreign matter. See his movements in "The Daemon of Socrates." Lord, *what beauty there is in these lusty sallies and this variation, and more so the more nonchalant and fortuitous they seem.*

(3) *It is the inattentive reader who loses my subject, not I. Some* word about it will always be found off in a corner, which will not fail to be *sufficient* [*bastant*], although it may be concise. I seek out change indiscriminately and tumultuously. My *style* and my *mind* alike go wandering. (III. 9, 761, emphasis mine)

This text echoes Montaigne's text that was analyzed earlier: all the previously stated poetic principles are reaffirmed, sometimes in the *same terms*. It will be recalled that in the first text, Montaigne concludes by noting (1) that in the logic of his system of exposition, "stories" and "quotations" often go "outside of [his] subject" and bear "the seeds of a richer and bolder material"; and (2) that between these stories and quotations there sounds a "subtler note," a resonance that should be taken into consideration. In the latter text the same problems provide the impetus for his poetic reflection. It is as if poetics, too, demands the same system of resumptions and resonances as that necessary for the smooth functioning of the essay as reflective text. In repeating himself, Montaigne shows that he is conscious of the rhetorical difficulties raised by his text. And this time the new metaphors lead us to an essential point: What is the logic that allows the fragments, in spite of their extreme heterogeneity, to constitute *a unity?*

In the first sequence of Montaigne's text quoted above, this unity is described as the *resonance* of a series of stories: there is a unity of "fantasies," but it is "oblique," transverse. What may appear as wandering—a total lack of order—is in fact an *exigency* characteristic of essayistic writing. The second sequence develops this theme by invoking Plato and Plutarch, very freely interpreted. Montaigne focuses, in a sense, on the aporetic and—in certain aspects—"polyphonic" side of Plato's early dialogues in order to reaffirm a characteristic I have mentioned earlier: the *Essays* open dialogue form. But he also takes up an aspect of Plutarch's *Moral Works*—providentially devoted to Socrates' daemon—in order to be more specific. In the first sequence, Montaigne has said: "My fantasies

follow one another, but sometimes it is from a distance, and look at each other, but obliquely"; relying on Plutarch, he specifies that the "subjects" are produced only *incidentally*. Definite *intention* and *plan* do not guide and punctuate the scansion of what the essay proposes: rather, the multiplicity and initial heterogeneity of the elements of the work determine the appearance of particular utterances. Thus what matters to the essayist is not the classical question of rhetorical *inventio*—finding something to say—nor that of *dispositio*—putting in order what has been found. Rather it is a problem of *complicatio*, which consists in producing, as Barthes will say of the *Text*, "theory, critical combat, and pleasure simultaneously . . . with intellectual things (*Roland Barthes*, 90). As Montaigne says earlier in the essay from which I have taken the passage commented upon, "The one who does not guide others well, guides himself well; *and the one who cannot produce effects, writes Essays*" (emphasis mine). Our question—what logic permits the heterogeneous fragments of the essayistic text to constitute a unity?—should, then, be posed more specifically in these terms:
(1) What is the constitutive method of the essayistic text?
(2) What sort of effects does it intend?
On these questions, the *Essays* are quite clear:

> The ancients do not fear these changes, and with a wonderful grace they let themselves be tossed in the wind, *or seem to*. (III. 9, 761, emphasis mine)

It is possible to interpret the reservations expressed by the words "or seem to" as a deliberate calculation on Montaigne's part—to say that Montaigne, either by natural inclination or by conviction, would find pleasure in leading his reader astray, all the while knowing perfectly well where he is going and where he is taking his reader. Such a reservation is generally credited to the account of that Montaigne who is considered to be a strategist of meaning and an apologist of digressive allusion, in order to assert some continuity of meaning between his diverse fragments. In short, this passage can be interpreted in the most economical sense: one need but read between the lines to understand that there is an underlying idea structuring the text. Such an interpretation seems to be confirmed by the third sequence of the text quoted above: "It is the inattentive reader who loses my subject, not I." The author remains master of meaning.

There are at least three arguments that weaken such an interpretation. (1) It leaves no place for the productivity linked to the intrinsic form of the essay. (2) It disregards Montaigne's affirmation of the writer's status with regard to the text: "To him," writes Montaigne of the poet-essayist, "we must certainly concede mastery and preeminence in speech" (III. 9, 761). (3) In addition, such an interpretation should be categorically rejected because its underlying assumptions—that the text is based on the author's pleasure in leading the reader astray and on his ultimate mastery of the text's meaning—inevitably lead to the evasion of the other difficulties presented by the text. Thus Montaigne, seeking to make his thought clear, writes:

> The titles of my chapters do not always embrace their matter; often they only denote it by *some mark*, like those other titles, *The Maid of Andros, The Eunuch*, etc. (III. 9, 761, emphasis mine)

It is possible to see here no more than a kind of casual indifference to the stylistic or rhetorical rule concerning the relation between the *title of a work* and the *content of the work* itself, an indifference that may be accounted for simply enough in aesthetic or psychological terms. Thus René Jasinski can write, commenting on this passage: "Assuredly the title does not work without a touch of imagination [*fantaisie*]. . .. But let us *modify the title*. Let us underline the humor in "Of Coaches." Or let us *substitute* another title that corresponds to the deep meaning! . . . Everything becomes immediately clear.

By asserting the "deep meaning" of the text, hypostatized *against* the multiplicity of facets and the multitude of thoughts and ideas it produces, the *form* of the text is once more denied any productivity of its own. In such an approach, there is an instrumental conception of the expository mode of a work that makes for a quick resolution of the problems. Remove this, change that: but what remains of the work? Why did the essayist choose this mode of presentation and organization of is thoughts if one can so easily suppress everything that, according to the familiar stereotyped canons, is taken for pure ornamentation or a slip of the pen?

Clearly, we must follow a different path if we are to understand what is taking place in the *Essays*. Montaigne says of his titles that they "denote by some mark" the matter of the *Essays*. Why not take him seriously and try to discover what this "mark" may allude to and what its significance may be?

In my opinion, the answer to this question can be found in the third sequence of the text I have quoted above, where Montaigne writes: "It is the inattentive reader who loses my subject, not I."

This is an affirmation that one spontaneously tends to interpret as follows: the montage of stories, examples, and so on in the essay, the exploded and chaotic aspect of construction, are surface effects; in fact, Montaigne always knows where he is going. All that's necessary is to find *the* guiding thread. This sort of interpretation resembles those discussed earlier: again, the author's intention becomes the central "motif" of the essay and the rest is relegated to the simple role of ornamental "grotesques": stories, examples, and so on.

Only in the language of paradox can it be said that an essay is "tossed in the wind" and *at the same time* that it merely "seems" to be "tossed." Indeed, the most characteristic feature of a Montaignian essay is this altogether original kind of "disjunctive synthesis" (Deleuze) of opposite terms, contradictory fragments, and the like. But to accept and understand this, one must see the difference between the instances that Montaigne calls arbitrary—"fortuitous," as he puts it—and those he calls necessary. The essayist in Montaigne—and the "secret" of the genre he created is to be found principally at this level—does not affirm that the same thing is both necessary and arbitrary: *"necessity" always refers to the mode of exposition, constitution, and functioning* of the always heterogeneous elements of the essayistic text, *whereas "arbitrary"* refers only to what the text sets forth ("thoughts," "ideas," "judgments," etc.), elements that "fall" like simple effects of the work's functioning and that must be connected first of all to its formal structure.

Neither the "deep meaning" nor the psychological identity of the author, nor the "style" are of real use in showing that *in spite of everything* there is unity and meaning in the essayistic work. One must have recourse instead to the particular mode of treatment or arrangement of the stories, examples, maxims, and other elements. The structuration of the essay in no way originates in a dualist logic of content and form, latent and patent, an opposition between deep and surface structure: it cannot be said that the chaotic succession of the elements entering into the essay's composition is arbitrary only in appearance and actually becomes a necessary order for the attentive reader. There is not first an idea or concept that is then followed by "illustrations" made up of anecdotes, witticisms, quotations, and the like. Instead, *from the very beginning and at an identical semantic and formal level*, there are heterogeneous series of stories, examples, maxims, and the rest.

What Montaigne affirms as necessary, first and foremost—and this is the theoretical affirmation running through the *Essays*—is *chaos*, or, in Montaigne's own terms, "diversity": "And two opinions identical in the world never existed, any more than two hairs or two grains," writes Montaigne, concluding his first published book. *"Their most universal quality is diversity."* What returns, what comes again—while remaining quite irreducible to a punctual identity of the psychological, gnoseological, or material type is Chaos—the multiplicity and diversity of suppositions, words, ideas, and things, the infinite variations of reality and life. To realize this, one need only interrogate "things" by going beyond the concepts that are supposed to "express" them:

> I ask what is "nature," "pleasure," "circle," "substitution." The question is one of words, and is answered in the same way. "A stone is a body." But if you pressed on: "And what is a body?"—"Substance."—"And what is substance?" and so on, you would finally drive the respondent to the end of his lexicon. (III. 13, 818–819)

The method of exposition and composition of the essay and the type of effects corresponding to it are in the image of this multiplicity, this variety, and it is this that makes their character fundamentally paradoxical for us. For instead of affirming the identity and the return of the "idea," the "thought," or the "intention" *one* and *united*, the form of the essay, inverting the classic problematic of the exposition of the *Idea* in general, is such that it can affirm the identity and the "eternal" return only of a chaos in which several ideas will shine, in which several "bold" subjects will be born, but this time in a totally "fortuitous" manner:

> Lord, what beauty there is in these lusty sallies and this variation, and more so, the more nonchalant and fortuitous they seem. (III. 9, 761)

For this reason, attention must be given to the formulation of Montaigne's poetic theses. Thus, Montaigne does not say: the *reader in general* can "lose my subject," but rather the "inattentive" reader. From what I have tried to show, the inattentive reader is not at all, quite obviously, the careless, casual, or unintelligent reader, but rather the one who expects the essayistic work to produce only effects with a monological or singular meaning. The "inattentive" reader is also the one who expects the essayist to affirm from the first the unity in origin of the essay's preexisting and self-evident contents—in short, to settle matters once and for all. Finally, the "inattentive" reader is the one who reverses the perspective by taking a given "fallout" (*retombée*), a given punctual effect that the essay produces in the course of reading, as the text's *meaning* or the author's *intention*. Thus the reader generalizes the *partial effects* that are produced by the literary machine at work in the essay and takes them as the essay's meaning.

BASTANT, ANTE. adj. Sufficient. *Renaut n'en prit qu'une somme bastante* [Renaut took only a sufficient sum]. LA FONT. *Orais. Louville, avec Mme Maintenon contraire, n'était pas bastant pour être de la conférence* [Louville, with Mme Maintenon opposed, was not strong enough to prevail]. ST. SIM. 101, 75 *Obsolete.*

HIST. 16 C. *D'autres forces assez bastantes pour faire un avant-garde* [Other forces strong enough to form a vanguard]. CARL. I, 40. *Aux besoins extraordinaires, toutes les provisions du monde n'y scauraient baster* [All the provisions in the world cannot suffice for extraordinary needs]. MONT. I, 317. *Cette âme sera capable d'une très saincte amitié, la sincérité et la solidité de ses moeurs y sont déjà bastantes* [This soul will be capable of a very holy amity, the sincerity and solidity of its ways are already enough]. ID. III, 73.

ETYM. Ital. *bastare* 'to suffice, to endure, to be preserved'; from a root meaning 'to sustain, to bear', found also in *bât* 'packsaddle', *bâtir* 'to build', *bâton* 'stick, staff' q.v.

—LITTRE

BASTANT, ANTE. adj. The *s* is pronounced. That which suffices, which suits, which satisfies. *Ces vivres ne sont pas bastantes pour me nourrir* [These provisions are not enough to feed me]. *Ces raisons ne sont pas bastantes pour me persuader* [These reasons aren't sufficient to convince me]. *Cette caution n'est pas bastante pour me contenter* [This guarantee isn't enough to satisfy me].

BASTER. The *s* is pronounced. Formerly meant to 'to suffice' and is still used in the proverbial phrase *Baste pour cela* 'who cares!' or simply *Baste* 'pass, I'm satisfied.' This word came into use only in the time of Queen Catherine de Médicis, as Borel noes.

—FURETIERE, *Dictionnaire Universel*, 1690

(Slaktine Reprints, Geneva, 1970)

Although he refuses any explanation that relies on the singleness of the author, meaning, or "style," Montaigne does not revert to the mere attentiveness of the reader to account for the unity of the work. He does not surreptitiously reintroduce on the one hand what he rejects on the other. What is it, then, that makes one have the experience, in spite of everything, that the arrangement of the heterogeneous parts that constitute an essay forms a certain *totality*?

At first, Montaigne's answer to the question may appear sybilline:

> Some word about it will always be found off in a corner, which will not fail to be sufficient (*bastant*), although it may be concise. (III. 9, 761)

What can be the nature of such a "word"? How can a word be said to be "sufficient"? Further, what must the power of a word be to give us a text as fragmented as an essay on the principle of its organization and justify its motley appearance? This is clarified in another text, where Montaigne deals with the unity so characteristic of the essayistic work:

> My book is *always one*. Except that at each new edition, so that the buyer may not come off completely empty-handed, *I allow myself to add, since it is only an ill-fitted patchwork, some supernumerary emblems*. (III. 9, 736, emphasis mine)

Once more Montaigne gives us to understand in the form of a paradox the specificity of the unity of his *Essays*: the book is always one and yet it is an "ill-fitted patchwork." The "soldering" (*soudume*)—a favorite term in Montaigne—is always lacking, and yet the essay is not constituted in an arbitrary manner: somewhere, there is always a "sufficient word" (*mot bastant*), a "concise" word, a "supernumerary emblem" that enables the essay to function as a totality and gives it its unity. But the "sufficient word" is not the latent or original meaning that one can always end up finding again with a little "attentiveness"; it is a "paradoxical element" of the "Snark" or "Jabberwocky" type: it is a complicated word—that is, a word that *complicates* stories, *envelops* significations, conceals riches that no preconceived notion will ever subsume. The "sufficient" word is a Pandora's box from which anything and everything may escape, but whose contents can never be known in advance. For this reason, its potentialities can be deployed only by means of certain *literary strategies*, certain ways in which stories and thoughts are brought together in a montage.

To situate in a theoretical context what we understand by the expressions "sufficient word" or "supernumerary emblem," we may turn to the concept elaborated by Giles Deleuze, under the categories of the *dark precursor* or *Differentiator*, in his *Différence et Répétition*. "Every system," Deleuze writes, "contains its dark precursor that assures communication between border series. . . . In every case it is a matter of knowing how the precursor exercises this role" (156–157). A little further on, Deleuze adds: "We call *disparate* [*dispars*] the dark precursor, this *difference in itself* (to the second degree) that brings into relation the series that are themselves heterogeneous or disparate. In each instance, its space of displacement and its process of disguise are what determine the relative magnitude of the differences brought into relation."

Now, a careful reading of Montaigne's texts will show that there is nothing less arbitrary than the choice of *titles* or "words" that Montaigne assembles in order to submit them to multiple variations. Contrary to Jasinski, who sees arbitrariness in Montaigne's choice of titles, I would be inclined to say that nothing is more essential to the play of the text (in other instances this can be a word or notion constantly running through the text: "experience," "coach," etc.) than the choice of a given title—but with the essential reservation that such a "title" no longer acts through its *identity*, whether the identity be "nominal" or "homonymic." Indeed, as frequently occurs in Montaigne, the title no longer appears as the identity of a signified, of an "obviated' theme, but, according to Deleuze's rigorous formulation, as the "differentiator" of distinct signifieds, which "*secondarily* produce an effect of resemblance of the signifieds as an effect of identity in the signifier" (ibid.)—and, I might add, in the word, notion, or title. In Montaigne—at least as I read him with reference to Deleuze—the "differentiator" in question may equally well be called "sufficient word," "concise word," or "supernumerary emblem" because these words and emblems" play identical roles in the economy of a Montaignan text.

Take as an example the essay entitled "Of Drunkenness" (II. 2)—the majority of Montaigne's essays could be similarly analyzed. Between the *signifying* series of "vices" and the *signified* series of different types of "intoxication" that Montaigne, seemingly improvising, parades before us, no equality, no semantic identity is established: of the two series paired by the dark precursor "drunkenness," one always exceeds or stimulates the indeterminate character of the other. Better: the respective determinations of each series are constantly exchanged with those of the others without ever reaching equilibrium. To put it another way: no prior definition of "vice" can ever exhaust the indefinite "variety" of figures (and effects) of intoxication. Without the potency of the esoteric word "intoxication," the essay—the text of this essay—would have been impossible. But this is because the text is literally nourished by the gap (écart)—or, if you prefer, the (irreducible, generative) difference—that the word "drunkenness" establishes by assembling a multitude of themes that without it could never have been brought together. Faced with the infinite variety of figures assumed by "intoxication," where can we *pigeonhole*, how above all we can *qualify* the given forms it may take: intoxication that is *poetic*, or *prophetic*, and so on? Clearly, it is not enough to assert that the essay is a mode of incompletion or simply that it is "informal": this is the same illusion that leads us to say that a text does not belong to any *genre* and to accept the existing genres as necessary forms. It is not by its rhetorical deficiency, but rather by the excess of forms it brings into play, that the essay invents the *form* in which, as I shall seek to demonstrate, it plays in its turn the role of "precursor"—that is to say, in which, by mobilizing the resources of multiple genres at the same time, it provokes, as Barthes puts it, a veritable "mutation" of the modern text. Here is the first part of the answer to the question of the essay's unity: the "sufficient" word can in no way be dissociated from the series (of stories, examples, maxims, dialogues, poems, and the rest) that it puts into play. The very logic of the paradoxical and sufficient word is to render obsolete and insignificant the rhetorical question of the beginning and the end, the before and the after, as prerequisite to any possible narration or discourse. Moreover, in this logic of the "sufficient" word, the rhetorical frontier separating the proper meaning from the figural, the metaphorical from the literal, and above all, the narrative from the discursive, no longer exists. In an essay, one can think and "discourse" with stories, poems, metaphors, and myths. The "sufficient" word always plays on at least two series of heterogeneous significations, making them resonate and communicate without, however, being their cause; it complicates things by multiplying stories, and within them, it brings about new distinctions by having each series branch into new series of other stories.

Now it can be seen why the logic of the essay is a logic of *complicatio*: through a paradoxical word heterogeneous series are put into communication and made to resonate without being subsumed. But there will always be a hiatus between the series, and only the "sufficient" word will maintain a connection between them. The starting point is the genre of "words"—"drunkenness", "cripple," and the rest—though the essayist is interested not in their meaning but in the "worlds" they enclose. Thus the essay takes on a given scope, follows a given path, etc., proportional to the subjects that are "complicated" in this way. Its entire "organization"—as well as its effects—depends on this. Thus it is a false problem to look for the plan of an essay. Finding a coherent one—which is not at all impossible—can happen only by chance.

There is one pitfall to be avoided: it is possible to give the "sufficient word" an identity and simplicity that distort comprehension of the overall mechanism at work in the essay. With the "sufficient word," contrary to what happens for a concept, stories remain complicated at the same time that series continue to be separated. And regardless of the operations effected on the basis of a paradoxical word, it does not cease to complicate those series it brings into relation, despite their heterogeneity, and to multiply their significations. The flash of light is always apparent, but not the "dark precursor" that announces it. More specifically: this type of "dark precursor," the "sufficient word," is sought after in order to complicate things, and not to simplify them or lessen their import. The aim is not to make the reader's task easier, but rather to teach how to decipher the signification of words that spring out of chaos and the "perpetual movement" of all things. It is for this reason that the essay is drawn to images and metaphors. For this reason, it can only manifest itself—in every sense of the term—through fragments:

> I do not want a man to use his strength making me attentive and to shout at me fifty times: "*Or oyez!*" ["Now listen"] in the manner of our heralds. The Romans used to say in their religion "*Hoc age*" [Give Heed"], as we say in ours "*Sursum corda*" ["Lift up your hearts:]: these are so many words lost on me. (II. 10, 301)

The essayist wants "to deal with people who themselves have told themselves this (to 'give heed'); or who, if they have their '*Hoc age*,' have a substantial one with a body of its own" (ibid., 302). The "simple and artless" style that Montaigne defends will be that which "strikes": "difficult rather than boring, remote from affectation, irregular, disconnected, and bold: each bit making a body in itself; not pedantic, not monkish, not lawyer-like, but rather soldierly" (I. 26, 127). The problem of the compositional originality of an essay is not resolved by changing the title, by drastically carving up the text, or by having recourse to psychologemes! Suppressing or simply changing the title of an essay such as "Of Coaches" only discards a bothersome word: what makes up the unity of the text is broken; it is reduced to formless *patchwork*.

THE ESSAY

Among all the terms that relate to the literary genres, the word Essay is certainly the one that has given rise to the most confusion in the history of literature; since Montaigne used the term to describe his writings, "essay" has served to designate works that are so diverse from a formal point of view, and so heterogeneous from a thematic point of view, that it has become practically impossible to subsume a single, definitive type of text under this term. Since the 17th century, the lexeme *Essay* has been used to describe any prose text of medium length wherein an informal tone prevails and the author does not attempt an exhaustive treatment. This meaning goes back to the first edition of the *Dictionnaire de l'Academie* (1798): "This is still said of certain works called thus either by modesty or because the author did not propose to explore in depth the subject he treats." And, in fact, in contrast to the *Treatise* or *Summa*, Essay constantly refers to a wide variety of works that have nothing in common but the absence of system and a relative "brevity."

"Essays" are to be found in nearly all fields and all periods: in physics for example (*Essai sur la nature de l'air*, Mariotte, 1676), and also in botany (*Essays élémentaires sur la botanique*, J.J. Rousseau, 1771), in mineralogy (*Essai de mineralogie des Monts-Pyrenees*, Abbé Pelasson, 1781), in mathematics (*Essai philosophique sur les probabilités*, Laplace, 1814) and quite obviously, in poetics (*L'air et le songes, Essai sur l'imagination du mouvement*, Gaston Bachelard, 1947) and in philosophy (*Essay on Human Understanding*, John Locke, among hundreds of others, 1690).

Today, the word Essay is still used to describe the most diverse and sometimes the most contradictory genres: under the Essay rubric are ranged autobiographical text, memoirs, journals, critical studies—exemplified by Sartre's *Situations* or Butor's *Repertoire(s)*—and even dialogues—for example, those of Plato or Diderot. Lukács's *Soul and Form* includes even Schopenhauer's *Parerga* and practically all Kierkegaard's works within this category. Indeed, for a very long time, if a prose text represented a relatively personal point of view on any subject, it was automatically classified as an Essay.

Though infatuation for this term and its borrowing for the denomination of other genres is not unconnected with the considerable success and influence of Montaigne's *Essais* (1580–588), it was not Montaigne who gave this term all the meanings it has carried since the Middle Ages. Coming from the Latin *exagium*, which signified both *exact weighing* and, by extension, *ordeal*, then *examination*, the lexeme *Essai* and the verb *Essaier* 'to try' already existed in commonly used locutions such as *faire l'essai* 'try out' or *mettre a l'essai* 'put to the test'. We know what Montaigne has made of this word and we can easily guess what philosophers, scholars, and writers will derive from it after the Renaissance: with the emergence of "experimental science" and philosophical taste for the concrete "obser-vation" of "facts," a word like "essay" will become a most useful and pre-cious term. A polysemic word par excellence, "essay" can designate at one and the same time a trial (experimental, moral, physical), an examination (of conscience or of resources) and an exercise, an athletic trial: thus, in the story of *Petit Jehan de Saintré*, we find: "to play ball, throw bars, rocks and fiery stakes, and all other essays" (Hamel 1959). The verb *essaier* 'to try', for its part, is also used in the language of corporations which de-mand that after six years of apprenticeship a worker must be *essaié* 'tried', that is, *judged* by the jury. *Essaier* is thus *mettre à l'essai* 'put to the test' and also, at the same time, *faire l'essai* (*l'experience*) *de, éprouver, et subir:* 'try out (experience), put to the test, and suffer' (Hamel, ibid.). Therefore, it is not surprising to see this term describe such heterogeneous "works," from the Renaissance to our own time: to write an Essay, it is enough to avoid a learned tone, to keep it "short," and to propose putting something (an idea, body, thing) to the test of one's own reflection.

As can be seen, use of the substantive "Essay" does not raise a major difficulty: insofar as it depends upon the decision—if not arbitrary, at least *contingent*—of a writer, it represents a historical event that one cannot help but ratify. On the other hand, the creation of the *genre* of Essay by Montaigne was not accomplished without problems. A unique case in the annals of literature, the Essay is the only literary genre to have resisted in-tegration, until quite recently, in the taxonomy of genres. No other genre ever raised so many theoretical problems concerning the origin and defi-nition of its Form: an atopic genre or, more precisely, an *eccentric* one insofar as it seems to flirt with all the genres without ever letting itself be pinned down, the literary essay such as Montaigne bequeathed it to posterity has always had a special status. No doubt, by virtue of the mul-tiplicity of contradictory principles governing its organization—the pace "by leaps and gambols" of its style, the absence of a unique or unified sub-ject, its philosophical "incompleteness," its disrespect for the rhetorical norms of plan and progression, (in short, of composition)—Montaigne's *Essays* have not ceased to be the object of a mechanism of "disavowal" that historically has taken the following form: on the one hand, devalorization and rejection: "The essay is a degenerate, impossible genre, not very serious and even dangerous" (the attitude of Pascal and Malebranche, for example); and on the other hand, valorization and reappropriation: "Moreover, this belongs to me and I have always said so" (such is the attitude of Gide or Valéry). What is remarkable here is that in a systematic fashion the first argument generally bears on the "form" of the Essay and the second on its "content" (Boase 1935). This helps explain why the study of Montaigne's *Essays*—and through them, that of Genre—has always comprised two movements that have not always blended: a time in which the *philosophical* point of view prevailed (What is Montaigne's "thought"?) and one in which the *formal* and *generic* point of view dominated instead. As we know, if the first question received an incalculable number of "answers," the second was never directly taken into account until relatively recently. Indeed, if the much debated "thought" of Montaigne seems comparatively well "understood" today, the form of the genre and certain "supernumerary" and eccentric effects that it still enables the essay to produce at the expense of the most scrupulous commentator, continue to be the object of open debate.

In the books where the question of genre is tackled head on, the appearance of the Essay and its mode of organization are usually related to the general context from which the *Essays* emerged. The by now classic example of this type of approach is that of Pierre Villey (*Les sources et l'evolution des "Essays" de Montaigne*, 1908), who, analyzing the cultural and philosophical environment of the period when Montaigne composed his *Essays* makes them derivative of the multitude of genres and subgenres that were still in fashion during the Renaissance: the *Adages* and *Apophtegmes* of Erasmus, the *Lectiones antigua* of Caellius Rhodiginus, the *Golden Letters* of Guevara, as well as the mass of compilations, commentaries, Lessons and *Moralia* that dominated the intellectual scene. In such a context, the *Essays* appear as the reaction, "in an overflowing century" (Montaigne), of the Renaissance man to the slightly dusty picture of classical Antiquity: it would be a matter of "making a new inventory," of taking new bearings and making a fresh start in thought. It is the existence of these "genres" that would explain, among other things, the variety of forms and the multiplicity of themes that traverse Montaigne's *Essays*: here, the Essay appears "incomplete" and "not composed" only to the "modern" mind. The Essay does not arise from a literary void, but from a "literary field" that has disappeared.

Much the same idea is found in Hugo Friedrich (1968), for whom the

Essay appears as the manifestation of an "anti-scholastic" movement of liberation that explains and favors the emergence and triumph of the "open form" and the "taste for mélanges."

Though such an approach can quite obviously account for a given thematic or stylistic aspect of the Essay, it nonetheless remains fundamentally extrinsic and far too descriptive. It is better at showing that which, in the Essay, belongs to other genres, than in concretely presenting what belongs to it alone.

In a more recent study, focusing on the history and the form of the Essay genre—which he assimilates to the more general notion of *self-portrait*—Michel Beaujoir (1980) has tried to surmount these theoretical difficulties. He convincingly shows that, despite its incontestable utility, this type of interpretation nevertheless misses the essential: namely, the importance of the *rhetorical practice* in existence at the time the Essay first appeared. For Beaujoir, that the essay could be regarded for so long as a discourse without "origin" and "without precedent" is less because the contemporaneous sub-genres and the Essay's supposed transformation of them have been forgotten than because modern criticism has "repressed" the rhetorical "matrix" that conditioned the mode of functioning and the organization of *all* the genres of the Renaissance. It is this dimension that would explain, among other things, the *timeless* and *utopic* character of the Essay; standing out against the background of an absent structure stemming from the Commonplaces (*Loci*) of rhetorical *Inventio* and rhetorical Memory, it always reflects a "phantasm of community foreign to history" and a "subject" that is impersonal and transhistoric.

Hence the permanence of the Esasy's *themes*—it is the Book of the Self confronting Value, the Imaginary, the Ideological, and the eternal return of Stupidity; hence the persistence of the Figures (*Figura*): Desire, bliss, Death, the Body, Grief, Time, the Symbolic, etc. Thus, from Saint Augustine's *Confessions* to *Roland Barthes by Roland Barthes*, by way of Rousseau's *Reveries* or Nietzsche's *Ecce Homo*, if we do not always apprehend the *same* man, it is always the same "type of memory, both very archaic and very modern, by which the events of an individual life are eclipsed by the recollection of an entire culture" (Beaujour 1977). The "disorder" and the absence of philosophical completeness in the Essay are, in the final analysis, only apparent: distracted by Montaigne's anti-rhetorical attitude or by the modern (narcissistic) "prejudice" that makes us favor the *topoi* of "psychoanalytic vulgate" to the detriment of rhetorical *topoi*, we take for "poetic license" and radical originality what in reality is heavily coded. An adequate rhetoric is what we lack: the Essay is gibberish without origin only for those without Memory.

Less *empirical* in its proceedings, this approach permits us to render a better account of the most salient features of this "impossible" genre, the Essay, but it is not certain that it escapes the "reflex of reduction" (Sollers) that characterizes the other types of analyses. The Essay is, once more, related to a unique "origin," a unique "source." In other words, if it is true that when one negatively or privatively defines the Essay as an "incomplete" text, without order, etc., one only perpetuates the misunderstanding of the influence of rhetorical schemas; and if consequently it is necessary to return to these "sources," it nonetheless remains true that the Essay is not confined to pure and simple *repetition* of these schemas: a text that is not in appearance rhetorically "composed," the Essay is nonetheless a "constituted" text on the formal plane. Consequently, rather than merely taking an inventory of what it *owes* to Rhetoric, one must also *show at the same time* what it has done with this inheritance. Therefore, it is important to raise the capital problem of the *general economy* of the essayistic text insofar as it constitutes a specific "work" and insofar as it has at its disposal an "operatory" power (Galay 1977) that is not homogeneous *with any preconceived rhetorical schema.*

Having renounced the economy of the philosophical "system" commanded by the idea of Mastery, and having dismissed the economy of Literary Genres insofar as it commands the ordered exchange of the different modes of enunciation (narration or discourse), the Essay appears historically as one of the rare literary texts whose apparent principal task was to provoke a "generalized collapse" of the economies of the rhetorically coded text: in fact, what is most important to the essayist is neither the problem of *Invention*: finding something to say; nor that of rhetorical *Disposition*: putting in order what has been found (Barthes 1970); nor that of *Knowledge*: speaking of Being, Truth, etc.; but, finally, that of *Complication*. As Barthes says, in the spirit of Montaigne, it is a question "with intellectual things . . . of combining . . . *at the same time* theory, critical combat, and pleasure" (Barthes 1975). That is, outside the "presentative synthesis" that rhetoric offers and outside the philosophical system or Treatise ("closed," "monosemic," and "dogmatic"), there remains, for the one who has renounced all Mastery, the possibility of a writing as "procedure," or as Barthes puts it a "tactics without strategy" (Barthes, ibid.). Together with the outlines, the written exercises, and the fussy precisions of composition, the entire "scene" of language as a warlike *Topos* and battlefield (of Faculties and Theses) is "gone beyond" in a deporting movement. Indeed, what offers food for thought, what allows us to experiment with the Essay as writing, as a unique Form, is the possibility of a "plural" text made up of multiple networks "that interact without any one of them being able to dominate the others": an "ideal" text that neither assumes an ultimate signified nor merely repeats the Same, but is a "galaxy of signifiers . . . it has no beginning; it is reversible; we gain access to it by several entrances, none of which can be authoritatively declared to be the main one" (Barthes 1970). In this sense, the Essay refers less to the genres and to the rhetorical repertoire—these are only two of the possible "entrances"—than to the power (*dunamis*) of the specific "procedures" that it brings into play in order to elaborate its rhetoric and to produce its effects (Galay, ibid.).

Born *practically* and *aesthetically* with Montaigne, and reappearing sporadically in the history of literature (Beaujour 1980), the Essay still had to be born *theoretically*: with essayists like Nietzsche (for example *Ecce Homo*, the *Gay Science*), Paul Valéry (*Les Cahiers* or *Rhumbs* and *Tel Quel*) and above all recently with Roland Barthes, this genre judged "unclassifiable" for a long time, was finally able to make its "theoretical entrance" into the history of literature and the theory of literary genres.

WORKS CITED

Barthes, Roland. 1970. *S/Z*. Paris: Seuil, coll. "Tel Quel."

————. 1975. *Roland Barthes par Roland Barthes*. Paris: Seuil, coll. "Ecrivains de Toujours."

Beaujour, Michel. 1977. Autobiographie et autoportrait. *Poétique* 32, November.

————. 1981. *Miroirs d'encre, rhétorique de l'autoportrait*. Paris: Seuil.

Boase, Alan M. 1935. *The Fortunes of Montaigne: A History of the Essays in France, 1580–1669*. London: Methuen.

Friedrich, Hugo. 1975. *Montaigne*. Paris: Gallimard.

Galay, Jean Louis. 1977. Problèmes de l'oeuvre fragmentaire: Valéry. *Poetic* 31, September.

Hamle, S. 1959. "Expérience-Essai": Contribution à l'étude du vocabulaire de Montaigne. *Bibliothèque de la Société des Amis de Montaigne*, July–December: 20–32.

de Montagine, Michel. 1957. *The Complete Works of Montaigne: Essays, Travel Journals, Letters*. Trans. Donald Frame. Palo Alto: Stanford University Press.

CARL H. KLAUS
....

ESSAYISTS ON THE ESSAY [1989]

Five years ago, I set out to design a graduate course on the nature of
the essay, a course in which I hoped to engage students in a theoretical
investigation of the form. As a preliminary part of my planning, I went
off to the library and the MLA Bibliography to compile a reading list, only
to discover that I was venturing into territory that literary and rhetorical
theorists had barely set foot on, much less explored in any systematic way.
Oh yes, I found learned studies of Montaigne, Addison and Steele, Lamb,
the eighteenth-century periodical essay, the Romantic personal essay, the
modern essay. But the essay itself, the whole territory—its boundaries, its
terrain, its deep interior—that was a place only a few scholars had chosen
to visit. It remains almost as uncharted today, except for a lengthy review
article by Chadbourne, documenting how little has been done not only in
America, but also in England and on the Continent, to map the world of
the essay and develop a theory of its form. So it is that I decided to consult
the essayists themselves as an alternative source of commentary on the
form.

At the beginning of my search, I already had on hand several passages
and pieces about the essay, from Johnson's dictionary definition of it as "a
loose sally of the mind" to White's celebration of it as the "excursion" of "a
self-liberated mart" (vii), so I had reason to hope that I might find several
more. Since that time, I have collected material by some forty essayists, as
varied as Montaigne, Bacon, Addison, Johnson, Hazlitt, Lamb, Thoreau,
Howells, Lukacs, Woolf, Priestley, Chesterton, Krutch, Daiches, Huxley,
Adorno, Kazin, Hoagland, White, Thomas, Gass, and Hardwick. Some of
their comments are as brief as Bacon's aphorisms, some as ample as the
habitual digressions of Montaigne. Some of their remarks come in the
form of prefaces, others in the form of reviews. But most of their commentary is to be found in essays entirely devoted to the essay. The essay
on the essay, it would seem, is a subgenre itself, as Hilaire Belloc implied
when he wrote "An Essay upon Essays upon Essays."

All in all, these self-reflexive statements and pieces engage a wide range
of issues and problems concerning the purpose of the essay, the subject

matter of the essay, the form of the essay, the length of the essay, the variety of the essay, the essay and other forms of writing, the style of the essayist, the voice of the essayist, the personality of the essayist, the mind of the essayist, the knowledge of the essayist, the composing process of the essayist, the essayist and the reader, the essayist and the culture, the essayist and the journalist, the essayist and the critic, the essayist and the scholar, the essayist and truth. Varied as the essayists are in the topics they discuss, the contexts of their discourse, and the backgrounds they bring to the discussion, they seem to me to hold surprisingly similar ideas about the essay—ideas strikingly at odds with notions of it that are purveyed by most literary guidebooks and composition textbooks.

The harmony I perceive in their thinking first caught my attention when I noticed a tendency among essayists from every period and culture to define the essay, or their own essayistic practice, by setting it off against highly conventionalized and systematized forms of writing, such as rhetorical, scholarly, or journalistic discourse. So, too, I repeatedly found them invoking images and metaphors suggestive of the essay's naturalness, openness, or looseness as opposed to the methodicality, regularity, and strictly ordered quality of conventional prose discourse. Montaigne, of course, is the first to make such a contrast: "The scholars distinguish and mark off their ideas more specifically and in detail. I, who cannot see beyond what I have learned from experience, without any system, present my ideas in a general way, and tentatively. As in this: I speak my meaning in disjointed parts. . ." (824). Given Montaigne's well known commitment to follow "my natural and ordinary pace, however off the track it is," "to let myself go as I am" (297), to "seek out change indiscriminately" (761), it was hardly surprising to me that he should make such a contrast between the scholars and himself, between their "system" and his "disjointed parts." But Montaigne's "disjointed parts" also led me to think of the phrases that Bacon uses to describe his aphoristic essays—"dispersed meditations" (239) and "fragments of my conceites" (238)—phrases which suggest that at least in describing their essayistic practice these two might not be quite so different as they are often made out to be. Indeed, in The Advancement of Learning, Bacon concludes a brisk defense of aphoristic over methodical writing with a pithy antithesis which makes clear that for him, as for Montaigne, the essay is neither a mode of proof, nor of persuasion, but of inquiry: "And lastly, aphorisms, representing a knowledge broken, do invite men to inquire further; whereas methods, carrying the show of a total, do secure men, as if they were at furthest" (173).

Montaigne, admittedly, is concerned with reflecting his own process of in-quiry, whereas Bacon aims to provoke inquiry in others. Yet both essayists describe their practice in terms that emphatically distinguish essayistic form and purpose from the methodical discourse that dominated classical rhetoric and medieval scholasticism.

The persistence, indeed the codification, of this contrast can be seen in a surprising statement from one of Addison's *Spectator* papers: "Among my Daily-Papers, which I bestow on the Publick, there are some which are written with Regularity and Method, and others that run out into the Wildness of those Compositions, which go by the Name of Essays" (IV 186). When I first read this passage, I was struck by the sharpness with which Addison formulates the distinction between "Regularity and Method" on the one hand, and "Wildness" on the other, as well as by the detail with which he develops the contrast in the remainder of the piece. But a later reading led me to see that this brief passage also contains a notable revelation—that, contrary to prevailing descriptions of his work, Addison does not classify all of his *Spectator* papers as essays. Anything "written with Regularity and Method," as indicates elsewhere, he consid-ers to be "a Set Discourse" (II: 465); thus he only applies "the name of *Es-says*" to papers that "run out into . . . Wildness." Addison's keen awareness of the differences in his two kinds of papers can be seen in the clear-cut contrast he draws between the composing processes he follows in each case: "As for the first, I have the whole Scheme of the Discourse in Mind, before I set Pen to Paper. In the other kind of Writing, it is sufficient that I have several Thoughts on a Subject, without troubling myself to range them in such order, that they may seem to grow out of one another, and be disposed under the proper Heads" (IV: 186). And to solidify the contrast, he identifies the precedents for each type: "*Seneca* and *Montaigne* are pat-terns of writing in this last Kind, as *Tully* and *Aristotle* excel in the other" (IV: 186). Indeed, given his neoclassical bias, Addison goes on to make a detailed case for "Methodical Discourse," arguing that in this form an author's "thoughts are more intelligible and better discover their Drift and Meaning . . . than when they are thrown together without Order and Connexion" (IV: 186). The firmness with which Addison distinguished between his two types of *Spectator* papers can be seen in an earlier formu-lation of virtually the same contrast: "When I make Choice of a Subject that has not been treated of by others, I throw together my Reflections on it without any Order or Method, so that they may appear rather in the Looseness and Freedom of an Essay than in the Regularity of a Set Discourse" (II: 465). Here, too, as in the other discussion of his composing process, Addison reveals that despite his neoclassical allegiance to "Order or Method," he knows enough from his firsthand experience of writing to acknowledge that the essay allows him the "Freedom" to explore ideas, to engage material "that has not been treated of by others."

Having put together this small segment in a history of ideas of the essay, I realized that Johnson's well-known dictionary definition, though often cited as a striking invention, is actually an ingenious condensation of received ideas about its form. Johnson's complete definition, in fact, concludes with an antithesis that closely echoes Addison's version of the contrast, as well as Addison's neoclassical preference for methodical discourse: "an irregular, indigested piece, not a regular, orderly performance." But Johnson, too, is so widely experienced a writer that when he turns to thinking about the essay in detail, at the opening of a piece for *The Rambler*, he also recognizes the special advantages of the essay over methodical forms of writing:

The writer of essays escapes many embarrassments to which a large work would have exposed him; he seldom harasses his reason with long trains of consequences, dims his eyes with the perusal of anti- quated volumes, or burthens his memory with great accumulations of preparatory knowledge. A careless glance upon a favourite author, or transient survey of the varieties of life, is sufficient to supply the first hint or seminal idea, which enlarged by the gradual accretion of mat- ter stored in the mind, is by the warmth of fancy easily expanded into flowers, and sometimes ripened into fruit. (201)

Indeed, as if to enact this stylized vision of an essay's accidental, easy and natural gestation—from a "careless glance" to a "seminal idea" to a "ripened . . . fruit"—Johnson expands his seminal idea about the essay into two paragraphs of reflection on the unpredictable and uncontrollable aspects of essay writing, which in turn lead into a meditative essay on the uncertainties of life.

By this point in my story, it might seem that the contrast itself has become so conventionalized as to be a mere commonplace, a convenient but largely formulaic way of writing about the essay or launching an es- say upon some other subject. Yet, its persistence over so long a period of time—not only from Montaigne to Johnson, but from Johnson to the present—suggests that it must contain a significant element of truth, or belief, or value for those who invoke it. In this case, it seems to be an inescapable, even imperative, way for these essayists to define and affirm what they also refer to as the "freedom" of the essay—its independence from the strictures and structures that govern other forms of discourse. Their preoccupation with this quality is reflected in the numerous synonyms and metaphors for freedom that pervade their comments. Howells, for example, refers to the essay's "essential liberty" (802), Chesterton to its "leisure and liberty" (2), Williams to its "infinite fracture" (323), Kazin to its "open form" (ix), Hoagland to its "extraordinary flexibility" (27), Lopate to its "wonderfully tolerant form" (1), Epstein to its "generous boundaries" (34), and Hardwick to its "open spaces" (xiv). By persistently invoking such expansive phrases along with such a sharp contrast, these essayists seem to be conceiving of the essay as a unique genre—a form of writing whose distinguishing characteristic is its freedom from any governing aspect of form. Strictly speaking, then, they seem to be portraying it as an antigenre, a rogue form of writing in the universe of discourse. Or as Adorno puts it, "the law of the innermost form of the essay is heresy" (171).

This conception of the essay, as antigenre, can also be seen in a very pointed contrast between the essay and the article that has dominated the thinking of essayists throughout the twentieth century. So pervasive is this distinction in their commentary that it seems to have the status for them of a self-evident truth. The earliest explicit use of it that I have been able to find occurs in a column by Howells, dating from 1902, in which he laments the time "when the essay began to confuse itself with the article, and to assume an obligation to premises and conclusions" (802). Though Howells does not venture to say when the change took place, he clearly contrasts the article's "premises and conclusions" with the essay's "wandering airs of thought" (802). This echoing of the persistent dichotomy between methodical and natural discourse, between strict and open form, can also be heard in more recent versions of the contrast between essay and article. Krutch, for example, calls the essay "manmade as opposed to the machine-made article" (19); Hoagland, in a similar spirit, asserts that "Essays don't usually boil down to a summary, as articles do, and the style of the writer has a 'nap' to it, a combination of personality and originality and energetic loose ends that stand up like the nap on a piece of wool and can't be brushed flat" (25–26). As these examples suggest, the contrast of essay and article is often defined in terms of a dichotomy between organic and mechanistic form, and, by extension as an epitome of the conflict between humanistic and technological values.

The point of contrast that arouses modern essayists more than any other, however, is the distinction they make between the personal orientation of the essay and the factual orientation of the article. As Weeks puts it, the essay "does not deal in statistics or belabor an argument as does a magazine article. . . . The essay is an experience which you the reader share with the writer—you share his laughter, delight, or pity; you share a deepened understanding or a quickening of the spirit in a style that does not date" (81). In one form or another, this particular dichotomy is discussed more intensely and at greater length than any other issue they engage. Some of the intensity can be traced to the fact that modern essayists have perennially witnessed editors and readers being lured away from the essay by the utilitarian appeal of the article. Indeed, as early as 1881, Stephen considered "our magazines and journals" to be so "radically changed" that it was "easier to write about essay-writing than to write an essay oneself" (65). With the onset of World War I, and the numerous economic, political, and social upheavals that followed, magazine editors found themselves compelled to satisfy a persistent demand for highly informed articles about the most pressing and complex issues of the day. By the early 1930s, the changing editorial policies had become so widespread that essayists such as Gerould openly spoke out against "the spectacle of the old-line magazines forsaking their literary habit, and stuffing us month after month, with facts, figures, propaganda, and counter-propaganda . . ." (Information 393). By the early 1950s, Krutch considered the situation to be so far gone that "The very word essay . . . is avoided with horror, and anything which is not fiction is usually called either an 'article,' a 'story,' or just 'a piece'" (18).

The essayists' quarrel with the article, though obviously provoked in part by the competition for magazine space, seems to be rooted in their opposition to the fact-dominated conception of knowledge they perceive in the article. This opposition is reflected in their tendency to portray the article as being so heavily made up of "facts," "figures," and "statistics" that it allows no room for the personal experience, personal thought, or personal voice of the essayist. Given this extreme dichotomy, they depict the article, in turn, as being out of touch with human concerns. As Knitch puts it, "The magazines are full of articles dealing statistically with, for example, the alleged failure or success of marriage. Lawyers discuss the law, sociologists publish statistics, and psychologists discuss case histories," but "one man's 'familiar essay' on love and marriage might get closer to some all-important realities than any number of 'studies' could" (19). Krutch's remarks also reveal that their skepticism is aroused not so much by a scorn of facts per se as by a distrust of specialized "studies," whose heavy reliance on factual information they regard as symptomatic of an ill-placed confidence in the reliability of highly systematized—and thus highly impersonal—approaches to knowledge. Ultimately, then, they seem to be implying that the article embodies a naively positivistic approach to knowledge, an approach that fails to recognize the essentially problematical nature of things. Gass is especially emphatic on this score in his satiric portrait of the scholarly article: "It must appear complete and straightforward and footnoted and useful and certain and is very likely a veritable Michelin of misdirection; for the article pretends that everything is clear, that its argument is unassailable, that there are no soggy patches, no illicit inferences, no illegitimate connections . . . In keeping with his attack on the certitudes of the article, Gass portrays the essay by contrast as having a disinterested engagement in the play of ideas, and thus as making no special claims about the truth of its observations: "The essay is unhurried (although Bacon's aren't); it browses among books; it enjoys an idea like a fine wine; it thumbs through things. It turns round and round upon its topic, exposing this aspect and then that; proposing possibilities, reciting opinions, disposing of prejudice and even of the simple truth itself—as too undeveloped, not yet of an interesting age" (25). This conception of the essay, as embodying an inherently skeptical, and therefore antimethodical, approach to knowledge, is most fully developed by Adorno, who offers a seemingly inexhaustible set of variations on the theme of the essay's "heresy":

> Luck and play are essential to the essay (152). The essay does not obey the rules of the game of organized science . . . the essay does not strive for closed, deductive or inductive, construction (158). As the essay denies any primeval givens, so it refuses any definitions of its concepts (159). In the essay, concepts do not build a continuum of operations, thought does not advance in a single direction, rather the aspects of the argument interweave as in a carpet (160). The essay . . . proceeds so to speak methodically unmethodically (161). Discontinuity is essential to the essay (164).

Radical as these statements are in their rebellion against any systematized form of thought, they are, I think, no more extreme than Montaigne's contrast between the "system" of "the scholars" and his "disjointed parts," or than Johnson's contrast between the scholar's "long train of consequences" and the essayist's "fancy." Indeed, the continuity of their thought is reflected in Adorno's equation of "the neopositivists," whom he opposes, "with Scholasticism," to which Montaigne contrasted himself (160). Whereas both the neopositivists and scholastics adhere to "the traditional concept of method," the essay, according to Adorno, "takes the anti-systematic impulse into its own procedure" (160). So, the history of ideas of the essay comes full circle, and in doing so it calls attention, I believe, to the essayists' profound motive for persistently drawing so sharp a contrast between the essay and methodical prose discourse. By virtue of being free from the systematized form of such discourse, the essay offers a means of liberating the essayist from the systematized form of thinking imposed by such discourse. Thus, Montaigne declares "My Style and my mind alike go roaming" (761). So, too, Hoagland asserts that "because essays are directly concerned with the mind and the mind's idiosyncracy, the very freedom the mind possesses is bestowed on this branch of literature that does honor to it, and the fascination of the mind is the fascination of the essay" (27). Ultimately, then, the essayists seem to conceive of the essay as a place of intellectual refuge, a domain sacred to the freedom of the mind itself.

Given this conception, some readers, I imagine, must be wondering how essayists account for the formal essay—that type of prose in which "the author," according to Abrams, "writes as an authority, or at least as highly knowledgeable, and expounds the subject in an orderly way." Surprising as it may be, this long-honored subgenre, which repeatedly turns up in literary handbooks, histories, and encyclopedias, does not seem to figure in the thinking of essayists, not even in the thinking of Hazlitt and Stephen, who survey the work of their predecessors and thus might be inclined to organize their surveys in terms of a distinction between it and the informal essay. In fact, this commonplace distinction is discussed only by Lopate, and he brings it up only to call it into question, noting that "it is difficult even now to draw a firm distinction between the two, because elements of one often turn up in the other, and because most of the great essayists were adept at both modes" (1). The closest that any of the others comes to making such a distinction is when Epstein mentions in passing that "there are formal essays and familiar essays" (27), or when Smith declares that "Bacon is the greatest of the serious and stately essayists—Montaigne the greatest of the garrulous and communicative"

(40), or when Huxley distinguishes among three different kinds of essays—those that focus primarily on "the personal and the autobiographical," those that turn their attention outward to the "concrete-particular" aspects of "some literary or scientific or political theme," and those that "work in the world of high abstractions" (v–vi). But in elaborating their distinctions, neither Smith nor Huxley refers to the "formal" essay, or to any of the logical, systematic, and tightly organized qualities that are usually associated with it. Ultimately, most essayists simply do not recognize such a thing as the formal essay, presumably because it embodies the very antithesis of what they conceive an essay to be. They recognize, of course, that Bacon's manner is highly impersonal, and that he inclines to "work in the world of high abstractions," but they do not seem to think of him as having established a particular type of essay.

Most essayists, in fact, do not tend to classify essays at all, and the few who do make gestures in that direction offer little more than loose classificatory listings, such as Epstein's assertion that "there are literary essays, political essays, philosophical essays, and historical essays" (27), or Hardwick's observation that "most incline to a condition of unexpressed hyphenation: the critical essay, the autobiographical essay, the travel essay, the political—and so on and so on" (xiii). Classifications more rigorous than these would be inconsistent with the essayists' basic view of the essay as being deeply allied to the free play of thought and feeling. Accordingly, Epstein observes that "The essay is in large part defined by the general temperament of the essayist" (27). In keeping with this view, White playfully suggests the hopelessness of trying to classify essays, for, as he sees it, "There are as many kinds of essays as there are human attitudes or poses, as many essay flavors as there are Howard Johnson ice creams" (vii). In much the same spirit, Montaigne conveys the hopelessness of trying to classify human character and behavior: "I do not attempt to arrange this infinite variety of actions, so diverse and so disconnected, into certain types and categories, and distribute my lots and divisions distinctly into recognized classes and sections" (824). As these passages suggest, the antimethodical impulse of essayists probably also has something to do with their tendency to stay away from elaborate systems of classification.

Though they oppose methodical discourse, the essayists are careful to make clear that they consider the essay to be a highly disciplined form of writing. Indeed, their insistence on its freedom from conventionalized form and thought probably makes them all the more intent on dispelling any notion that the essay is a free-for-all form of writing. White is especially pointed on this issue: "And even the essayist's escape from discipline is only a partial escape: the essay, although a relaxed form, imposes its own disciplines, raises its own problems, and these disciplines and problems soon become apparent and (we all hope) act as a deterrent to anyone wielding a pen merely because he entertains random thoughts or is in a happy or wandering mood" (viii). Montaigne, "disjointed" though he professes himself to be, also sounds the same note of caution: "I go out of my way, but rather by license than carelessness. My ideas follow one another, but sometimes it is from a distance, and look at each other, but with a sidelong glance" (761). Even Adorno makes a point of asserting that the essay "is not unlogical; rather it obeys logical criteria in so far as the totality of its sentences must fit together coherently" (169). Each of these passages clearly affirms a belief in coherence, but coherence of an unusual kind, as Montaigne suggests in his playful image of "ideas" that "follow one another . . . from a distance, and look at each other, but with a sidelong glance."

This view of coherence, as Montaigne implies, is based not on mere surface continuity from one statement to the next, but on a deep connection between ideas—on a cohesion so powerful that ideas seem to be animated by an awareness of their affinities to each other no matter how far apart, or how unrelated, they may seem to be. By personifying his ideas in this way, Montaigne is evidently trying to bear witness to the drama of thought itself—a drama in which ideas, like characters, often seem to assume a life of their own, and thus to develop and interact with each other in surprising and fascinating ways. Indeed, Montaigne apparently seeks to encourage just such developments—to "go out of my way, but rather by license than carelessness." In one sense, of course, this explicitly formulated intention may be seen as evidence of Montaigne's dedication to his role as essayist—that is, to essay, to test, to try out, to explore something, in this case his ideas. In another sense, these statements may be seen as confirmation of a desire to write in a way that authentically replicates the natural flow of his thoughts, as borne out by his assertion that "My style and my mind alike go roaming" (761). Yet his statement bespeaks so self-conscious, so deliberate, an intention to "go out of my way" as to be somewhat at odds with the genuinely purposeless or directionless movement implied by the activity of roaming—to be more in keeping with the spirit of Adorno's assertion that the essay "proceeds, so to speak, methodically unmethodically." In fact, in this same set of reflections on his writing, Montaigne reveals what may well be the ultimate motive behind his generally digressive behavior, when he exclaims, "Lord, what beauty there is in these lusty sallies and this variation, and more so the more casual and accidental they seem" (761). The clear implication of this statement, I think, is that Montaigne intends his "roaming," his "lusty sallies," to be seen as an elaborate fiction—as an imitation, rather than an actual replication, of his mind in action. Indeed, in his very next statement, Montaigne declares that "It is the inattentive reader who loses my subject, not I. Some word about it will always be found off in a corner, which will not fail to be sufficient, though it takes little room" (761). So, it would appear that Montaigne is always in control of his thoughts, or aspires to be, letting them roam just enough so that they seem to be as "casual and accidental" as possible, yet keeping them sufficiently in check so that they do ultimately "follow one another" and "look at each other."

I have dwelt on these reflections of Montaigne because they embody a sophisticated conception of essayistic form that is echoed in various ways by subsequent essayists. According to this conception, the essay evidently calls for a delicate set of mental adjustments, attuned both to giving the mind a free rein and to reining it in, so that the form of the essay will appear to reflect the process of a mind in action, but a mind that is always in control of itself no matter how wayward it may seem to be. In other words, the essay is conceived as being based on an idea somewhat akin to the principles of organic form, yet also akin to the principle of artful artlessness. Addison hints at this complex quality when he says that in writing an essay "it is sufficient that I have several Thoughts on a Subject, without troubling my self to range them in such order, that they may seem to grow out of one another, and be disposed under the proper Heads" (IV: 186). Gerould explicitly defines this complex principle when she asserts that "The basis of the essay is meditation, and it must in a measure admit the reader to the meditative process. . . . An essay, to some extent, thinks aloud; though not in the loose and pointless way to which the 'stream of consciousness' addicts have accustomed us" (Essay 412). Gass affirms the same principle when he speaks of Emerson as having "made the essay into the narrative disclosure of thought . . . but not of such thinking as had actually occurred. Real thought is gawky and ungracious" (34). Huxley redefines it as "Free association artistically controlled," in trying to account for the "paradoxical secret of Montaigne's best essays." And Adorno codifies the paradox in his idea of the essay's methodical unmethodicality.

Given this conception of essayistic form, the essayists, in turn, tend to see the meaning of an essay as residing not so much in any particular idea or point that it happens to affirm, as in its display of a mind engaging ideas. So, for example, Kazin claims, "In an essay, it is not the thought that counts but the experience we get of the writer's thought; not the self, but the self thinking" (xi). Hoagland similarly asserts that "through its tone and tumbling progression, it conveys the quality of the author's mind," and thus he concludes that "the fascination of the mind is the fascination of the essay" (27). And Gass declares that "the hero of the essay is its author in the act of thinking things out, feeling and finding a way; it is the mind in the marvels and miseries of its makings, in the work of the imagination, the search for form" (19–20). In each of these statements, as in others, the essayists focus so deliberately on the image of the author in the process of thinking that they tend to see the essay as embodying something very much like the drama of thought, or what Hardwick refers to as "thought itself in orbit." Lopate, for example, asserts "that, in an essay, the track of a person's thoughts struggling to achieve some understanding of a problem is the plot, is the adventure" (1). Adorno shifts the dramatic focus from the essayist thinking to thought in action by asserting that "the thinker does not think, but rather transforms himself into an arena of intellectual experience, without simplifying it" (160–61). And Lukács views the drama in such abstract terms that he does not even allude to the essayist, but conceives of the essay instead as enacting the experience of thought itself: "There are experiences, then, Which cannot be expressed by any gesture and which long for expression. From all that has been said you will know what experiences I mean and of what kind they are. I mean intellectuality, conceptuality as sensed experience, as immediate reality, as spontaneous principle of existence . . . " (7). None of the essayists actually goes so far as to remove the essayist entirely from the scene of the essay, not even Lukács, though his comments date from the pre-Marxist, idealist phase of his thought. Indeed, he explicitly notes that "The hero of the essay was once alive, and so his life must be given form; but this life, too, is as much inside the work as everything is in poetry" (11).

Most essayists, in fact, give special attention to the role of the essayist in the essay, and not only through their concern with the flow of an author's thoughts, but also through their preoccupation with an author's implied personality. The importance that they attribute to personality is reflected in the fact that almost all the essayists I have examined implicitly or explicitly make it a defining feature of the essay, and not just of the "familiar" essay. As Daiches puts it, "the essay, however serious and objective in intention, can be defined as a reasonably short prose discussion in which the personality of the author in some degree shapes the style and tone of the argument" (4). This emphasis on personality is reflected in a tendency, especially among the nineteenth-century essayists, to discuss their predecessors primarily in terms of the changing moods or aspects of personality that they find in their essays, and occasionally to judge them for what they deem to be an inappropriate manner, as Hazlitt does Johnson for being "always upon stilts" (101). Hazlitt's judgment in this case turns out to be reflective of norms that have prevailed throughout the nineteenth and twentieth centuries. The basic premise of these norms, as Stephen puts it, is that "no literary skill will make average readers take kindly to a man who does not attract by some amiable quality" (69). According to these norms, the essayist in Benson's view should have the "power of giving the sense of a good-humored, gracious and reasonable personality" (59). In keeping with these same norms, Woolf asserts that "the voice of the scold should never be heard in this narrow plot" (217), and Hardwick observes that "pompously self-righteous, lamely jocular forays offend because an air of immature certainty surrounds them" (xvii). As these remarks suggest, and as Gass makes clear,

> This lack of fanaticism, this geniality in the thinker, this sense of the social proprieties involved (the essay can be polemical but never pushy) are evidence of how fully aware the author is of the proper etiquette for meeting minds. . . . If there is too much earnestness, too great a need to persuade, a want of correct convictions in the reader is implied, and therefore an absence of community. (24)

In view of their concern for engaging readers, "for meeting minds," it should come as no surprise that the essayists' conception of personality is on the whole as complex and delicately attuned as their overall conception of essayistic form. Woolf hints at the complexity when she speaks of personality as "the essayist's most proper but most dangerous and delicate tool" (222). A few sentences later she defines the complexity in the form of another paradox—"Never to be yourself and yet always—that is the problem" (222). This paradoxical conception of the essayist's persona as being at once an authentic reflection of personality and a fictionalized construction of personality can be traced in part to the practices of the periodical essayists, whom Hazlitt describes as having "assumed some fictitious and humorous disguise, which, however, in a great degree corresponded to their own peculiar habits and character" (95). In a similar fashion, Lamb's playful preface to his essays makes clear that what Elia "tells us, as of himself, was often true only (historically) of another." But even in the absence of self-evidently fictitious disguises, the essayists tend to discuss personality in terms that suggest they see it as involving a subtle combination of actual and fictional qualities. In an unpublished review of Hazlitt, for example, Lamb notes that "This assumption of a character, if it be not truly (as we are inclined to believe) his own, is that which gives force & life to his writing" (303). Similarly, Benson's previously cited remark that "the charm" of an essayist "depends upon his power of giving the sense of a good-humored, gracious and reasonable personality" seems to imply that such a personality is not a literal reflection of the essayist's own nature, but something that the essayist is capable of projecting, "of giving the sense of," in writing. Weeks likewise observes that "Style is at once the man himself and the shimmering costume of words which centers your attention" (81). This complex interplay between the essayist's authentic self and the self in "costume," between the actual and the fictional personality, is clearly delineated by White:

> The essayist arises in the morning, and, if he has work to do, selects his garb from an unusually extensive wardrobe: he can pull on any sort of shirt, be any sort of person, according to his mood or his subject matter—philosopher, scold, jester, raconteur, confidant, pundit, devil's advocate, enthusiast. . . . There is one thing the essayist cannot do, though—he cannot indulge himself in deceit or in concealment, for he will be found out in time. (vii–viii)

So it would seem that essayists explicitly recognize an intimate connection between role-playing and essay-writing, even as they affirm that the roles they play must be deeply in tune with their inherent nature.

It is one thing, however, to create the impression of a particular "sort of person"; it is quite another matter to do so at the same time that one is projecting the impression of a particular "meditative process." At first thought, of course, there might appear to be no problem here, since the two impressions presumably must be in harmony with each other—the personality giving direction to the meditative process, and the meditative process in turn revealing the most distinctive aspects of the personality. But as the essayists define personality, it seems to refer to a public aspect of self, something that one can put on as easily as if it were a "costume" or "garb," whereas a meditative process presumably involves the private aspect of one's self. Paradoxically, then, the essayists apparently conceive of the essay as somehow conveying a multistable impression of the self, an impression that projects the self in both its private and public aspects, in the process of thought and in the process of sharing thought with others. As Gerould puts it, "An essay, to some extent, thinks aloud." As Gass puts it, "The unity of each essay is a unity achieved by the speaker for his audience as well as for himself, a kind of reassociation of his sensibility and theirs" (35). As Hoagland puts it, "the artful 'I' of an essay can be as chameleon as any narrator in fiction" (26).

As the essayists see it, then, the essay, far from being a form of nonfiction, is a profoundly fictive kind of writing. It seeks to convey the sense of a human presence, a human presence that is indisputably related to its author's deepest sense of self, but that is also a complex illusion of that self—an enactment of it as if it were both in the process of thought and in the process of sharing the outcomes of that thought with others. Considered in this light, the essay, rather than being the clear-cut, straightforward, and transparent form of discourse that it is usually considered to be, is itself a very problematic kind of writing. So, it should not be confused either with article-writing and theme-writing, or with exploratory writing and expressive writing. As Priestley says, "it is a pity that other types of prose composition which could easily be given such a title as 'theme; 'thesis,' or 'article,' should bear the name [of essay]" (8). Given the essayists' view of it, the essay clearly calls for different ways of writing and different ways of reading from these other types of prose. It calls for using and understanding language as a symbolic form of action. To illustrate what this might entail is clearly beyond the scope of this piece—is presumably the purpose of other pieces in this book. For the moment, then, my only concern is to urge a rethinking of the essay, and to suggest that any rethinking of it might best begin with a consideration of what the essayists themselves have had to say about it.

WORKS CITED

Abrams, M. H. "Essay." *A Glossary of Literary Terms.* New York: Holt, Rinehart and Winston, 1981. 55–56.

Adorno, T. W. "The Essay as Form." Trans. Bob Hullot-Ketitor. *New German Critique.* Spring–Summer 1984: 151–71.

Bacon, Francis. *The Advancement of Learning.* Ed. William Aldis Wright. London: Oxford, 1963.

_____. *The Essays.* Ed. John Pitcher. New York: Viking Penguin, 1985.

Belloc, Hilaire. "An Essay upon Essays upon Essays." *One Thing and Another*. London: Hollis and Carter, 1955.11–14.

Benson, Arthur Christopher. "The Art of the Essayist." In Vol. 4 of *Modern English Essays*. 5 vols. Ed. Ernest Rhys. London: Dent, 1922.50–63.

Bond, Donald F. ed. *The Spectator*. 5 vols. London, Oxford, 1965.

Chadbourne, Richard. "A Puzzling Literary Genre: Comparative Views of the Essay." *Comparative Literature Studies* 20 (1983): 133–53.

Chesterton, G. K. "On Essays." *Come to Think of It*. London: Methuen, 1930.1–5.

Daiches, David. "Reflections on the Essay." *A Century of the Essay*. New York: Harcourt, 1951.1–8.

Epstein, Joseph. "Writing Essays." *The New Criterion*. June 1984: 2634.

Gass, William. "Emerson and the Essay." *Habitations of the Word*. New York: Simon and Schuster, 1985.9–49.

Gerould, Katharine Fullerton. "An Essay on Essays." *The North American Review*. December 1935: 409–18.

_____. "Information, Please!" *The Saturday Review of Literature*. 29 Dec. 1934: 393–95.

Hardwick, Elizabeth. Introduction. *The Best American Essays 1986*. Ed. Elizabeth Hardwick. New York: Ticknor & Fields, 1986. xiii–xxi.

Hazlitt, William. "On the Periodical Essayists." In Vol. 6 of *The Complete Works of William Hazlitt*. London: Dent, 1931. 91–105.

Hoagland, Edward. "What I Think, What I Am." *The Tugman's Passage*. New York: Random House, 1982. 24–27.

Howells, William Dean. "Editor's Easy Chair." *Harper's Magazine*. October 1902: 802–03.

Huxley, Aldous. Preface. *Collected Essays*. New York: Harper and Row, 1960. v–ix.

Johnson, Samuel. *A Dictionary of the English Language*. London: W. Strahan, 1755.

_____. "Rambler No. 184." In Vol. 5 of *The Yale Milton of the Works of Samuel Johnson*. Ed. W. J. Bate and Albrecht B. Strauss. New Haven: Yale UP. 1969. 200–04.

Kazin, Alfred. "The Essay as a Modern Form." The Open Form: Essays for our Time. New York: Harcourt, 1961. vii–xi.

Krutch, Joseph Wood. "No Essays, Please." *The Saturday Review of Literature*. 10 March 1951: 18–19, 35.

Lamb, Charles. *The Essays of Elia*. London: Dent, 1929.

_____. Unpublished Review of William Hazlitt's *Table Talk*. Lamb as Critic. Ed. Roy Park. Lincoln: U of Nebraska P, 1980. 299–307.

Lopate, Phillip. "The Essay Lives—In Disguise." The New York Times Book Review. 18 Nov. 1984: 1, 47–49.

Lukács, Georg. "On the Nature and Form of the Essay." *Soul and Form.* Trans. Anna Benstock. Cambridge: MIT, 1978. 1–18.

Montaigne. *The Complete Works.* Trans. Donald M. Frame. Stanford: Stanford UP, 1957.

Priestley, J. B. Introduction. *Essayists Past and Present.* New York: Dial Press, 1925. 7–32.

Rucker, Mary K. "The Literary Essay and the Modern Temper." *Publications in Language and Literature* 11 (1975): 317–35.

Smith, Alexander. "On the Writing of Essays." *Dreamthorp: A Book of Essays Written in the Country.* Portland, Maine: Thomas Bird Mosher, 1913. 23–46.

Stephen, Leslie. "The Essayists." *Men, Books, and Manners.* Minneapolis: U of Minnesota P, 1956. 45–73.

Thomas, Lewis. "Essays and Gaia." *The Youngest Science.* New York: Viking, 1983. 239–48.

Thoreau, Henry David. *The journal of Henry David Thoreau.* 14 vols. Ed. Bradford Torrey and Francis H. Allen. Salt Lake City: Gibbs M. Smith, 1984.

Weeks, Edward. "The Peripatetic Reviewer." *Atlantic Monthly.* Aug. 1954: 81–82.

White, E. B. Foreword. *Essays of E. B. White.* New York: Harper and Row, 1977. vii–ix.

Williams, William Carlos. "An Essay on Virginia." *Imaginations.* New York: New Directions, 1971. 321–24.

Woolf, Virginia. "The Modern Essay." *The Common Reader.* New York: Harcourt, 1956. 216–27.

Zeiger, William. "The Exploratory Essay: Enfranchising the Spirit of Inquiry in College Composition." *College English* 47 (1985): 454–66.

This study was completed with the assistance of an Old Gold Summer Fellowship (1987), for which I am grateful to the University of Iowa.

Of the essayists whose comments I have gathered thus far, only Thoreau does not concur in seeing the essay as a natural or open form of writing, but his divergence is occasioned only by a preference for the even "more simple, less artful" way of communicating thoughts in his journal (III: 239).

The compelling appeal that this contrast has had for essayists may be seen in the shaping influence that it evidently had on Lamb's Elian persona, as he makes clear in "Imperfect Sympathies," when he distinguishes between "imperfect intellects (under which mine must be content to rank)" and "systematizers," between those whose "minds" are "suggestive" and those whose minds are "comprehensive," between those who "are content with fragments and scattered pieces of Truth" and those who strive for "ideas in perfect order and completeness" (Essays 69–70).

See Rucker for a highly detailed account of the essay's declining appeal during the first half of the twentieth century. Given her restricted historical orientation, she necessarily interprets the conflict between essay and article as a distinctly modern phenomenon, rather than as a twentieth century manifestation of a long-standing conflict between the essay and methodical discourse.

Thus while I am in sympathy with Zeiger's desire to encourage "the spirit of inquiry in college composition," I consider his distinction between the "expository essay" and the "exploratory essay" to be potentially as misleading as the distinction between the "formal" and "informal" essay. Indeed, his conception of the "expository essay" is virtually identical to the methodical discourse that essayists have long opposed; and his conception of the "exploratory essay" does not seem to recognize any difference between the actual nature of mental exploration and the symbolic form of mental exploration that essayists attribute to the essay.

R. LANE KAUFFMANN

....

THE SKEWED PATH: ESSAYING AS UNMETHODICAL METHOD [1989]

> *There will always be much of accident in the essentially informal, this un-methodical, method.*
> —*Walter Pater*

Is the essay literature or philosophy? A form of art or a form of knowledge? The contemporary essay is torn between its belletristic ancestry and its claim to philosophical legitimacy. The Spanish philosopher Eduardo Nicol captured the genre's uncertain status when he dubbed it *"almost* literature and *almost* philosophy" (207). The problem is hardly a new one. It goes back to what Plato called the "ancient quarrel" between poetry and philosophy, and more recently to the German romantic theorist Friedrich Schlegel, who called for a mode of criticism which would be at once philosophical and poetic. But today, when the status of critical discourse is up for grabs, reflecting the crisis of knowledge in the universities, the question of the essay takes on a new urgency. Now the predominant form of writing in the human sciences, it cannot avoid the challenge to define itself according to the prevailing standards of scientific knowledge and method.

Despite the essay's interdisciplinary prominence, it has fallen largely to literary critics and theorists to debate the generic status of the form. In Anglo-American letters, this debate is unavoidably filtered through the long-standing question of the nature and function of criticism. A century or so ago, Walter Pater and Oscar Wilde evoked criticism as art, while Matthew Arnold and others held it to the less glamorous role of mediating the great tradition. Nowadays, matters are less simple. The case for creative criticism is being made in North American universities by deconstructionists, a school of avant-garde theorists who challenge the conventional distinction between literary and critical discourse. Since, as Nietzsche observed, no discourse can escape rhetorical figuration, should criticism not give up the pretense of being a neutral metalanguage and join in the fun of writing, drawing upon the freedom and techniques available to all forms of expression?

The deconstructionist position is understandable as a reaction both to sterile academic criticism and to the scientistic ethos of modern society. But the move to blur the distinctions between art and criticism is no more advisable now than it was a hundred years ago, when Wilde exhorted the critic to be an artist and flee the "dim, dull abyss of fact" (16). Indeed, the move is chancier now, because it may further undermine the already weak position of humanistic study in the universities and in society at large. By associating criticism with *l'esprit de frivolité*, deconstructionists may suppose that they are tweaking the nose of positivism. But they risk abandoning the field to positivistic method by trivializing other modes of inquiry. Whatever the intent, to insist that criticism and philosophy are not different in kind from literature is surely to weaken the essay's claim to be a legitimate medium of critical inquiry—a claim on which its future in the human sciences is bound to depend in large measure. Several important questions emerge in this regard. What are the cognitive and philosophical claims, and what is the methodological status, of the critical essay? Can these claims be honored without disowning the rhetorical flexibility and spontaneity long associated with the genre? Must one choose between the essay as literature and the essay as philosophy, or can it be both, to the detriment of neither? The aim of the present essay is to explore the answers given to these questions by several important modern theorists and to draw some conclusions as to the place of the essay in the contemporary human sciences.

I.

Walter Pater may be credited with having rediscovered the essay as the "strictly appropriate form of our modern philosophical literature . . . . the essay came into use at what was really the invention of the relative, or 'modern' spirit, in the Renaissance of the sixteenth century" (174–75). Pater's assumption that a continuous "modern" sensibility motivates the essay since Montaigne seems slightly anachronistic today. The serenity we find in Montaigne's writings (and to some extent in Pater's as well) is harder to come by nowadays. To be sure, the essay is still "an expression of the self thinking," as Alfred Kazin wrote in 1961 to introduce *The Open Form*. But the essaying self is much attenuated. One can no longer seriously pretend that the essay (or anything else) expresses "the individual's wholly undetermined and freely discovered point of view" (Kazin x). Since Marx and Freud, discovering one's point of view has come to mean discovering what determines it. One finds now a roughly inverse proportion between self-affirmation in a piece of discourse and the degree of philosophical seriousness accorded it. To read Montaigne now is to realize that the contemporary essayist travels under a more rigid protocol, within more carefully patrolled boundaries. Going through the disciplinary checkpoints of the knowledge industry, the essayist (the masculine pronoun will be used in this text) must declare his intentions. Are his writings subjective or objective? Opinion or knowledge? Classified as opinion, they may pass; few will take them seriously in any case. But if they claim to know something, they must be accompanied by the proper documents certifying their use of scientific method, and showing the fruits of its application. Whereas Montaigne wrote with one eye on the world and the other on himself, the modern essayist, *sub specie academiae*, works with one eye on the object of study while the other nervously reviews the methods by which he is authorized to know or interpret.

The unity of experience one encounters in Montaigne's writings was not given but achieved, forged in the midst of the civil and religious wars of the late sixteenth century. The medieval worldview was shattered, the Copernican revolution had begun, education and public life were chaotic, the wrenching paradigm shift toward modernity was under way (Barfield 14). Montaigne's serene individualism was anchored in the stoical and humanist traditions of *culture de rame*, combining self-cultivation and practical wisdom (Friedrich 323). Only this inner security can account for his exemplary "negative capability," the high tolerance for doubt and contingency which pervades his work.

Pater shrewdly identifies Montaigne's essays with the dialectic method of Plato's dialogues. Both forms, dialogue and essay, convey the flow of discursive reasoning, with or without the presence of an interlocutor. Both genres cut a circuitous path, approaching truth obliquely, registering the contingencies of occasion. The method of both genres is, for its genuine practitioners, "coextensive with life itself; . . . there will always be much of accident in this essentially informal, this unmethodical method" (Pater 185–86). Like Socrates, Montaigne has the wisdom of his ignorance; he knows that he knows not. Unlike Socrates, however, Montaigne is a true skeptic: he suspects that certain knowledge is unattainable through reason. Throughout his essays, he mocks human pretensions to systematic knowledge, whether in scholastic dogma, medicine, or humanist educational reforms. "I do not see the whole of anything," he informs us. "Nor do those who promise to show it to us" (Montaigne 219). The great scientific and geographical discoveries of the sixteenth century are for him only proof that we were once deceived by our certainties and will doubtless be so again. His only doctrine is the "docta ignorantia," "learned ignorance"—the wisdom that comes from accepting nescience and finitude as part of the human condition. This stance did not entail turning away from the pursuit of truth or learning; but Montaigne reveals in the *quest* for knowledge, the pleasure of the chase, not its goal. He flouts the humanist equation of method with systematic presentation (Gilbert 69–73). As taught in the schoolbooks, the purpose of method was to facilitate knowledge by reducing all subjects to the bare essentials, thereby saving the student or reader from the idle *curiositas* of meandering authors and from the trouble of discovering the material for himself. Scorning the humanists' well-marked shortcuts, Montaigne preferred the crooked path of actual experience.

His use of the term *Essais* to name his writings was already a methodological choice (Friedrich 353–56). To essay is to experiment, to try out, to test—even one's own cognitive powers and limits. The word connotes a tentative, groping method of experience, with all its attendant risks and pleasures. Montaigne may digress from a topic but not from himself: "It is the inattentive reader who loses my subject, not I. . . . I seek out change indiscriminately and tumultuously. My style and my mind alike go roaming" (761). Montaigne cannot be dismissed as a self-absorbed humanist ideologue. To watch the self navigating a world in flux has little or nothing to do with narcissism and everything to do with close observation and critical reflection. "I do nothing but come and go. My judgment does not always go forward; it floats, it strays. . . . Nearly every man would say as much, if he considered himself as I do" (426). Long before Rimbaud's discovery that "*je est un autre*," Montaigne had recognized the decentered quality of selfhood. Long before Freud, he had debunked the uninterpreted self as a reliable foundation for knowledge: "Our dreams are worth more than our reasonings. The worst position we can take is in ourselves" (427). Montaigne appeals instead to mobility and chance. "I take the first subject that chance offers. They are all equally good to me. And I never plan to develop them completely" (219). His strategy of anticipated digression evokes the *ordo neglectus*, the insouciant style cultivated by the Renaissance man of the world (Friedrich 350, 359–64). He refers to himself ironically as "a new figure: an unpremeditated and accidental philosopher" (409). For Montaigne, there is no unbridgeable gap between self and world; subject and object are one: "I am myself the matter of my book." (2) His essays constitute not only a mode of writing but a form of life; they are inseparable from the sentient self of the essayist.

His refusal to separate self from method, the living subject from the experienced object, places Montaigne on the far side of the epistemological divide inaugurated by Sir Francis Bacon, for whom methodological self-renunciation was the necessary price of progress. Bacon conceived method as a way of screening out the passions and prejudices of the knowing subject, the better to enlist nature in the service of human ends. Though Montaigne did not foresee the imminent triumph of scientific method, his own "unmethodical method," grounded in the somatic self, is already an implicit critique of instrumental reason (Friedrich 153–55). Instinctively refusing to accommodate the constraints of systems, Montaigne rubs modernity against the grain. Or is it precisely this refusal which makes him our contemporary? Systems need the individual subject only as a foundational principle. They need only the subject qua rational being: "Je pense, donc je suis," wrote Descartes. To which Valero would reply: "Parfois je pense, parfois je suis." Montaigne managed to think and to exist at the same time.

Notwithstanding Pater's invocation of a "relative" or "modern" spirit extending from Montaigne's century to our own, the intellectual conditions of the modern essay are no longer those of the essayist from Bordeaux. Intervening is what Max Weber called the progressive rationalization or "disenchantment" of the world. The triumph of secular reason over religious authority, the social and political upheavals of western Europe and the rise of the bourgeoisie, the expansion of printing and the public sphere—all of these things initially multiplied the possibilities of the individual. But with the advent of mass media and the commercialization of public discourse, along with the exponential increase and specialization of knowledge and information, culture grew increasingly instrumentalized. Thought became fragmented, the individual attenuated. The essay moved away from the meditative self-portrait into more specialized forms. This process was not linear or uniform; it varied by national and cultural context. Sometimes it took the form of unbridled subjectivism: Karl Kraus rebuked the *feuilletonistes* of late nineteenth-century Vienna for their narcissistic impressionism (Janik and Toulmin 79–80). In England, in contrast, the personal essay dropped out of sight between Lamb and Beerbohm, giving way to journalistic reviewing, in which the critic functioned as "the middle-man, the interpreter, the vulgariser" (Hunecker 151) The habitual essayist, lamented Virginia Woolf, "must skim the surface of a thought and dilute the strength of personality" (304) The tissues of experience had hardened; the essayist's dialogue with the world no longer flowed easily, as in Montaigne, through the prose membrane of the essay. Nor was this condition to be alleviated, *pace* Woolf, by, "triumphs of style" or by "knowing how to write." The growing instrumentalization of culture affected not only the producers of the essays but also their consumers, shaping the habits and expectations of the reading public. Surveying the previous half century of British essay writing, Woolf could still assert in the 1920s that the essay's sole purpose was to give pleasure (293). "Today tastes have changed," Auden would write a few years later, explaining the decline of the essay as a form of belles letters by the diminishing interest of modern readers in authorial subjectivity: "We can no longer derive any pleasure from the kind of essay which is a fantasia upon whatever chance thoughts may come into the essayist's head" (396).

Perhaps the best evidence of the specialization of modern thought is the rigid distinction usually drawn between the essay and systematic philosophy. Eduardo Nicol, an exponent of strict generic boundaries, defines the essay as a marginal genre of philosophy. In his view, the essayist's job is to speak of sundry issues in a nontechnical style to a general public, to illuminate particular phenomena against the background of ideas. The essayist and the true philosopher practice distinct modes of cognition: the philosopher methodically follows up the threads joining one problem to another rather then remaining attached, like the essayist, to the strand linking the single fact to an isolated problem or idea. Moreover, they stand in opposite relation to the genre as a medium of presentation: "For the born essayist, the essay is a way of thinking; for the born philosopher, the essay is an occasional form, a convenient way of setting forth his conclusions." While the philosopher rehearses his ideas in private before publishing them, the essayist's practice is "like a theatre of ideas in which the rehearsal and the final performance are combined." (Nicol 207–13; my trans.) Nicol does not deny the essay its place as a legitimate minor form; he insists only that the essayist accepts the rules and lesser status of the genre and that he not try to claim the prestige of philosophy, the inherently superior calling. For the result would be chaos—a "confusion of genres." Nicol rebukes Jose Ortega y Gasset, the greatest Spanish philosophical essayist (and in temperament close to Montaigne) for just such a blurring of genres. Protesting the tendency of Ortega and his compatriots (especially Miguel de Unamuno) to make the self and its surrounding, rather than truth, the protagonists of their essay. Nicol lays down the law:

"One must either serve the self or serve philosophy" (239). The choice is ultimately between ideology and science; between *doxa*, mete opinion, and *episteme*, scientific knowledge (150). Nicol's distinction ratifies the alienation of thought from lived experience which Montaigne protested in his essays. But the modern critical-philosophical essay—as instanced not only by Unamuno and Ortega but also by Walter Benjamin, Theodor W. Adorno, Roland Barthes, and Jacques Derrida, to name but a few—rebels against Nicol's law. Instead of bowing to philosophical systems, the essay—if one may adopt Adorno's device of personifying the genre to characterize the aims of its practitioners—refuses to subordinate its own impulses to norms handed down from above. It flouts the imperialism of scientific method while trespassing over the boundaries of the academic disciplines. At its most combative, modern philosophical essayism recalls Nietzsche's taunt in *Twilight of the Idols* that the will to system betrays lack of integrity (*Portable* 470).

I I.

Though it was Pater who first designated the essay as the "strictly appropriate form of our modern philosophical literature," it was Central Europeans schooled in the German Idealist tradition who did most to justify this designation. Thinkers in this tradition, from Lessing to Adorno, considered thought inseparable from its mode of presentation (*Darstellung*). The German romantics Schlegel and Novalis held that, through ironic self-reflection, "minor" genres such as aphorism, fragment, and essay could give form to speculative inquiry of the highest order (Lacoue-Labarthe and Nancy). Like the Idealism from which it derived, romantic essayism was largely eclipsed by the positivistic turn in European thought in the second half of the nineteenth century. By the turn of the present century, however, conditions allowed for the resurgence and fuller development of philosophical essayism (Luft 18–22, 100–21). Vitalist and aestheticist thinkers were in revolt against positivism and scientific method. Wilhelm Dilthey and Georg Simmel were trying to establish an independent methodology for the *Geistestvissenschaften* ("human sciences"). Along with Simmel, writers such as Robert Musil, Rudolph Kassner, and György Lukács were producing brilliant essays in cultural criticism.

In his 1911 collection, *Soul and Form*, Lukács, a young Hungarian critic, inquires into the plight of the modern essay, which he identifies with criticism (Kritik). How is it, he asks, that the writings of the greatest essayists, by giving form to a vital standpoint, or weltanschauung, managed to transcend the sphere of *science* and attain a place next to art, "yet without blurring the frontiers of either"? How does such form "endow the work with the force necessary for a conceptual re-ordering of life, and yet distinguish it from the icy, final perfection of philosophy" (1)? Whereas the modern essayist uses the occasion of reviewing the works of others to formulate his essential questions, Plato, for Lukács the original and greatest essayist, needed no "mediating medium" and was able to pose his questions directly to life. Having lost Plato's golden age, when man's "essence" and his "destiny" were in harmony, the modern essayist finds no Socrates ("the typical life for the essay form") to serve as a vehicle for his own ultimate questions. The symbols and experiences drawn from other works do not suffice. The modern essay "has become too rich and independent for dedicated service, yet it is too intellectual and multiform to acquire form out of its own self," leading most critics to adopt a certain frivolity as their very "life-mood" (13–15). Lukács maintains that the essayist is by nature a precursor to a grand system, awaiting "the great value-definer of aesthetics, the one who is always about to arrive. . . . [the essayist] is a John the Baptist who goes out to preach in the wilderness about another who is still to come, whose shoelace he is not worthy to untie." But is the essayist then a mere harbinger who is rendered superfluous by the arrival of the grand system (16)? There is a deep ambivalence in Lukács's messianic longing for a system. His desire for wholeness (hardly uncommon in Central Europe on the eve of World War I) registers a partial protest against the fragmentation of modern life; but Lukács hesitates, sensing that such transcendence would involve sacrificing his individuality to a higher ideal. In this pre-Marxist phase of his work, Lukács concludes that the essay's unfulfilled longing is "a tact of the soul with a value and an existence of its own. . . . The essay is a judgment, but the essential, the value-determining thing about it is not the verdict (as is the case with the system) but the process of judging" (17–18).

The method of the modern essayist—that of commentary and critique—is no longer "co-extensive with life." He needs other works, other lives, to give meaning to his own. Indeed, as a specialist in cultural commentary, he has become a "mediating medium." Is it the essayist's destiny to find himself by losing himself? Not the way Lukács went about it—as one may observe by way of epilogue to his early theory of the essay. After becoming a communist in 1918 and participating in the Hungarian revolution, he went on in the 1920s to write *History and Class Consciousness*, the most influential work of Marxist philosophy since Marx. Placing Marxist theory under the aegis of the Hegelian category of totality, Lukács in effect opted for a secular version of the System he had heralded in messianic tones in his earlier work. Forced immediately to recant his Hegelian-Marxist synthesis, he nevertheless remained in the Party, which he regarded as his "ticket to history." Lukács's self-sacrifice to the idea of totality is mocked by the Stalinist system at whose service he placed himself, and his Marxist works are haunted by his earlier defense of the essay's fragmentary and solitary authenticity.

There is irony in the fact that his recanted work stimulated a countering, anti-Hegelian school of thought: the critical theory of the Frankfurt School, which used Lukács's own insights to criticize the totalizing pretensions of his Hegelian Marxism (Jay). The defense of the essay's philosophical legitimacy was continued by two members of this school: Walter Benjamin and Theodor W. Adorno. In the methodological introduction to his 1928 study of German baroque tragic drama, Benjamin draws a line between knowledge, which may be possessed, and truth, which may only be represented: "For knowledge, method is a way of acquiring its object; . . . for truth [method] is self-representation, and is therefore immanent in it as form." Whereas philosophy as system "weaves a spider's web between separate kinds of knowledge in an attempt to ensnare the truth as if it were something that came flying in from the outside," Benjamin posits a nonacquisitive ideal for philosophy: truth as the representation of ideas. He sees in the discontinuous treatise or esoteric essay, which he compares to a mosaic, the proper form of this alternative philosophy: "Representation as digression—such is the methodological nature of the treatise. The absence of an uninterrupted purposeful structure is its primary characteristic. . . . The value of fragments of thought is all the greater the less direct their relationship to the underlying idea" (27–30). Thus began Benjamin's career of experimenting with fragmentary forms in criticism, forms displaying little or no "uninterrupted purposeful structure," ranging from treatise and commentary to surrealist pastiche, essay, and thesis. His "micrological" way of theorizing from particulars (the epithet is from Schlegel) had an ethico-ontological rationale. Benjamin saw his task as that of "redeeming" concrete phenomena from the refuse of history as they were abandoned by systems in their march to generalization. To this end, he used surrealist montage to light up cultural phenomena in a sudden "profane illumination." Whereas the pre-Marxist Lukács had assigned only provisional value to the essay's fragmentariness, Benjamin's prose experiments made fragmentation the heart of his method. Adorno, in turn, developed Benjamin's ideas into a full-scale theory of the essay. In his 1931 inaugural address at the University of Frankfurt, Adorno argued that the essay was the appropriate form for contemporary philosophy. Since traditional philosophy had failed in its effort to grasp the whole of reality through self-sufficient reason, it was time to give up stale systems and to rely instead on the essay as a more sensitive method of philosophical interpretation. The essay approached its objects in a spirit of "exact fantasy"—combining respect for the object's complexity with an element of imaginative freedom altogether lacking in systems. Fragmentary and experimental in form, the essay would be polemical in intent: "For the mind (Geist) is indeed not capable of producing or grasping the totality of the real, but it may be possible to penetrate the detail, to explode in miniature the mass of merely existing reality" ("Actuality" 132–33). Seconding Benjamin's endorsement of fragmentation as the essay's source of truth, Adorno's theory represents an unequivocal rejection of Lukács's Hegelian-Marxist validation of totality and system. Adorno's 1958 "The Essay as Form" presents his definitive theory of the essay as a critique of systematic method. The essay is said to reject the identity principle upon which all systems are based—the epistemological assumption that their network of concepts mirrors the structure of reality; that subject and object of cognition are ultimately identical. It also refuses the ontological priorities of systems—their privileging of the timeless over the historical, the universal over the particular (158). Instead of subsuming particular phenomena under first principles and hardened concepts, the essay form rhetorically mediates its own concepts, urging their "interaction" in the cognitive process while refusing to simplify that process. Proceeding in "methodically unmethodical fashion" (160–61)—Adorno echoes Pater, wittingly or not—the essay refuses to surrender its element of "fantasy" to the vain project of capturing the object within a rigid logical or conceptual framework. The essay observes a "pleasure principle" which mocks the stern "reality principle" of official thought (168–69). But it does not follow mere whim or fancy: "determined by the unity of its object" (165), the task of the critical essay, as Adorno notes elsewhere, is to follow "the logic of the object's aporias" ("Cultural Criticism" 32). Since the object—for Adorno, always part of social reality—is itself contradictory, "antagonistic," the essay is structured in such a way that it could always, at any point, break off. It thinks in fragments just as reality is fragmented, and gains its unity only by moving through fissures, rather than by smoothing them over." Flouting the Cartesian precept to articulate continuously and exhaustively, moving from the simplest elements to the most complex, the essay dismisses the pretense that thought could achieve total comprehension of its objects. "Discontinuity is essential to the essay; its concern is always an arrested conflict" ("Essay" 161–64). But this "discontinuity" is relative. The essay makes up in aesthetic stringency what it forfeits in logical precision or discursive continuity. Instead of trying to present arguments in a foolproof deductive sequence, the essay's arguments "interweave as in a carpet" (160). In its rhetorical transitions, the essay, like music—Adorno regarded Schoenberg's serial method of composition as a model for philosophical form—"establishes internal cross-connections . . . . co-ordinates elements, rather than subordinating them" (169–170). Defying the "scientific mentality, which bans rhetoric in favor of an allegedly neutral language, the essay thus "rescues a sophistic element" (168).

From Adorno's analogies, which emphasize the essay's aesthetic texture and transitions, one may infer that the rhetorical function of essaying is not merely to transmit the essayist's thoughts but to convey the feeling of their movement and thereby to induce an experience of thought in the reader. This notion would support Lukács's claim that the crucial thing about the essay's judgment is not the verdict but the process of judging. For Adorno (contrary to Nicol), the rhetorical-aesthetic dimension of presentation does not vitiate but rather enhances the essay's truth claims; it "obeys an epistemological motive" (164). This is true of Adorno's essayism. Without using the label, his theory tacitly identifies the essay with his agenda of "negative dialectics," or dialectics without synthesis or identity (Adorno, *Negative Dialectics*). Adorno's antinomian method is enacted rhetorically through paradox, irony, oxymoron, and chiasmus. In such expressions as "methodically unmethodical," "exact fantasy," and "arrested conflict," the dialectical play of opposites works against the illusion of stasis, identity, or totality, allowing the reader to feel the motion of transgressing epistemological taboos and boundaries. To read Adorno's essays is to be compelled to think dialectically. Their form is negative dialectics, crystallized.

As though in final reproach to the later Lukács for his obeisance to systems and "judgments," Adorno concludes by identifying the essay form with permanent revolt against orthodoxy of any kind: "The essay's innermost formal law is heresy" (171; trans. altered). The paradox of heresy as law marks Adorno's theory and practice of the essay. Constantly reenacting the obligatory heresy against perceived orthodoxy, his own writings come to resemble less an open-minded process of judging than a predetermined verdict. As he relentlessly inveighs against systems, his method finally becomes one itself (Wohlfarth 979). Instead of dissolving received standpoints, his method stakes out a position; it takes a stand.

In this respect, Adorno's practice of the essay is diametrically opposed to that of Montaigne. The individual is still the focus of experience, as in Montaigne's essays, but the function of subjectivity has changed considerably. In contrast to Montaigne's affirmation of the self in its richness and contingency, Adorno practices a self-restraint which is at once epistemologically and rhetorically motivated. The essay, for Adorno, tends toward "the liquidation of opinion or standpoint, including the one from which it begins" (166; trans. altered). So that the subject may experience the object without dominating it, the personality is kept in abeyance. It is true that Adorno's writings reveal an unmistakable persona, despite their forbidding philosophical style. But the speculative freedom and playfulness of Montaigne's essays, and their unabashed self-reference, are implicitly proscribed in Adorno's essays as breaches of philosophical protocol. The essay takes on the methodological role of "exact fantasy" in the service of negative dialectics. So it may be said that, in Adorno, the essay is subtly reinstrumentalized in its very critique of instrumentalization.

III.

Central to the theories examined above is the historical conflict between fragmentary and totalizing modes of thought—between essay and system. The crisis of contemporary thought may be described in terms of this dilemma. On the one hand, in an era of totalitarianism, the inherent tendency of systems to closure, and their operational role in what has been called the "political economy of truth" (Foucault, "Truth" 131–33), continue to make the system suspect as an epistemological and discursive norm. On the other hand, the fragmentary-essayistic mode championed by some critics harmonizes with the accelerating compartmentalization of knowledge in academic institutions and in society at large. If critical thought does not aspire in principle to comprehend the entire sociocultural complex in which it operates but remains content with constructing allusive montages in a limited domain, it risks becoming uncritical and begins to reproduce rather than challenge the status quo. The response to this dilemma in the works of the French poststructuralists Jacques Derrida, Jean-François Lyotard, Roland Barthes, and Michel Foucault constitutes the most significant development in contemporary Continental essayism. These thinkers, no less than the Frankfurt School critical theorists, have felt the magnetic pull of philosophical systems—whether phenomenological, structuralist, Marxist, or psychoanalytical. And like the German theorists (the later Lukács being the obvious exception), the French poststructuralists have by and large resisted the systematic temptation by privileging fragmentation as an aesthetic and methodological principle. The two schools of theory diverge in their respective justifications of this principle. For the German theorists—still working, albeit critically, within a humanist-idealist paradigm—essayistic fragmentation serves two aims. First, it preserves freedom of imagination as a necessary moment of the essaying process; and second, it signals that the knowing subject in the process no longer plays the constitutive role reserved for it in idealist systems. Nut defers instead to the object of cognition, following the "logic of its aporias." Contrariwise, the French theorists (the francophile Benjamin anticipates the poststructuralist view in this respect), extending the German post-Hegelian critiques of idealism and wishing to eliminate all vestiges of Cartesianism and humanism from their thinking, pronounce the Subject anachronistic and the Author dead. They are apt to justify discursive discontinuity with reference to the play of language or textuality operating autonomously, with no conscious subject in control (Barthes, "Work"), or to the libidinal vagaries and intensities which are found conspicuously at play even in critical or theoretical discourse (Lyotard, *Economic* 292– 301). Lyotard exposes the lingering pieties and authoritarian power claims of theory conceived as metalanguage or master discourse, advocating instead a "paganized" discourse in which the search for truth becomes an "affair of style" ("Apathie" 9–10). If the Frankfurt School theorists regard consciousness as the locus of ideology and the scene of critical thought, the poststructuralists are preoccupied instead with language and discourse, looking less to epistemology than to avant-garde art and aesthetics for their discursive models. A utopian ideal in either case, the essay is for the German theorists a *cognitive* or *epistemic* utopia; for the French thinkers it would be, to use Roland Barthes's phrase, a "utopia of language" ("Lecture" 8).

This is not to suggest that the two schools have equal investments in the genre. The German thinkers ascribed to the essay the heroic role of defending critical and creative thought against the encroachments of instrumental reason, as embodied in systems. In contrast, the French thinkers have resisted identifying their projects with established genres, even questioning the very notion of genre (Derrida, "Lot"). They have at times distanced themselves from the essay in particular (Lyotard, Economic 303), mistrusting discourses of self-representation, whether the self appears in the foundational role of the Cartesian cogito or in the more congenial guise of Montaigne's essays. Despite such demurrers, the French theorists belong well within the tradition of philosophical essayism. It is telling that both Foucault and Barthes, systematic critics of bourgeois individualism in their early works, make the self in distinct ways a central concern of their late works, and each pays final homage to the essay as well. Citing the desire to "stray afield of oneself" as the motivation of his work, Foucault defines the essay as "the living substance of philosophy. . ., an 'ascesis,' *askesis*, an exercise of oneself in the activity of thought" (Use 8–9).

More significant in the present context than their differences is the fact that both schools respond, in overlapping historical phases, to the conditions of contemporary knowledge and research by producing essays as unmethodical method. Whatever their differences in terminology, both schools rebel against the primacy of systems and method. Both refuse demands for absolute objectivity—demands which usually mean bowing to another's construction of the object. These theorists propose not epistemological anarchy but rather the methodological recognition of contingency. In a passage on method in *Of Grammatology*, Derrida writes of deconstruction's (momentary) departure, along a "traced path," from the age of logocentrism: "The departure is radically empiricist. It proceeds like a wandering thought on the possibility of itinerary and of method. It is affected by nonknowledge as by its future and it ventures out deliberately. . . . We must begin wherever we are" (162). But neither school practices straightforward empiricism; both view thought as rhetorically and textually mediated. The essay's rhetorical method is not the traditional invention based on manipulation of catalogued topoi or commonplaces: "Topological thinking . . . knows the place of every phenomenon, the essence of none" (Adorno, "Cultural Criticism" 33). Theorists of both schools refuse to separate the acts of thinking and writing, to regard writing as a mere instrument of thought. Faced with Nicol's option to serve the self or serve philosophy, they refuse the alternative. Unlike the systematic philosopher who rehearses his thoughts in private, deleting all traces of contingency from his discourse, the essayist, mindful that all thought is circumstantial, reflects on the circumstances of his own discourse, making them serve the thought at hand.

Revealing rather than concealing its rhetorical character, the essay carries on its Socratic mission; the critical discussion of culture in the public sphere. In practice, if not always in theory, both schools would agree with

Adorno—who echoes Max Bense (420)—that the proper function of the essay is the critique of ideology ("Essay" 166). Its principal activity is the critical interpretation of tests. For this reason, theories of the essay necessarily have a hermeneutic dimension. The essay's mode of cognition is, in Wilhelm Dilthev's terms, "ideographic" rather than "nomothetic," concerned with understanding particular cases rather than with finding general laws. Max Bense's argument that the essay's method is "experimental" (417–18, 424) may be taken in a nonpositivistic sense: the essay makes heuristic and bermeneutical "probes" of phenomena, without utilitarian or universalizing intent. Of the hermeneutical principles common to the essayism of both (German and French) schools of theory, the most basic one is that there is no unconditioned standpoint. That is why the essayist must continually reflect on the context of discourse, and why in its very form the essay will bear traces of that contextualitv. The interpretive practices of Adorno and Derrida show striking parallels. In their approach to texts, both negative dialectics and deconstruction operate as negative or "heretical" hermeneutics; each approach has been likened to "negative theology" (Buck-Morss 90; Handelman 98–129). As readers, both Derrida and Adorno seek the anomaly, the exception which thwarts the rule. As critics, both play with binary oppositions to undermine traditional metaphysical hierarchies, showing not how to construct texts or systems of interpretation but how to undo canonical ones. And as theorists, both Adorno and Derrida are ultimately driven by philosophical systems in their very attempt to deconstruct these systems. Unfortunately, under the present conditions of knowledge and its dissemination, in which even the subtlest critical model is destined for commodification, the work of each theorist has tended to become mechanized, reified by its adherents, as though the price of its popularity were parodic exaggeration of the programmatic tendencies latent in each mode of essaying.

As these examples show, the essay's task is more difficult than ever, combining—to return to my initial example—the disciplinary functions of literary criticism with the broader one of ideology-critique. In the former, intradisciplinary capacity, the critical essayist must stay abreast of the considerable advances in techniques of analysis; he must be a specialist. In the broader capacity of counterideologist, however, he must relate cultural experience to the larger social complex—a complex in which the critic may, at certain junctures, find himself in strategic alliance with art against the imperial claims of theory. But it seems unlikely that justice can be done to both functions by a mode of criticism which plunges into the text or artwork on the work's own terms. The venerable plea for creative criticism, renewed by American deconstructors (for example, Hartman, *Criticism*), might be compatible with the claim that the essay practices unmethodical method: "unmethodical" insofar as it draws on the unregulated faculties and energies of art, the essay is "methodical" insofar as it bends to the more prosaic chores of humanistic knowledge—not only discovery but interpretation, commentary, synthesis. The dual function of criticism is not helped, however, by pretending that art and criticism are one. That art involves critical thinking, and that criticism may also create, as Wilde observed, does not justify abolishing the distinction. Criticism becomes uncritical when it thinks of itself as art, among other reasons because it thereby invites itself to be consumed as art, rather than as argument. Literary analysis of critical texts should attempt to illuminate the cognitive claims of the essay, not (necessarily) to undermine them—as though arguments could be answered merely by pointing accusingly at their rhetorical construction.

Precisely how paradigms of knowledge and their forms of presentation will change in response to cybernetic technology is an open question. Lyotard sees the essay as a form which will follow the pragmatics of postmodern science, practicing avant-garde experimentation in its search for new rules, new statements, and creative instabilities (*Postmodern* 81). Gregory L. Ulmer's *Applied Grammatology* tries to harness the new technology's progressive potential by codifying and adapting the method of Derrida's critical essays to electronic media, thus making it more accessible as a model both to academic essayists and to students in the classroom. But Derrida's method, though not immune to routinization, contains an unmethodical moment, the moment of imagination, which refuses to he programmed; attempts to program it anyway would generate more nonsense and dogma than insight. Ulmer's project not only downplays the friction between the epistemological dynamics of postmodern science and its current socioeconomic organization; it also assumes that a liberating force inheres in technical procedures rather than in their application in specific contexts, whether critical or artistic. No *esprit de finesse* attaches automatically to the essay, as any reader knows and as one sees in the instrumentalization of the form since Montaigne. The moment of freedom, of rebellion against *l'esprit géométrique*, is not a given of the genre; it must be reinvented each time an essayist sits down to write. Whether the form manifests a subtle mind or a square one depends very much on the essayist.

IV.

The career of the essay is more than a matter of local interest for literary theory and criticism. Embodying as it does the perennial dialectic between the individual thinker and established thought systems, the genre invites reflection by philosophical anthropology as well. Like other cultural forms, the essay responds not only to changing external conditions but also to the stratum of the specifically human. This stratum does not evolve in isomorphic relation to society or technology. If it did, one could hardly begin to account for the chronic feelings of nostalgia, lost innocence, and crisis which have marked modern consciousness, motivating the major critiques of modernity at least since Rousseau. Insofar as artistic and critical form answer to this stratum, they continue to express residual needs which remain unfulfilled or repressed by civilization in its technical and societal modalities. As long as instrumental reason reigns, and as long as its injunctions prevail in society, the essay's aim will be to redress the imbalance through the critical interpretation of culture, as culture both registers and resists those injunctions. This does not mean that the essay clings to dated models of individuality, such as Montaigne's "honnête homme," but neither does it discard autonomy as an obsolete ideal. Nor does one promote the essay's aims by naively opposing the spontaneous, unmethodical moment of essaying to its critical or methodical moment. Only a commitment to maintain the tension between the two moments can keep the essay from getting mired in either faddism or dogmatism. The choice now is not between unbridled subjectivity and the absolute system; these are only ideal types, theoretical constructs. The situation of the modern essayist is better captured by Friedrich Schlegel's aphorism: "To have a system or not to have one—both are equally deadly for the mind. One has little choice but somehow to combine the two" (31; my trans.). In the current critical landscape, there are powerful temptations both in systems and in antisystems. Both are preemptive, colonizing modes of thought: wherever one finds oneself, the terrain has been mapped, the roads and lanes well laid out in advance. The contemporary situation calls for a less programmed, more venturesome mode of response, a kind of thought at once fragmentary and holistic, not governed by exclusive principles, whether systematic or unsystematic in nature. Perhaps the faculty most required of the modern critic is what Keats, admittedly to different purpose, once termed "Negative Capability, that is, when man is capable of being in uncertainties, Mysteries, doubts, without any irritable reaching after fact and reason" (350). For Keats, this faculty in a "great poet" meant that "the sense of Beauty overcomes every other consideration, or rather obliterates all consideration." Possession of this faculty would bring the essayist to a less extreme result, to an equipoise, restoring "all consideration" without eliminating the "sense of Beauty." It would lead, epistemologically speaking, to a qualified skepticism, allowing the essayist to entertain systems, to glean their energies and insights, without entirely succumbing to them. At the same time, it would enable him to resist the siren call of antisystems, with their reverse absolutism and methodological velleities. (Who, if not the essayist, will deconstruct the deconstructors?)

Toward the end of his career, Roland Barthes acknowledged that he had produced "only essays, an ambiguous genre in which analysis vies with writing" ("Lecture" 3). With its avowed antinomian character—its mosaic form, its unmethodical method—is the essay not inherently a pluralistic and interdisciplinary genre? At once "writing" and "analysis," literature and philosophy, imagination and reason, it remains the most propitious form for interdisciplinary inquiry in the human sciences. Its task is not to stay within the well-charted boundaries of the academic disciplines, nor to shuttle back and forth across those boundaries, but to reflect on them and challenge them. To accept the prevailing divisions and to stay dutifully within them would betray the essay's mission of disciplined digression. The essay's irregular path ("method" comes from the Greek *meta* and *bolos*: "along the way or path") registers the element of contingency which is common to all forms of genuine query. "Methodic groping is a kind of comradeship with chance—a conditional alliance," Justus Buehler has observed; "far from being, as some philosophers believe, the sign of weakness in a man or a method, [it] is the price that the finite creature is naturally obliged to pay in the process of search" (84–86). So perhaps it is truer to say that essaying is an extradisciplinary mode of thought. Entering the road laid down by tradition, the essayist is not content to pursue faithfully the prescribed itinerary. Instinctively, he (or she) swerves to explore the surrounding terrain, to track a stray detail or anomaly, even at the risk of wrong turns, dead ends, and charges of trespassing. From the standpoint of more "responsible" travelers, the resulting path will look skewed and arbitrary. But if the essayist keeps faith with chance, moving with unmethodical method through the thicket of contemporary experience, some will find the path worth following awhile.

WORKS CITED

Adorno, Theodor W. "The Actuality of Philosophy." *Telos*, 31 (Spring 1977): 120–33.

_____. "Cultural Criticism and Society." In *Prisms*. Trans. Samuel and Shierry Weber. London: Neville Spearman, 1967.

_____. "The Essay as Form." *New German Critique* 32 (Spring 1984): 151–71.

_____. *Negative Dialectics*. Trans. E. B. Ashton. New York: Seabury Press, 1973.

Auden, W. H. "G. K. Chesterton's Non-fictional Prose." In *Forewords and Afterwards*. New York: Random House, 1974.

Barfield, Owen. "The Rediscovery of Meaning." *The Rediscovery of Meaning and Other Essays*. Middletown, Conn.: Wesleyan University Press, 1985.

Barthes, Roland. "From Work to Text." In *Image-Music-Text*. Ed. and trans. Stephen Heath. New York: Hill and Wang, 1977.

_____. "Lecture in Inauguration of the Chair of Literary Semiology, Collége de France." October, 8 (Spring 1979): 3–16.

Benjamin, Walter. *The Origin of German Tragic Drama*. Trans. John Osborne. London: New Left Books, 1977.

Bense, Max. "Über den Essay und seine Prosa." *Merkur* 3. (1947): 414–24.

Buchler, Justus. *The Concept of Method*. New York: Columbia University Press, 1961.

Busk-Morss, Susan. *The Origin of Negative Dialectics*. New York: Free Press, 1977.

Derrida, Jacques. "La loi du genre/The Law of Genre." *Glyph* 7 (1980): 176–232.

_____. *Of Grammotology*. Trans. Gayatri C. Spivak. Baltimore: Johns Hopkins University Press, 1976.

Foucault, Michel. "Truth and Power." In *Power/Knowledge: Selected Interviews and Other Writings*. 1972–1977. Ed. Colin Gordon, trans. Colin Gordon et al. New York: Pantheon, 1980.

_____. *The Use of Pleasure*. Trans. Robert Hurley. New York: Random House, 1986.

Friedrich, Hugo. *Montaigne*. Trans. Robert Rovini. Paris: Gallimard, 1968.

Gilbert, Neal W. Renaissance Concepts of Method. New York: Columbia University Press, 1960.

Handelman, Susan. "Jacques Derrida and the Heretic Hermeneutic." In *Displacement: Derrida and After*. Ed. Mark Krupnick. Bloomington: Indiana University Press, 1983.

Hartman, Geoffrey. *Criticism in the Wilderness*. New Haven: Yale University Press, 1980.

Hunecker, James. "Concerning Critics." In *A Modern Book of Criticisms*. Ed. Ludwig Lewisohn. New York: Boni and Liveright, 1919.

Janik, Allan, and Stephen Toulmin. *Wittgenstein's Vienna*. New York: Simon and Schuster, 1973.

Jay, Martin. *The Dialectical Imagination: A History of the Frankfort School and the Institute of Social Research, 1923–1950*. Boston: Little, Brown, 1971.

Kazin, Alfred. "Introduction: The Essay as a Modern Form." In *The Open Form: Essays for Our Time*. Ed. Alfred Kazin. New York: Harcourt Brace, 1961.

Keats, John. "Four Letters." In *Criticism: The Major Statements*. Ed. Charles Kaplan. New York: St. Martin's, 1975.

Lacoue-Labarthe, Philippe, and Jean-Luc Nancy. *The Literary Absolute: The Theory of Literature in German Romanticism*. Trans. Philip Barnard and Cheryl Lester. Albany: State University of New York Press, 1988.

Luft, David S. *Robert Musil and the Crisis of European Culture, 1880–1942*. Berkeley: University of California Press, 1980.

Lukács, Georg. *History and Class Consciousness: Studies in Marxist Dialectics*. Trans. Rodney Livingstone. Cambridge, Mass.: MIT Press, 1971.

————. *Soul and Form*. Trans. Anna Bostock. Cambridge, Mass.: MIT Press, 1974.

Lyotard, Jean-Francois. "Apathie dans la théorie." *Rudiments païens*. Paris: Union Générales d'Editions, 1977.

————. *Economic libidinale*. Paris: Minuit, 1974.

————. *The Postmodern Condition: A Report on Knowledge*. Trans. Geoff Bennington and Brian Massumi. Minneapolis: University of Minnesota Press, 1984.

Montaigne, Michel. *The Complete Essays of Montaigne*. Trans. Donald M. Frame. 1965. Reprint. Stanford: Stanford University Press, 1981.

Nicol, Eduardo. *El problema de la filosofía hispánica*. Madrid: Tecnos, 1961.

Nietzsche, Friedrich. *The Portable Nietzsche*. Trans. and ed. Walter Kaufmann. New York: Viking, 1982.

Pater, Walter. *Plato and Platonism*. 1893. London: Macmillan, 1912.

Schlegel, Friedrich. *Kritische Schriften*. Munich: Hanser, 1964.

Ulmer, Gregory L. *Applied Grammatology: Poste-Pedagogy from Jacques Derrida to Joseph Beuys*. Baltimore: Johns Hopkins University Press, 1985.

Wilde, Oscar. "The Critic as Artist." In *Plays, Prose Writings, and Poems*. London: Dent and Sons, 1975.

Wohlfarth, Irving. "Hibernation: On the Tenth Anniversary of Adorno's Death." *MLN*, 94 (1979): 756–87.

Woolf, Virginia. "The Modern Essay." In *The Common Reader*. 1st ser. 1925. 2d ser. 1932. New York: Harcourt Brace, 1948.

WHAT HAPPENED TO THE PERSONAL ESSAY? [1989]

The personal or familiar essay is a wonderfully tolerant form, able to accommodate rumination, memoir, anecdote, diatribe, scholarship, fantasy, and moral philosophy. It can follow a rigorously elegant design, or—held together by little more than the author's voice—assume an amoebic shapelessness. Working in it liberates a writer from the structure of the well-made, epiphanous short story and allows one to ramble in a way that more truly reflects the mind at work. At this historical moment the essayist has an added freedom: no one is looking over his or her shoulder. No one much cares. Commercially, essay volumes rank even lower than poetry.

I know; when my first essay collection, *Bachelorhood*, came out, booksellers had trouble figuring out where to stock it. Autobiography? Self-help? Short stories? I felt like saying, "Hey, this category has been around for a long time, what's the big deal?" Yet, realistically, they were right: what had once been a thriving popular tradition had ceased being so. Readers who enjoyed the book often told me so with some surprise, because they hadn't thought they would like "essays." For them, the word conjured up those dreaded weekly compositions they were forced to write on the gasoline tax or the draft.

Essays are usually taught all wrong: they are harnessed to rhetoric and composition, in a two-birds-with-one-stone approach designed to sharpen freshman students' skills at argumentation. While it is true that historically the essay is related to rhetoric, it in fact seeks to persuade more by the delights of literary style than anything else. Elizabeth Hardwick, one of our best essayists, makes this point tellingly when she says: "The mastery of expository prose, the rhythm of sentences, that pacing, the sudden flash of unexpected vocabulary, redeem polemic. The essay . . . is a great meadow of style and personal manner, freed from the need for defense except that provided by an individual intelligence and sparkle. We consent to watch a mind at work, without agreement often, but only for pleasure."

Equally questionable in teaching essays is the anthology approach, which assigns an essay apiece by a dozen writers according to our latest notions of a demographically representative and content-relevant sampling. It would be more instructive to read six pieces each by two writers, since the essay (particularly the familiar essay) is so rich a vehicle for displaying personality in all its willfully changing aspects.

Essays go back at least to classical Greece and Rome, but it was Michel de Montaigne, generally considered the "father of the essay," who first matched the word to the form around 1580. Reading this contemporary of Shakespeare (thought to have influenced the Bard himself), we are reminded of the original, pristine meaning of the word, from the French verb *essayer*: to attempt, to try, to leap experimentally into the unknown. Montaigne understood that, in an essay, the track of a person's thoughts struggling to achieve some understanding of a problem *is* the plot. The essayist must be willing to contradict himself (for which reason an essay is not a legal brief), to digress, even to risk ending up in a terrain very different from the one he embarked on. Particularly on Montaigne's magnificent late essays, free-falls that sometimes go on for a hundred pages or more, it is possible for the reader to lose all contact with the ostensible subject, bearing, top, bottom, until there is nothing to do but surrender to this companionable voice, thinking alone in the dark. Eventually, one begins to share Montaigne's confidence that "all subjects are linked to one another," which makes any topic, however small or far from the center, equally fertile.

It was Montaigne's peculiar project, which he claimed rightly or wrongly was original, to write about the one subject he knew best: himself. As with all succeeding literary self-portraits—or all succeeding stream-of-consciousness, for that matter—success depended on having an interesting consciousness, and Montaigne was blessed with an undulating, supple, learned, skeptical, deep, sane, and candid one. In point of fact, he frequently strayed to world subjects, giving his opinion on everything from cannibals to couches, but we do learn a large number of intimate and odd details about the man, down to his bowels and kidney stones. "Sometimes there comes to me a feeling that I should not betray the story of my life," he writes. On the other hand: "no pleasure has any meaning for me without communication."

A modern reader may come away thinking that the old fox still kept a good deal of himself to himself. This is partly because we have upped the ante on autobiographical revelation, but also because Montaigne was writing essays, not confessional memoirs, and in an essay it is as permissible, as honest, to chase down a reflection to its source as to admit some past shame. In any case, having decided that "the most barbarous of our maladies is to despise our being," Montaigne did succeed, via the proto-psychoanalytic method of *Essais*, in making friends with his mind.

Having taken the essay form to its very limits at the outset, Montaigne's dauntingly generous example was followed by an inevitable specialization, which included the un-Montaignean split between formal and informal essays. The formal essay derived from Francis Bacon; it is said to be "dogmatic, impersonal, systematic, and expository," written in a "stately" language, while the informal essay is "personal, intimate, relaxed, conversational, and frequently humorous" (New Columbia Encyclopedia). Never mind that most of the great essayists were adept at both modes, including Bacon (see, for example, his wonderful "Of Friendship"); it remains a helpful distinction.

Informal, familiar essays tend to seize on the parade and minutiae of daily life vanities, fashions, oddballs, seasonal rituals, love and disappointment, the pleasures of solitude, reading, going to plays, walking in the street. It is a very urban form, enjoying a spectacular vogue in eighteenth- and early nineteenth-century London, when it enlisted the talents of such stylists as Swift, Dr. Johnson, Addison and Steele, Charles Lamb, William Hazlitt, and a visiting American, Washington Irving. The familiar essay was given a boost by the phenomenal growth of newspapers and magazines, all of which needed smart copy (such as that found in the *Spectator*) to help instruct their largely middle-class, *parvenu* readership on the manners of the class to which it aspired.

Although most of the *feuilletonistes* of this period were cynical hacks, the journalistic situation was still fluid enough to allow original thinkers a platform. The British tolerance for eccentricity seemed to encourage commentators to develop idiosyncratic voices. No one was as cantankerously marginal in his way, or as willing to write against the grain of community feeling, as William Hazlitt. His energetic prose style registered a temperament that passionately, moodily swung between sympathy and scorn. Anyone capable of writing so bracingly frank an essay as "The Pleasures of Hating" could not—as W. C. Fields would say—be all bad. At the same time, Hazlitt's enthusiasms could transform the humblest topic, such as going on a country walk or seeing a prizefight, into a description of visionary wholeness.

What many of the best essayists have had—what Hazlitt had in abundance—was quick access to their blood reactions, so that the merest flash of a prejudice or opinion might be dragged into the open and defended Hazlitt's readiness to entertain opinions, coupled with his openness to new impressions, made him a fine critic of painting and the theater, but in his contrariness he ended by antagonizing all of his friends, even the benign, forgiving Charles Lamb. Not that Lamb did not have *his* contrary side. He, too, was singled out for a "perverse habit of contradiction," which helped give his "Elia" essays, among the quirkiest and most charming in the English language, their peculiar bite.

How I envy readers of *London* magazine, who might have picked up an issue in 1820 and encountered a new, high-spirited essay by Hazlitt, Lamb, or both! After their deaths, the familiar essay continued to attract brilliant practitioners such as Stevenson, DeQuincey, and Emerson. But subsequently, a little of the vitality seeped out of it. "Though we are mighty fine fellows nowadays, we cannot write like Hazlitt," Stevenson confessed. And by the turn of the century, it seemed rather played out and toothless.

The modernist aesthetic was also not particularly kind to this type of writing, relegating it to a genteel, antiquated nook, *belles lettres*—a phrase increasingly spoken with a sneer, as though implying a sauce without the meat. If "meat" is taken to mean the atrocities of life, it is true that the familiar essay has something obstinately nonapocalyptic about it. The very act of composing such an essay seems to implicate the writer in humanist-individualist assumptions that have come to appear suspect under the modernist critique.

Still, it would he unfair to pin the rap on modernism, which Lord knows gets blamed for everything else. One might as well "blame" the decline of the conversational style of writing. Familiar essays were fundamentally, even self-consciously, conversational; it is no surprise that Swift wrote one of his best short pieces on "Hints Toward an Essay on Conversation", that Montaigne tackled "Of the Art of Discussion", that Addison and Steele extensively analyzed true and false wit, that Hazlitt titled his books *Table Talk*, *Plain Speaker*, and *The Round Table*, or that Oliver Wendell Holmes actually cast his familiar essays in the form of mealtime dialogues. Why would a book like Holmes's *The Autocrat of the Breakfast Table*, a celebration of good talk that was so popular in its time, be so unlikely today? I cannot go along with those who say "The art of conversation has died, television killed it," since conversation grows and changes as inevitably as language. No, what has departed is not conversation but conversation-flavored writing, which implies a speaking relationship between writer and reader. How many readers today would sit still for a direct address by the author? To be called "gentle reader" or "*hypocrite lecteur*," to have one's arm pinched while dozing off, to be called to attention, flattered, kidded like a real person instead of a privileged fly on the wall—wouldn't most readers today find such devices archaic, intrusive, even impudent? Oh, you wouldn't? Good, we can go back to the old style, which I much prefer.

Maybe what has collapsed is the very fiction of "the educated reader," whom the old essayists seemed to be addressing in their conversational remarks. From Montaigne onward, essayists until this century have invoked a shared literary culture: the Greek and Latin authors and the best of their national poetry. The whole modern essay tradition sprang from quotation. Montaigne's *Essais* and Burton's *Anatomy of Melancholy* were essentially outgrowths of the "commonplace book," a personal journal in which quotable passages, literary excerpts, and comments were written. Though the early essayists' habit of quotation may seem excessive to a modern taste, it was this display of learning that linked them to their educated reading public and ultimately gave them the authority to speak so personally about themselves. Such a universal literary culture no longer exists; we have only popular culture to fall back on. While it is true that the old high culture was never really "universal"—excluding as it did a good deal of humanity—it is also true that without it, personal discourse has become more hard-pressed. What many modern essayists have tried to do is to replace that shared literary culture with more and more personal experience. It is a brave effort and an intriguing supposition, this notion that individual experience alone can constitute the universal text that all may dip into with enlightenment. But there are pitfalls on the one hand, it may lead to cannibalizing oneself and one's privacy; on the other hand (much more common and to my mind, worse), is the assertion of an earnestly honest or "vulnerable" manner without really candid chunks of experience to back it up.

As for popular culture, the essayist's chronic invocation of its latest bandwagon fads, however satirically framed, comes off frequently as a pandering to the audience's short attention span—a kind of literary ambulance chasing. Take the "life-style" pages in today's periodicals, which carry commentaries that are a distant nephew of the familiar essay: there is something so depressing about this desperate mining of things in the air, such a fevered search for a generational *Zeitgeist*, such an unctuously smarmy tone of "we," which assumes that everyone shares the same consumerist-boutique sensibility, that one longs for a Hazlittean shadow of misanthropic mistrust to fall between reader and writer. One longs for any evidence of a distinct human voice—anything but this ubiquitous Everyman/woman pizzazzy drone, listing tips for how to get the most from your dry cleaner's, take care of your butcher block, or bounce back from an unhappy love affair.

The familiar essay has naturally suffered from its parasitic economic dependency on magazines and newspapers. The streamlined telegraphic syntax and homogenized-perky prose that contemporary periodicals have evolved make it all the more difficult for thoughtful, thorny voices to be tolerated within the house style. The average reader of periodicals becomes conditioned to digest pure information, up-to-date, with its ideological viewpoint disguised as objectivity, and is thus ill-equipped to follow the rambling, cat-and-mouse game of pet-verse contrariety played by the great essayists of the past.

In any event, very few American periodicals today support house essayists to the tune of letting them write regularly and at comfortable length on the topics of their choice. The nearest thing we have are talented columnists like Russell Baker, Ellen Goodman, Leon Hale, and Mike Royko, who are in a sense carrying on the Addison and Steele tradition; they are so good at their professional task of hit-and-run wisdom that I only wish they were sometimes given the space to try out their essayistic wings. The problem with the column format is that it becomes too tight and pat, one idea per piece. Fran Lebowitz, for instance, is a very clever writer, and not afraid of adopting a cranky persona, but her one-liners have a cumulative sameness of affect that inhibits a true essayistic movement. What most column writing does not seem to allow for is self-surprise, the sudden deepening or darkening of tone, so that the writer might say, with Lamb: "I do not know how, upon a subject which I began treating half-seriously, I should have fallen upon a recital so eminently painful. . . ."

From time to time I see hopeful panel discussions offered on "The Resurgence of the Essay." Yes, it would be very nice, and it may come about yet. The fact is, however, that very few American writers today are essayists primarily. Many of the essay collections issued each year are essentially random compilations of book reviews, speeches, journalism, and prefaces by authors who have made a name for themselves in other genres. The existence of these collections attests more to the celebrated authors' desires to see all their words between hardcovers than it does to any real devotion to the essay form. A tired air of grudgingly gracious civic duty hovers over many of these performances.

One recent American writer who did devote himself passionately to the essay was E. B. White. No one has written more consistently graceful, thoughtful essays in twentieth-century American language than White; on the other hand, I can't quite forgive his sedating influence on the form. White's Yankee gentleman-farmer persona is a complex balancing act between Whitmanian democratic and patrician values, best suited for the expression of mildness and tenderness with a resolute tug of elegiac depression underneath. Perhaps this is an unfair comparison, but there is not a single E. B. White essay that compares with the gamy, pungent, dangerous Orwell of "Such, Such Were the Joys . . ." or "Shooting an Elephant." When White does speak out on major issues of the day, his man-in-the-street, folksy humility and studiously plain-Joe air ring false, at least to me. And you would never know that the cute little wife he describes listening to baseball games on the radio was the powerful *New Yorker* editor Katharine White. The suppression or muting of ego as something ungentlemanly has left its mark on *The New Yorker* since, with the result that this magazine, which rightly prides itself on its freedom to publish extended prose, has not been a particularly supportive milieu for the gravelly voice of the personal essayist. The preferred model seems to be the scrupulously fair, sporting, impersonal, fact-gathering style of a John McPhee, which reminds me of nothing so much as a colony of industrious termites capable of patiently reducing any subject matter to a sawdust of detail.

The personal, familiar essay lives on in America today in an interestingly fragmented proliferation of specialized subgenres. The form is very much with us, particularly if you count the many popular nonfiction books that are in fact nothing but groups of personal essays strung together, and whose compelling subject matter makes the reading public overlook its ordinary indifference to this type of writing. Personal essays have also appeared for years under the protective umbrella of New Journalism (Joan Didion being the most substantial and quirky practitioner to emerge from that subsidized training ground, now largely defunct); of autobiographical-political meditations (Richard Rodriguez, Adrienne Rich, Vivian Gornick, Marcelle Clements, Wilfrid Sheed, Alice Walker, Nancy Mairs, Norman Mailer), nature and ecological-regional writing (Wendell Berry, Noel Perrin, John Graves, Edward Hoagland, Gretel Ehrlich, Edward Abbey, Carol Bly, Barry Lopez, Annie Dillard); literary criticism (Susan Sontag, Elizabeth Hardwick, Seymour Krim, Cynthia Ozick, Leslie Fiedler, Joyce Carol Oates), travel writing and mores (Mary McCarthy, V. S.

Naipaul, Joseph Epstein, Eleanor Clark, Paul Theroux), humorous pieces (Max Apple, Roy Blount, Jr., Calvin Trillin), food (M. F. K. Fisher). I include this random and unfairly incomplete list merely to indicate the diversity and persistence of the form in American letters today. Against all odds, it continues to attract newcomers.

In Europe, the essay stayed alive largely by taking a turn toward the speculative and philosophical, as practiced by writers like Walter Benjamin, Theodor Adorno, Simone Weil, E. M. Cioran, Albert Camus, Roland Barthes, Czeslaw Milosz, and Nicola Chiaromonte. All, in a sense, are offspring of the epigrammatic style of Nietzsche This fragmented, aphoristic, critical type of essay-writing became used as a subversive tool of skeptical probing, a critique of ideology in a time when large, synthesizing theories and systems of philosophy are no longer trusted. Adorno saw the essay, in fact, as a valuable counter-method.

> The essay does not strive for closed, deductive or inductive construction. It revolts above all against the doctrine—deeply rooted since Plato—that the changing and ephemeral is unworthy of philosophy, against that ancient injustice toward the transitory, by which it is once more anathematized, conceptually. The essay shies away from the violence of dogma. . . . The essay gently defies the ideals of [Descartes'] *clara et distincta perceplio* and of absolute certainty. . . . Discontinuity is essential to the essay . . . as characteristic of the form's groping intention. . . . The slightly yielding quality of the essayist's thought forces him to greater intensity than discursive thought can offer, for the essay, unlike discursive thought, does not proceed blindly, automatically, but at every moment it must reflect on itself. Therefore the law of the innermost form of the essay is heresy. By transgressing the orthodoxy of thought, something becomes visible in the object which it is orthodoxy's secret purpose to keep invisible.

This continental tradition of the self-reflexive, aphoristically subversive essay is only now beginning to have an influence on contemporary American writers. One saw it first, curiously, cropping up in ironic experimental fiction—in Renata Adler, William Cass, Donald Barthelme, John Barth. Their fictive discourse, like Kundera's, often resembles a broken essay, a personal/philosophical essay intermixed with narrative elements. The tendency of many postmodernist storytellers to parody the pedantry of the essay voice speaks both to their intellectual reliance on it and to their uneasiness about adopting the patriarchal stance of the Knower. That difficulty with assumption of authority is one reason why the essay remains "broken" for the time being.

In a penetrating discussion of the essay form, Georg Lukács put it this way: The essay "is a judgment, but the essential, the value-determining thing about it is not the verdict (as is the case with the system), but the process of judging." Uncomfortable words for an age when "judgmental" is a pejorative term. The familiar essayists of the past may have been non-specialists—indeed, this was part of their attraction—but they know how to speak with a generalist's easy authority. That is precisely what contemporary essayists have a hard time doing: in our technical age we are too aware of the advantage specialists hold over us. (This may explain the current confidence the public has in the physician-scientist school of essayists like Lewis Thomas, Richard Selzer, Stephen Jay Gould, F. Gonzalez-Crussi, Oliver Sacks: their meditations embedded in a body of technical information, so that readers are reassured they are "learning" something, not just wasting their time on *belles letttres*.) The last of the old-fashioned generalists, men of letters who seemed able to write comfortably, knowledgeably, opinionatedly on everything under the sun, were Edmund Wilson and Paul Goodman; we may not soon see their like again.

In *The Last Intellectuals*, Russell Jacoby has pointed out the reticence of writers of the so-called generation of the sixties—my generation—to play the role of the public intellectual, as did Lionel Trilling, Harold Rosenburg, C. Wright Mills, Irving Howe, Alfred Kazin, Daniel Bell, Dwight Macdonald, Lionel Abel, etc., who judged cultural and political matter for a large general readership, often diving into the melee with both arms swinging. While Jacoby blames academia for absorbing the energies of my contemporaries, and while others have cited the drying up of print outlets for formal polemical essays, my own feeling is that it is not such a terrible thing to want to be excused from the job of pontificating to the public. Ours was not so much a failure to become our elders as it was a conscious swerving to a different path. The Vietnam War, the central experience of my generation, had a great deal to do with that deflection. As a veteran of the sixties, fooled many times about world politics because I had no firsthand knowledge of circumstances thousands of miles away (the most shameful example that comes to mind was defending, at first, the Khmer Rouge regime in Cambodia), I have grown skeptical of taking righteous public positions based on nothing but simpatico media reports and party feeling. As for matters that I've definitely made up my mind about, it would embarrass me, frankly, to pen an opinion piece deploring the clearly deplorable, like apartheid or invading Central America, without being able to add any new insights to the discussion. One does not want to be reduced to scolding, or to abstract progressive platitudes, well founded as these may be. It isn't that my generation doesn't think politics are important, but our earlier experiences in that storm may have made us a little hesitant about mouthing off in print. We—or I should say I— have not yet been able to develop the proper voice to deal with these large social and political issues, which will at the same time remain true to personal experience and hard-earned doubt.

All this is a way of saying that the present moment offers a remarkable opportunity for emerging essayists who can somehow locate the moral authority, within or outside themselves, to speak to these issues in the grand manner. But there is also room, as ever, for the informal essayist to wrestle with intellectual confusion, to offer feelings, to set down ideas in a particularly direct and exposed format—more so than in fiction, say, where the author's opinions can always be disguised as belonging to characters. The increasing willingness of contemporary writers to try the form, if not necessarily commit themselves to it, augurs well for the survival of the personal essay. And if we do offend, we can always fall back on Papa Montaigne's "*Que sçay-je?*": What do I know?

WHAT IS READING?
IT'S EATING ON THE SLY [1994]

It's also a clandestine, furtive act. We don't acknowledge it. It confuses. Reading is not as insignificant as we claim. First we must steal the key to the library. Reading is a provocation, a rebellion: we open the book's door, pretending it is a simple paperback cover, and in broad daylight escape! We are no longer there: this is what real reading is. If we haven't left the room, if we haven't gone over the wall, we're not reading. If we're only making believe we're there, if we're pretending before the eyes of the family, then we're reading. We are eating. Reading is eating on the sly.

Reading is eating the forbidden fruit, making forbidden love, changing eras, changing families, changing destinies, and changing day for night. Reading is doing everything exactly as we want and "on the sly."

And what hooks do we read as we become strangers in joy? Those that teach us how to die.

For example Montaigne, our textual grandfather.

"Montaigne." This is the title of a short text by Thomas Bernhard that I read with delight as "The Tale of Writing." A crafty tale, written in a single flight, at the pace of a single race, miming the scene of concealed reading.

The title announces: "Montaigne." I might think, like you, that this text will deal with Montaigne the author. Will it be a portrait? "Montaigne" in the nude, plain "Montaigne," announces nothing beyond Montaigne. "Montaigne" puts us in a state of Montaigne.

So we think this will be a portrait of Montaigne or that it will return to Montaigne, the head of the text.

And this is where the text starts, by fleeing. In flight. Written to flee a death threat. The flight and the fugitive's panting will trace the text's path and rhythm. Taking off from "Montaigne," the narration and narrator race in Montaigne's direction:

In order to flee my family and therefore my executioners, I took refuge in a corner of the tower, and without light and hence without maddening the mosquitoes against me, I had taken from the library a book which after I had read a few sentences turned out to be by Montaigne with whom I am, *in a certain intimate and actually enlightening way, a relative more than with anybody else.*[1]

Montaigne whom he loves best. And the whole of this short adventure deals with that choice in darkness.

This is how it starts and it then goes on to tell the adventure of reading that hook. The text is a real lesson in writing, paragraph by paragraph, step by step, as if you were inside the tower and climbing step by step—I won't tell you if it is up or down—in complete obscurity.

The text flees paragraph by paragraph. "Montaigne" comes to an end in twenty-two steps or paragraphs—twenty-two bounds. Since you read with your body, your body paragraphs. The steps are almost comparable in size. Sometimes a bit shorter or a bit longer. And they are all equally dense and urgent.

It is immediately about the essential experiences of our lives. No sooner do we enter than we take flight. In the first paragraph we already have a series of directions. And each one of them will be pursued, none of them will be abandoned by the text. However, for the major part of this text, we run and flee in the dark: "I took refuge in a corner of the tower, and without light . . . . I had taken . . . . a book. . . . In absolute darkness I had taken a book from the library." A blind choice, I choose precisely Montaigne, with whom "I am . . . a relative more than with anybody else." I choose from amongst them all—and without having chosen him, hence *blindly*—my relative.

Montaigne with whom I am, in a certain intimate and actually enlightening way, a relative more than with anybody else.

Here's the light, in the relationship with Montaigne. It is an enlightening relationship. Third paragraph:

On the way which led me to the tower, where as I have said I did not put on the light because of the mosquitoes, I tried very consciously, with the greatest concentration, to guess which book I had picked up on the shelf, but all the philosophers who went through my head, were all possible philosophers except Montaigne.[2]

The light comes from inside, the book comes through the head (mine). Montaigne comes to him from within, like necessity itself.

This is already a lesson in true reading; reading we cannot dissociate from our lives. Reading, which establishes another universe of light and dark to that of the outside world, and which is obviously the prolongation of the universe of writing. This happens in intimacy, where sunlight does not reign, reigned over by another light.

That is what we do, we pick up something in the dark. We don't know what we will pick up. We always do this: we pick up a book, but we don't know why. And it happens to be our parent, since the only way to find our real parent is to pick up a book in the dark. It is mysterious. Maybe it is the parent on the shelf that has chosen us, but it can't be explained. Anyway, this is the way we happen on those books that will change our lives. Of course we have at least heard a signifier, but we do choose in this completely blind way and it turns out to be light. This is how Montaigne comes to Bernhard: as the totally unexpected and completely hoped for. All the philosophers go through his head except Montaigne. A subtle scene of overinvestment. The desire for Montaigne is so strong that he doesn't expect Montaigne. And Montaigne comes on the condition of being unexpected. He is absolutely unexpected. There must be an absence of light, plus light in the sentence in order to find Montaigne. Because, of course, light comes from inside and you cannot account for the arrival of light in your life and your head through books. Bernhard insists on this:

So I read *my* Montaigne with the shutters locked in the most absurd way because it was extremely painful to read without artificial light.[3]

It was unimaginable—so he read Montaigne in complete darkness.

Eventually, we reach the point where Bernhard has read Montaigne and has come to this sentence:

Let us hope that nothing happened to him. [N. B., Hélène Cixous's emphasis.] This sentence was not from Montaigne, but from my family, which was looking for me and roaming round the foot of the tower in search of me.[4]

"Let us hope that nothing happened to him." We can taste all the sugar and salt and bitterness of this sentence once we have read everything that precedes it. On a realistic level the parents appear to be worried (I'm talking about the contents of the sentence, not about the intervention of the sentence in the text). If we have a sense of irony we hear: we hope he hasn't read anything, that nothing has happened in that terrible tower, in particular that Montaigne hasn't arrived, etc. . . .We could unravel the sentence forever. One world is being swallowed by another. I was reading Montaigne until the sentence came. The continuity is wonderful. Bernhard doesn't say whether this sentence is inside or outside. The sentence bumps into him. It is imagined as if it were a dream. Are you in your dream or are you already outside? The sentence that has just been uttered: is it still in the dream or is it already outside? Is it in the book or is it in you? It is delocalized. There is hesitation as to the sentence's origin because, after all, Montaigne isn't Montaigne: he is "my family." Montaigne and "my family" pass through the same parental place.

Now we don't know whether this sentence, which is the last sentence of the book, is heard inside or outside the tower. Just as we don't know whether the book happens inside or outside.

Why did Bernhard need to take refuge in the dark tower—Montaigne's tower, obviously—unless it was to save his life, which had been threatened since his earliest childhood by his executioner-family. Things are clear in the dark library. It concerns the deadly war waged between children and parents, this war that turns in circles and began before us all: fear and destruction weave their web between children and parents; you want to kill me, says one, no, you're the one who wants my death, says the other. And it's true, each one kills the other, on either side of the book: the object of passion. It's true: those who love texts incite the hatred of those who don't. It's true: one can kill for a book, for a poem. For or against. One can kill a poet on account of poetry. It's true: poetry—what poison to those who can't take it. For between us, readers and antireaders, there are crimes prompted by jouissance.

Our murders are decided in an obscure and violent relation to jouissance, in jealousy so dark, primitive, and remote we don't even see it. There, in the shadows, a scandalous scene of deprivation is played out: the parent would like to starve the child or at least use hunger to keep hold of him or her. And all this is not without love, not without hate.

If in the past I was frightened to death to take a lump of sugar from the sugarbowl in the dining room; today I am frightened to death to take a book from the library and I am even more frightened to death if it is a philosophy book, like last night.

In the beginning they told you: you must not drink this water, because it is poisoned. If you drink this water, you arc heading for disaster, if you read this book, you are heading for disaster. They lead you into the forest, they put you in dark children's rooms, to disturb you, they introduce you to people you immediately recognize as those who will destroy you.[5]

We recognize the old grandiose and threatening hymn: you will not drink, you will not eat, you will not read, you will not write, otherwise, you will die.
And they call reading a sin, and writing is a crime.
And no doubt this is not entirely false.
They will never forgive us for this Somewhere Else.

Let's come back to the first words of this text; all this is done only "in order to escape." The text has been written in order to escape, to escape the family, etc. Here is the last paragraph:

> I read my Montaigne with the shutters locked in the most absurd way because it was extremely painful to read without artificial light. . . . Let us hope that nothing happened to him. This sentence was not from Montaigne, but from my family who were looking for me and were roaming round the foot of the tower in search of me.

We are still in the dark. Without artificial light: but not without light. We must be as refined as he is, everything is, so to speak, clear.
I come back to the beginning of the text. The text takes off at full speed, in order to escape. The escape is not carried out. All the while the others are there down below.
There is a relationship between reading and what engenders the need, the urgency of reading: you can't have one without the other. To escape . . . I read. That's the mystery of reading. And no realism. One must stay on the side of the text. Accepting the fact that reading is carried out "with the shutters locked." It's both true and not true. We must constantly have one foot in one world and one in the other. This does not belong to the fantastic: it is misleading in Kafka's manner. You believe you are on a path, but you're on another, you're on that one, etc. Such is the relation between reading and writing. In the same way this text is written by the light of an inner Montaigne, in the dark. We write in the dark, we read in the dark:

they are the same process.

NOTES

1   Thomas Bernard, "Montaigne," *Die Zeit*, October 8, 1982, no. 41.

2   *Ibid.*

3   *Ibid.*

4   *Ibid.*

5   *Ibid.*

RACHEL BLAU DUPLESSIS

f-WORDS: AN ESSAY ON THE ESSAY
[1996]

In 1969, the Belgian artist Marcel Broodthaers prepared several tampered versions of *Un coup de dés jamais n'abolira le hasard*. On the cover, Broodthaers's name was given as author. My own quandary, in the spirit of that voracity, would be whether to offer "The Essay as Form" or *A Room of One's Own* by Rachel Blau DuPlessis. In Broodthaers' Mallarmé, a version called "Image," each of the lines is found blackened over, creating design across the fold but effacing all the words within a constructivist geometry. These black Montessori sticks of varying lengths and widths—indicating line segments, but as an array of unreadable cul-de-sacs—are only temporarily charming. The analytically motivated *foutisme* of conceptual art makes the words into an unreadable visual "image" and icon by imprinting over the barely interpretable "images" of Mallarmé's own hermetic obscurity. For its charm—its play with erasure and dark design, with transforming writing into a visual text—does depend on the continued availability of that poem from other sources. To the degree that the version alludes to official gestures of effacement, like censored documents from an FBI file, these blacked-out lines evoke the problematic politics of censorship. Thereupon one yearns for even the dark opacity of Mallarmé's words because they validate the valuable privilege of reading and writing *what we will*. (*f*-words to date: *foutisme, effacement*, FBI, that last to stand, perhaps awkwardly, for the possibilities of state-fortified censorship and other political repressions of texts and writers.)

Another gesture of beginning would be Woolf's in the diary of 1899; her age is seventeen. Taking a book by Isaac Watts with the suggestive title of *Logick, or, the right use of Reason, with a variety of rules to guard against error in the affairs of religion and human life as well as in the sciences*, Woolf cuts pages from her own diary to fit his binding, and then glues them not only to Watts, inside his book, but uses Watts's pages, also glued together, to hide the existence of her own. She does so precisely to write *what she will*. And the hiding of her work is a poignant, discerning gesture and can be read within her mid-adolescent writing life as raising questions of autonomy, property, claims to privacy, and selfhood (De Salvo 1989, 248–50). This book was, apparently, bought for its binding, not for the title and its ironic allegories. But the Watts title still makes a statement about turning method against itself. Woolf uses the book physically; its curious Logick of open-and-shut rules protect her from those guards and guardians of intellectual and moral method who, as she said thirty years later, "save us so much thinking" by propounding such axioms as "Cats do not go to heaven. Women cannot write the plays of Shakespeare"(Woolf [1929] 1957, 48).

Both Woolf and Broodthaers claim the book by saying it is a space in which one wants to make or leave one's mark as freely as possible. The book is just one institution of cultural accumulation; he also claimed the museum, she disclaimed the university. One gesture makes a book keep the secret of her writing; it is deftly marginal, deftly embedded. Her visual text calls us to register fear, cunning, and the hope of uncensored writing annealed to and sandwiched invisibly into treatises on propriety. His visual text frets replacement and effacement, fingering those strings, and firmly, *fortissimo*. Each is differently motivated, but both are methodological critiques of method. Her gesture places Watts's words—indeed whole pages—"over" hers; his gesture paints inked-out blocks over words, deposing Mallarmé's text. The gender issues of access and authority are rather stark in these examples, but taking the two together one can say that writing on the side, through the interstices, between the pages, on top of the writing, constructing gestures of suspicion, writing what one will (what one wills), writing over the top, writing a reading, writing an untransparent text, writing into the book—all these practices and more frame the essay.

This is an essay (my essay) about the essay. Essay is always opposite. Well, often opposite. Oppositional. How does the essay function? What is it taxonomically? The adjective *autobiographical* often used for this manner of work flails and gasps—it is an inadequate descriptor, even though some people may take the stance denominated "I." These are works of "reading"—for essays are acts of writing-as-reading. Acts of trying out, as the French root *essayer* says. It seems as if the essay mode, in our generation, was impelled by the social and cultural force of "1968"—and its motivations—as these forces and events coalesced and influenced "reading." There was a particular flash point of interpretation among women, who began, as "68ers" (in Meredith Tax's phrase) to decode all the multifarious and dispersed signs by which gender had been inscribed. The questions of interpretation, of reading the signs by which one had been read, had similarly, and prior to 1968, become central to a number of cultural practices based in historical idioms (e.g. "race"; the colonized and the colonizer) and ethical ones (e.g. questions of becoming and of justice). It is clear that this desire to descry the ideologies and powers at work in one's own sociocultural formation is one strong source for the contemporary essay.

The practice of "reading" became a vital and earth-shattering act within one's investigative and imaginative life, quite charged with questions of access, consumption, positioning, pleasure, scrutiny, ingestion, interpretation, agenda setting. Reading the signs; crossings, as cross-signs, sighs inside signs, reading as cosigning, as if one also owned, had signed for, cultural materials and was not simply their object, or their dutiful consumer. It was worth your life to "get" a specific book or text or document or event, to undertake it, to ingest it, to deturn it, even to detox it—a reading beyond reading, an impelled and propulsive reading. The word analysis should be able to stand for this, but it doesn't get the lift and loft of feeling-thinking about ideology and event. The word *deconstruction*, so often suggestive, did not uniformly offer a justification to seek political meaning with a defined ethical stake within the world. This kind of "reading" aroused serious personal emotions of pain and pleasure, grief and joy via cultural participation. These paradigm-changing moments on a mass or collective scale—a political conversion leading to serious growth in interpretive nuance; the notion that cultural acts play on our fibers . . .—all this was expressed within the essay.

But if contemporary essays are works of sociopersonal "reading," they are also works of "wrought," a thinking that occurs by the physical elaboration of language, a work and a working in language, not only a working through something intellectually or emotionally. Not language for a summary of findings, but language as the inventor of findings. *Wrought* is the past participle of *work*; but I thought (wrongly, but willfully) that *wreaking* was a related word. *Reading* and *wreaking* make a euphonious pair. However *wreaking* is at the far end of essay in its real meaning—its wrath, its venting, its drive. If *wreaking* could be altered somewhat—its propulsions made positive instead of vengeful, one would have the sense of the essay's energy, its wayward reach into utopic desires. Jed Rasula's *This Compost*, an ethnopoetic book of wisdom-essays, also offers a neologism for the activity of making and seeking: writing and reading fused together is *wreading*—a need-filled kneading of texts (Rasula 2002, 11–12). And *wreaking* and *wreading* are what interesting essays get to, one way or another, offering knowledge in passionate and cunning intersections of material, in ways excessive, unsummarizable, and (oddly, gloriously) comforting by virtue of their intransigent embeddedness and their desire, waywardly, to riffle and roam.

The word *poetic* for this kind of writing serves as a marker of untransparent textuality, in the realm of wreaking/wrought. The poetic study, the study as poem, poetic criticism, prose-poem expositions, criticism as fancy fictive acts that awoke to find them true—all these possibilities come to pool in the essay because of its enactment of a praxis. It is the genre showing how *poesis* itself turns back and forth between the discursive statement and the medium itself. The essay does a thinking that is of language in all its rhetorical density and snarls, its emotional evocations, associations, burrs, leaps, expostulations, and fleshliness. Sociality and textuality meet in the essay. It is not aesthetic only, not political only, but aesthetico-political.

The contemporary essay can offer a particular kind of social autobiography: "coming out" stories, "social reading," or community stories. These are readings offered by, and of writers from formerly semisilenced, disparaged social locations—from woman, black, gay, Latino/a, Asian, lesbian—all claiming "voice." Particularism, the local, the nuance of place and idiom—our essay, one mode, has become travel writing into our past, our communities, an ethnography by citizens. At best, the unrolling narratives of pressure, prejudice, conversion, engagement, the precise articulation of speech and writing out of repression, assimilation, and marginalization are dramas well suited to the essay. The essay will serve for the bricolage of tools and packs, the space or continent to be trekked, the stamina and passions of both investigation and findings, the affirmations and their compromises. Given that the essay is all margin, marginalia, and interstitial writing, it rearranges, compounds, enfolds, and erodes the notion of center in textually and socially fruitful ways. Claiming a palpable liberation and a permanent engagement with one's social space, even with one's personal history, is one keynote of the essay in our time. Sometimes this freedom is enlivening, and sometimes it is enervating, its happy truths a religious structure of feeling to which some may be agnostic. It is an efflorescence of difference, now perhaps, and with no little irony, reaping hegemonic fruits.

Another essay mode offers an account of a main character, a character launched much like heroines of novels, in which self-fashioning and accounts of exemplary moments are central. As the concern for individual subjectivity is exploded in literary criticism, as the word "self" became, so curiously, taboo in certain contemporary theorizing practices, "selfhood" and "quest" and "growth" and "narrative coherence" reemerge in this writing. If one kind of identity writing is ethnography, if the work of poet-critics from modernism on suggests an epistolary mattedness, the post office, the blog and listserv, flying and flyting in all directions, this set of essays offers the classic realist novel of *Bildung*. Indeed, Woolf has called the self "the essayist's most proper but most dangerous and delicate tool" (Woolf [1925] 1962, 274). Woolf accomplished an effacement of self: her final work is done under the suggestive rubric of "anon." The essay's f is like the definite integral sign in mathematics, and self-integration is sometimes the watchword of this material, but f is also the sign of effacement, of a function between. For both what one knows and what one doesn't fully know can provoke writing. Hence for me "identity" is hardly the thing speaking; what speaks is something more fugitive. It is vulnerability fissioning within being.

Faced with all that, one might tend to say—essay? it's short but personable writing in prose, and it speaks from the heart (wherever that is). Essays tend to call the genre into question, which theory about genre does anyway, so it sometimes seems as if the essay is lots of modes, not one mode, a set of intersections of intention. Some but not all are "autobiographical"; some, but not all, are discursive; some, but not all, are heteroglossic; some, but not all, are theoretical, and on and on. Indeed, Réda Bensmaïa argues that the essay is not a genre, nor even several and mixed genres, but becoming itself: "a moment of writing before the genre, before genericness—or as the matrix of generic possibilities" (Bensmaïa 1987, 92). This offers a symptomatic aura of specialness to the essay, as if it were the universe one second before its big bang dispersion. It's not that the essay is unsusceptible to genre "definition"; it's rather that the nature of the essay asks one to resist categories, and it starts with itself.

There is some frank arousal within essay function, essay being the genre of spiritual arousal, of social mourning, of political fury as a kind of melody and the sense of a new day dawning. While this time may be (quite implausibly) redeemed, the essayist, skeptical and dubious (even of her-/himself, not to speak of the time), is acting to sift, against hegemonic narratives that would efface them, the debris and the wasted shards, the details that tell us why we are so. This is the "task to brush history against the grain" with penetrating bits of trouble, of the troubled, of the troubling (Benjamin 1969, 257). This nexus of arousal, fury, passion and hope, along with cunning scrutiny of social and cultural texts learned, in necessity, through the scrutiny of official lies, should tell us again why this essay-function was reborn out of (loosely) the long reverberations of the sixties in US thought. It's not so much before genre as under history.

The essay is restless. It is like a kind of travel writing, a voyaging, partial and never satisfied, always a little too hungry or full . . . a little too thirsty, or in the precarious condition of having drunk some strange new kind of water, wine, coffee or *eau de vie*. . . . the view you came five thousand miles for shrouded in clouds, or too sunny, too hot, giving you a headache . . . a particular mix, in short, of satisfied and un-.

Is it possible to synthesize these vectors—to offer any centers around which this writing clusters? What joins tendencies in the essay is probably a renewed attentiveness to materiality, to the material world, including the matter of language. While this attention can also sometimes split into two, emphases on either textual materiality or biographical/ historical/ topographical materiality, the real interest comes when these are fused: when textuality and social practices both compel attention to materiality. The essay is a way of representing struggle, crossings, and creolized exploration. Essays can be tested by the degree and tension of the struggles and passions with which they reverberate.

So while there are probably always essays, it only feels like a moment for The Essay when there is some materialist coagulation of meaning in the formal choice, when critique joins with passion inside language that materializes that passion as rhetoric; when interested and situated knowledge is exposed in its vibrancy; when people have undergone changes that resonate in all felt areas—ethical, intellectual, emotional, visceral, political. For "subject position" is "language position." Notice the tones in which you are fluent; then add the tones in which you stutter. You're beginning to get it. When a situated practice of knowing made up by the untransparent situated subject—as if figuring out on the ground, virtually in the time of writing—explores (explodes) its material in unabashed textual untransparency, conglomerated genre, ambidextrous, switch-hitting style, that's it: *f*-words. The essay.

What is taken (by some) as rhetoric or style or manner (these offered, damningly, as if they were detachable technologies of writing) is in the essay a way of knowing. A path. In some old woods, in the middle of something. The path of rhetoric *is* the path of knowledge. The digression is the subject. The polyvocal collage, the unmatted plurality, the tonal glissades, the upstart mischief, undecorous, suspicious, the probing, the backtracking, the outbursts, the resistances *are* a large measure of the essay's findings.

Essay is the play of speculation. The test of the essay is whether it opens a space for the reader, rather than closing one. The essay is interested and agnostic, situational and material, presentational, investigative, and heuristic. Writing an essay comes from curiosity and need—the need to examine opinions and contradictions, and to interrogate cultural materials, especially those taken for granted. The essay has an ethos of porous, lambent, intense examination, an antiauthoritarian play of perpetual dialectics.

It is a text whose ideal state (that's a paradox), as articulated by Woolf, Adorno, and Benjamin (and by the critics Bensmaïa and Good speaking of Barthes and of Montaigne), contests any notion that writing or thinking leads to unity, system, abstraction, mastery. Indeed, "its structure negates system" (Adorno 1991, 17). The essay, as Adorno argues, protests against all of the "rules" of method (codified by Descartes)—claims of totality and continuity, claims of universality, claims that any concept emerges from a tabula rasa and independent of language, independent of its materiality. Essays can emerge from continuous free association, like Freud's "dream work," a way of reading the rebus of signs thrown into the conscious mind or found in the real, a tactic of inventive discovery proposed by H. D. in *Tribute to Freud* and other of her essays.

Driven, the essay is also relaxed, casual, humane. Humane, it is also angry, resistant, unrelaxed—passionate and driven. What has caused this double gesture? A political provocation and spiritual intuition both lead to the ethos of the essay. Writing an essay does not imply a proper (meaning objective) distance from something but a significant proximity to it, an implication. A being implicated. In fact, a being consumed. Even when the essay crackles with authority, it is not authoritarian. Even when it's partial, it is never particularist. The essay, without ever claiming to be the messiah is messianic; it engineers rhythms of conversion; it raises and rouses readers, changes the little auricular feathers at its readers' ears.

The ethics of essay is most stringent: it involves the rejection of mastery. Adorno argues that the essay "abjures the ideal" of its own certainties as it moves into the force field created by its insights (Adorno 1991, 161). And yet the essay is also a response made in a smallness and minority so exacting it can be almost arrogant. A fine line. The essay can seem to be a genre of sensibility, expressing the fetishized individual, in various postures of apparent self-revelation. "Personal" may be an easy way of summarizing the upstart quality, the gestures of emancipation and inter-rogation that fuel the essay with situated, nonobjective thought. But it is not the most thorough way.

I am or was once writing this as a reluctant child prepared a written report on "the liver." Her tears, in fact, had stained my wooden desk, and she had labeled them "Koré's tears" with a little note taped next to the stains, now gone. In an earlier essay, "For the Etruscans," another child's shout up through the strained passages of the house, raising the question of "fig newtons," or a riff on "ricotta" seemed to evoke, for some people, the perpetual interruptibility, including self-interruptibility, of women try-ing to do cultural work.

So I have, so to speak, a personal stake in this question. Why are the *Pink Guitar* essays taken as personal? Is it because women's words must be (ipso facto) personal? Is it because the risk of the heterogeneric, of the tonal swoops may seem like a personal boldness? Is it because people reading any pronoun like "I" forget that what they are reading is not life but "biographemes"—selected, made—a work of art. The very danger of the personal is memorialized in this heavy word, a clinical term clearly de-signed to ward off any charge of unmediated spill (Miller 1991, 9 and 19). So what, then, does the word *personal* mean applied to *The Pink Guitar* whose autobiographical moments number barely twenty? Are these too many moments? Does the word mean no more than "situated thinking": the challenge "to the sustaining fiction of objectivity, distance, and neu-trality in critical studies"? (DuPlessis 1990, viii). Does the word *autobio-graphical* get used sentimentally, to suggest "unmediated" and authentic? Or does it suggest a constructed, selected, "fiction of memory" (in Sidonie Smith's phrase) (Smith 1987, 45)? But though rare enough if one were to catalogue or number them—the glimpses of parts of "life" lived at one address or another, 317, 211, now 413, are finally only glimpses. I have told you relatively nothing.

However, that work spotlighted sudden, abrupt moments, intransigent, brimful of contradictions—a dream, an encounter: insoluble. It seems the suddenness and the amorality of the transition, and the intransigence of the contradiction are arresting. Further, these essays (I mean mine, oth-ers' as well) evoke from the reader a set of emotions and responses al-lowably more varied and juiced-up, more open-ended than what is asked by the general/normal material one reads. They ask for affective read-ing, to use the term Steve McCaffery highlights from Deleuze (McCaffery 2001, 42). Because readers have been moved, moved inside *their* lives, they think I have been more autobiographical than I generally have been. The readerly arousal to pleasure created by the essay generates the aura of autobiography. For who has not wanted to get some boards and nails after reading *Walden?*

Yet an essay is arguably a very un-narcissistic mode, for it maintains a notion of service, of the exemplary use of the ego or its testing disso-lution within a cultural project. To illustrate, the person who speaks as "bell hooks"—a remarkable nom de plume given what she wants—says that the essay writes at and "about the points where the public and the private meet, to connect the two" (hooks 1989, 2). Precisely. What people mean when they claim "the personal" is often the reverberation of collec-tivity. The essay is (to borrow from Nancy Miller) "positional"; positional-ity, not personality is central. The essay expresses community, even when apparently singular, and hence allows us to apprehend communitarian yearnings via what seems to be a private play of thought. Far from being exercises in narcissism, in gaining a personal voice, essays are practices in multiplicity, in polyvocality, in other opinions intercutting, in heteroge-neous, faceted perspectives. In short, essays are not a way of "gaining a voice" but of losing one in the largeness of something else.

My argument is abrupt, unregenerate, somewhat willful and over-stated: the essay is transpersonal, collective, based not on *I* but on *we* and *it* (and other pronouns too). Indeed, the pronominals are so unimaginably interrelated, that perhaps only invented pronouns (as Hélène Cixous in-vents *hesheit*) can intimate the social meaning of the essay. Transpersonal; even if apparently autobiographical, essay is more fundamentally collec-tive, the sound of a *we*—an I dissolving back and forth into a listening, and sometimes speaking, other. The voice of the essay at base makes a collective, not a personal speculation.

The collective upsurge behind the apparently individual subject in the essay is most visible at stress points of political desire and anxiety. In "Sor-ties," talking a psychoanalytic language of universal gender conditions, Cixous suddenly bursts out with this collective "song":

There is no invention possible, whether it be philosophical or poetic, without there being in the inventing subject an abundance of the other, of variety: separate-people, thought-/people, whole populations issuing from the unconscious, and in each suddenly animated desert, the springing up of selves one didn't know—our women, our monsters, our jackals, our Arabs, our aliases, our frights" (Cixous 1986, 84).

The purely psychoanalytic subject splits like a fig, and out come the multiple seeds of social dynamics evoking a variety of rich allusions and narratives; these are a collectivity inside an individual, with some notable ethnic anxieties. In this polysocial collectivity, this "peopling" the individual has turned itself inside out, becoming social (Cixous 1986, 86).

Given the rejection of mastery, the arrogant minority, the glimpses of intimate moments, the tracking of a wayward mind thinking, one can also see why the essay has been summed up by the term *feminine*. Extravagance—said Thoreau—wanders around, eccentric, excessive, overdoing it in the strangest ways—why, it's a description at one and the same time of The Essay and The Female of the Species. *Feminine* is a difficult and untrustworthy word—but it makes an exciting gesture, points to a major alteration of thought, a certain wayward turning of practice. And all the negatives of the feminine, the overdone, the exaggerated, the brazen, the wrongheaded, the prone to error, the needing correction, the lack of *mesura*, the overspill, the loss of boundaries: all these become positive rhetorics. The essay embodies, and can claim, a feminized space: of interruption, of beginning again and again, of fragmentation, of discontinuities. But most in its distrust of system, its playful skepticism about generalization. And interest in the small, the odd, the quirky, the by-the-side, the thing changeable, the viewer changeable too. Skepticism even about one's own self-interested positions.

Yet I resist the term "feminine" or regard it with a wary suspicion. Given a 1950s adolescence, "feminine" means some pretty repressive things with burdensome social implications. I can't shake off these things even with repeated exposures to poststructuralist theory, in which "feminine" indicates an untheorizable, excessive writing practice, an untrammeled space beyond symbolic/logocentric order, a practice of immoderation, insubordination, and transgression to which women have a privileged relation. I don't think women as a group are (forever and ever) any more or less in process, indeterminate, fluid, beyond the cultural compact, that is, any more "feminine" than any particular men might be (although some men have power even to be feminine). It is a powerful enabling myth to think so, and it has led to compelling work of resistance and critique, but it is a faith claim. And try as one might to recuperate it, binarist meanings of *feminine* confuse me as a common reader whenever the term *"feminine"* is used to praise antipatriarchal urgencies or some zone imagined beyond the symbolic order. Indeed, there seem to be two completely opposite uses of this term in contemporary thinking: as affirming infinite free-play and as reaffirming the rigid manacles of gender binarism.

I think style and form are strategies of acquiescence and resistance, and the important question is how these rhetorics are used by writers (with what ideology and agency motivating the rhetorics) and how they are perceived by critics (with what ideology and situated reading practices). Hence one may choose, with authorial agency and wary senses of risk, those rhetorics that are (for whatever reason) currently called "feminine." I have said this since "For the Etruscans" (1979). But I said it in a certain tricky way, playing with that choice of "feminine" rhetoric—that is with collage, suture, association, tonal glissades, evocation of the quotidian and unsolemn, interruption, jumpcuts. Hence "For the Etruscans" was widely taken to defend "feminine" language. However, what I actually said is that all rhetorical choice was situational and that nonhegemonic rhetorical strategies are often grasped by groups (women as "ambiguously non-hegemonic") in need of oppositional statement.

Still, it's important to consider the descriptor *feminine* to see what it has offered to significant theorists and polemicists who have used it. "The Laugh of the Medusa" by Hélène Cixous is one of the great twentieth-century manifestoes (Cixous 1980). Like many manifestoes, it exhorts the creation of something that is rhetorically palpable, so the new time that is urged as coming in history is already present in its own prose. The insurgent force of the prose catapults us into the future perfect, with its fecund confusions of present and future tense. It is a work millennial, apocalyptic, and filled with that interplay between political and spiritual energies often found in feminist essays. In this work, exchanges among pronouns claim a new community—a border crossing among third person, second person, and first person, both singulars and plurals. The desire for a "feminine writing" occurs to undermine the central Freudian tenet of gender asymmetry: castration or lack. All logos-centered writing is interpreted as "writing the [male; universalized] body"; her response is that the body of the woman must also write itself (a much misunderstood point). She insists that a fecund plurality of penile forms are the snakes on the Medusa head. Hence that scare head (symbolizing castration) is viewed instead as an affirmative copia of penile and orgasmic/clitoral abundance. With the knowledge of the multisexual female (the new bisexual in Cixous's terms), the phallic period in world history is ended (Cixous 1980, 252). Woman's insurgent laughter around a "vatic [i.e. liberatory] bisexuality" "which doesn't annul differences but stirs them up, pursues them" will break up the deep ideological laws of castration and female repression (Cixous 1980, 254). So the operable term in this essay should really be *écriture bisexuelle* or *polysexuelle*; her *f*-word *feminine* is a polemical gamble.

Similarly Luce Irigaray proposes that the main concepts of psychoanalysis have taken no account of female presence or desire, so the system is not even so much binary as monistic. It is a model of one, in which women are seen by "hom(m)ology" to men, and thus mis-seen. This "economy of the same" should be refused. Her proposal of the term "feminine" then makes a collection point or site for all the excluded materials: maternal pleasure, clitoral presence, the formation of the daughter, a new rhetoric—a whole counter symbolic order of real interplay between two sexes that depends on asserting the powers of the female sex (Irigaray 1985). The counter symbolic order (heterogeneity) has not been construed as a phallic order, and it does not depend on the postulate of loss in the formation of the sexes. She sees as in a vision not one vs. the Other, but a play of "bothness." Irigaray thus hypothesizes a true hetero-sexual (which means a person whose sexuality is heterogeneous; at other times a self-stimulating woman independent of the heterosexuality we know) for a new economy of representation, a practice of "heterogeneity." The unleashed female imaginary, valued and active, is a necessary precondition for the establishment of true heterogeneity, and grows from a triangulation among sexuality, rhetoric, desire. So the heterogeneous involves a multidirectional, whimsical, passionate language, and it involves desires that seems to transpire at once in rhetorical need, social urgency, and sexual organs. Heterogeneity slides into the term "feminine" in Irigaray when the *precondition* for the establishment of a new symbolic order (assuming value to all aspects of femaleness) is taken *as* that symbolic order. In both Cixous and Irigaray, although without total exactness, the term "feminine" is a synonym for heterogeneity, multiplicity, and poly-sexual affirmation.

To call non-linear structures, cross-generic experiment, collage, non-narrative play with subjectivity, temporality, and syntax—by the name of "feminine" follows the French feminism of Cixous and Irigaray. One could nod approvingly, as does Joan Retallack in *The Poethical Wager*, accepting the word—mainly but not totally. "It is the women (among experimental poets) who—for the first time in large numbers using "feminine" formal processes—are presenting us with our strongest, most challenging models of literary feminisms" (Retallack 2003, 144). This is actually an argument that demands, rightfully, that the poetry of "established feminist circles" not be considered the only feminism in poetry, which must include works of "the experimental feminine" (that is, works by women using experimental rhetorics). Yet in "feminine," Retallack chooses a term that reinvokes the very rigidity it wanted to criticize, a term that has specific social connotations and non-liberatory uses (Retallack 2003, 141).

The female use of the "feminine" is especially striking for Retallack; she calls it the poethical—a radical changing of rhetorics, genres, and modes of writing that challenges thought, perception, and subjectivity. Her more absolutist heteronym, the equally provocative Genre Tallique says, "Feminist writing occurs only when female writers use feminine forms"; that "only" creates difficulties (Retallack 2003,127). I only wish I could be so certain. For instance, this means that no man could ever write a feminist work, even in feminine forms; further, this is a polemical argument taking feminism away from more rhetorically stolid women, so it is quite exclusionary. Also, it depoliticizes, or appropriates the term "feminism" and makes it the property of specific rhetorical, modal and genre choices. Certainly a rhetorical choice has historical and situational meaning—it is precisely a wager in Retallack's terms, not an absolute. But more than that, a rhetoric is only part of a politics—necessary but not sufficient.

Then in other of her essays, Retallack is not so certain that "feminine" is the best term for what she wants: "Our best possibilities lie in texts/ alter-texts where the so-called feminine and masculine take migratory, paradoxical, and surprising swerves to the enrichment of both,/n/either, and all else that lies along fields of limitless nuance" (Retallack 2003, 113). That "so-called" hints that the gender binarist terms are only a stepping stone to something postbinarist and possibly postgender—"a culture of reciprocal alterity" of the genders and dynamic (social and literary) uses of the possibilities of masculine and feminine by anyone and everyone. Would it not be more useful, for such a dialectic, to leave the terms feminine and masculine in the category of the to-be-sublated?

The category "feminine writing" has been so evocative because "feminine" serves as collection site for a variety of rhetorical/ethical theories that open the utopian possibility of serious intellectual and social change in the realm of gender. The term valorizes the demeaned or minoritized. And then the word evokes a fundamental change of everything, everywhere. Yet saying that there already exists a space ("the feminine") for this change begs the question, or slides across the question, of political and social struggle that could bring about this level of change. It is under these aroused rubrics of a social transformation that one can understand such an unpromising and confusing term as "feminine." But only as a cover word, an encoded word. Just as the term "personal" veils the plurality inside one subject, the gender-hybrid subject, and community, so the word "feminine" is a flat cover term that veils its real meanings. If one wants to say transgressive, hybrid, antihegemonic rhetorics, why not do so in these words? *"Feminine"* names a suggestive site of what is yearned for in these essay-manifestoes: female (as human) agency beyond oppressions, sexual plurality, political change, cultural struggle. Sometimes the *f*-word *feminine* is a stand-in for reaffirming situated materiality (an old idea of female bodies, as if men's bodies did not suffer materially, were not subject to buffetings). I should, in any event, want to substitute untranscendent, situated materiality of body and text as a source for thought and mainly forget about the word *"feminine."* Or affirm that the loss of any mind-body split is an ideological goal. All thought being so situated, so invested (in-*f*-ested), the issue is finding and tracking materiality and interests, not denying them.

The reason it has been blinding to call a certain rhetoric "feminine" is that it seems to credit our gender (speaking as Herself) with a style disruptive of hegemony. Yet it is not impossible (and can be seen, for example, in some of Charles Olson's essays) that this radical, rousing style can be coupled with ancient, patriarchal gender tropes. Thus any call for the "feminine" in discourse is interesting only when crossed with a feminist, or otherwise liberatory, critical project; rhetorical choices are only part of a politics. There are my *"onlys."* And further—no matter what kind of writing, it is important to understand it by assiduously maintaining feminist (gender-oriented) reception for all writing—one of the richest achievements of this creative period.

Thus collectivity, heterogeneity, positionality and materiality (although veiled under the terms *personal, autobiographical,* and *feminine*) buoy the essay, give it the density of texture, the sense of implication, the illusion of completeness in a form that embodies its own fragmentation. The essay is the mode in which material sociality speaks, in texts forever skeptical, forever alert, forever yearning.

—fugitive, fissured, finding, effrontery, factor, fragmented, "feminine," foutisme, if, effort, foxy, fate, fancy, far & farthest, fast, field, function, effervescent, factitious, findings, feelings, effusion, flounce, forage, farrago, furious, forte, forth, flame, fluid, fronts, freed, fibers, riff, "force field," freely, fold.

WORKS CITED

Adorno, Theodor. *Notes to Literature*, vol. 1. Trans. Shierry Weber Nicholsen. New York: Columbia University Press, 1991.

Atkins, G. Douglas, *Estranging the Familiar: Toward a Revitalized Critical Writing*. Athens: University of Georgia Press, 1992.

Benjamin, Walter. *Illuminations*. Trans. Harry Zohn. New York: Schocken Books, 1969.

Bennett, James. "The Essay in Recent Anthologies of Literary Criticism," *Sub Stance* 60/18, 3 (1989): 105–111.

Bensmaïa, Réda. *The Barthes Effect: The Essay as Reflective Text*. Trans. Pat Fedkiew. Minneapolis: University of Minnesota Press, 1987.

Butrym, Alexander. ed. *Essays on the Essay: Redefining the Genre*. Athens: University of Georgia Press, 1989.

Caserio, Robert. "The Novel as a Novel Experiment in Statement: The Anticanonical Example of H. G. Wells," in Karen Lawrence, ed. *Decolonizing Tradition: New Views of Twentieth-Century "British" Literary Canons*. Urbana: University of Illinois Press, 1992: 88–109.

Cixous, Hélène. "The Laugh of the Medusa." Trans. Keith Cohen and Paula Cohen. *New French Feminisms*, in Elaine Marks and Isabelle de Courtivron, eds. Amherst: University of Massachusetts Press, 1980: 245–264.

Cixous. "Sorties: Out and Out: Attacks/ Ways Out/ Forays," in Cixous and Catherine Clément, *The Newly Born Woman*. Trans. Betsy Wing, Foreword by Sandra Gilbert. Minneapolis: University of Minnesota Press, 1986: 63–132.

DeKoven, Marianne. "Male Signature, Female Aesthetic: The Gender Politics of Experimental Writing." In *Breaking the Sequence: Women's Experimental Fiction*. Ed. Ellen Friedman and Miriam Fuchs. Princeton: Princeton University Press, 1989: 72–81.

De Salvo, Louise. *Virginia Woolf: The Impact of Childhood Sexual Abuse on Her Life and Work*. Boston: Beacon Press, 1989.

DuPlessis, Rachel Blau. *The Pink Guitar: Writing as Feminist Practice* (1990). Tuscaloosa: The University of Alabama Press, 2006.

Good, Graham. *The Observing Self: Rediscovering the Essay*. London: Routledge, 1988.

Goldwater, Marge. *Marcel Broodthaers*. Introduction by Marge Goldwater. Minneapolis: Walker Art Center and New York: Rizzoli, 1989.

hooks, bell. *Talking Back: Thinking Feminist, Thinking Black*. Boston: South End Press,1989.

Irigaray, Luce. *Speculum of the Other Woman* (1974). Trans. Gillian Gill. Ithaca: Cornell University Press, 1985.

Irigaray. *This Sex Which is Not One* (1977). Trans. Catherine Porter with Carolyn Burke. Ithaca: Cornell University Press, 1985.

Irigaray. "The Three Genres" (1987). Trans. David Macey, in *The Irigaray Reader*, Margaret Whitford, ed. Cambridge: Basil Blackwell, 1991: 140–153.

Joeres, Ruth-Ellen Boetcher and Elizabeth Mittman, eds. *The Politics of the Essay: Feminist Perspectives*. Bloomington: Indiana University Press, 1993.

Lukács, Georg. *Soul and Form*. Trans. Anna Bostock. Cambridge: MIT Press, 1971.

Mailhot, Laurent. "The Writing of the Essay." Trans. Jay Lutz, in *The Language of Difference: Writing in QUEBEÇ(ois)*, Ralph Sarkonak, ed. *Yale French Studies* 6 (1983): 74–89.

Mallarmé, Stéphane. *Mallarmé*. Trans. Anthony Hartley. Baltimore: Penguin Books, 1965.

McCaffery, Steve. *North of Intention: Critical Writings, 1973–1986*. New York: Roof Books, 1986.

McCaffery. *Theory of Sediment*. Vancouver: Talonbooks, 1991.

McCaffery. *Prior to Meaning: The Protosemantic and Poetics*. Evanston, IL: Northwestern University Press, 2001.

Miller, Nancy K. *Getting Personal: Feminist Occasions and Other Autobiographical Acts*. New York: Routledge, 1991.

Rasula, Jed. *This Compost: Ecological Imperatives in American Poetry*. Athens: The University of Georgia Press, 2002.

Retallack, Joan. *The Poethical Wager*. Berkeley: University of California Press, 2003.

Rix, Helmut. "La scrittura e la lingua." Mauro Cristofani, ed. *Etruschi: Una nuova immagine*. Florence: Giunti Gruppo Editoriale, 2000: 199-227.

Smith, Sidonie. *A Poetics of Women's Autobiography*. Bloomington: Indiana University Press, 1987.

Woolf, Virginia. *A Room of One's Own* (1929). New York: Harcourt, Brace & World, Inc., 1957.

Woolf. "The Modern Essay." *The Common Reader, First Series* (1925). London: The Hogarth Press, 1962: 267–281.

Woolf, "'Anon'" and the Reader." Brenda Silver, ed., *Twentieth Century Literature: Virginia Woolf Issue* 25, 3/4 (Fall/Winter 1979), 397–398.

ESSAYING THE FEMININE:
FROM MONTAIGNE TO KRISTEVA [1997]

The symbolic categories *masculine* and *feminine* usually align themselves with biological and social distinctions between *male* and *female*, *man* and *woman*, but they needn't always, as is clear in our ability to speak of a masculine woman or a feminine man without raising any questions about chromosomes or genitalia. Masculinity and femininity may in fact be organized around various loci of distinction.

Virginia Woolf, for instance, makes them a matter of dominance and submission in both the public and private spheres. Woolf identifies the masculine with "the creature, Dictator as we call him when he is Italian or German." Father we call him at home, "who believes that he has the right, whether given by God, Nature, sex or race is immaterial, to dictate to other human beings where they shall live, what they shall do," a stance that must be countered by a feminine "attitude of complete indifference" to the pomp and circumstance, the costumes, the patriotic sentiments that characterize the "manly qualities" leading to war.[1]

Julia Kristeva formulates the distinction in terms of time: "Female subjectivity would seem to provide a specific measure that essentially retains *repetition* and *eternity* from among the multiple modalities of time known through the history of civilization," in contrast to "a certain conception of time as project, teleology, linear and prospective unfolding; time as departure, progression, and arrival—in other words, the time of history."[2]

It is still possible in these structures to associate *masculine* with the male human being and *feminine* with the female. But Kristeva herself warns,

> The fact that these two types of temporality (cyclical and monumental) are traditionally linked to female subjectivity insofar as the latter is thought of as necessarily maternal should not make us forget that this repetition and this eternity are found to be the fundamental, if not the sole, conceptions of time in numerous civilizations and experiences, particularly mystical ones. The fact that certain currents of modern

feminism recognize themselves here does not render them fundamentally incompatible with "masculine" values.[3]

Many French theorists, Kristeva among them, carry the terms *masculine* and *feminine* to a level of abstraction at which they become principles or modalities without specific human referents. Thus, Kristeva postulates a female principle repressed, denied, and exiled by the Masculine Logos.[4] In other words, "the feminine," as everything left out by language, can't be articulated by either men or women. Such theorists have been criticized on the grounds that in accepting "the premise that language and experiences are coextensive," postulating language to be a male construct whose operation depends on women's silence and absence," and "perceiving the project of representation [of women] as invalid," they "may settle for a textual 'femininity' unconnected to real women."[5]

The concept of textual femininity—of all that can never be said lying between and beneath the words on the page—unattached to some human form whose breasts and belly, swollen like the Venus of Willendorfs, insist upon its femaleness, has appeal (and not just for those men who use it to calm their queasiness about the exclusions women complain of: "But you see, dear lady, my femininity is just as repressed as yours"). It accurately, if paradoxically, reflects the female sense of functioning as a cipher in a symbolic system that does not represent her at all, her sense, that is, of not being a real *anything*, woman or otherwise, but only "the blank in the symbolic chain, its hole."[6]

And yet—historically, culturally, existentially—there have been real women (as there have been real men): not just modalities but cellular constructs, warm and wet and fragrant and surprisingly durable, occupying some space, some time, who have (whether reasonably or not) believed themselves not men and have therefore experienced some difference whereby they have been known to represent themselves as women. I can't prove this statement, of course. I only know it in my bones. The nature of their womanness may well be influenced by their function as silences in male-dominated language: their negativity, their dissidence, as Kristeva would have it.[7] But it is *theirs*, it attaches to them as female human beings as it does not to male human beings, because they bear the weight of centuries of living according to certain terms, under a certain law, as it were, which has marked them experientially as a separate caste. Thus, the feminine is more than a symbolic category.

In my writing, I try to sustain a kind of intellectual double vision: to see the feminine *both* as that which language represses and renders un-representable by any human being, male or female, *and* as that which in social, political, and economic terms represents experiences peculiar to the female. I want my femininity both ways—indeed, I want it as many ways as I can get it. I am the woman writer. Don't ask me for impregnable argument. As far as I'm concerned, my text is flawed not when it is am-biguous or even contradictory, but only when it leaves you no room for stories of your own. I keep my tale as wide open as I can. It's more fun this way. Trust me.

Like the French feminists, I subscribe to the premise that the world we experience is itself an immense text that in spite of its apparent complex-ity has been made in Western thought to rest on a too-simple structural principle opposing reason to emotion, activity to passivity, and so on, ev-ery pair reflecting the most basic dichotomy—"male" and "female." Like them, I seek to disrupt the binary structure of this text, or Logos, through *l'écriture féminine*, which "not only combines theory with a subjectivism that confounds the protocols of scholarly discourse, it also strives to break the phallologic boundaries between critical analysis, essay, fiction, and poetry."[8]

Hence I write essays in the Montaignesque sense of the word: not the oxymoronic "argumentative essays" beloved by teachers of composition, which formalize and ritualize intellectual combat with the objective of demolishing the opposition, but *tests*, trials, tentative rather than conten-tious, opposed to nothing, conciliatory, reconciliatory, seeking a mutuality with the reader which will not sway her to a point of view but will incor-porate her into their process, their informing movement associative and suggestive, not analytic and declarative.

"If my mind could gain a firm footing," writes Montaigne, "I would not make essays, I would make decisions; but it is always in apprentice-ship and on trial."[9] In fact, the details of Montaigne's life demonstrate that he was fully capable of making decisions; in his essays he sets aside that capacity. "Thus his starting points are not intended to engage a war of opinions," says John O'Neill of the Montaignesque writer, "they are rather subjunctive alliances for the sake of exploring what hitherto had been shared terrain. By the same token, the conclusions reached are not meant to be absolute, but only what seems reasonable as a shared experi-ence." And, as O'Neill points out, "Montaigne found thinking difficult because he rejected the easy assembly of philosophy and theology careless of man's embodied state," aware that the "loss in scholastic abstractions is that they can be mastered without thought and that men can then build up fantastic constructions through which they separate the mind from the body, masters from slaves, life from death, while in reality nothing matches these distinctions."[10]

Preference for relation over opposition, plurality over dichotomy, embodiment over cerebration: Montaigne's begins to sound like a feminist project. Which is not to say that Montaigne was a feminist. ("You are too noble-spirited," he was able to write to the Comtesse de Gurson when she was expecting her first child, "to begin otherwise than with a male."[11]) But whether intentionally or not, Montaigne invented, or perhaps renewed, a mode open and flexible enough to enable the feminine inscription of human experience as no other does. The importance of this contribution has been largely overlooked, perhaps because many of Montaigne's statements, as well as his constant reliance on prior patriarchal authority, strike one as thoroughly masculine, and also because the meaning of essay has traveled so far from Montaigne's that the word may be used to describe any short piece of nonfiction, no matter how rigid and combative.

"Thus, reader, I am myself the matter of my book," Montaigne writes in his preface to the essays. "You would be unreasonable to spend your leisure on so frivolous and vain a subject."[12] In claiming this plural subjectivity, he is clearly aware that he has made writing do something new: "Authors communicate with people by some special extrinsic mark; I am the first to do so by my entire being, as Michel de Montaigne, not as a grammarian or a poet or a jurist."[13] Not much later, Francis Bacon, the first English writer of "essays," would shape modern scientific method thus: "Generally let every student of nature take this as a rule—that whatever his mind seizes and dwells upon is to be held in suspicion, and that so much the more care is to be taken in dealing with such questions to keep the understanding even and clear."[14] How differently Montaigne perceives the human psyche in essays that are, as Virginia Woolf notes, "an attempt to communicate those a soul . . . to go down boldly and bring to light hidden thoughts which are the most diseased; to conceal nothing; to pretend nothing; if we are ignorant to say so; if we love our friends to let them know it."[15]

This image of descent and retrieval echoes Woolf's description elsewhere of the experience of the woman writer as a dreaming fisherman whose imagination sweeps "unchecked round every rock and cranny of the world that lies submerged in the depths of our unconscious being," seeking "the pools, the depths, the dark places where the largest fish slumber," until it smashes against the rock of "something, something about the body, about the passions, which it was unfitting for her as a woman to know." This problem, "telling the truth about my own experiences as a body, I do not think I solved," says Woolf.[16] In such an adventure, Montaigne has the advantage, his embodiment and his awareness of it owning at least marginal cultural acceptability. Even so, his task is hardly easy, Woolf writes, for he must be "capable of using the essayist's most proper but most dangerous and delicate tool," the self: "that self which, while it is essential to literature, is also its most dangerous antagonist."[17]

It is this quality in Montaigne that Woolf admires, and often imitates in her own essays, despite her self-doubt: "this talking of oneself, following one's own vagaries, giving the whole map, weight, colour, and circumference of the soul in its confusion, its variety, its imperfection."[18] Not command of the mind and the world, but communication with the mind and its world forms Montaigne's purpose. "I do not portray being: I portray passing," he states, characterizing his project as "a record of various and changeable occurrences, and of irresolute and, when it so befalls, contradictory ideas: whether I am different myself, or whether I take hold of my subjects in different circumstances and aspects."[19] By embracing contradiction, Montaigne never permits himself a stance sturdy enough for gaining sovreignty over himself, his fellow creatures, or any of the other natural phenomena objectified by scientific discourse.

Unlike Montaigne, Bacon had no qualms about his footing. All a man need do was dislodge the idols of his mind—rooted in human nature, idiosyncracy, social intercourse, and philosophical dogma—and he would see plain the objective world, the world "out there," the world of principles uncontaminated by human flux and context. Human nature being pretty much as Bacon thought it was, "prone to suppose the existence of more order and regularity in the world than it finds,"[20] Bacon's detached view prevailed over Montaigne's messy, shifting, "domestic and private" engagement with "a life subject to all human accidents." For the past four hundred years, people may have read Montaigne for delight, even for wisdom, but most have turned to Bacon for direction to "the truth." And now, from the very products of Baconian practice, those trained in "scientific objectivity," we are learning that one cannot observe reality without changing it and that even physics, that quintessential exercise in intellectual aloofness, is not actually the impartial scrutiny of phenomena "out there" but is rather "the study of the structure of consciousness."[21]

In rejecting the concept of himself as a self-consistent entity, purged of peculiarity, coherent through time and separate from the external processes he observes and records, Montaigne seems curiously contemporary, capable of grasping as Bacon would probably not what Michael Sprinker describes as "a pervasive and unsettling feature in modern culture, the gradual metamorphosis of an individual with a distinct, personal identity into a sign, a cipher, an image no longer clearly and positively identifiable as 'this one person.'"[22] "We are all patchwork," Montaigne writes, "and so shapeless and diverse in composition that each bit, each moment, plays its own game. And there is as much difference between us and ourselves as between us and others."[23] His use of the essay form reflects this sense of fragmentation.

Montaigne's essays are not strictly autobiographical if we accept the conventional definition of autobiography, the story of a person's life written by himself, wherein "story" is a narrative, that which has a beginning, middle, and (problematic) end: linear, continuous, coherent, chronological, causal. But insofar as the "life" in autobiography—selflifewriting—is a construct of the writing/written self, it has at least submerged narrative elements that may be read even when they are not explicit in the autobiographical text.[24] With its "'stuttering,' fragmented narrative appearance,"[25] Montaigne's form helps him to avoid "the original sin of autobiography," the use of hindsight to render his narrative logically consistent,[26] as well as to mitigate the "split intentionality" between Montaigne the man and the discursive "I."[27] A collection of personal essays literally stutters—begins, halts, shifts, begins anew—in a partial and piecemeal literary enterprise that may go on, as Montaigne's did, for twenty years, ending or, more precisely, reaching "not their end but their suspension in full career"[28] only with death.

"To the extent that we impose some narrative form onto our lives," Phyllis Rose writes, "each of us in the ordinary process of living is a fitful novelist, and the biographer is a literary critic."[29] So, too, the autobiographer, whose interpretive task is complicated by a double authority and at least a triple subjectivity, since autobiography is the written (the root so demands) story (the word leaves room for the confabulative possibilities in the process) one tells oneself (first, always) and the wider world (some of whom, at least, are strangers), at some distance from the events and the responses of the subject (also oneself) to those events, about oneself. But the task may be more than complicated, it may be impossible, for the female autobiographer, who has been entitled—historically, culturally, linguistically, critically, that is, politically—to neither authority nor subjectivity. I distinguish the female autobiographer here because I believe her situation to be genuinely separable from that of any other selflifewriter. Margaret Homans articulates the type of difference I have in mind neatly in her discussion of the novels of Toni Morrison, Alice Walker, and Margaret Atwood:

> Indeed, among scholars who accept the primacy of language, one of the most vexed questions in feminist literary criticism is whether or not anything differentiates women's relation to discourse from other literary revolutions (modernism is the example most often cited), or from the discourse of other marginalized groups, such as colonial writers, or racial and ethnic minorities . . . . These novels differentiate between two kinds of marginality: while victimization takes relatively overt forms with respect to race or nationality, the silencing and oppression experienced by women as women are masked as their choice.[30]

Thus, in the paradigm Elaine Showalter borrows from anthropologists Edwin and Shirley Ardner, because women, like minorities, occupy the "muted" cultural sphere, they must use the language of the "dominant" sphere if they expect to be broadly understood, because those who dominate will not trouble to learn their language.[31] Since the dominant language, organized on the basis of sexual polarity, controls the way we all look at the world,[32] and since "complicity with an oppressive male authority is a shared women's experience,"[33] a woman's capacity for uttering what is distinctive about her self's life is especially blunted. Her mutedness tends to become muteness.

Even leaving aside the crude but common identification of autobiography as a record of the great deeds of great men, one finds that until quite recently almost every discussion of the autobiographical project employs the generic "he." The hidden assumption that the self in selflifewriting is masculine is not, of course, surprising, but the absence of surprise does not signify the absence of pain. If we are all, in fact, fitful novelists, and the novel is a male genre; if the biographer and autobiographer are literary critics, and literary criticism is a male genre; then the female practitioner of *life*, let alone of selflifewriting, is inauthentic, forced to tell a story that is not hers. The act of telling, the act of writing about the telling, the very language of the telling and the writing exclude her experientially and aesthetically from her autonomous existence, make her function in the existence of an other, leave her at best skewed and strained, at worst silent as the grave.

How does the fitful novelist learn to inscribe his life/text? Here is the privileged process feminist criticism reveals: The writer, in imitating and recombining the inscriptions available to him from the context he calls culture, is literally the author of his being, with the authority to insert his own text forcefully into the world-text, which will validate the terms of his text, his way of being in the world. And once he lifts his pen to make of his inscription an artifact, his act joins the lineage of such acts, authorized by them, authorizing them, entering "the metaphor of literary paternity" wherein

> a literary text is not only speech quite literally embodied, but also power made manifest, made flesh. In patriarchal Western culture, therefore, the text's author is a father, a progenitor, a procreator, an aesthetic patriarch whose pen is an instrument of generative power like his penis. More, his pen's power, like his penis's power, is not just the ability to generate life but the power to create a posterity to which he lays claim.[34]

Ah yes, we've met this man before: He is the father of sons.

The female fitful novelist possesses no such paternal authority. Her attempts to tell herself the story of herself are cast in a syntax and lexicon demanding that she be the object, not the author, of desire—the stuff, not the spinner, of dreams. Not for her the pen/penis but only envy of the pen/penis. She lives as a lack. "A lot is being said today about the influence that the myths and images of women have on all of us who are products of culture," writes Adrienne Rich.

> I think it has been a peculiar confusion to the girl who tries to write because she is peculiarly susceptible to language. She goes to poetry or fiction looking for her way of being in the world, since she too has been putting words and images together; she is looking for guides, maps, possibilities; and over and over in the "words' masculine pervasive force" of literature she comes up against something that negates everything that she is about: she meets the image of Woman in books written by men.[35]

What she sees in the mirror of these texts may be beautiful or hideous, but it is always unutterably alien. Yet if she tries to articulate her self, these are the features that she limns: not who she is but who she is for the man who desires / does not desire her. Of her own desire she knows almost nothing. How can she in a world-text whose language is predicated, according to the fathers of psychoanalysis and linguistics, upon lack and rupture? In that context, the child learns to speak only to name what is absent, irretrievably lost: the body of the mother, riven from the child by the father, who introduces the wider social world founded on sexual difference. According to Jacques Lacan, without the phallus, then, the point of division, the child does not enter language—the process of signifying what is missing—and will not become an "I."[36] In this account, woman is confined to the role of the Other—cipher, secret, naught—who confers but does not derive meaning. In the grammar of the phallus—the I, I, I— she can't utter female experience.

"It is from the Other that the phallus seeks authority and is refused,"[37] and refusal sounds like just what's called for here. One alternative linguistic scheme might be based in plenitude and continuity. Suppose we say that instead of loss of the maternal body (which female children are "forbidden" less radically than male children) as the means of entering the symbolic order, the child luxuriates in the language spilling from that body freely and sweetly as milk until—so closely does she identify with the source of this pleasurable flow, so abundantly does she love the mother—she begins to reciprocate. And even after the two part, as the child's growing body and boundless curiosity dictate they must, they use words to signify their profound connection to each other and to all those (beginning with the father, phallus and all) who, over time, are drawn into their company. A writer, novelist Abby Frucht reflects, "doesn't look with her eyes, she looks with her words. She doesn't listen with her ears, she listens with her words. She doesn't touch with her fingers, she touches with her words."[38] Language may be imagined as a series of acts, both generous and generative, which do not mourn absence but affirm presence: word as glance, as sigh, as caress.

My concern here is not which of these linguistic views is correct— both are metaphors for a process still not fully understood—but which one permits all the figures caught up in it the richest development. The interpretive models we choose matter. The person who believes that in universal grammar the sentence "has a perpetrator and a victim, and often a blunt object, which is usually 'the,'"[39] does not occupy the same world as the one who supposes the sentence to hold two entities, who are often particularized by "the," in relation to each other. The woman who theorized language along the lines of intimacy might elude the text that phallogocentrism has coerced her into inscribing and tell some altogether different tale.

In 1929, Virginia Woolf caught glimpses of women writing "as women write, not as men write,"[40] but she predicted that it would be a century before they realized their capabilities, and we've got more than a quarter of that span to go. Still, there are signs, there are visions of what woman's writing might look like. Here's one I particularly like, Hélène Cixous's description of "a feminine textual body" as

> always endless, without ending: there's no closure, it doesn't stop, and it's this that very often makes the feminine text difficult to read. For we've learned to read books that basically pose the word "end." But this one doesn't finish, a feminine text goes on and on and at a certain moment the volume comes to an end but the writing continues and for the reader this means being thrust into the void. These are texts that work on the beginning but not on the origin. The origin is a masculine myth. . . . The question, "Where do I come from?" is basically a masculine, much more than a feminine question. The quest for origins, illustrated by Oedipus, doesn't haunt a feminine unconscious. Rather it's the beginning, or beginnings, the manner of beginning, not promptly with the phallus in order to close with the phallus, but starting on all sides at once, that makes a feminine writing. A feminine text starts on all sides at once, starts twenty times, thirty times, over. [41]

Without specific examples, to which Cixous seems constitutionally averse, this definition is merely suggestive, however; and Woolf, though generally a marvel of precision, quotes a "man's sentence" readily enough but never sets down a comparable "woman's sentence." She does note some possible qualities of a woman's book—brevity, broken sentences and sequences—and of the sensibility producing it, most tellingly that "men were no longer to her 'the opposing faction'"[42] or perhaps even the objects of any particular interest at all.

The trick, as Woolf prescribes it, is somehow to "bring out and fortify the differences" between masculine and feminine creative powers and enable a woman to write "as a woman" even though "it is fatal for any one who writes to think of their sex,"[43] and Woolf does not resolve this apparent dilemma. Can one *be* "woman," *do* "woman," but not *think* "woman"? And if one can't, will one truly expire? Well, probably not. A writer always writes out of difference, not just of gender but of every circumstance, and awareness of her idiosyncracies is likely to strengthen her work if only because it enhances her control of them. For a constellation of reasons, among them her own abuse in childhood,[44] sexual awareness may appear more problematic to Woolf then to many other writers. Such possible overreaction aside, however, her call for an androgynous mind undistorted by sex-consciousness may be construed as a matter not so much of attitude toward sex as of cognitive style. Woolf prefers the "union of man and woman" in the mind over their division into "opposing factions": a distinctively feminine (or possibly androgynous, but not masculine) view.

As my gropings here suggest, despite my instruction by a host of gifted feminist critics, I certainly don't yet have a clear vision of what women's writing might be. *Pace* Jacques Lacan, I know that the phallus is no transcendental signifier—nor transcendental anything else, as far as I'm concerned—but I don't know what my transcendental signifier is, if indeed there is any such thing, which I doubt, since the whole concept seems far too *located* to express my experience of the world. My "I" seems simply not to be the male-constructed "I." It is more fluid, diffuse, multiplex (giddy, duplicitous, and inconstant, I think men have called it). Maybe we need another sort of signifier for the female self—the "O" might be a logical choice, or rather a whole string of Os: OOOOO. That's me.

The fact of the matter, though, is that when I sit down at my desk to tell a story, I can't begin, "OOOOO woke this morning to the song of a cardinal in the fig tree outside the back door." Radical feminist writers like Monique Wittig and Mary Daly experiment with techniques for reinventing reality by exploding patriarchal linguistic patterns. But in passages like this one—

The Powers to break the framers' frameworks are within women. Discovering our Lust of Be-ing, we can easily swing open the doors to our freedom. We work to attain the Prudence of Prudes, the Courage of Crones, the Distemper of Dragon-identified fire-breathing Furies. Furiously focused, we find our Final Cause.[45]

—all those hyphens and capital letters and puns and alliterations give me a wicked case of intellectual indigestion, and after twenty pages I'm too dyspeptic to go on. If I want to speak plainly to you about particulars—and I do, more than anything else—I must use the language that I know you know.

I want a prose that is allusive and translucent, that eases you into me and embraces you, not one that baffles you or bounces you around so that you can't even tell where I am. And so I have chosen to work, very, very carefully, with the language we share, faults and all, choosing each word for its capacity, its ambiguity, the space it provides for me to live my life within it, relating rather than opposing each word to the next, each sentence to the next, "starting on all sides at once . . . twenty times, thirty times, over": the stuttering adventure of the essay.

NOTES

1 Virginia Woolf, *Three Guineas* (New York: Harcourt Brace Jovanovich, 1966), pp. 58, 107.

2 Julia Kristeva, "Women's Time," Trans. Alice Jardine and Harry Blake. *Signs* 7 (Autumn 1981): 34.

3 Ibid., p. 35.

4 Domna C. Stanton, "Language and Revolution: The Franco-American Dis-Connection," in *The Future of Difference.* Ed. Hester Eisenstein and Alice Jardin (Boston: G. K. Hall, 1980), p. 75.

5 Margaret Homans, "'Her Very Own Howl': The Ambiguities of Representation in Recent Women's Fiction," *Signs* 9 (Winter 1983): 186, 187.

6 Stanton, "Language and Revolution," p. 76.

7 According to Stanton, ibid., p. 75.

8 Ibid., pp. 73, 80.

9 Michel de Montaigne, "Of Repentence," *Selections from the Essays.* Ed. and trans. Donald M. Frame (Arlington Heights, IL: AHM Publishing Corp., 1973), p. 75. Cf. Kristeva's notion of the subject "in process/on trial" (the French *process* means both) in "Women's Time."

10 John O'Neill, *Essaying Montaigne: A Study of the Renaissance Institution of Writing and Reading* (London: Routledge and Kegan Paul, 1982), pp. 9, 32, 69.

11 Montaigne, "Of the Education of Children," in *Selections*, p. 10.

12 Montaigne, "To the Reader," in *Selections*, p. 3.

13 Montaigne, "Of Repentence," p. 76.

14 Francis Bacon, "The Four Idols," from *Novum Organum, in A World of Ideas*, ed. Lee A. Jacobus (New York: St. Martin's Press, 1983), p. 337.

15 Virginia Woolf, "Montaigne," *The Common Reader* (New York: Harcourt Brace & World, 1953), p. 66.

16 Virginia Woolf, "Professions for Women," *Women and Writing*, ed. Michèle Barrett (New York: Harcourt Brace Jovanovich, 1979), pp. 61, 62.

17 Virginia Woolf, "The Modern Essay," *The Common Reader*, p. 222.

18 Woolf, "Montaigne," p. 59.

19 Montaigne, "Of Repentence," p. 75.

20 Bacon, "The Four Idols," p. 332.

21 Gary Zukav, *The Dancing Wu Li Masters* (New York: Bantam Books, 1980), p. 31.

22 Michael Sprinker, "Fictions of the Self: The End of Autobiography," in *Autobiography: Essays Theoretical and Critical*, ed. James Olney (Princeton: Princeton University Press, 1980), p. 322.

23 Montaigne, "Of the Inconsistency of Our Actions," p. 48.

24 Louis A. Renza, "The Veto of the Imagination: A Theory of Autobiography," in *Autobiography*, p. 41.

25 Ibid., p. 279.

26 Georges Gusdorf, "The Conditions and Limits of Autobiography," in *Autobiography*, p. 41.

27 Renza, "The Veto of the Imagination," p. 279.

28 Woolf, "Montaigne," p. 67.

29 Phyllis Rose, *Parallel Lives: Five Victorian Marriages* (New York: Alfred A. Knopf, 1983), p. 6.

30 Homans, "'Her Very Own Howl,'" p. 198.

31 Elaine Showalter, "Feminist Criticism in the Wilderness," *Critical Inquiry* 8 (Winter 1981): 200.

32 Elaine Marks and Isabelle de Courtivron, eds., *New French Feminism: An Anthology* (Amherst: University of Massachusetts Press, 1980:, p. 4.

33 Homans, "'Her Very Own Howl,'" p. 200.

34 Sandra M. Gilbert and Susan Gubar. *The Madwoman in the Attic: The Woman Writer and the Nineteenth-Century Literary Imagination* (New Haven: Yale University Press, 1979), p. 6.

35 Adrienne Rich, "When We Dead Awaken: Writing as Revision," *On Lies, Secrets, and Silence: Selected Prose 1966–1978* (New York: W. W. Norton, 1978), p. 39.

36 Numerous explanations of this Lacanian account are available. For a particularly lucid one, see Terry Eagleton, *Literary Theory* (Minneapolis: University of Minnesota Press, 1983), pp. 163–74.

37 Jacqueline Rose, "Introduction—II," *Feminine Sexuality: Jacques Lacan and the école Freudienne*, ed. Juliet Mitchell and Jacqueline Rose, tr. Jacqueline Rose (New York: W. W. Norton, 1982), p. 51.

38 Abby Frucht, "The Objects of My Invention," *The New York Times Book Review*, 11 April 1993, p. 24.

39 Russ Rymer, *Genie: An Abused Child's Flight from Silence* (New York: Harper Collins, 1993), p. 27.

40 Virginia Woolf, *A Room of One's Own* (New York: Harcourt Brace Jovanovich, 1957), p. 27.

41 Hélène Cixous, "Castration or Decapitation?" tr. Annette Kuhn, *Signs* 7 (Autumn 1981): 53.

42 Woolf, *A Room of One's Own*, p. 96.

43 Ibid., pp. 91, 96, 108.

44 For a study of this formative factor, see Louise DeSalvo, *Virginia Woolf: The Impact of Childhood Sexual Abuse on Her Life and Work* (Boston: Beacon Press, 1989).

45 Mary Daly, "New Archaic Afterwords," to *The Church and the Second Sex* (Boston: Beacon Press, 1985), p. xxvii.

CYNTHIA OZICK
....

SHE — PORTRAIT OF THE
ESSAY AS A WARM BODY [1998]

An essay is a thing of the imagination. If there is information in an essay, it is by-the-by, and if there is an opinion in it, you need not trust it for the long run. A genuine essay has no educational, polemical, or sociopolitical use; it is the movement of a free mind at play. Though it is written in prose, it is closer in kind to poetry than to any other form. Like a poem, a genuine essay is made out of language and character and mood and temperament and pluck and chance.

And if I speak of a genuine essay, it is because fakes abound. Here the old-fashioned term poetaster may apply, if only obliquely. As the poetaster is to the poet—a lesser aspirant—so the article is to the essay: a look-alike knockoff guaranteed not to wear well. An article is gossip. An essay is reflection and insight. An article has the temporary advantage of social heat—what's hot out there right now. An essay's heat is interior. An article is timely, topical, engaged in the issues and personalities of the moment; it is likely to be stale within the month. In five years it will have acquired the quaint aura of a rotary phone. An article is Siamese-twinned to its date of birth. An essay defies its date of birth, and ours too. (A necessary caveat: some genuine essays are popularly called "articles"—but this is no more than an idle, though persistent, habit of speech. What's in a name? The ephemeral is the ephemeral. The enduring is the enduring.)

A small historical experiment. Who are the classical essayists that come at once to mind? Montaigne, obviously. Among the nineteenth-century English masters, the long row of Hazlitt, Lamb, De Quincey, Stevenson, Carlyle, Ruskin, Newman, Arnold, Harriet Martineau. Of the Americans, Emerson. It may be argued that nowadays these are read only by specialists and literature majors, and by the latter only when they are compelled to. However accurate the claim, it is irrelevant to the experiment, which has to do with beginnings and their disclosures. Here, then, are some introductory passages:

One of the pleasantest things in the world is going a journey; but I like to go by myself. I can enjoy society in a room; but out of doors, nature is company enough for me. I am then never less alone than when alone.
—William Hazlitt, "On Going a Journey"

To go into solitude, a man needs to retire as much from his chamber as from society. I am not solitary whilst I read and write, though nobody is with me. But if a man would be alone, let him look at the stars.
—Ralph Waldo Emerson, "Nature"

I have often been asked how I first came to be a regular opium eater; and have suffered, very unjustly, in the opinion of my acquaintance, from being reputed to have brought upon myself all the sufferings which I shall have to record, by a long course of indulgence in this practice purely for the sake of creating an artificial state of pleasurable excitement. This, however, is a misrepresentation of my case.
—Thomas De Quincey, "Confessions of an English Opium Eater"

The human species, according to the best theory I can form of it, is composed of two distinct races, the men who borrow, and the men who lend.
—Charles Lamb, "The Two Races of Men"

I saw two hareems in the East; and it would be wrong to pass them over in an account of my travels; though the subject is as little agreeable as any I can have to treat. I cannot now think of the two mornings thus employed without a heaviness of heart greater than I have ever brought away from Deaf and Dumb Schools, Lunatic Asylums, or even Prisons.
—Harriet Martineau, "From Eastern Life"

The future of poetry is immense, because in poetry, where it is worthy of its high destinies, our race, as time goes on, will find an ever and surer stay. There is not a creed which is not shaken, not an accredited dogma which is not shown to be questionable, not a received tradition which does not threaten to dissolve. . . . But for poetry the idea is every-thing; the rest is a world of illusion, of divine illusion.
—Matthew Arnold, "The Study of Poetry"

The changes wrought by death are in themselves so sharp and final,

and so terrible and melancholy in their consequences, that the thing stands alone in man's experience, and has no parallel upon earth. It outdoes all other accidents because it is the last of them. Sometimes it leaps suddenly upon its victims, like a Thug; sometimes it lays a regular siege and creeps upon their citadel during a score of years. And when the business is done, there is a sore havoc made in other people's lives, and a pin knocked out by which many subsidiary friendships hung together.
—Robert Louis Stevenson, "Aes Triplex"

It is recorded of some people, as of Alexander the Great, that their sweat, in consequence of some rare and extraordinary constitution, emitted a sweet odor, the cause of which Plutarch and others investigated. But the nature of most bodies is the opposite, and at their best they are free from smell. Even the purest breath has nothing more excellent than to be without offensive odor, like that of very healthy children.
—Michel de Montaigne, "Of Smells"

What might such a little anthology of beginnings reveal? First, that language differs from one era to the next: there are touches of archaism here, if only in punctuation and cadence. Second, that splendid minds may contradict each other (outdoors, Hazlitt never feels alone; Emerson urges the opposite). Third, that the theme of an essay can be anything under the sun, however trivial (the smell of sweat) or crushing (the thought that we must die). Fourth, that the essay is a consistently recognizable and venerable—or call it ancient—form. In English: Addison and Steele in the eighteenth century, Bacon and Browne in the seventeenth, Lyly in the sixteenth, Bede in the eighth. And what of the biblical Koheleth—Ecclesiastes—who may be the oldest essayist reflecting on one of the oldest subjects: world-weariness?

So the essay is ancient and various: but this is a commonplace. There is something else, and it is more striking yet—the essay's power. By "power" I mean precisely the capacity to do what force always does: coerce assent. Never mind that the shape and inclination of any essay is against coercion or suasion, or that the essay neither proposes nor purposes to get you to think like its author—at least not overtly. If an essay has a "motive," it is linked more to happenstance and opportunity than to the driven will. A genuine essay is not a doctrinaire tract or a propaganda effort or a broadside. Thomas Paine's "Common Sense" and Emile Zola's "*J'accuse*" are heroic landmark writings; but to call them essays, though they may resemble the form, is to misunderstand. The essay is not meant for the barricades; it is a stroll through someone's mazy mind. Yet this is not to say that there has never been an essayist morally intent on making an argument, however obliquely—George Orwell is a case in point. At the end of the day, the essay turns out to be a force for agreement. It co-opts agreement; it courts agreement; it seduces agreement. For the brief hour we give to it, we are sure to fail into surrender and conviction. And this will occur even if we are intrinsically roused to resistance.

To illustrate: I may not be persuaded by Emersonianism as an ideology, but Emerson—his voice, his language, his music—persuades me. When we look for superlatives, not for nothing do we speak of "commanding" or "compelling" prose. If I am a skeptical rationalist or an advanced bio-chemist, I may regard (or discard) the idea of the soul as no better than a puff of warm vapor. But here is Emerson on the soul: "when it breathes through [man's] intellect, it is genius; when it breathes through his will, it is virtue; when it flows through his affection, it is love." And then—well, I am in thrall, I am possessed; I believe.

The novel has its own claims on surrender. It suspends our participation in the society we ordinarily live in, so that—for the time we are reading—we forget it utterly. But the essay does not allow us to forget our usual sensations and opinions; it does something even more potent: it makes us deny them. The authority of a masterly essayist—the authority of sublime language and intimate observation—is absolute. When I am with Hazlitt, I know no greater companion than nature. When I am with Emerson, I know no greater solitude than nature.

And what is most odd about the essay's power to lure us into its lair is how it goes about this work. We feel it when a political journalist comes after us with a point of view—we feel it the way the cat is wary of the dog. A polemic is a herald, complete with feathered hat and trumpet. A tract can be a trap. Certain magazine articles have the scent of so-much-per-word. What is indisputable is that all of these are more or less in the position of a lepidopterist with his net: they mean to catch and skewer. They are focused on prey—i.e., us. The genuine essay, in contrast, never thinks of us; the genuine essay may be the most self-centered (the politer word would be subjective) arena for human thought ever devised.

Or else, though still not having you and me in mind (unless as an exemplum of common folly), it is not self-centered at all. When I was a child, I discovered in the public library a book that enchanted me then, and the idea of which has enchanted me for life. I have no recollection either of the title or of the writer—and anyhow very young readers rarely take note of authors; stories are simply and magically *there*. The characters included, as I remember them, three or four children and a delightful relation who is a storyteller, and the scheme was this: each child calls out a story-element—most often an object—and the storyteller gathers up whatever is supplied (blue boots, a river, a fairy, a pencil box) and makes out of these random, unlikely, and disparate offerings a tale both logical and surprising. An essay, it seems to me, may be similarly constructed—if so deliberate a term applies. The essayist, let us say, unexpectedly stumbles over a pair of old blue boots in a corner of the garage, and this reminds her of when she last wore them—twenty years ago, on a trip to Paris, where on the banks of the Seine she stopped to watch an old fellow sketching, with a box of colored pencils at his side. The pencil wiggling over his sheet is a grayish pink, which reflects the threads of sunset pulling westward in the sky, like the reins of a fairy cart . . . and so on. The mind meanders, slipping from one impression to another, from reality to memory to dreamscape and back again.

In the same way Montaigne, in our sample, when contemplating the unpleasantness of sweat, ends with the pure breath of children. Or Stevenson, starting out with mortality, speaks first of ambush, then of war, and finally of a displaced pin. No one is freer than the essayist—free to leap out in any direction, to hop from thought to thought, to begin with the finish and finish with the middle, or to eschew beginning and end and keep only a middle. The marvel of it is that out of this apparent causelessness, out of this scattering of idiosyncratic seeing and telling, a coherent world is made. It is coherent because, after all, an essayist must be an artist, and every artist, whatever the means, arrives at a sound and singular imaginative frame—or call it, on a minor scale, a cosmogony.

And it is into this frame, this work of art, that we tumble like tar babies, and are held fast. What holds us there? The authority of a voice, yes; the pleasure—sometimes the anxiety—of a new idea, an untried angle, a snatch of reminiscence, bliss displayed or shock conveyed. An essay can be the product of intellect or memory, lightheartedness or gloom, well-being or disgruntlement. But always there is a certain quietude, on occasion a kind of detachment. Rage and revenge, I think, belong to fiction. The essay is cooler than that. Because it so often engages in acts of memory, and despite its gladder or more antic incarnations, the essay is by and large a serene or melancholic form. It mimics that low electric hum, sometimes rising to resemble actual speech, that all human beings carry inside their heads—a vibration, garrulous if somewhat indistinct, that never leaves us while we wake. It is the hum of perpetual noticing: the configuration of someone's eyelid or tooth, the veins on a hand, a wisp of string caught on a twig, some words your fourth-grade teacher said, so long ago, about the rain, the look of an awning, a sidewalk, a bit of cheese left on a plate. All day long this inescapable hum drums on, recalling one thing and another, and pointing out this and this and this. Legend has it that Titus, emperor of Rome, went mad because of the buzzing of a gnat that made her home in his ear; and presumably the gnat, flying out into the great world and then returning to her nest, whispered what she had seen and felt and learned there. But an essayist is more resourceful than an emperor; and can be relieved of this interior noise, if only for the time it takes to record its murmurings. To seize the hum and set it down for others to hear is the essayist's genius.

It is a genius bound to leisure, and even to luxury, if luxury is measured in hours. The essay's limits can be found in its own reflective nature. Poems have been wrested from the inferno of catastrophe or war, and battlefield letters too: these are the spontaneous bursts and burnings that danger excites. But the meditative temperateness of an essay requires a desk and a chair, a musing and a mooning, a connection to a civilized surround; even when the subject itself is a wilderness of lions and tigers, mulling is the way of it. An essay is a fireside thing, not a conflagration or a safari.

This may be why, when we ask who the essayists are, it turns out—though novelists may now and then write essays—that true essayists rarely write novels. Essayists are a species of metaphysician: they are inquisitive—also analytic—about the least grain of being. Novelists go about the strenuous business of marrying and burying their people, or else they send them to sea, or to Africa, or (at the least) out of town. Essayists in their stillness ponder love and death. It is probably an illusion that men are essayists more often than women (especially since women's essays have in the past frequently assumed the form of unpublished correspondence). And here I should, I suppose, add a note about maleness and femaleness as a literary issue—what is popularly termed "gender," as if men and women were French or German tables and sofas. I *should* add such a note; it is the fashion, or, rather, the current expectation or obligation—but there is nothing to say about any of it. Essays are written by short of it. John Updike, in a genially confident discourse on maleness ("The Disposable Rocket"), takes the view—though he admits to admixture—that the "male sense of space must differ from that of the female, who has such an interesting, active, and significant inner space. The space that interests men is outer." Except, let it be observed, when men write essays: since it is only inner space—interesting, active, significant—that can conceive and nourish the contemplative essay. The "ideal female body," Updike adds, "curves around the centers of repose," and no phrase could better describe the shape of the ideal essay—yet women are no fitter as essayists than men. In promoting the felt salience of sex, Updike nevertheless drives home an essayist's point. Essays, unlike novels, emerge from the sensations of the self. Fiction creeps into foreign bodies; the novelist can inhabit not only a sex not his own, but also beetles and noses and hunger artists and nomads and beasts; while the essay is, as we say, personal.

And here is an irony. Though I have been intent on distinguishing the marrow of the essay from the marrow of fiction, I confess I have been trying all along, in a subliminal way, to speak of the essay as if it—or she—were a character in a novel or a play: moody, fickle, given on a whim to changing her clothes, or the subject; sometimes obstinate, with a mind of her own; or hazy and light; never predictable. I mean for her to be dressed—and addressed—as we would Becky Sharp, or Ophelia, or Elizabeth Bennet, or Mrs. Ramsay, or Mrs. Wilcox, or even Hester Prynne. Put it that it is pointless to say (as I have done repeatedly, disliking it every moment) "the essay," "an essay." The essay—an essay—is not an abstraction; she may have recognizable contours, but she is highly colored and individuated; she is not a type. She is too fluid, too elusive, to be a category. She may be bold, she may be diffident, she may rely on beauty, or on cleverness, on eros or exotica. Whatever her story, she is the protagonist, the secret self's personification. When we knock on her door, she opens to us, she is a presence in the doorway, she leads us from room to room; then why should we not call her "she"? She may be privately indifferent to us, but she is anything but unwelcoming. Above all, she is not a hidden principle or a thesis or a construct: she is *there*, a living voice. She takes us in.

JOHN D'AGATA
·······················

INTRODUCTION [2007]

Five thousand years ago, the people of Sumer could dig just a few feet into the ground and eventually find water pooling up around them. The name of their home—Mesopotamia—was given to it in fact because it lay between the shores of the Tigris and Euphrates, "the place between two rivers." They believed, not unreasonably, that they came from the water, that their home was the first to emerge from the ocean and to bring into the world a shape out of chaos.

They invented civilization.

They invented agriculture.

They made the first alcohol, first kiln, first loom, first wheel, first road, first city, and the first government on earth. The laws that they established were the first legal codes, their taxes the first system of levies.

Consequently, around 3200 BCE, the Sumerians developed a way of keeping track of their progress, advancing these successes even further over time with a rudimentary series of scratches in clay that we recognize today as the first system of writing.

They developed it into a form for recording their transactions—

From a cultivated field, which is situated in the valley of Liù-Bel, Itti-balatu, the son of Nabu-iddin, has made a purchase of six talents of wheat from Tashmitum-damqat, son of Shigua. Tashmitum-damqat has counted the money, the full price of that crop from the field in Liù-Bel, on Ululu thirteenth, the seventh year of Cyrus.

They developed a kind of warranty—

Bel-akha-iddin, son of Bel-epish, spoke unto Bel-shum-iddi, son of Mu-rashu, saying: "As to the ring in which an emerald has been set in gold, I guarantee that for twenty years the emerald will not fall from the gold ring. If the emerald falls from the gold ring before the expiration of twenty years, Bel-akha-iddin, son of Bel-epish, will pay to Bel-shum-iddi, son of Murashu, ten manas of silver," as witnessed by Khatin, son of Abu-nu-emuq, on Elul eighth, the thirty-fifth year of Artaxerexes.

They even established the first-known marriage contract—

I, Rimum, son of Shamkhatum, have taken for my wife and spouse, Bashtum, daughter of Belizunu, in the witness of Uzibitum, priest of Shamash, the son of Addiya. The bridal present shall be ten shekels of gold. If, after receipt of this, Bashtum to her husband, Rimum, shall say "You are not my husband," she shall be strangled and cast into the river. If Rimum, her husband, to Bashtum shall say "You are not my wife," he shall pay her ten additional shekels. I swear this by Shamash, Marduk, and my king Shamshu-ilu-na.

And so, this is how it began. Not poetry or stories or dramas or songs. This is how writing began. The first thing we thought of doing after inventing this new tool was account for all the stuff we had, the stuff we'd lost, the stuff that was owed to us.

Indeed, it's estimated that over 90 percent of what the Sumerians wrote down only served an administrative function. The roots of writing are planted it seems in the worst kind of nonfiction imaginable: informational, literal, nothing about it mattering beyond the place it held for facts.

It's upsetting to think that this is what our genre evolved from, but even more so that some still think the genre hasn't evolved. Are we working toward information, or are we working toward art?

It's not very clear sometimes.

For me, the lyric essay has been a way of defining what I like about the genre by pitting it against what I don't.

I was cocky about this for a while.

I said some things about memoir that I probably now regret.

Ditto concerning criticism, journalism, all narratives, et cetera.

At one point, I had a very clear understanding of what I believed this was and wasn't.

But it's been a year now since my teacher Deborah Tall passed away, and according to Jewish tradition it's time that her headstone be placed at her grave. This feels like she's really gone.

I'm less willing, these days, to offer definitions.

On the day that somebody dies, you want never to go to sleep. And now that a year's gone by, I want the lyric essay to be whatever it wants to be.

I know that that's not very useful.

Every semester I inherit undergraduates from our introductory work-shops who've been taught that anything goes when it comes to lyric essays.

I want to tell them just the opposite.

Just the opposite isn't true.

Last fall, after her death, I spent an afternoon with my box of stuff from college. Most of it was junk: tests I could never pass today; essays I would never write; a petrified piece of rotini pasta that Diane Ackerman had left behind at a dinner before her reading.

Underneath a hat, however, crumpled at the bottom of the cardboard box, I found a yellowed fax that Deborah had once sent.

To: John D'Agata
From: Deborah Tall
4/14/93

I was still a sophomore, and I think she was on the road. I picked it up in the English Department's office at my college and probably read it a dozen times before I reached my dorm.

John, Just saw this in the new *Georgia Review* and thought of you. Hang it over your desk. Lose no sleep. Also heard from someone else that this is a very good book. See you next week. Deborah

It was a review of Jim Galvin's now-classic *The Meadow*, a book that we've since embraced in the nonfiction community, but one that reviewers had difficulty placing at the time. "The book defies categorization in its mix of philosophy, memoir, aesthetics, imagination, and documentary observa-tion," the reviewer initially wrote.

But I'm reminded of what Latin American historian Eduardo Galeano wrote in the preface to *Memory of Fire*: "I don't know to what literary form this voice of voices belongs. I don't know if it is novel or essay or epic poem or chronicle. . . . Deciding robs me of no sleep. I do not believe in the frontiers that, according to literature's customs officials, separate the forms.

Somehow, over the years, I became a customs official. I wrote a manifesto. I visited people's schools to indoctrinate their students.

"What you're looking for," Deborah wrote me, in another note that I saved from my junior year of college, "is a kind of essay propelled not by its information, but rather by the possibility for transformative experience. You're talking about the lyric. A lyric form of the essay."

Is that too simple for us today? Is that too soft for academia? Can we still keep a thing alive without consulting the owner's manual for its breathing apparatus?

It's not that anything goes. Nor that there were ever rules for succeeding in this form. It's that everything in nonfiction—this genre of crop receipts, of warranties, of marriage contracts—has the potential to be turned into something that is better, more potent, more artful, shaped.

I want us to be transformative. I think that if we are, we might not ever die.

Let's start over, then. Can we?

We could go back, if we wanted to, to 2700, five full centuries after writing was invented.

The Sumerians, at this point, are still using their technology exclusively for commerce. Thanks to this, however, the first city on the planet has grown from an outpost of one reed temple and five mud huts that once housed an estimated twenty-seven people, to a city of 80,000 stretching two and a half square miles.

Oral history tells us that the gods at that time, looking down at the Sumerians, noticed the new markets, the new apartment blocks, the clanging carts on paved streets, the potters and the butchers and the prostitutes and jewelers all screaming out for customers, scribbling out receipts.

In fewer than three generations, according to archaeologists, the Sumerians came to constitute the highest concentration of humans on the planet.

Four thousand times more dense than the world had ever seen.

The gods were looking down, it's said, because we'd never been so noisy.

They decided that that was enough.

They decided to send a flood.

For seven days and seven nights, the Tigris and Euphrates rivers overcame their banks, pushed rapidly through the city, dissolved it back into the earth. The home of the Sumerians was rendered, once again, indistinguishable from the nothing that it originated from.

We have geological records that confirm this flood occurred.

We have an oral history that says everybody died.

One tradition, however, says that a young man by the name of Ziusudra was spared by the gods for the sake of novelty. They granted him immortality, invited him to heaven.

Before he left, however, just in case there were survivors, Ziusudra inscribed a list onto the blankness of the world about how he thought humans might rebuild their broken culture.

This, we think, was somewhere around 2600. Six hundred years before the first poem was ever written. Eight hundred years before the story of Gilgamesh was told.

This not only is the start of world literature as we know it, it's the start of an alternative use of nonfiction in the world.

What Ziusudra left behind was more than information. It's the first recorded document of instructional observation, a catalog of do's and don'ts that gestures beyond itself, the first attempt by a human mind to communicate an idea with imaginative expression, an essaying through a speaker's own experience of the world in order to make a shape where there previously was none:

THE LIST OF ZIUSUDRA

In those days—in those far remote days—in those nights—in those far-away nights—in those years—in those long ago years—at that time when wise ones knew how to speak, the oldest, the wisest, knew how to speak with the goldest of words, but they did not write anything down.

Friends, let me give you the instructions that the elders gave to me. Let me give you advice, and please don't neglect it. The instructions of our elders are precious in life. We should comply with them.

First of all, don't ever buy a donkey that excessively brays, for this is the kind of animal that will split your midriff.

Neither should you buy a prostitute from the street, for hers is a mouth that will bite.

You should not ever buy a house slave either, for he is a weed that will make you sick.

You should not ever hire a freedman to help you, for he knows that he can get away with lying in the shade.

And do not ever buy a slave girl from the palace, for they are usually sold from the bottom of the barrel.

Don't loiter about when there is a quarrel in progress, and try not to ever be a witness to one. Don't get into any quarrels, nor cause one, talk about one.

Stand aside from quarrels altogether, in fact, for you should take another road in life.

You should not disgrace yourself, should not tell lies, should not boast or gossip or deliberate for too long.

You should not draw water from a well you can't reach: for this will make you suspicious to those who are near.

You should not set to work using only your eyes, for possessions are not multiplied by only looking at them.

And you should not drive away a powerful man from your home, for that is like destroying the outer wall of your house.

Instead, by grasping the neck of a large ox you can cross a mighty river, and likewise by moving alongside the paths of mighty men you will go very far in life.

Understand, though, that when we are talking about bread it is easy to say, "Sure, I will give some to you," yet the time of actual giving can be as distant as the sky.

The eyes of the slanderer always move like a spindle.

The garrulous man fills his grain bag while the haughty one brings his empty.

He who works with leather will eventually work his own. And a weak wife will always be seized by fate.

For fate, dear friends, is like a wet bank. It is always going to make you slip.

BRIAN LENNON
· ·

LYRIC AS NEGATION [2007]

I associate the essay with an intellectual dynamic that has always seemed fundamentally at odds, to me, with "lyric" song. Perhaps that reflects the distance of the classical studies in the background of several prominent lyric essayists from my own background in philosophy—which to me is European Romantic prosaic philosophy, beginning with Kant and ending, for now at least, with Derrida. Of course, Georg Lukács, the Hungarian revolutionary commissar and founder of Western Marxism, wrote a still highly influential essay on the essay in his pre-Communist youth, assessing Plato as the original and greatest essayist of all—but he meant this as a mark of Plato's famous hostility to poetry more than anything else.

The essay is *negative*, as "nonfiction," its genus, is negative: not a fourth genre, but the negation of genre. Where drama promises public spectacle, and poetry retains its cachet as the origin of the language arts, "nonfiction" offers only *not fiction*, the refusal or denial of fiction. Nonfiction refuses that with which we associate rapture and transport, the pleasures of the imagination in a world of regimented time. The very idea of it strikes one sometimes as boring and pitiable, like the figure of Bartleby the Scrivener, whose complete introversion is a monument to the death in meaningless work. Even the *Encyclopædia Britannica* concedes that "nonfictional prose seldom gives the reader a sense of its being inevitable, as does the best poetry or fiction." Nonfiction cannot answer the question, "Would I die if I were prevented from writing?"

This thoroughly prosaic nature of the debased modern essay is, I take it, what the prefix "lyric" is intended to countermand. But the negative, the "non-," of "nonfiction" gives us something of Bartleby's quiet violence, the almost satanic calm with which he prefers not to obey and refuses to be budged in his preference. This negative force, this violence, is what enables nonfiction to oppose coercion even as it also serves it and, in a way that debates about truth and fiction often only hint at, offers us the ethical experience of writing, of the writing of power and the power of writing. To negate fiction is, in a sense, to create truth—a gesture whose burden of *conscience* is greater than craft-based scenarios of trust and readerly expectations allow. To experience writing ethically is to understand that writing is never harmless, never just a song.

The "lyric" in "lyric essay," then, like the "creative" in "creative nonfiction," positivizes the negative. But the negative remains, which is one reason that the question *What is it?* seems to follow the nonfiction-plus generic hybrid more lasciviously than it does, say, the fiction-minus of "documentary fiction." There are two issues here. One is taxonomy: in 2007, the third centennial of the birth of Carolus Linnaeus, we are more than ever beholden to the idea that our ideas are *things*, that our ordering forms are in the world itself, rather than in our talk about the world. The question "Why are we talking about the essay?"—what *function* does it serve in our talking—yields to the question "What is it?" The other is the culture industry and the market, in which classified "things" are exchanged as products. (Lukács, in his signature contribution to Marxist ideology critique, called this *Verdinglichung*—a literal translation might be "thingification"—and it is adumbrated clearly in the pre-Marxist work: "The essay form has not yet, today, travelled the road to independence which its sister, poetry, covered long ago—the road of development from a primitive, undifferentiated unity with science, ethics and art.") New genres are new products, of course, for consumers of creative writing: above all, the captive, self-captivating market of alienated pre-professionals—Bartlebys—seeking its advanced degrees.

On the one hand, then, the "lyric essay" is a *university* problem—the problem of how to describe divisions, departments, fields, practices, artifacts of knowledge. We cannot *talk* about anything without, so to speak, making it a thing. But all of us must, also, sometimes, sell those things, to "make a living": and so here it is an arts community problem, a problem of art practice and art careers as well. And making it, marketing it, in our culture, means personalizing it.

Historically, nonfiction prose genres include religious and secular didactic and polemical writing, autobiographical writing of many kinds, including writing never intended for publication, and philosophical writings, including the aphorism and the imagined dialogue. "Personal" writing in the sense now familiar to us is either a new formation or a venerable tradition, depending on whether the Renaissance strikes one as a very long time ago. The appearance or disappearance of the ego, as in often abused notions of the death of the author, is hardly a determinant of genre in any case, and it goes without saying that egoistic self-assertion is in and of itself neither good nor bad, neither progressive nor regressive.

Still, the "land rush toward the personal essay," as Douglas Hesse put it in "The Recent Rise of Literary Nonfiction: A Cautionary Assay," was hardly innocent of the competition for prestige, or merely for justification, in the disciplinary university. "To put it crassly," Hesse wrote (not crassly at all), "in a landscape crowded with scholars, one way to gain *Schreibensraum* is to declare new territories open for colonization. Suddenly there are not only virgin texts to explore but a virgin genre, not only countries but continents. And like early priests or prospectors, scholars who first stake claims will not only publish more richly but also largely determine future citizenship in the territory. . . . Naming this territory by asserting the literariness"—or, we might say, the "lyricity"—"of the essay is a gesture with corporate as well as individual payoffs."

The essay as form, lyric or no, is not indigenous to the literary culture of the United States—though we do have our own inheritance and our own culturally specific modifications of the form. Nonexhaustively, these include the foundational writings of Hamilton, Madison, and Jay; the humorist and romantic traditions of Twain and Poe; American Transcendentalism; a vast wealth of twentieth-century social and literary criticism; and the literature of philosophical pragmatism. Etymologically, the essay is French, and while "creative nonfiction" as practiced in our own context today reflects the secular self-interest and the ruminative nonchalance of the "idle" Montaigne, it seems little influenced by the polemical skeptic who defended cannibals. Writing in 1991, Hesse suggested that this was part of a backlash against what he called "postmodern theory." By 2005, when I obtained my first full-time teaching position partly on the basis of my "creative nonfiction," it seemed to me that the scales had tipped, and that while my own work continued (then) to be dismissed in some quarters as overly intellective, there was clearly a kind of delirium out there, a backlash against the backlash, if you will, for the new experimental "lyric" essay. (In 2007, I am no longer so sure—or so aware.)

It is, of course, *Verdinglichung* once more to suggest that anything that flouts any convention at all is a capital-*E* Essay. Misguided as it may be, however, this approach is the better one, in so far as it opens the door farther than it shuts it. And in truth, the door opens itself. Though I admire the tradition of "essayism" in my own country—a tradition beginning with the Federalist Papers and ending, for the time being, with the New Journalism and the American reception of deconstruction—the Essay with which I feel the keenest kinship lived once upon a time in German-language modernism, to which I have no biographical or other natural connection, a purely elective affinity. The attraction for me lies in the fact that in the writings of Robert Musil, Siegfried Kracauer, the young Lukács, and others one can read the theory of the essay next to its practice, as well as an anti-academic tendency refreshingly different from our native variety here in the United States, which tends to be more broadly anti-intellectual. For if the academic study of literature and the pedagogy of creative writing subordinate appreciation to analysis and inspiration to method, a notion of "pure writing" preserves the injustice while merely changing its direction. This is the head-heart dilemma that a pragmatic and utilitarian, if paradoxically wasteful national culture must resolve by valorizing one of its terms. We all know which one. Hesse observes simply, and correctly, that "the ideologies of literary nonfiction mirror the culture in which it is taught and read." The "creative" in our "creative writing" stands for the natural, the real, the organic, the pure, in implicit contrast with the artifice of mere writing. Must we say the same of the lyric essay?

But the "lyric" in lyric essay is perhaps less a claim than a *demand* for form, in Lukács's own extended sense of that term: at least, this is how I still find it useful. If the lyric essay "manifesto" that launched *Seneca Review*'s publishing program in the new genre was more factive and descriptive than rhetorical and polemical, as I would have preferred—announcing, rather than demanding a change in the way things are done— it also hesitated, meaningfully, in that positivization. This hesitation, this doubt, I think now, was and remains something more—potentially, at least—than the alienated, self-effacing modesty of the materially comfortable middle-class individualist, as it is so often read—*theorized*—by impresarios of the personalized essay. *Essayismus*, the term that Musil used for his own union of art and science, of aesthetics and ethics, and of form and content in composition, is the bad conscience of "creative writing," we might say, in the same way that Canada is the bad conscience of the United States. When Theodor Adorno, writing in German, used the phrase "creative writing," he wrote it in English—to mark it as an American invention, to be sure, but also as a performance of his own understanding of writing and the experience of the foreign. This writer, who spent part of his productive life in exile in the United States and who learned to write as ferociously well in English as in his mother tongue, understood the essay as a *traveler*. "The way the essay appropriates the concept" he wrote in "The Essay as Form,"

is comparable to the conduct of someone stuck in a foreign country speaking its language, instead of assembling it from elements as is done in school. He will read without a dictionary. . . . As certainly as such learning remains exposed to error, so does the essay as form, it pays for its affinity with open intellectual [*geistigen*] experience with a lack of any security, which the norm of established thought fears as death.

Adorno's essay as form rejects academic bureaucracy, but it also resists easy anti-intellectualism; it insists on the carnivalesque, on the aspect of play in writing, without exalting play as somehow closer to nature. The essay aspires to the condition of music *in* thought, not in dismissing thought; it pursues unreason with and through reason. It is a permanent failure that keeps trying. In the end, the essay turns against even itself. Most importantly, for Adorno, the essay is a form of "negative dialectics," the self-critique of the socially privileged: a way of grappling with, as he put it, "the guilt of a life which purely as a fact will strangle other life," and the coldness which made Auschwitz possible, as well as the coldness required to live *after* Auschwitz.

If this ethical dimension is missed in the theory of the lyric essay, it is not, perhaps, absent from its practice. For the Montaigne who wrote *Que sais-je?* (What do I know?), which appeals so to the personal essayist, is the same Montaigne who wrote, "We may well call [cannibals] barbarians in regard to the rules of reason, but not in regard to ourselves, who surpass them in every sort of barbarity." Montaigne as critic of modernity: can the lyric essay do that?

But if lyric is the "unhappy" song of the self not contentedly, but anxiously alone among (its) others—claiming, in its declassifying division, a place in a world of shared meaning, rather than seceding—then *lyrikos* can be *polemos*. Today, we need it to be.

WHAT IS A LYRIC ESSAY?
PROVISIONAL RESPONSES [2007]

Shhhh—not so loud! That's my first reaction to the question, *So what's a lyric essay?* I want to protect the LE. I want to give it the bigger, roomier coat of E to hide in. I want it underground, under the radar. When asked its age at the admissions booth, as honest LE begins to say *Me? I'm twel—* I'll be the one poking it in the back, saying *She's ten! Let's go!*

I know novelists who are more at home in the essay than the novel (though they wouldn't agree or admit). I know poets whose poems— whose whole books—look suspiciously like lyric essays (see the late, brilliant Tom Andrews' *Random Symmetries*). It's that such people call themselves *novelists* and *poets* mostly. Why the emphasis? Why the disguises? Then again, I say of my own prose: "Oh, it's a piece on this or that." I like to say "piece." That way, it could be mistaken, at first mention, for a dance or a sculpture or a musical composition. "Piece" suggests heft and objecthood. Ongoingness in a series. A partial nature (somewhere's a whole, and here, I offer a sliver/shard/relic). "Piece" is, I realize, also not so up front.

So what's the trail I'm intent on throwing you off?

I, the poet, have felt at times like I need to confess. *Mom, Dad, sit down. I have to tell you something* (held breaths all around, here it is, they saw it coming): *I love sentences. I think I've always loved sentences. I just didn't know it until . . . recently. I mean, I love both lines and sentences. They each give me something the other can't—and I want to live with them both.* I imagine their deflation. They were prepared for one or the other. But this . . . *lyric* stuff people are talking about—you're into *that*? Just *choose*, they'd say. Decide already! What's *with* your generation?

I once submitted an essay to a Famous Editor with a note that read "Enclosed is a lyric essay, blah, blah, blah, . . . and he sent it back saying, "Yes, good, we'll take it et cetera, but shouldn't 'lyric' be something *someone else* says about your essay?" Yikes. What a cringe. I've been jittery about the term ever since because, yeah, now that he mentioned it, it seems kind of . . . embarrassing. Actually, really embarrassing. "Lyric," like a compliment, might best be bestowed. Might best be graciously accepted—like "poetic." One might best earn it, in others' estimation. Like r-e-s-p-e-c-t.

"Well, you're lucky, you write *lyric* essays," a poet/essayist once said to me. I'm pretty sure I *retorted*—something about my Works Cited pages. Because by "lyric" I think she meant "easy, the way a poem is easy; not requiring research."

The lyric essay may be, most essentially, an epistolary form—as I suspect The Essay itself is, most essentially. This is probably why it feels weird to read my work aloud. I'm not sure essays really lend themselves to readings—unless they are funny. And if you're not really, primarily, funny—well, it's weird. If essays behave like letters addressed to A Reader, and if the letter, as a form, provides a space for communion between friends (one repairs to a place of solitude to read the little gift, to allow the essence of the distant friend to fill up the space) then reading aloud (at a bookstore, say) a letter already written/sent/received (i.e.: published) is a strange kind of excess. Too public. Overkill. MySpace-ish. And reading a "lyric" essay aloud? That can be as bad as saying, "And now I'll do a poem I wrote for my beloved. . . Ahem!" You have to leave big dramatic pauses to indicate white space. Inflect the italics. And the ever-troublesome issue of conveying quotes forces you to claw the air with crook'd fingers, Little Bunny Foo-Foo style.

Amusing terms collect around the lyric essay: some LEs are not "text-bound" apparently. Some films are called "essays." Composer Samuel Barber wrote two Essays for Orchestra. I, myself, in the last month, have suggested to some writers that their (very lyric) essays might be best realized as performances (with lights and various speakers moving on and off). I've suggested the addition of pictures to certain essays, thus inadvertently promoting a thing called "the graphic essay." And yet—I'm uncomfortable stretching the term "essay" too far. Silly Putty used to make me nervous in the same way when stretched, especially when it spread the face of a comic-book character, making it slowly wide, then tall, then transparent until it wore through entirely and the face's features blew around in the breeze like a ripped flag.

The essay—the sensation of writing and reading the thing—comes to me best, most clearly, by way of an old association—a game I used to play as a kid with ants. An ant would be walking across the sidewalk and I'd put my finger in front of it like a log; the ant would nearly bump up against the log, think the better of it, sniff, pick up some clue, and then choose another path. And then I'd put my finger down in front of *that* path. And there and there and there. The ant never got tired or gave up and sat down (crying, lamenting, exhausted . . . no!). Such a tiny life force, such ferocity of purpose! Dumb ant! Brilliant ant! I tried out all those feelings. The ant just kept moving. And changing direction. In response to. Those are the moves (engagement and veering), that's the energy (a jagged, overall grace and doggedness) I associate with the essay.

Eventually I'd get tired and the ant would get to go—home, I guessed. *Home*, though? Maybe it would resume its path—the path it had in mind all along, before I came and knocked out all the routes. Maybe it bought, with all that rerouting, a new idea about home, and made up a new destination with its thinking. Maybe the ant family was so large, so fluid, so capacious in its reception of travelers, that my ant could duck in to any tunnel and call it *home*. Maybe in recounting its day, as it must have at some point (how else to explain its long absence to the clan) it learned to say something different than "lost" or "thwarted" and retooled all that confusion into "meandering" and "journey" while sitting around a cozy pile of sugar with the kids late at night. These too—the luck, the stories, the courting of unknowns—mean "essay" to me.

"That was a nice, lyrical description, those ants," one might say. Or, "that ant-association illustrates the lyric essay very nicely." Well, I'm glad if that's the case, but really the term "lyrical" is only a way of being true. Maybe the term is best employable as a conversation starter—about the essay, or about any form. Let's transpose the question for a minute: What is a lyric painting? (Well, it describes *something* about movement and gesture.) A lyric film? (Not so many words, lots of gesture, palpable atmospheres, no color or an abundance of it.) A lyric yoga class? (Right sense of flow and linkage between poses; nice pacing, not too many words). And a lyrical salad? (Essayist Carl Klaus recently made me one, both neatly composed and full of surprises). A lyrical driving style? (My friend Greg Gensheimer has perfected something called "the international turn"—a nicely controlled tossing of kids up against each other, followed by a quick and soft recovery). A lyrical sermon? (Rev. Rebecca Clouse, 5/6/07, Gloria Dei, Iowa City: all pedal to the metal, yet full of cycle, full of structure.) A lyrical peony? (Heavy in blooming, cool even in heat.) A lyrical cook? (My husband, Jed Gaylin, who makes all the garnishes edible.) And now we're in a conversation, an effort to refine, complicate, enlarge a point.

It's a good question—this "What is a lyric essay?" question that *Seneca*

Review and its editors have been framing and serving and allowing us to expound on for years now. It *continues* to be a good question because it recurs with the honest insistence of a child's question when s/he knows that a solid singular answer is suspect, or is simply not to be had. It's a question whose answers are best dosed out—lest you overwhelm the kid with too much information all at once.

Q: Where's the little LE?

A: I don't know—outside playing somewhere, I guess. If he's not crying, he's happy.

Interpretation: Benign neglect is good for kids and the lyric essay.

Insistent Question: So for the purposes of this issue of *Seneca Review*, what then is a lyric essay?

Sidelong Wish: May we—readers and writers both—remain in a state of wonder about just that. May we value novelty enough to protect it. And since the reasons for questioning elemental things change as we get bigger, may we, as the Magic 8 Ball so often suggests, *Ask Again Later*.

REALITY, PERSONA [2009]

REALITY

1

These are the facts, my friend, and I must have faith in them.

2

What is a fact? What's a lie, for that matter? What, exactly, constitutes an essay or a story or a poem or even an experience? What happens when we can no longer freeze the shifting phantasmagoria which is our actual experience?

3

During the middle of a gig, Sonny Rollins sometimes used to wander outside and add the sound of his horn to the cacophony of passing cabs.

4

Have you ever heard a record that makes you feel as good as Stevie Wonder's *Fingertips—Part 2*? I haven't. It's so *real*. When you listen to the record, you can hear a guy in the band yelling, "What key? What key?" He's lost. But then he finds the key, and *boom*. Every time I hear that guy yelling, "What key?" I get excited.

5

Soul is the music people understand. Sure, it's basic and it's simple, but it's something else 'cause it's honest. There's no fuckin' bullshit. It sticks its neck out and says it straight from the heart. It grabs you by the balls.

6

The most essential gift for a good writer is a built-in, shock-proof shit detector.

7

Ichiro Suzuki, the first Japanese position player in the major leagues, has unusually good eyesight and hand-eye coordination and works extremely hard at his craft, but his main gift is that he's present in reality. If he's chasing a fly ball, he doesn't sort of watch the ball; he really, really, really watches the ball. When sportswriters ask him questions, he inevitably empties out the bromide upon which the question is based. Once, after running deep into foul territory to make an extraordinary catch to preserve a victory, he was asked, "When did you know you were going to catch the ball?" Ichiro said, "When I caught it."

8
Don't waste your time; get to the real thing.

9
Jennicam first went up in 1996; it went offline several years later. Every two minutes of every hour of every day, an image from a camera in Jenni's apartment was loaded onto the web. In her FAQ, Jenni said, "The cam has been there long enough that now I ignore it. So whatever you're seeing isn't staged or faked. While I don't claim to be the most interesting person in the world, I do think there's something compelling about real life that staging it wouldn't bring to the medium."

1 0
Act naturally.

1 1
Somewhere I had come up with the notion that one's personal life had nothing to do with fiction, whereas the truth, as everybody knows, is nearly the direct opposite. Moreover, contrary evidence was all around me, though I chose to ignore it, for in fact the fiction both published and unpublished that moved and pleased me then as now was precisely that which had been made luminous, undeniably authentic by having been found and taken up, always at a cost, from deeper, more shared levels of the life we all really live.

1 2
People are always asking me when I'm going to make "real movies." These are my real movies. Nothing could be more real than the movies I make.

13

Making up a story or characters feels like driving a car in a clown suit.

14

Only the truth is funny (comedy is not pretty; definition of comedy: pulling Socrates off his pedestal).

15

Nicholson Baker is a comic personal essayist disguised, sometimes, as a novelist. His work is most appealing when he lavishes more attention upon a subject than it can possibly bear: broken shoelaces, say, in *The Mezzanine* or an innocuous line of Updike's in *U and I*. It wouldn't work if, instead of a shoelace, it was the Brooklyn Bridge, or if, instead of Updike, it was Proust: Baker's excessive elaboration wouldn't be funny or interesting. His style feeds upon farcical and foppish topics (e.g., his essay on the history of the comma). Baker is an unapologetic celebrant of gadgets, appliances, contraptions, machines, feats of engineering. His pseudo-scientific lyricism serves him well—seems oddly illuminating—when he's overanalyzing the physics of straws or the opening of *Pigeon Feathers*. His point appears to be that nothing is beneath interest.

16

Attention equals life or is its only evidence.

17

"Why do you take photographs so constantly, so obsessively? Why do you collect other people's photographs? Why do you scavenge in second-hand shops and buy old albums of other people's pasts?"
"So that I'll see what I've seen."

18

We are poor passing facts,
warned by that to give
each figure in the photograph
his living name.

19

In the end I missed the pleasure of a fully imagined work in which the impulse to shape experience seems as strong as the impulse to reveal it.

20

Plot, like erected scaffolding, is torn down and what stands in its place is the thing itself.

21

—praise for matter in its simplest state, as fact.

22

There isn't any story. It's not the story. It's just this breathtaking world— that's the point. The story's not important; what's important is the way the world looks. That's what makes you feel stuff. That's what puts you there.

23

Shooting must be done on location, and props and sets must not be brought in (if a particular prop is necessary for the story, a location must be chosen where this prop is to be found); the sound must never be produced apart from the images or vice versa (music must not be used unless it occurs where the scene is being shot); the camera must be hand-held; the film must be in color, and special lighting is not acceptable; optical work and filters are forbidden; the film must not contain superficial action (murders, etc. must not occur); temporal and geographical alienation are forbidden (that is to say, the film takes place here and now); genre movies are not acceptable; the director must not be credited.

24

The most political thing I can do is try to render people's lives, including my own, in a way that makes other people interested, empathetic, questioning, or even antipathetic to what they're seeing—but that somehow engages them to look at life as it's really lived and react to it.

25

Verboten thematic: secular Jews, laureates of the real, tend to be better at analyzing reality than recreating it: Lauren Slater, *Lying*; Harold Brodkey, most of the essays; Phillip Lopate's introduction to *The Art of the Personal Essay*; Vivian Gornick, pretty much everything; Leonard Michaels, nearly everything; Melanie Thernstrom, *The Dead Girl*; Wallace Shawn, *My Dinner with André*; Jonathan Safran Foer, "Primer for the Punctuation of Heart Disease"; Salinger's later, consciousness-drenched work (I know I'll love the Buddhist-inspired meditations he's been writing the last forty years in his bunker). Less recently, e.g., Marx, Proust, Freud, Wittgenstein, Einstein.

2 6

The first resurrection of Christ is the heart of the backstory for the holiday of Easter and the original deification of Jesus. On the cross, he said that he would rise three days after his death. After he died of crucifixion, disbelieving Pilate and the Romans placed him in a cave and sealed the door with a boulder. On the third day, the boulder moved, Christ emerged, told his followers thank for your devotedness, etc. This is where Doubting Thomas gets his due. The risen Christ has Thomas actually feel the mortal wound (see the painting by Caravaggio for visualization). Jesus proves to all disbelievers that he really is the son of God. He will return on Judgment Day. Up to heaven and he hasn't been heard from since. (The last Christian died on the cross.)

2 7

The writing class has met every Wednesday afternoon for the past few years: twenty women, a retired dentist, and my father, now 96. Although he's been plagued by manic-depression for fifty years and has received electroshock therapy countless times, in almost every piece he presents himself as a balanced okaynik, Mr. Bonhomie. He's always thrown a stone at every dog that bites, but in one story he sagely advises his friend, "You can't throw a stone at every dog that bites." His children from his first marriage, from whom he's estranged, didn't attend his 90TH birthday party, but now they do, bearing gifts. He's been bald since he was 40, but now his hair is only "nearly gone." My mother, who died at 51, dies at 60. His voice in these stories is that of a successful tough guy: "She was dressed to the nines in flame-red shorts and a low-cut halter that showed her heart was in the right place." My dad, Sam Spade. His Waterloo was failing ever to see or call his childhood sweetheart, Pearl, after he had lost his virginity with a woman he met at a Catskills resort (the woman who became his first wife). In real life, at age 68, when he was visiting his sister, Fay, in Queens, Fay bumped into Pearl at the Queens Center Mall, got Pearl's number, and suggested that my dad call her. Again, he couldn't bring himself to call—which is a great, sad story. But in the story he wrote, he calls her, they get together, and "Eleanor" tells "Herb": "Please don't be so hard on yourself. It happened. It's all water under the bridge now. You did what you thought was right for you then. I understand. Maybe I didn't then. But it's all over now. That year, Joe and I got married, so I guess it's all worked out for the best, right?" This was, according to my father, the "toughest thing I've ever written—painful. It hurt deep down just to write it, more than 53 years after it happened." I want it to hurt more. My father and mother divorced shortly before her death thirty years ago, and they had, by common consent, an extremely bad relationship. But it's now a "solid-as-Gibraltar marriage." My father, asking for time off from his boss, tells him, "I'm faced with a palace revolution, and the three revolutionaries at home are getting ready to depose the king." The king he wasn't. I want him to write about forever having to polish the queen's crown according to her ever-changing and exacting specifications. I want to ask him, What did that feel like? What is it like inside his skin? What is it like inside that bald, ill dome? No aerial views or airy glibness. Please, Dad, I want to say: only ground-level, which at least holds the promise of grit.

2 8
Daniel Johnston, a manic-depressive singer and songwriter whose early songs were recorded on a $60 stereo, has a cult following (recipient of praise from Kurt Cobain and Eddie Vedder), due primarily to the unglamorous, raw, low-quality production of his music, which chronicles his mental illness.

2 9
All the best stories are true.

3 0
That person over there? He's doing one thing, thinking something else. Life is never false, and acting can be. Any person who comes in here as a customer is not phony, whereas if a guy comes in posing as a customer, there might be something phony about it, and the reason it's phony is if he's really thinking, "How am I doing? Do they like me?"

3 1
He is to be accepted and forgiven because his faults are the sad, lovable, honorable faults of reality itself.

3 2
A didactic white arrow is superimposed on the left- and right-hand panels, pointing almost sardonically at the dying man. (These arrows, Francis

Bacon's favorite distancing device, are sometimes explained as merely formal ways of preventing the viewer from reading the image too literally. In reality, they do just the opposite and insist that one treat the image as hyperexemplary, as though it came from a medical textbook.) The grief in the painting is intensified by the coolness of its layout and the detachment of its gaze. It was Bacon's insight that it is precisely such seeming detachment—the rhetoric of the documentary, the film strip, and the medical textbook—that has provided the elegiac language of the last forty years.

33

Life isn't about saying the right thing, and it's certainly not about tape-recording everything so you have to endure it more than once. Life is about failing. It's about letting the tape play. Boswell, *Life of Johnson*. Jean Stein, *Edie*. *The Education of Henry Adams*. Geoffrey Wolff, *The Duke of Deception*. Julian Barnes, *Flaubert's Parrot*.

34

If you was hit by a truck and you were lying out in that gutter dying, and you had time to sing one song, one song people would remember before you're dirt, one song that would let God know what you felt about your time here on earth, one song that would sum you up, you telling me that's the song you'd sing? That same Jimmie Davis tune we hear on the radio all day? About your peace within and how it's real and how you're gonna shout it? Or would you sing something different? Something real, something you felt? Because I'm telling you right now: that's the kind of song people want to hear. That's the kind of song that truly saves people. It ain't got nothing to do with believing in God, Mr. Cash. It has to do with believing in yourself.

35

Reality-based art is a metaphor for the fact that this is all there is, there ain't no more.

36

The world is everything that is the case.

PERSONA

37

And I shall essay to be.

38

The book is written in the first person, but that "I" is the most deceptive, tricky pronoun. There are two of us. I'm a chronicler of this character at the center who is, but in the necessary sense not, me. He doesn't have my retrospect nor my leisure. He doesn't know what's around the next bend. He's ignorant of consequences. He moves through the book in a state of innocence about the future, whereas of course I as the writer, from the time I begin writing the first paragraph, do know what the future holds. I know how the story is going to turn out.

39

Painting myself for others, I have painted my inward self with colors clearer than my original ones. I have no more made my book than my book has made me.

40

Cinéma vérité looks for performers in everyday life; without them, you really haven't got footage. Some people have whatever that quality is that makes them interesting on film—a kind of self-confidence or self-assuredness mixed, perhaps, with a degree of vulnerability—and other people don't have it, but as a filmmaker you know it when you see it. You have to sense that there's something real behind the so-called performance.

41

Johnny Carson, asked to describe the difference between himself and Robert Redford, said, "I'm playing me."

42

In *Essays of Elia*, Charles Lamb turned the reader's attention to the persona, the unreliable mask of the "I," not as an immutable fact of literature but as a tool of the essayist in particular, who, if he or she wants to get personal, must first choose what to conceal. These peculiarities—the theatrical reticence, the archaism, the nostalgia, the celebration of oddity for its own sake—are regular features of Lamb's essays, and they helped to change the English (and American) idea of what an essay should be. Even when personal essayists don't flaunt their power to mislead us, even when we no longer expect belle-lettrists to write old-fashioned prose, we still expect essays to deliver that same Elian tension between the personal and the truly private and to tell stories that are digressive and inconclusive.

Most of all, we expect personal essayists to speak to us from behind a stylized version of themselves, rather than give us the whole man—as Montaigne or Lamb's favorite devotional writers seem to do—or a more-or-less representative man like the *Spectator* of Addison and Steele. Lamb wasn't the only Romantic essayist who wrote this way; Hazlitt soon followed suit, so did De Quincey and Hunt. But Lamb was the first. Ever since Elia, eccentricity has been the rule.

43
Autobiography can be naively understood as pure self-revelation or more cannily recognized as cleverly wrought subterfuge.

44
When I state myself, as the Representative of the Verse—it does not mean—me—but a supposed person.

45
I'm not interested in myself per se. I'm interested in myself as theme-carrier, as host.

46
A novelist-friend, who can't not write fiction but is flummoxed whenever he tries to write nonfiction directly about his own experience, said he was impressed (alarmed?) by my willingness to say nearly anything about myself: "It's all about you and yet somehow it's not about you at all. How can that be?"

47
One is not important, except insofar as one's example can serve to elucidate a more widespread human trait and make readers feel a little less lonely and freakish.

48
"The soul must become its own betrayer, its own deliverer, the one activity, the mirror turned lamp"—which could and should serve as epigraph to Alphonse Daudet, *In the Land of Pain*; Fernando Pessoa, *The Book of Disquiet*; Michel Leiris, *Manhood: A Journey from Childhood into the Fierce Order of Virility*.

49

Andy Kaufman went way beyond blurring the distinction between performer and persona, past the point where you wondered what separated the actor from the character; you wondered if he himself knew anymore where the boundaries were drawn. What did he get out of such performances? The joy of not telling the audience how to react, giving that decision—or maybe just the illusion of such decision-making—back to the audience. Afterward, he typically stayed in character when among fellow performers, who resented being treated like civilians. On his ABC special, the vertical hold kept rolling, which the network hated because it didn't want viewers to think there was anything wrong with their TV sets when in fact the problem was by design.

50

In Lorrie Moore's story "People Like That Are the Only People Here," the putatively fictional account of a writer whose toddler is diagnosed with cancer, characters are named only by the roles they play: the Mother, Husband, Baby, Surgeon, Radiologist, Oncologist. The Mother discusses the possibility (the Husband emphasizes the financial necessity) of writing about the experience. When the story was published as fiction in the *New Yorker*, it was accompanied by a photo of Moore and a caption, "No, I can't. Not this! I write fiction. This isn't fiction." About the story, Moore has said, "It's fiction. Things didn't happen exactly that way; I reimagined everything. And that's what fiction does. Fiction can come from real-life events and still be fiction." The Mother is a writer and teacher who is already writing each scene as she experiences it. If this isn't a story about Moore and her baby, what is it about? The deep ambivalence writers have about using their personal lives to make a living. Even as the Mother agonizes about taking notes, she's diligently observing the environment, gathering data about cancer that will both help her child and (bonus!) make the story she'll write a better one. God, embodied as the manager of Marshall Field's, informs the Mother that "to know the narrative in advance is to turn yourself into a machine. What makes humans human is precisely that they do not know the future." The writer, of course, writing the story, does know what the ending will be, has planned it, lived through it. And the Mother also knows the future. When they leave the hospital with their baby, the Husband expresses gratitude for the people they've met, and the Mother responds, "For as long as I live, I never want to see any of these people again." The Mother will see those people, over and over again:

she'll spend a great deal of time and effort recreating them; writing the story, she insures that those people will always be with her. The Mother is angry at the world for paying to read such a story, but she's also angry at herself for profiting from not only her own life and pain but that of her family and all the families who shared their time in the pediatric oncology ward with her. She's angry that she can't leave these people behind, or the worry behind, or the fundamental truth that a part of living, of breathing, of surviving, is to exploit those human relationships in order to make our own stories, in order to live.

5 1

The source of my crush on Sarah Silverman? Her willingness to say unsettling things about herself, position herself as a fuck-me/fuck-you figure, a bad-good girl, a JAP who takes her JAPpiness and pushes it until it becomes the culture's grotesquerie: "I was raped by a doctor—which is, you know, so bittersweet for a Jewish girl." "I don't care if you think I'm racist; I only care if you think I'm thin." "Obviously, I'm not trying to belittle the events of September 11TH; they were devastating, they were beyond devastating, and I don't want to say especially for these people or especially for these people, but especially for me, because it happened to be the same exact day that I found out that the soy chai latte was, like, 900 calories."

5 2

A Hero of Our Time, gentlemen, is in fact a portrait, but not of an individual; it is the aggregate of the vices of our whole generation in their fullest expression.

5 3

The man who writes about himself and his time is the man who writes about all people and all time.

5 4

Was Keats a confessional poet? When he talks about youth that grows "pale and specter-thin, and dies," he's talking about his kid brother Tom, who died of tuberculosis. But he's talking about more than that. The word "confessional" implies the need to purge oneself and to receive forgiveness for one's life. I don't think that's what confessional poetry is about at all. I think it's a poetry that comes out of the stuff of the poet's personal life, but he's trying to render this experience in more general and inclusive, or what used to be called "universal," terms. He's presenting himself as a representative human being. He's saying, "This is what happens to us as human beings in this flawed and difficult world, where joy is rare." Sylvia Path is certainly one of the outstanding "confessional" poets, but when Path entitles a poem "Lady Lazarus," she's trying to connect herself to the whole tradition of pain and death and resurrection. She's not presenting herself as Sylvia Plath, but as part of a larger pattern.

55

This is the wager, isn't it? It's by remaining faithful to the contingencies and peculiarities of your own experience and the vagaries of your own nature that you stand the greatest chance of conveying something universal.

56

Self-study of any seriousness aspires to myth. Thus do we endlessly inscribe and magnify ourselves.

57

A man's life of any worth is a continual allegory.

58

What is true for you in your private heart is true for all men.

59

All our stories are the same.

60

Every man has within himself the entire human condition.

61

Deep down you know you're him.

ACKNOWLEDGMENTS
....

I am entirely grateful to the following graduate students who assisted me in the production of this anthology: Micah McCrary, Colleen O'Connor, Ryan Spooner and a big thank you to Jennifer Tatum who organized the group. Tina Simpson was a steadfast and invaluable help as my assistant under the undergraduate research mentor initiative through the Dean's Office at Columbia College Chicago. Kenneth Daley, Chair of the English Department at Columbia College, provided critical early subvention for the book. And thanks to Kim Kupperman for taking this project on— it was years in the offing when essay anthologies were considered box office poison.

This anthology is dedicated to—who else?—Phillip Lopate.

PERMISSIONS

. . . .

"The Decay of Essay-Writing" originally appeared in *Essays*, Volume I, by Virginia
    Woolf (Harcourt Brace, 1967) and is reprinted by permission.
"Montaigne" originally appeared in *The Common Reader* by Virginia Woolf
    (Harcourt Harvest, 1984) and is reprinted by permission.
"The Modern Essay" originally appeared in *The Common Reader* by Virginia Woolf
    (Harcourt Harvest, 1984) and is reprinted by permission.
"On the Nature and Form of the Essay" originally appeared in *Soul and Form*,
    translated by Anna Bostock (MIT Press, 1974), and is reprinted by permission.
"Preface" by Christopher Morley originally appeared in *Modern Essays* (Harcourt
    Brace, 1921) and is reprinted by permission.
"The Essay as Form" by Theodor Adorno originally appeared in *Telos* (Number
    60, Summer 1984), translated by Bob Hullot-Kentor and Frederic Will, and is
    reprinted by permission.
"The Essay—Is It Literature?" originally appeared in *What Do I Know? Reading,
    Writing, and Teaching the Essay* by Robert Antwan (Boynton/Cook, 1987) and is
    reprinted by permission.
"The Logic of the 'Sufficient Word' in the Montaignian Essay" originally appeared
    in *The Barthes Effect: The Essay as Reflective Text*, by Réda Bensmaïa, Pat Fedkiew
    trans., (University of Minnesota Press, 1987) and is reprinted by permission.
"Essayists on the Essay" by Carl Klaus originally appeared in *Literary Nonfiction:
    Theory, Criticism, Pedagogy*, edited by Chris Anderson (Southern Illinois
    University Press, 1989) and is reprinted by permission.
"The Skewed Path: Essaying as Unmethodical Method" by R. Lane Kauffmann
    originally appeared in *Essays on the Essay: Redefining the Genre*, edited by
    Alexander Butrym (University of Georgia Press, 1989) and is reprinted by
    permission.
"What Happened to the Personal Essay" originally appeared in *Against Joie de
    Vivre* by Phillip Lopate (University of Nebraska Press, 1989, rpt. 2008) and is
    reprinted by permission.
"What is Reading? It's Eating on the Sly" originally appeared in *Three Steps on the
    Ladder of Writing* by Hélène Cixous, translated by Sarah Cornell and Susan
    Sellars (Columbia University Press, 1994) and is reprinted by permission.
"Essaying the Feminine: From Montaigne to Kristeva" originally appeared in *Voice
    Lessons: On Becoming a (Woman) Writer* by Nancy Mairs (Beacon Press, 1997)

and is reprinted by permission.

"*f*-words: An Essay on the Essay" originally appeared in *Blue Studios: Poetry and its Cultural Work* by Rachel Blau DuPlessis (University of Alabama Press, 2006) and is reprinted by permission.

"She: Portrait of the Essay as a Warm Body" originally appeared in *Quarrel and Quandary* by Cynthia Ozick (Random House, 2001) and is reprinted by permission.

"Introduction to Special Issue" originally appeared in *Seneca Review*, by John D'Agata (Seneca Review, 2007, volume 37, no. 2) and is reprinted by permission.

"Lyric as Negation" originally appeared in *Seneca Review*, by Brian Lennon (Seneca Review, 2007, Vol 37, no. 2) and is reprinted by permission.

"What is the Lyric Essay? Provisional Responses" originally appeared in *Seneca Review*, by Lia Purpura (Seneca Review, 2007, volume 37, no. 2) and is reprinted by permission.

"Reality, Persona" by David Shields originally appeared in *Truth in Nonfiction*, ed. David Lazar (University of Iowa Press, 2008) and in different form in *Reality Hunger* (Knopf, 2010) and is reprinted by permission.